Labor's Story

LABOR'S STORY

AS REPORTED BY THE AMERICAN LABOR PRESS

Edited By

Gordon H. Cole

EDITOR, *The Machinist*
International Association of Machinists, AFL-CIO

Leon Stein

EDITOR, *Justice*
International Ladies' Garment Workers' Union, AFL-CIO

Norman L. Sobol

EDITOR, *Local 1-S News*
Retail, Wholesale and Department Store Union, AFL-CIO

Community Publishers
Glen Cove, New York
1961

CONTENTS

Labor Cartoons on Pages: 14, 18, 36, 49, 56, 68, 91, 101, 117, 144, 154, 162, 163, 175, 188, 198, 211, 214, 234, 251, 253, 266, 275, 287, 299, 315.

Introduction

Many forces have contributed to the building of the United States into freedom's mightiest arsenal. One of the greatest of these is Union labor, the men and women whose ingenuity and skill and productivity are unsurpassed anywhere in this troubled world. The unity and spirit of American labor have helped to make the American standard of living a model for the world.

The story of American labor is a proud and exciting story. It is also the least told story. With a few noteworthy exceptions, the commercial press—the newspapers and the magazines, have not chosen to tell the story of American labor, its triumphs and its accomplishments, its skill and its productivity.

The rare occasions when some part of labor's story finds its way into the pages of the commercial press are almost always times of strife. The daily newspapers seldom cover the world of the shop, of advances in labor-management relations, of labor's substantial contributions to the community, of the history of sacrifice and devotion through which the unions have been built by working people as the American way to achieve the American standard of living.

The founding fathers of America looked upon the press as an essential medium of information and education in a complex society. They understood that a free people can achieve unity only if every group has the opportunity to be heard, only if every group can express its position on the issues and the problems of the day and have those expressions read.

The commercial press has long since ceased to provide an open forum for diverse and conflicting views. The steady consolidation of American newspapers has reduced the competition of ideas and news coverage as well as the competition for advertising and circulation revenue.

In 1910, for a population of ninety-two million Americans there were 2,600 daily newspapers. In 1961 for a population of more than one hundred seventy-five million Americans, there are less than 1750 daily newspapers. In more than 90 per cent of American cities where dailies are published there is no newspaper competition.

As the newspapers have grown and prospered, the voice of protest in their editorial and in their news columns has been muted. Today, almost the only newspaper space available for dissent is in the labor press.

By comparison with the commercial press, the labor press is a handful of periodicals, none of them issued daily, most of them understaffed, many of them without adequate illustrations or skilled typography and almost all of them put together by editors who make up in devotion what they lack in professional training.

The odds are against the labor press as a countervailing journalistic force. The union member to whom it addresses its appeal is the daily target of bulging newspapers, shrieking televised messages, slick magazines that pull and haul. Only once a week or fortnight or month the printed voice of his union—thin indeed by comparison—comes through the mail or into the shop.

It is smaller in size, has less white space, few or no features or comics or prizes or puzzles or "cheese cake" pictures. In many cases it has no advertisements. Moreover, it misses the powerful drama of sex, murder and crime.

Yet, in its all too small, too few and too solidly printed pages it deals with the world that is of utmost urgency to working people and their families. In its most primitive form the labor publication may be the work of a volunteer committee from the third floor back nightshift, set down in laboriously cut, mimeographed stencils and carrying little more than notices of births, deaths and marriages.

Yet, such is the power of even the mimeographed word that for the group laboring in that small wedge of America's huge production plant this is "their" paper in the sense that no other one is. The same kind of proprietary attachment is felt by the worker toward the paper that comes from his union's local, district council or general office.

Although small in size and generally cramped in format, labor papers reflect the widening horizons of workers' interests. The papers themselves have played an important part in achieving this expansion of interest. Their pages reflect the unanimity of conviction that workers' welfare is inseparable from community well-being, national prosperity and international peace. They insist that the fact of union membership, far from detaching a worker from community responsibilities, rather strengthens the bond.

In this sense, labor papers make no pretense at "dispassionate" or "impartial" editing. They acknowledge and define their point of view as being that of the union member and then present their accounts of pending legislation, collective bargaining, political developments and economic fluctuations accordingly. They admit the purpose of agitating as well as educating.

They are also beginning to reflect an increased professionalism. Techniques tested in the commercial press are frequently being adapted by labor editors. Through their International Labor Press Association, labor editors meet with faculties of schools of journalism, sponsor workshops and seminars, exchange views with labor reporters of the general press. The calibre of the writing, the depth of its perception of issues and human values that clash at the bargaining table and that are resolved in the pay envelope and trade union programs have reached a level that compares most favorably with reporting in the general press.

In many communities where monopoly ownership has replaced

competitive journalism in the commercial press, the labor press is emerging as the last champion of change, the only remaining voice of a loyal opposition. Soon after his election, President John F. Kennedy declared: "I have had the opportunity of reviewing a number of union publications and I am convinced that the astute handling of the election issues brought new understanding of their significance to millions of union members across the land."

We hope that this volume, an anthology of the labor press between 1955 and 1960, will provide all the evidence needed to prove the case for greater, more balanced coverage of the labor story in the general press. It is a proud story; its heroes and heroines are the 17,000,000 union members who furnish the energy and the skills that keep America free and prospering.

We hope, too, that for many it will also be a revelation of the extent to which the cause of good unionism coincides with the cause of good citizenship. The working men and women of this nation and the leaders they choose to represent them through their unions are fully aware of the grave responsibilities confronting them in these challenging times.

They accept with pride the assignment given them by President-elect Kennedy, who, in a message to the 1960 ILPA Convention, declared: "Our job is just starting. The complexity of the problems which we face in the 1960's and our attempts to meet them will require a high degree of public understanding and public support. To this end, I look to the labor press as an essential medium of education."

—The Editors

I

Trade Unions In Action

EDITORS' NOTE

Working people formed unions as a protest against the arbitrary and sometimes thoughtless exercise of economic power by their corporate employers. The employees wanted a voice in deciding their own rates of pay, their hours of work and the health and safety conditions under which they work.

The economic strength that union members brought to the negotiating table made them partners in determining corporate practices on wages, hours and working conditions. The Government's role in peacetime has been limited largely to guaranteeing employees the right to join the union of their own choice and to mediating difficult disputes.

Despite the folklore to the contrary, collective bargaining in the United States and Canada has developed as a system of local, plant by plant bargaining. Wages and conditions are adjusted through negotiations to local problems and local preferences or to the standards of the region or the immediate industry.

Even the big master contracts that set wage patterns for an industry or for a far-flung corporate giant are normally supplemented by local negotiations.

This system of negotiation has been remarkably successful. Over the years some 97 per cent of the hundreds of thousands of negotiations between labor and management result in agreement on wages and conditions without the loss of an hour's work. Strikes are the exception, not the rule in labor-management negotiations.

For these reasons, the primary assignment of the labor press is to bring to union members the facts about the industry, about the area, about the national economy. Union publications are the only publications available to the rank and file members which present the facts from the workers' viewpoint, that interpret events with sympathy and understanding of the economic and social problems of the wage earner.

The labor press is virtually the only press which supports union members when they are forced out on strike. It is the only press which reports the handling of grievances and champions the organizing efforts of non-union employees.

The articles, news stories and editorials in this section of *Labor's Story* faithfully reflect the bread and butter activities of unions. The steel strike is treated in detail as an example of one of the greatest, successful strikes in American labor history. It won important support from the entire labor press.

Chapters in this bread and butter section deal with labor's basic economic problems: the runaways, the changing South, safety, apprenticeship and technological change and unemployment.

1 | COLLECTIVE BARGAINING

WHAT'S BEHIND YOUR WAGE INCREASE?

*Tom Donahue, director, Contract Dept., Local 32B,
in Building Service Employee, June 1955*

It was meeting night shortly before the Union's biggest contract was to expire. The hall was crowded. Joe Smith stood up in the back of the hall and suggested that wages were the most important issue for the new contract, that "prices seem to be going up every week" and the Local ought to concentrate on a wage increase.

Frank Jones, who's 63, said he thought wages were important but that "the Union ought to start thinking about the future" — in his view "pensions should be the first issue."

Bill Johnson, who just took his wife home from the hospital last week after an operation, said he thought that "an increase in welfare benefits, in hospital and surgical allowances," should be first.

And so it went—a young member rose to say that the union ought to get more vacations and holidays, the fellow who lost two days' pay last week because he was out sick thought sick leave should be the prime issue, the fellow who didn't think he was getting his proper share of overtime thought the Union ought to tighten up the clause requiring rotation of overtime, and so on. Each member had his own particular problem. Each wanted to see it solved this year in this contract.

This "thrashing out" of conflicting views, this effort to arrive at a common opinion, is an important part of the answer to what's behind your wage increase. It is the beginning of a process called "collective bargaining."

During the last twenty years the trade union movement has really come into its own and with it has developed an extensive system of collective bargaining. The last ten years have seen a steadily rising cost of living and steadily rising wage rates following along behind. In some cases union members have caught up or even gotten ahead a bit; in others, they've fallen behind for a time. But, overall, the trend of wage rates for union members and the amount of purchasing power which those rates reflect, has been very definitely up.

Your wage increase represents a part of the total picture of national wage movements and is conditioned by all of the hundreds of factors which affect you and your job. The theater owner, the building operator, the local school board, the department store owner, the ball park operator and all the other people who employ Building Service members are all affected by changes in the national economy and changes on the local scene as well.

But whatever the national or local picture, your Union is in there, trying to do a job for you, trying to answer facts with facts and match figures with figures, in a continuing effort to insure you and the other members of your Local the best possible conditions through collective bargaining.

The process of collective bargaining is not easy to describe. It is a long and complicated business, and there are as many varieties of it as there are stars in the sky. But we can get some idea of its essential parts if we follow the process in a specific case. Let's take a look at what happened after the meeting described above.

After all the arguments were given, the members named a negotiating committee. This committee met immediately after the regular meeting. They spent hours talking over the proposals to be made to the employer, deciding what and how much they should ask for, what things were important, what things didn't seem solid enough to warrant much attention. But always there was the central theme, "What can we get that will benefit the most people?" Then came the strategy sessions planning where they could give a little and where they'd stand fast, and what the line of approach on each issue would be.

Meetings with the employer were scheduled and the pressure began building. Members began discussing the ever-present questions of "Will we have to strike to get what's right? Should we strike? Can we win?" Many a silent prayer was uttered for the success of the negotiations.

The chairman of the negotiating committee shot off a quick request to the International's Research Department for some facts and figures to back up the argument. What are comparative wage rates? What's happened to the cost of living? What's the industry pattern and can we fit into it? What are the economic trends in the industry?

The chairman also contacted the local newspapers and made them aware of the issues in the situation and tried to get the Union's position across to the public effectively so that the Union would get a measure of public support.

Then the meetings began. "How long did the Union think it could keep getting increases," the employer wanted to know. Was there no end to this kind of thing? If they kept on, they'd all be out of jobs and he'd be out with them. Best thing he could do was give them the keys to the place and let them take over the busi-

ness. (There's always some "crying" of this sort by the boss.)

The Union people let him get this off his chest. Then, they told him a few things: How tough it was to support a family on the wages he was paying; that it was okay for him to sit back and tell them the world was coming to an end if they got an extra couple of bucks a week and how they were putting him out of business, but last year's profit statement didn't look half as sick as some of their pay envelopes when the wife got through with weekly grocery shopping. They'd be willing to settle right now for a share of the profits but he needn't tell them about the lean years unless he's willing to split the profits in the good years!

Anyway, that's how it all began. The meeting lasted hours, seemed to accomplish nothing. The bargainers sat through another meeting with no success. Still more meetings were held, both sides jockeying for position and getting their arguments across. Facts and figures clashed, personalities got into the discussion occasionally. The room temperature, and blood pressure, rose and fell with each turn.

Between meetings there were frantic searches for missing facts, and talks with leaders of other unions— to compare notes on benefits won, on union strength, on the way the economy was heading. Periodically, the members were consulted, asked would they compromise on this point, stand firm on that.

Finally the issues became narrowly defined, and the bargaining sessions grew shorter. Each side did a good bit of give-and-take, and at last —after endless hours and weeks of negotiations—an agreement was hammered out and signed, with the members voting on the final terms.

Collective bargaining is just what the word implies. It is an attempt to work out the best possible "bargain" for a group of members under a given set of circumstances.

No, the Union didn't get everything it wanted or felt entitled to. The employer gave more than he felt he should have and didn't get all he felt entitled to either. But the Union did make progress. It did get another rung up the ladder, and the whole business of collective bargaining, of two sides sitting down and discussing their ideas and differences and coming to a mutually agreeable settlement, had once again proved its worth.

If the parties hadn't been able to work it out between them, they still could have tried a few other aids to collective bargaining before they came to a strike situation. The state or federal mediation agency could have been called on to send someone in to try to compromise the differences, or they could have agreed to the appointment of "fact-finders" who'd look into the issues and recommend a settlement. If both methods failed, they could have agreed to submit the whole thing to an arbitrator and let him decide. The value of each of these approaches, of course, will depend on the particular situation.

Anyway, that's how this business of collective bargaining works. The variations are limitless but the basic approach is the same.

So, the next time anyone asks you what you think about your latest wage increase, stop and think. Think about what you got and how you got it. Think about what part you played in getting it, and if you're not satisfied, consider what you can do about doing a better job next year.

LABOR'S GOALS AT THE BARGAINING TABLE

Elmer E. Walker, IAM secretary-treasurer,
in The Machinist, December 5, 1957

Basically labor's goals at the bargaining table will continue to be beamed toward established and time-honored objectives: higher wages—to provide a rising standard of living; increased leisure time—to enjoy the benefits of higher living standards; protection against arbitrary treatment on the job; safe and healthful working conditions; and a degree of security against different kinds of emergencies and financial strains.

These, then, are the principal ingredients out of which labor will concoct its bargaining demands. The exact proportions in which they will be used will vary depending upon the needs and desires of the employees involved, the nature of the industry, the level of existing collective-bargaining gains, and so forth,

Wages, of course, will continue to be an important ingredient in labor's goals. Wages are the bread and butter of unionism. For workers in organized industries who already have achieved a fairly high level of wages, new increases are essential as a means of sharing in the constantly increasing productivity of our economy. In low-wage industries, higher wages are also needed to grant workers a fairer share in existing standards of living and levels of productivity.

Beyond the tangible goals which I have outlined, labor will be striving toward one other goal which is fundamental to its own future success and to the well-being of the nation as a whole. That goal is the steady perfection of the collective-bargaining process.

We of management and labor who work in the field of collective-bargaining know that the contract is not the end, but only the beginning, of the process. For the administration of an existing contract is essential both to the success of that contract and as the foundation for future contract negotiations.

The contract which is poorly administered fails in its purpose, just as a law which is not enforced fails to accomplish its purpose. And the union and the management which cannot get together on the interpre- tation and just administration of ex- isting contract clauses can hope for nothing but dissension when the contract is up for renegotiation.

ON MANAGEMENT RIGHTS

Paul L. Phillips, president of the United Papermakers and Paperworkers, in United Paper, November 30, 1959

We haven't seen statistics on the subject, but our guess would be that more strikes have been caused this year by "management rights" than any other collective bargaining is- sue.

"We have lost our right to man- age," cry the corporate prophets of a holy war against unions . . . "we must," they say, "take a firm stand now to regain sacred rights eroded away by years of soft bargaining."

Anyone with half a grain of sense knows that management has the same right to manage today that it had before corporations faced labor across a bargaining table. The real difference between the days before unions and now is that today we have developed employee rights to parallel management rights.

Essentially what is called the bat- tle of management rights is really a campaign by management to take away hard-won employee rights.

What are these rights? How were they gained? What effect do they have upon efficient management of an enterprise?

Employee rights are products of law or union negotiations. Minimum standards of wages and hours . . . safety and health . . . are among employee rights established by law. Without legislative action by organ- ized labor most of those employee rights would still be in the dream rather than the enforcement stage.

It has been the job of union nego- tiators to raise and extend these minimum rights.

Our government has recognized this union responsibility as good for the nation by stating (in the federal labor law) that it is the policy of the United States to "encourage col- lective bargaining." The same law limits the scope of collective bar- gaining to "wages, hours and condi- tions of work."

Over the years, the National La- bor Relations Board, the agency re- sponsible for enforcing this policy, has built a vast body of law defining what is meant by "conditions of work."

Thus, the Board says that an em- ployer commits an unfair labor prac- tice by refusing to negotiate on such matters as pensions, vacations, group insurance, holidays, etc. . . . but it also says that the union has no (damn, if you please) business try- ing to bargain about who the boss will hire, where he sells his product and for how much, etc.

It should not be concluded from this that the right to negotiate on employee rights was given to unions by the government or the NLRB . . . that right had already been estab- lished over the years in thousands of labor agreements . . . the law merely confirmed that right.

BARGAINING DEMANDED BY PUBLIC WORKERS

Federation News (Chicago), April 25, 1959

The wider use of collective bar- gaining processes by public em- ployees in order to boost wages and cut unemployment is being pushed by the State, County and Municipal Employee's Union.

The union's international execu- tive board has approved a call to its 1,600 affiliated local unions "to press in the months ahead for the conclusion of collective bargaining agreements providing substantial wage increases."

"For years," the board statement declared, "the income of public employees has trailed behind that of the better-organized workers of private industry, serving to depress wage levels throughout the country."

Indicating the importance of higher income for public employees, the union pointed out that state and local government service is continuing to expand, even in time of recession. This area is expected to employ a larger share of the work force in the future.

In October 1958, production workers received an average of $374 a month. Yet full-time state government employees in the United States, including governors, administrators and other top-paid personnel, received an average of only $355 a month in the same period.

DEMOCRATIC NATURE OF BARGAINING RESULTS IN NOVEL CONTRACTS

AFL-CIO News, March 30, 1957

Old gimmicks — and a few new ones — still find their way into modern collective bargaining contracts.

They range from two dozen free bagels (a hard-coated sinker shaped like a doughnut but made out of bread rather than cake)—to $100 contributions for study in foreign countries.

The New York State Dept. of Labor — taking a moment out from more serious work — has come up with a survey of novel clauses in union-management contracts.

The free bagels—two dozen of 'em —go at the end of every working day to members of the Teamsters employed by New York City bagel bakers.

"The (contract) provision seems," the department's Industrial Bulletin comments, "to be unclassifiable under any general category."

Another Teamsters local, under contract with a brewery, has a clause which permits free and unlimited consumption of the employer's product during specified working hours.

The $100 travel allowance for study abroad turned up in a contract held by Community Social Agency Employees Local 1707, of New York City, a unit of the State, County and Municipal Employees. Twenty-five days' paid leave goes with it.

Quite a few New York State local unions, the department's researchers found, have agreements which give a worker a paid holiday on his birthday. One between the Painters and contractors on Staten Island goes a step further. It provides a $5 bill for the celebrant with the compliments of his boss.

The Machinists have a contract that assures full pay to members quarantined because of contagious disease. Some employers under contract to Local 3, Brotherhood of Electrical Workers, pay for two weeks of jury duty.

Among other agreements turned up by the department were company payment for eyeglasses broken during working hours; the right of an employee to retain ownership of an invention; paid coffee breaks (which are becoming increasingly common) and three hours off for blood donations.

"Contractual variety in fringe benefits and working conditions is a reflection of the democratic nature of the collective bargaining process," the Bulletin says.

"In the Act"

SEAMAN

WAGE INCREASES THAT MAKE SENSE

Voice of Cement, Lime and Gypsum Workers, May 1958

In recent months various cement companies have written in their official publications articles alluding to wage increases that workers receive.

These cleverly written articles sing the same old familiar tune: "Companies must make a profit to survive;" "Higher wages mean higher prices;" "Profits are needed to buy new plants and machinery;" "Wage increases must be based on productivity to be a real wage increase;" and "Raising wages to increase purchasing power doesn't really help the economy to prosper."

Let's consider the first point: profits are needed by (cement) companies to survive. Available figures since 1947, which marked the start of normal operations for the cement industry after a war-time halt in production, show that the net profits of 22 leading cement companies have increased by 260%. During the same period of time the average hourly earnings of production workers in the cement industry have increased only 72%. Apparently cement companies are not suffering from a lack of sustained profits.

In addition to this, since 1947, 30

new cement plants have been built and at least 26 existing plants are known to have completed expansion or improvement programs in 1957 alone.

As for the second point, that higher wages mean higher prices, we might call to the attention of a few cement companies that from 1947 to the end of 1957 the price of cement has increased 68.9% while during the same period of time the real average hourly earnings of production workers in the industry increased only 48%. Average hourly earnings include vacation pay, holiday pay, overtime and other premium pay.

Obviously the price increases have far outrun the costs involved in paying increased wages.

The third point that profits are needed to buy new plants and machinery is the most unrealistic point of all. Just why consumers should be forced to pay higher prices for cement in order to finance the expansion of companies in the industry is hard to understand.

This position is made even more incomprehensible when one stops to think that one of the basic ideas of our free enterprise system is that enterprises should obtain capital for expansion purposes through our existing financial institutions by making direct loans or by issuing additional stocks or bonds.

However, instead of following this procedure a great majority of cement firms have persisted in financing most of their expansion from internally generated funds, at the expense of the consumer, by charging higher prices for their product then would otherwise be the case.

Since we are discussing this question of using profits for expansion, a fact should be pointed out, which the cement companies that talked of wages and profits evidently forgot to mention. This fact is the higher depletion deductions given to the cement industry in computing their income taxes.

Just last year a court decision allowed a more favorable basis for figuring their 15% depletion allowance. As a result of this court ruling tax refunds have been applied for by cement companies for the years 1951 to 1956. This tax refund, which is estimated to range from $1 million for most of the smaller companies, up to $17 million for some of the larger companies, will go back into the industry's pockets.

Yet there is no great rush by these firms to reduce prices to reflect this windfall of money to be received.

Let's consider the next argument that wage increases must be based on productivity to be "real wage increases." We maintain that wages besides considering productivity must also take into account increases in the cost of living so that the living standards of workers are not reduced over a period of time.

However, even if wages must be based entirely on increased productivity, as the companies contend they should, then our wage increases in the industry have been and are now perfectly justified.

Specifically we point to the increase in the cement industry's productivity from 2.63 bbls. per man hour in 1947 to 4.24 bbls. in 1957, an increase of 61.2%. At the same time real weekly earnings of cement workers increased only 47.5%.

This definitely indicates a gap of 13.7% which increased wages have not yet filled.

In addition, since 1947, labor costs, as a percent of sales, have shown a marked decline, dropping from 26.6% in 1947 to 15.9% in 1957. This drop in labor costs was reflected in the profit made by 30 leading cement companies on their sales in 1957.

These firms made 15½c profit on every dollar of sales compared to a profit of only 5.9c earned by all manufacturing in 1957.

Let's examine the last point: that wage increases to bolster consumer purchasing power, are of little real help to the prosperity of the economy. Unfortunately we cannot accept the opinion of a few pseudo-economists, but instead we must turn to more informed economists such as Sumner Slichter of Harvard University or Leon Keyserling and many others who admit the advantage to the economy in having a large amount of consumer purchasing power distributed on a broad economic basis among workers.

And we might add in reference to this point that the so-called built-in stabilizers, such as guaranteed employment benefits, health and welfare plans and pensions are praised by both management and government in helping to strengthen our economy in times of recession.

These benefits, as well as sustained purchasing power of workers from wages, have generally been won through the persistent efforts of unions at the bargaining table with companies who otherwise would not have granted such benefits.

This outcry heard from various companies that substantial wage increases will be bad for the company, as well as the worker and the economy, is the same old tune sung by ultra-conservative firms who have consistently opposed any social or economic gains won by their workers.

SEVERANCE PAY PROVISIONS SPREADING

Guild Reporter, November 13, 1959

The Newspaper Guild, which pioneered the negotiation of severance pay for workers in this country, no longer has a monopoly on that contract benefit, the AFL-CIO Dept. of Research finds.

The increased pace of technology, coupled with spreading joblessness in recent years, has led to a sharp-step-up in the number of severance pay plans written into contracts, the department noted in its current Collective Bargaining Report.

About 25 per cent of all contracts —covering approximately 35 per cent of all workers under union contracts —now contain some severance pay provisions.

Fifteen years ago, however, the U.S. Department of Labor found severance pay guaranteed in only five per cent of contracts. This figure inched up to eight per cent by 1950, and to 16 per cent by 1956.

Since 1956, about two million additional workers have been covered by negotiated provisions for severance pay, mainly as the result of ne-

gotiations by the Auto Workers and the Ladies' Garment Workers.

The program recently negotiated by the Meat Cutters and the Packinghouse Workers with Armour & Co., to deal with worker problems arising out of automation was also noted.

One purpose of severance pay is to compensate the worker on dismissal "in some measure" for loss of such job rights as seniority, vacations and pensions.

In addition, termination pay plans "have gained increasing acceptance as a helpful and desirable means of easing the impact on workers of loss of employment."

"To some extent," the Report continues, "severance pay also may serve as a form of job protection. Particularly where the plan calls for relatively large severance payments, the employer may have a financial incentive to keep the worker on the job and to take steps other than layoff or discharge to meet changes in operating conditions."

⚬⚬

"All that serves labor serves the nation. All that harms labor is treason. If a man tells you he loves America yet hates labor, he is a liar. There is no America without labor, and to fleece the one is to rob the other."

—ABRAHAM LINCOLN

HAPPY DAY

The Machinist, June 14, 1956

Two or three weeks off with full pay will be easy to take this summer. The taking should be all the sweeter for remembering that it wasn't very many years ago that nobody thought of giving anyone in the shop a vacation with pay. That was something special for the folks in the front office. The shop would get its vacation on the next layoff.

All that has changed, of course, through collective bargaining by the union. It's a rare union agreement today that doesn't provide for one-, two- and three-week vacations for everybody—depending on length of service.

Actually, the vacation isn't free. Like everything else, we've had to earn it. In a sense, it's part of the general payoff for greater production we are able to turn out as a result of improvements in machinery—machinery producing so much that the economy can afford to give us all a chance to rest up and get a refreshed outlook on life.

As the machines continue to improve, we can ask for and expect to win longer and longer vacations with pay. Three weeks after 12 or 15 years is no longer a rarity. Four-week vacations are on the way. Already they are being written into some agreements for men and women with 20 and 25 years service. In another five years, they will probably be commonplace.

Our vacations serve more purposes than may meet the eye. They are a method of giving us the time to enjoy the wealth we help to create. At the same time, they represent a kind of shorter workweek—with the benefits taken once a year instead of by the week. And, they are real protection against layoffs when times are slack.

Figure it this way: if 100 employees in one shop take their vacations next month under the union contract, they will be absent from work two weeks apiece on the average. That's 200 weeks of work. Two hundred weeks of paid vacations mean fulltime work for 50 other men that month in that shop or a full year's work for four men.

Extend that across the country and you get a lot of work in industries where summer layoffs used to be traditional, every-year events.

Next year, if production keeps on increasing across the country and if the negotiating committee gets the proper support, maybe we can get a longer vacation.

IT'S THE LITTLE THINGS THAT HURT MOST, LETTER CARRIER'S WIFE TELLS SENATORS

AFL-CIO News, May 14, 1960

Mrs. Woodrow P. Gaines, wife of a union letter carrier, gave an eloquent reply to Administration opposition to a wage increase for government workers. Following are excerpts from her testimony before the Senate Post office and Civil Service Committee:

My husband has the top seniority among letter carriers in the Fort Lauderdale, Fla., post office by virtue of his 21 years service . . . but we have found that we cannot eat seniority privileges, nor can we cash them at the bank.

Many things which most families consider part of their normal routine are luxuries beyond a letter carrier's reach. My husband's best suit, for instance, is nine years old. I cannot remember, offhand, when we last saw a moving picture show.

If enjoyment costs money, it is beyond the Gaines family budget.

We have been blessed with four wonderful little boys, the oldest 10, the twins 7, and our youngest, 4. My husband's take-home pay has less buying power than it did before we started our family. Surely a couple should not be expected to remain childless merely for the privilege of the husband being a government employee!

Despite the fact that I, also, have to work and my husband takes odd jobs after his regular day's work is done, we had to take a second mortgage on our home. We have found it necessary to drop mortgage insurance and hospitalization insurance . . . . maintained for 10 years at great personal sacrifice . . . We have more indebtedness on our home than on the day we bought it.

I am a public stenographer working in our own home, and I have done this for five years. I average six to six and one-half hours sleep per night because there is not time for more. I am too busy supplementing my husband's salary, plus running a home and caring for four growing boys, whose growing feet require shoes and whose healthy appetites make a grocery expense that is a first on our budget.

To a wife and mother, it is the little things that hurt. When one 4-year-old begs, "Mamma, please rock me," it hurts that I am typing material that must meet a deadline.

Have you ever been placed in a position where you said a prayer that a little boy would not really lose his loose tooth for two more days because it was Wednesday and payday was Friday and there just wasn't any small change so the fairies could come? Have you ever known what it was to hunt in all the little teapots and containers to find 35 cents for a price of a child's school lunch ticket?

But, why should it be necessary to continue this narrative which I find is both distasteful and harrowing?

Certainly our failure to make ends meet is not the result of any extravagance or self-indulgence on our part. My husband is a high school graduate, possessed of a great deal of common sense, and like myself, a person of moderate tastes and desires. Neither of us drink nor do I smoke. My husband is a man who is respected in our community. We are both very proud of the fact that we work with youth groups, he holds an office on the executive board of the PTA, and is an active member of the Board of Stewards of the Methodist Church of which we are members.

Before our marriage I was trained in Business Administration and given half a chance could run the household well and save money for future needs, but the United States Government is not even giving us that half a chance.

Surely the United States of America—the richest and most powerful nation in the world—can afford to pay their letter carriers a decent salary so they can rear their children in pride and decency.

"So *that's* where the yellow went!"

STRIKES ARE 'MINUTE FRACTION' OF AMERICAN ECONOMIC LIFE

AFL-CIO News, December 13, 1958

The role of the strike in the overall picture of American collective bargaining and economic activity is so small as to be almost insignficant, a study by the AFL-CIO Dept. of Research shows.

In its Collective Bargaining Report, the department provides the 1957 figures on "the worker's ultimate weapon in his relation with his employer," as compiled by the Bureau of Labor Statistics, in their proper context, and makes the following points:

• "The 3,673 strikes represent only about 3 per cent of all collective bargaining situations. In 97 per cent of the cases, the parties concerned carried on their relations and settled their differences without any work stoppage.

• "The 1.39 million workers involved in strikes during 1957 were only 2 per cent of the non-agricultural work-force.

• "The total number of man-days idle, 16.5 million, was only 0.14 per cent of the total work-time of all workers and far less than the 40 million man-days lost because of on-the-job accidents. A total of 99.86 per cent of all work-time was carried on without interruption by strikes.

• "The days lost by strikes are an even smaller proportion of the total lost work-time represented by the enforced idleness of the unemployed."

The report lays to rest many public misconceptions that are often used to combat union organization.

It shows that relations between workers and their employers are growing better rather than worse, and that strikes are diminishing rather than increasing.

The number of 1957 man-days lost because of strikes was the lowest since 1931, except for 1940 and the war years. The total was less than in 1927—two decades ago—and about the same as in 1933. And since 1933 the work-force has increased by 70 per cent and union membership has multiplied six times.

"All but a small proportion of these 1957 walkouts revolved around basic improvements in wages, hours. supplementary benefits and other working conditions on the job," the report points out.

"These were the chief issues in about 80 per cent of the stoppages and responsible for over 90 per cent of the total work-time lost."

Strikes for union recognition have declined, the report points out, because the issue can be processed through the National Labor Relations Board. Union security caused only a few strikes either because many unions already have it or were able to negotiate it.

Jurisdictional strikes, which "normally receive very prominent attention in the press," accounted for less than 2 per cent of the man-days lost in 1957, largely because of machinery for settling such disputes developed by the AFL-CIO.

The typical 1957 strike, the figures show, involved relatively few workers and only a single plant or establishment — 76 per cent of all walkouts. Only 7 per cent of the stoppages were directed at companies or employer associations with 11 or more separate units.

The AFL-CIO economists cite a study by the National Industrial Conference Board which shows that 128 out of 194 unions surveyed constitutionally require authorization at both local and international levels before a group of workers can strike.

The report shows that about half of all international unions provide strike benefits, with payments in about one-third of all unions a flat amount ranging from $5 to $40 a week.

Demands for regulation of strikes "are often part of a well-organized campaign to reduce the effectiveness of trade unions," the report comments.

"The worker's right to strike is an integral part of the workings of a free society," it continues. "The right to strike is somewhat comparable to the farmer's right to refuse to plant a particular crop or a businessman's right to refuse to sell a particular product.

"It could be argued that an individual worker always has the freedom to work or not to work at a particular job for which he has been hired. But unless he also has the freedom to join with other workers and if necessary to act together with them in withholding his labor, this is but an empty right.

"The entire history of labor unions makes clear the fact that without the right to strike, the worker is helpless because his employer will automatically hold an insuperable advantage in bargaining with him."

THE REAL REASON MEN STAY OUT ON STRIKE

Oil, Chemical and Atomic Union News, December 7, 1959

The true causes of strikes and the real reasons men doggedly stay out on strikes many months long usually are overlooked by those people who try to answer all problems with arithmetic.

In any lengthy strike, those who oppose the strikers make much ado about the amount of wages lost by the strikers. The struck company usually issues press releases to remind the public and the strikers of the total wages sacrificed.

This leads, naturally, to the comment among outside observers that "The strikers never will make up for the wages they have lost, even if they win their demands."

To evaluate a strike on this basis is to miss the point. It is to be conceded that in many strikes, particularly those of long duration, the strikers sustain losses that would take many years to replace. But strikers seldom go out on the bricks for pennies-per-hour. Usually they strike because of a principle more valuable than money or because they have a frustrated feeling that rigid company positions have placed their backs to the wall.

This is the situation in the current Standard Oil-American Oil and Johns-Manville strikes. These men are not on strike for pennies; they are on strike for the protection of their very jobs and the working rules they need every day for the rest of their lives. They are on strike because they feel that they can no longer tolerate a situation in which the company calls all the shots and they have no say-so.

These strikes are five months old. There is no denying the amount of money they have lost. It probably averages close to $2,500 per man by now. But long ago these strikes went beyond the point of money-counting and became a matter of principle and pride.

The members struck because of a principle. It is pride that keeps them on strike. Whatever the cost finally may be, most of these members are much too proud to go back to work except on union terms and by majority vote of their fellow workers. To go back on any other basis would be to bow the head and bend the knee.

It is amazing that the money-counting types who manage American industry do not recognize the strength of pride in American working people. They may say such pride is foolish, impractical, stubborn and foolhardy if they wish, but they should recognize pride as something good and wonderful, too.

Perhaps the $100,000-a-year men do not need this sort of pride to sustain them in the battle of life. Perhaps they are sustained by success rather than by a conviction of righteousness—we wouldn't know.

But the people who have assumed more humble roles in life, the people who know that they will never be great or powerful or wealthy, place great store on pride. It gives them a sense of worthiness as members of the human race. They would rather go hungry than bend a knee.

Would those who try to evaluate strikes in dollars and cents want to see this pride destroyed? God grant that this shall never happen, for if it does the entire nation will be weaker and the human race itself will have slipped downward. God grant that a large percentage of the people always will be proud enough —yes, even stubborn enough—to stand for what they believe regardless of dollars and pennies.

WHY STRIKE?
A LINE IS DRAWN AGAINST ABUSE

San Jose Reporter, reprinted in Guild Reporter, September 11, 1959

Why strike?

The ultimate tool of labor relations is a two-edged implement, and people are always surprised when it cuts a little.

How can you possibly get back what you've lost in wages?

You can't. Why should you?

A strike occurs when a group of employees decides negotiations have reached the end of reason and a demonstration of solidarity and unwillingness to continue work without proper redress is called for.

Are all unions right when they strike? Of course not. All wars aren't right, nor are all politicians, all policemen, all wheeler dealers in the world of finance, all agents of the judiciary.

Why strike?

When a labor negotiation reaches a total impasse, the union has just two choices:

1. Give in.
2. Take a walk.

Where would labor be if there had never been a successful strike? Where would the country be?

You have only to consider where the wage earner once was to know where he'd be now.

Without the right to strike, a man in the great mass industries, a foundryman, perhaps, would be getting about $45 a week now. This is a fact even when all the external inciters to inflation are considered, wars, monetary manipulation, federal reserve hocus pocus and the governmental boondoggle of wayward spending.

Without the right to strike, a printer today would be drawing something like $40 a week in a town this size, for a six-day week.

The Great Spirit alone could guess what the average newspaper reporter would get; $18 a week perhaps, if he proved willing to work seven days a week, run errands of an evening, could give up eating lunch and showed willingness to take out $7 of the $18 a week in free passes to second rate movies and fourth rate boxing matches.

The first union was founded to circumvent abuse. This applies to abuse at the pay window as well as to the abuses of near-slavery and child labor.

There is nothing in the history of the world to indicate such abuse would have been abated by the good intentions of the political bodies and the best possible offices of the do-gooder reformers.

Abuse has been checked by drawing a line and standing on it.

The unions did the drawing.

The whole economy has benefitted. The farmer may never admit it, but this is why he gets more for his produce. The investor may not ever acknowledge the source of his well being, but today this chiefly is why he is able to clip gold crust off the edge of his coupons. Industrial management shows rare inclination to admit the existence, where labor relations figure, of economic fact, but this mainly is why management these days has something to manage.

The reason is this. The United States is a business nation. Business requires consumers. A consumer requires purchasing power. Nobody makes him a gift of it. A consumer has to earn, create and bargain for his purchasing power. He can't do it as a unit of one. Hence, the union.

The paycheck of practically every wage earner in the land is the size it is because of the existence of labor unions. This applies whether the wage earner belongs to a union or whether or not he ever heard of one.

And had there not always been implied the possibility of pressing the working man's claims by taking recourse to the picket line, the foundryman's first big pay raise would still be due.

The average man wouldn't have to worry about how big a yield his bond holdings might produce.

The average man wouldn't have any.

THE RIGHT TO STRIKE

Labor, November 28, 1959

A professor from the University of Maryland, a conservative institution, made some highly appropriate comments the other day on the issue of the right to strike. The professor, Harold F. Sylvester, aired his views in a letter to the Washington Star.

He said that "tensions created by the steel strike" have brought some people to the view that "workers have the right to strike only so long as they refrain from exercising it.

"It now appears," he added, "that a new doctrine is developing: The only permissible strike is the unsuccessful strike. So long as a particular strike does not seriously inconvenience the public, the strike may be tolerated. But as soon as it creates a pinch, 'something should be done about these conspiracies against the public'.

"The purpose of a strike," he continued, "is to put economic pressure on the employer and his customers. If it becomes unlawful the moment the employer or the customer inventories run short, then the right to strike means little indeed."

Clearly, Professor Sylvester has made a vital point at this time.

LABOR MUST RESIST THE 'HARDENING ATTITUDE'

Lee W. Minton, president, Glass Bottle Blowers Assn.,
in Glass Horizons, July 1959

More and more, in the field of labor relations, we hear talk of a "hardening attitude" on the part of some in management.

There are some, no doubt, who feel it is a good time to exploit the gigantic smear which political propagandists are trying to lay on all of union labor for the shortcomings of a minute percentage of leaders. These smear tactics are being employed not only in the legislative field but also at the bargaining table and in the field of organizing.

There are ruthless elements in some management quarters, too, who are eager to capitalize on the growing fears in the work force arising from inroads of automation. Those inclined to "talk tough" to unions might figure the time to bray the loudest is when workers are seeing others' jobs being wiped out and might be fearful of their own.

A third factor to be considered is the carefully promoted campaign to picture inflation as the nation's No. 1 danger and to portray union-won wage increases as the prime cause for inflation. This campaign represents a calculated effort to clothe unions in villain garments even before they reach the bargaining table.

The argument that union-won wage gains are the prime cause of inflation, of course, is a naive one; but, repeated frequently and in persuasive manner, it does damage to the union cause. When we consider the millions of Americans struggling today to make ends meet, the propaganda that workers' wages are causing inflation is a cruel one indeed.

How must the labor movement act to resist this warfare?

First of all, we must do everything possible to maintain and improve our economic strength. We can do this through organizing, through promoting more participation, more unity and feeling for the organizations of the AFL-CIO.

Strength is all-important, but its proper use is no less vital. If we are attacked in an irresponsible way, we must repulse the attack in a spirit of responsibility. This might seem difficult at times, but it is important to labor's long-term struggle.

COURAGEOUS HENDERSON STRIKERS SOLID IN FACE OF 'DOUBLE CROSS,' TROOPERS

Harry Conn (PAI), May 18, 1959

Henderson, N. C. — The textile mill's brilliant searchlights played on the strikers and state patrolmen congregating on the road leading to the mill entrance.

It was nearing 11 P.M. The second shift of strikebreakers was about to break. The strikers, many with 20, 30 or 40 years in the mill, gathered in small groups. After six months on strike their spirits were still high.

The troopers, using their flashlights, picked up nails and tacks from the road. "Nail pickers," someone shouted. There was laughter.

Suddenly the strikers started moving down the road away from the mill—and away from the searing searchlight. The troopers followed them. Small groups sang "Roll the Union On" and "Solidarity Forever."

"Here they come!"

The first car had Virginia tags. The strikers shouted at it, shaking their fists. Other cars zoomed by.

"Scab . . . filthy scabs . . . yellow . . . chicken . . . a scab is a scab until the day she dies . . . !"

The faces of the troopers were expressionless.

The cars moved by the shouting strikers in rapid succession. The figures inside were indistinguishable in the darkened, huddled groups. To the strikers they were job stealers, something to hate.

At 3 P.M. and 7 A.M. the scene is repeated. This is the surface coating of one of the biggest and most courageous strikes in Southern labor history—the strike of the Textile Workers Union of America against the Harriet-Henderson Cotton Mills.

This is a fight where the company holds most of the aces. It has obtained an injunction limiting picketing. It is recruiting strikebreakers out of county and out of state. And state troopers are, in effect, escorting the strikebreakers to and from work.

Dynamite explosions and gun fire are heard from time to time. More than $20,000 in rewards have been offered by the company, the union and others but no striker has been picked up. A vice president of the company admitted that "most" strikebreakers carry guns.

Strikers have been arrested for throwing dirt and rocks at cars. One scab's car has been turned over, nothing more serious. But the court seems to be under pressure to make examples out of these instances to discourage other strong action.

The union's answer to all this is one picket sign which reads: "Going For Broke."

This is precisely what the more than 1,000 strikers intend to do.

"As long as we've got a biscuit to eat I'm staying out until we get a contract," striker Johnny Martin declared. Martin, 51, first went to work in the mill when he was 12 years old.

"I'll never forget," he said. "I was in the sixth grade in school. Old John D. (the father of John D. Cooper, Jr., present president), led all the boys 12 or over out of school into the mill. We worked 60 hours a week and got $6.30."

As far as Martin is concerned "the union is the only answer. Life wouldn't be worth living without it. I know. I've worked with it and without it."

The rock-like solidarity of the strikers is something Cooper and townspeople cannot get over. "We all went out together and we'll all go back together," is a comment frequently heard among the strikers.

When the "false armistice" took place on April 17 this solidarity was put to the true test. Under the agreement the unionists thought that at least 500 strikers would be rehired but new strikebreakers had been employed without their knowledge, and only 25 strikers got jobs.

When these 25 realized what happened every single one of them dropped his tools and walked out to rejoin the picket line. And the strike has become a lockout.

Six months ago these strikers walked out of the mills when management refused to renew the old contract. The company president, aging John D. Cooper, Jr., demanded that an arbitration clause be deleted.

"If I'm going to run this plant efficiently we must not be forced into arbitration," Cooper told PAI later.

TWUA held the contract with the mills for 14 years. Cooper, himself, admits that the relationship was good—at least up until recent years.

The day after the strike, Nov. 17, Cooper opened up his mills. Not one of the 1100 workers would go through the picket lines. He shut the mill down for three months. On Feb. 16 he tried opening up the mills again. This time state troopers were on hand to escort strikebreakers through the picket lines.

Cooper admitted that several days before he opened the mills his attorney had called Gov. Luther Hodges' administrative assistant, and then handed the telephone to the Henderson mayor and the Vance County sheriff who requested the troops.

"After all, my attorney knew Ed Rankin (the Governor's assistant); the mayor and sheriff didn't," Cooper said.

Even with the troopers on hand only 57 union members went back to work. In the three months that followed some of these 57 returned to the strike and a few other unionists went back in the mill.

The union says the 57 figure is the highwater mark of unionists in the mill. Cooper told PAI he had no figures on this himself.

The bar to a settlement is the fact that some 700 strikebreakers are now holding down the jobs of the strikers. Not many more than 300 jobs are currently open and the company is recruiting strikebreakers fast with the intention of starting a third shift soon.

This has happened despite the fact that Gov. Luther Hodges, a former textile executive himself, warned Cooper that "your decision to begin a second and third shift at the mill will definitely heighten existing tensions in Henderson and Vance County and may actually result in bloodshed in spite of the best efforts of the law enforcement personnel."

Hodges participated in the negotiations which led up to the settlement that blew up.

He charged that the company "has intentionally or otherwise misled" him, the strikers and the Federal and state mediator.

The union was under the impression that there were only 437 strike-breakers in the mill. The Governor said there were 450 to 500 working. No figure was mentioned in the negotiations, but, as the Governor stated, "the clear impression given me and the mediators was that a substantial part of all jobs on the second and third shifts would be held for returning workers."

Asked by PAI why he did not, in good faith, mention the number Cooper replied: "Nobody brought it up. You didn't expect me to do it?"

Now the strike has settled down to a tense, long-range struggle. The TWUA has contributed a $100,000 fund to meet striker emergencies plus $5,000 a week for food for strikers and their families.

Funds are being contributed by North Carolina unions and other TWUA locals. But the hope for these strikers lies in the generous contributions of unionists from throughout the country.

"This fight is really the fight of the entire trade union movement," declares TWUA Regional Director Boyd Payton. "If we lose another key union center in the South it will not only be felt by these strikers but by every working man and woman all over this country—and in our economic and political life as well."

AFTERMATH OF THE HENDERSON STRIKE

Henderson, N. C. Freedom Fighter, July 26, 1960

Letter From Rhode Island

Following his visit to Rhode Island, where a "colony" of Henderson Freedom Fighters is living and working, David George received this letter from one of the families located there.

". . . we were so glad to see you and wish you could have stayed for supper with us. We are working every night (and) make 46 hours a week so far, and make more than we ever made there, and no one ever comes around and says anything to you. If we get behind they come and help . . . we are all enjoying it fine up here and hope we can make it our home from now on. We thank the Union there for all it did for us. We know God will take care of His children, and I know it because He put us to a test to see how strong our faith was, and I knew he would take care of us, and He has. Give our best regards to everybody, and ask them to pray for us all. We are starting a Henderson Club so I know you will hear from Cotton about it. Don't forget our Freedom Fighter, for we enjoy reading the news in it and I am making a History Book for my grandchildren to read some day . . . I hope you can read this . . . Mr. Cooper got all of my school days, and I got nothing but the love of God, and I had rather have that than anything. May God be with you all till we meet again,

(Mr. and Mrs.)....................J. ....

Henderson Members—Notice!

We have a number of immediate job openings for members of certain skills and experience—and we expect to have additional offers within the next few weeks. These openings are in textile mills in other states—100 per cent Union.

We need an up-to-date list of members who are willing and ready to accept such offers. There will be a special registration of all who are interested AT YOUR UNION HALLS.

National Readers Notice!

We are often asked by friends and well-wishers: "What can we send to Henderson, besides money, that will be especially helpful and welcome?"

The answer to this question will vary from time to time. But just now the answer is simple. Things most needed by most families are:

Bed sheets—Pillow Cases—Towels.

Some time back we received a very welcome and wonderful gift of 180 sheets from the Leaksville-Draper-Spray Joint Board, TWUA. These all were immediately distributed to 90 families (one pair to each family).

A Friend Indeed

One of those many, many wonderful people in all parts of the U. S.

and Canada who have done so much to help us is a retired railroad worker, living now in New Mexico. We have mentioned Dan Kelly before, but must do so again, because, through all the months of 1960 he has continued to send us a regular monthly donation of TEN DOLLARS. Maybe that amount does not sound so BIG to some people, but to us it seems an enormous contribution, and it warms our hearts as much as it helps to meet special needs.

HENDERSON TEXTILE STRIKERS, PROTESTING INNOCENCE, JAILED

AFL-CIO News, November 5, 1960

Eight officers and members of the Textile Workers Union, still protesting their innocence, have begun serving prison terms ranging from 2 to 10 years for participation in an alleged conspiracy to commit strike violence.

In an emotion-laden scene the unionists presented themselves at the Vance County courthouse here following denial of a long series of court appeals and failure of a last-minute bid to Gov. Luther H. Hodges for executive clemency.

While hundreds of TWUA members crowded around them singing "Solidarity Forever," the convicted unionists bade tearful farewells to their families before being led to waiting police cars.

Imprisoned were TWUA Vice Pres. Boyd E. Payton; TWUA Staff Representatives Charles E. Auslander and Lawrence Gore; Pres. Johnnie Martin of Local 578; and union members Warren Walker, Calvin Pegram, Robert Abbott and Malcolm Jarrell.

The eight had been convicted on charges of plotting a series of dynamitings in 1959 during the union's long strike against the Harriet-Henderson Cotton Mills. The dynamitings never took place.

Speaking on behalf of himself and the other men being imprisoned with

him, Payton told the gathering: "None of us has any desire to be a hero or a martyr. We'd much rather go home to our families. But the struggle to build the labor movement is just as worthwhile as the sacrifices for Christianity. Let's hold our heads high and face this test with courage."

Later, TWUA Pres. William Pollock stressed that the unionists were "victimized by a special agent of the police" who attempted to induce the men to bomb the struck plant and a power sub-station.

"TWUA," Pollock said, "has complete faith in the integrity of these men. We are deeply grieved at the hardships and sacrifices they are about to undergo. We know they will face their ordeal with the kind of courage that has always marked the struggle of textile workers for social justice."

Payton denied on behalf of all eight strikers that there was "any wrongdoing at Henderson." He went on: "There is no rancor nor bitterness in our hearts. Neither is there any burden upon our consciences."

Pres.-emeritus Emil Rieve commented: "After their persecutors are forgotten, history will know these eight men existed and that they tried to improve the lot of the little people."

IT'S COLD ON THE I-H LINE . . .
AND IN HARVESTER'S HEART

Jerry Dale in UAW Solidarity, December 22, 1958

It was cold in Chicago . . . the thermometer hovered around eight above. There were several inches of snow on the ground and flurries in the air.

A small group of pickets huddled around the big can with glowing briquets inside. Behind them stood the huge old McCormick works . . . empty and dreary-looking . . . a constant reminder of the Scrooge-like management which runs the giant International Harvester chain, the fourth largest corporation in the United States with which the UAW deals.

From a radio nearby came the strains of "Jingle Bells." The music seemed out of place, as indeed it was.

". . . It's a dirty thing this company is trying to do," Josef Biskowski was saying. "It wants to get rid of the older workers. It's trying to weaken our seniority protection and put the older people out on the street.

"Don't those executives know the world was not made for profit alone?"

Steamfitter Biskowski had a right to ask that question. At 56, he has spent 24 years of his life working for Harvester.

And he hastens to add, he's been a member of UAW Local 1308 from the very start.

"I think the company is deliberately dragging the negotiations out over Christmas and the cold weather," remarked Clarence Warr, a 62-year-old elevator operator. "They think we're going to panic. They just don't know us very well."

But Warr knows the company better than well. He's worked there for 32 years.

"We know their intentions all right," added Clarence Peeples, a member of the local's bargaining committee. "We've dealt with them before."

Like Biskowski, Peeples saw seniority as the No. 1 issue though, at 41, he is not one of the company's older workers.

"Actually, they're trying to chisel on a lot of things we've had in the old contract," he said. "Seniority is just one of them. They're trying to downgrade classifications; they're trying to cut down on sick benefits; they want more short work weeks."

Perennial layoffs were what bothered Joe Serna, Isaiah Williams and John Guerrero the most.

"First they work you overtime for a few months, then they push you out on the street," said Serna, a 50-year-old electric truck driver with 19 years' seniority. The other two, both low-seniority workers, agreed.

Stanley Klepczarek, 49, a hand trucker with 24 years' seniority, and with a sick wife and four kids at home, said simply: "The most important issue for me is more money."

At the nearby tractor works, a group of hammer men, members of UAW Local 1301, were picketing as a snowy darkness fell over the Windy City.

"There's nothing wrong with this company," exclaimed Walter Kulpa, a union member since 1937. His fellow pickets looked at him strangely.

"It's just that the people running it are lousy," Kulpa added with a grin. "They want you to produce till you drop dead. In our department production has increased at least 40 per cent, and with less people than we had before. I know, I've been here 22 years."

"We've got a foremen problem, too," added Charles Gay, a forge shop steward. "We have more foremen in our place than any other plant in America, and they justify their existence by riding the workers. Would you believe it, we have five foremen supervising 30 workers. That's where the profits are going."

Gay, at 49, has been with I-H for 24 years and a steward for 12.

"This is the time-study man's paradise," said Pat Muldoon, a 30-year man. "They'll use any excuse to retime a job and cut the rate. No job is safe."

"And they always time the fastest man," added Hilliard Sanders,

who's spent 15 years in the plant.

It was quite dark now. The snow had stopped, but even the warm fire could not halt the cold if you stepped away for a moment. The men were still talking. They've been there—talking and picketing—since Nov. 13. They will probably still be be there on Christmas night and perhaps even into the new year. They'll be there . . . at the tractor works . . . at McCormick . . . and at plant gates all over the country.

O'SULLIVAN VICTIMS HIT AGAIN BY T-H CRUSHER

AFL-CIO News, May 24, 1958

A National Labor Relations Board trial examiner has ruled that the Rubber Workers violated the Taft-Hartley Act by picketing and boycotting the violently anti-union O'Sullivan Rubber Co. It was the second heavy Taft-Hartley blow at the union and its Local 511 at Winchester, Va., in their conflict with O'Sullivan.

The examiner recommended that the NLRB order the local to cease picketing and advertising the boycott. He also recommended that the international be required to publish in its paper, the United Rubber Worker, a statement that the union has ended the boycott.

Local 511 struck O'Sullivan's on May 13, 1956 after months of company stalling on negotiations for a first contract.

The company brought in strikebreakers and continued operations on a curtailed basis. In April 1957, the company asked a decertification election which under Taft-Hartley would bar the strikers from voting. The election was held Oct. 18, 1957 and, with only strikebreakers casting ballots, the vote went overwhelmingly against the union.

The Rubber Workers continued to picket the Winchester plant and stepped up its boycott campaign of the "Nation's No. One Heel," the slogan used by the company.

In February 1958, the general counsel of the NLRB filed a complaint that the union's continuing picketing of the plant and its boycott campaign were unfair labor practices under Taft-Hartley.

The union, in hearings before Trial Examiner George A. Downing, claimed that the basic issue involved was the right to free speech. If the general counsel's charges were upheld, the union said, all unions would lose the right to tell the public about conditions in a plant involved in a labor dispute.

The picketing, it added, was "for organizational purposes by means of persuading the present employees of the company that they have impaired the welfare of all wage earners by taking the jobs of the pickets."

Downing held that the evidence in the O'Sullivan case is similar to that of the Curtis Brothers case in which the board ruled that picketing, if the union does not represent a majority of the employees in a plant, is in violation of the Taft-Hartley Act. The board's decision in the Curtis case, said Downing, is a binding precedent.

He recommended a similar cease and desist order against the international's nationwide boycott of O'Sullivan products.

KOHLER STRIKE ENTERS 4th YEAR; SOUND RELATIONS IS KEY ISSUE

Gervase N. Love in AFL-CIO News, April 13, 1957

SHEBOYGAN, WIS. — The grim and gallant strike of Auto Workers Local 833 against the Kohler Co. and its industrial feudalism has entered its fourth bitter year.

The third anniversary of the country's largest major strike came on April 5—"the unhappiest birthday in America," the strike committee called it.

The workers who once made plumbing wares are doggedly maintaining their court-restricted picket lines around the gray walls that enclose the plant in company-owned Kohler Village, near here.

At issue are some of the basic things that have been relegated to the history books in most areas of industrial relations — recognition by the company that workers are human beings and have an innate dignity that no employer can be allowed to deprive them of, and the right of the workers to live their own private and political lives as they see fit, in accordance with the law.

"There never has been true labor peace at Kohler," the strike committee said in an anniversary statement.

The committee said it is more confident of winning the strike than ever before.

"When the Kohler strike is setlleld," it said, "it will be because management has decided to join us in the effort to obtain a long range program for sound labor relations.

"We hope Kohler management comes to this conclusion soon. Until it does, we have no choice but to continue and enlarge our boycott campaign and our legal proceedings against Kohler. At the same time we will—as we always have—make every possible effort to promote and bring about a settlement."

There appeared little hope of an early settlement as the the strike went into another year. Only two months ago, Herbert V. Kohler, the company president, in a speech in Detroit urged other employers to refuse to bargain, to hire strikebreakers and to try and bust their unions.

Kohler workers have a long tradition of fighting management autocracy. It dates back to 1897, when the fathers and grandfathers of the present strikers organized a feeble union which struck, but was quickly beaten down.

The flame of industrial freedom flickered weakly for more than a generation—until 1934—then flared up again. Once more the workers formed a union, under the banner of the former AFL, and once again they took to the picket line.

The company resorted to butality. It armed scabs and guards who opened fire on a picket line from inside the plant, killing two pickets and wounding 47 other persons including a number of women and children. The national guard was called out to disarm the company goons and protect the strikers. A company union was formed, but for seven long years the AFL kept the plant under token picket lines.

Thus for 10 of the last 23 years, the Kohler plant has been struck.

Local 833 was organized when the company began kicking its company union around. It took eight months to negotiate the first contract. It wasn't a good agreement, but the union signed in the hope that the company would learn the advantages of peaceful relations and good-faith bargaining.

The hope proved futile. Negotiations were reopened as the first contract moved toward its expiration date, but there was no agreement on such basic issues as the union shop and the company's demand that a weak agreement be made weaker.

The old agreement died, and there was still no settlement. Kohler cancelled it, refusing to extend it until a new pact could be signed.

"You have to bargain with them," he told a reporter, "but you don't have to give them anything."

Finally, on April 5, 1954, the strike became effective. Once more Kohler recruited scabs and strong-arm men, armed them, and got an injunction limiting picketing. This time the company arsenal was confiscated by law enforcement officials before it could be used with the callousness of 1934.

"I am the law around here," Kohler told the pickets one day. "When I get through with you, you'll come crawling like worms, begging for your jobs."

The firm turned down every attempt at arbitration, whether made by the union or respected outsiders. It fired everybody connected with the union leadership. The union filed an array of charges against it with the National Labor Relations Board; a 112-day hearing has been held, but the trial examiner's report is not due until next summer.

The union initiated a nationwide boycott against Kohler products — portable electric light plants and air cooled engines as well as plumbing ware and fixtures—which has cost the firm millions of dollars in lost sales and is growing more widespread all the time.

The UAW has spent an estimated $11 million to keep the strike going, much of it coming from members of other unions.

Thus millions of dollars have been needlessly spent, millions of production manhours needlessly lost, and the seeds of no one knows how much hate needlessly sowed and nurtured because of Herbert V. Kohler, who made the mistake of thinking that a little money and a little power were enough to break not only his 3,400 employees, but the American labor movement.

(*Six years after the Kohler strike began, the National Labor Relations Board ruled that the company had, in effect, turned an economic strike into a massive unfair labor practice. The NLRB ordered the reinstatement of an estimated 3000 workers.*)

Chins Up

Lost my job, lost my car
My TV's on the bum,
Cupboard's bare, nothing there
Not a slice of chewing gum.
My unemployment insurance is gone,
There is no hope in sight
But the word comes from Augusta—
Everything's gonna be all right.
    Just keep those chins up,
    Just wait and see,
    Why comes the summer—
      prosperity.
The bills pile up, month by month,
My credit is all gone.
I'm worried sick, can't sleep at night
I toss and turn till dawn.
My dog's left home, my cat's gone, too;
There is no end in sight,
But the word comes down from Burning Tree—

Everything's gonna be all right.
    Just keep those chins up
    Just wait and see
    Why comes September—
      prosperity.
Down on the farm the well's run dry,
The chickens have the flu.
The cows won't calve, the bulls won't bull.
I don't know what to do.
The drought was bad, but the floods are worse,
I'm in an awful plight;
But comes the word from Gettysburg
Everything's gonna be all right.
    Just keep those chins up
    Just wait and see
    Why comes November—
      prosperity.
—JOE GLAZER
United Rubber Workers

PORTLAND PAPERS USE NEW WEAPON: STRIKE INSURANCE, $1 MILLION ACE-IN-HOLE

Oregon Labor Press, December 25, 1959

Strike insurance!

This is the ace-in-the-hole held by strikebreaking publishers of the Oregonian and Journal.

A strike insurance war chest of more than $17 million is held in a Montreal, Canada, bank. It is out of reach of United States courts and laws.

It can pay the Portland publishers up to $1 million in the present strike-lockout.

Each of them can collect $10,000 per day, up to $500,000, over a 50-day period.

Premium payments are deductible as a "business expense" for tax purposes.

Strike insurance enabled the publishers to bring in strikebreakers, some of them armed and with police records, to put down a legitimate effort of Portland newspaper unions to bargain collectively for fair and decent working conditions and wages.

Strike insurance is a potent new weapon for union-busting. It has been pioneered by the American Newspaper Publishers' Association.

Spearheading its development within the newspaper industry is Samuel Newhouse of New York, absentee owner of the Oregonian.

One reason why the publishers' strike insurance is held in Canada is that in 1956 the filing of such policies in New York was rejected by that state's Department of Insurance as "contrary to public policy."

The New York State Department of Insurance investigated charges that strike insurance actually encouraged publishers to force their employees out on strike.

The investigation was handled by the office of Jacob K. Javits, then attorney general of New York and now a Republican U. S. Senator from New York.

"On July 26, 1956," Javits reported, "I was advised by the Department of Insurance that the filings of each insurance company involved were rejected on the ground that approval of such coverage would be contrary to public policy."

But that didn't stop the newspaper publishers' association. They merely transferred their strike insurance to other companies and moved it into Canada, beyond the reach of U.S. laws.

Premiums for this insurance are high. Cost of the 50-day policy for one newspaper is $12,262.50 per year.

But payment of $24,525 has given the Portland publishers one million dollars and 50 days for their cold-blooded attempt to starve out their union employees.

Existence of newspaper strike insurance has been known for several years. But only last spring were the details of the plan made known. The American Newspaper Guild acquired copies of a memorandum of the Newspaper Publishers' Premium Fund Committee.

The plan was set up, according to the memorandum, by publishers to cover losses resulting from strikes.

Montreal Trust Company of Canada is the "escrow agent" to which all premiums are paid. This company issues strike insurance to newspapers on the advice of Elisha Hanson, general counsel for the American Newspaper Publishers' Association. Payments are made starting with the eighth day of a strike.

Armed with their new strike insurance weapon, the publishers of the Oregonian and Journal deliberately took positions in negotiations that obviously could not be accepted by the Stereotypers' Union. They refused to bargain in good faith. Other newspaper unions ran into the same arrogant attitudes in their negotiations with the publishers.

That the publishers deliberately provoked the strike seems clear also from the speed with which they brought to Portland an organized crew of professional strikebreakers.

Strike insurance and a pool of strikebreakers are the co-ordinated one-two punch adopted by anti-union newspaper publishers all over the country. This is the strategy in Westchester County, New York, where the Macy chain of newspapers has embarked on a union-busting campaign.

Even if Sam Newhouse has to pay out the $12,262.50 premium each year for each of his 14 newspapers, he is money ahead if he provokes a strike at only one of his operations.

Can a publisher insure himself against strike losses and then deliberately provoke a strike in order to collect money to finance a union-busting operation? This is clearly not the basis on which insurance policies are normally written.

This is the same as taking out fire insurance on a building and then deliberately setting fire to it in order to collect the insurance.

Newspaper unions are alert to the danger of strike insurance. It is a vicious and potent weapon in the effort to drive unions from newspaper plants. Combined with the equally-potent professional strikebreaker weapon, it becomes doubly dangerous.

The danger is not only to union members, but to any community where free collective bargaining for legitimate labor goals has been recognized as an American tradition.

WHEN A STRIKE ENDS

The Butcher Workman, November-December 1959

The Swift strike is over. Every incident in connection therewith should be relegated to the storehouse of memories.

That it was a bitter controversy, of course, cannot be denied. One of the aspects of man's relationship with man is that, often, we humans do not see eye-to-eye with each other. Ninety-nine times out of one hundred, this is good.

We would all be living in an archaic, medieval atmosphere if we just took things for granted. Every branch of science has improved because along the highways of progress there has been disagreement in scientific thinking. Trial and error eventually established the truth of a theory not fully agreed to.

In a labor-management relationship, however, it is unfortunate that national work stoppages occasionally occur. Neither labor nor management can say with absolute truthfulness, "We are without blame." It will always be debatable, depending upon which viewpoint we take, whether labor or management is wrong, and whether a strike should or should not have been declared.

Naturally, our organization feels that our membership was thoroughly justified in the recent Swift walkout. Likewise, we are sure the officials of Swift and Co. have their own opinions in the matter. The inevitable result, however, is that all bitter conflicts, whether in industry or among nations, must eventually be settled in the court of the great god "Compromise;" and so ended the Swift strike.

Our membership is satisfied with the settlement, and evidently Swift and Co. is also satisfied. Nothing can be gained, therefore, by our organization taking the position that, "We licked the tar out of Swift."

It would also be ill-considered on the part of any of the officials of Swift to take the position that, "We won because we did not give them everything they struck for."

When a strike ends, both sides in the conflict should learn something. They should remember that this is a world of give and take—a world of live and let live. In the storehouse of Swift strike memories, there should be a parchment upon which are indelibly written, for both sides to plainly see, the precepts upon which future negotiations should be based.

In the future, Swift officials should meet with union negotiators in the interests of their employees and will- ingly give as much as is safely possible. The negotiators for the union should approach the conference table with the idea in mind to ask for the membership only that which is safely possible and reasonably attainable.

So, the final curtain comes down upon the Swift strike. We pledge teamwork during every day of the existing two-year agreement, and we anticipate that the Swift concern will be equally cooperative. We wish Swift and Co., and all other packers who have signed our contracts, every success.

WHAT LABOR ASKS OF INDUSTRY

IUD Bulletin, July 1959

Nobody in the labor movement expects "any giveaway" in labor-management relations, Paul L. Phillips, president of the United Papermakers and Paperworkers, stated in addressing a recent IUD collective bargaining conference.

Phillips' address was entitled, "What Labor Wants of Management." He declared that labor is "under no illusion" that just because it wants something and proves that what it wants is fair, "management will come storming down Broad Street from the Union League and give it to us.

"In the final analysis, it is not the justice of the proposal or the persuasiveness of the union representative that wins improvements at the bargaining table. To be blunt, labor gets from management what labor is strong enough to take through the continuing and collective process of bargaining."

Phillips explained that if this amounted to a "primitive" concept, there nevertheless could not be—in his opinion—any collective bargaining without an appreciation of the "power relationship" between the parties.

"For real collective bargaining to exist, the membership of the union must h a v e the willingness and strength to take collective bargaining disagreements all the way down the line. . . . and I mean the picket line, too, if it's necessary."

Only the ability to withhold labor permits unions to have equality at the bargaining table, Phillips emphasized. Without that ultimate weapon, he added, "labor does not participate in collective bargaining but in collective begging."

Labor nevertheless does not view the labor - management relationship as a continuing "jungle battle" or any "life and death struggle," he stressed.

"The fact that we place the conflict between labor and management in the collective bargaining arena demonstrates that this must be a continuing relationship. Implicit in the concept of bargaining is the necessity for survival of both parties . . .

"It is rarely recognized, but just as employees organize to join unions to help themselves, they are at the same time organizing a force with a vested interest in the survival of the enterprise."

The difficulty, he added, lies in the fact that the concern with survival is not mutual on the part of the employer and the union. While the union seeks survival for the enterprise, he said, the same cannot often be said about employer concern for survival of the union.

Despite the apparent general acceptance of the idea of collective bargaining, the UPP president pointed out, large segments of management are unwilling to recognize that collective bargaining has a "permanent place" in our world.

Because the chairman of the National Labor Relations Board makes a certain speech one way or another, he said, "employers will not be persuaded to give up the use of prejudice, fear and interminable litigation to frustrate and defeat the desires of their employees to organize into unions. . . ."

He also pointed out that much of the opposition to union organization flows from NLRB rulings of recent years.

"I believe," he declared, "it is far more important at this time that we enforce existing law to encourage collective bargaining than to adopt new laws aimed squarely at harassing and weakening the trade union movement."

Phillips cited facts and figures showing that a false picture of labor power is being built in America. "Just think," he pointed out, "the jobs, the incomes, and family living standards of two of every three workers in this country are under the unilateral iron rule of employers whose power relationship to their employees has not changed one whit from the power relationship that existed between the medieval serf and his baron."

He further noted that all labor organization treasuries in the United States combined "hardly match the resources of a single large corporation in the paper industry."

Looking at the affluent society "in focus," Phillips stressed that if labor were so powerful, it would be expected that workers in Philadelphia would have a minimum wage of $2 an hour the year 'round in his industry.

"Sure the average wage in our union is well above $2, but did you ever hear of the six-footer who drowned crossing a stream that had an average depth of three feet?"

Labor wants management to compete on the basis of productivity and merchandising know-how, rather than by exploiting labor, Phillips emphasized. He stated that labor wants management to assume its share of responsibility for workers displaced by automation and other changes in the industrial process.

SUPREME COURT OF OUR INDUSTRY

The Electrical Workers' Journal, April 1959

For 40 years employers and employees in the electrical contracting industry have been getting along, voluntarily settling differences between themselves and living in peace. Both have prospered and the public has benefitted from better services uncomplicated by strikes.

The medium by which labor and management in the electrical contracting industry have done this, has been their Council on Industrial Relations.

Now exactly what is this Council? It is an organ composed of six representatives of the National Electrical Contractors Association and six members of the International Brotherhood of Electrical Workers. These members meet quarterly in various sections of the country and hear the cases brought before them.

These cases consist of matters in dispute, or interpretation of existing agreements. Both sides are heard and a decision is rendered. All decisions, by rules of the Council, must be unanimous, and here is a significant point: *never in the 40 years of the Council's existence has a decision been violated.*

We often hear today of various arbitration boards functioning throughout the country. The Council on Industrial Relations, in essence, is a judicial body rather than a mere arbitration organ. The fact that decisions must be unanimous, and that there is never a third party involved in its deliberations, makes it clear that the Council operates to effect just decisions, not merely compromises, that it strives to seek out errors and correct them. This is what makes it unique.

This is why our Council on Industrial Relations is far more valuable to the NECA and the IBEW and to the whole welfare of the electrical industry than any mere arbitration board could ever be.

Many cases are settled in advance of Council hearings because of the fact that the Council stands ready to hear cases. Many thousands of cases have been settled amicably by the individual employers and local unions bargaining in good faith, knowing that as a last resort this "Supreme Court of the Electrical Industry" is open to them.

The basic code of policy which has evolved from decisions of the Council rendered through the years, has set a pattern for local contractors and unions to follow, in solving their differences, making appeal to the Council unnecessary.

This code recognizes the fundamental rights of the employer and the employee and their mutual obligation to each other, to the industry and to the general public. It sets forth the policy of the industry on such vital matters as wages, union recognition, peaceful solution of industrial disputes, sacredness of negotiated contracts, worker participation in management, and the obligation of both parties to strive for efficiency in production.

All who serve on the Council are thoroughly acquainted with the problems and practices in the industry. They know that real stability can be attained only by rendering decisions which recognize the legitimate claims on the industry made by management, by labor and by the public it serves. When the members of the Council are in session they do not represent either NECA or the IBEW. They represent the Electrical Contracting Industry.

Obviously, the decisions made by the Council cannot please both disputing parties, and frequently they please neither. The record shows, however, that while complaints have been few, those registered are almost exactly divided between management and labor, which indicates that a fair, objective job is being done.

COLLECTIVE BARGAINING AT ITS BEST

Lee W. Minton, president, Glass Bottle Blowers Assn.,
in Glass Horizons, April 1960

In times of labor-management crisis, such as a major steel strike, public interest runs high in the problems of industrial relations. Just about everybody, expert and amateur alike, has a theory on "what ought to be done."

Probably the most serious shortcoming in our industrial philosophy is that the majority of Americans associate the entire concept of labor-union relations with the area of strife. Sadly, this negative attitude

is shared even by many who are active in union and management affairs.

There are a few rays of hope, however, which indicate a positive and dynamic philosophy of labor-management relations is gaining ground. When the steel strike of 1959 was settled, Secretary of Labor James P. Mitchell proposed that management and the union committtees continue meeting regularly to study functioning of the contract. Obvious benefit from this, of course, would be that any flaws could be remedied, or their damage limited, before they created a major breach in union and management relations.

The Glass Bottle Blowers Association was pleased to see the Secretary make such a recommendation. Our own union proposed such a procedure to the Glass Container and Fiber Glass Industry several years ago, and it was adopted. Results have been excellent.

Our philosophy—and we believe it must evenutally become the phisophy of all in labor and management—is that real collective bargaining is a continuing process, one that requires thoughtful, give-and-take effort by union and management month after month.

We also believe that a union must do more than merely make demands on an employer. Problems of an employer or an industry must necessarily be shared by the workers who earn their living in that industry, and they can share them best through their unions. In any industrial endeavor, both management and labor have an investment; management in terms of capital, labor in terms of skill, experience and seniority. In an enlightened labor-management relationship, each will strive to see that the other receives a fair return on his investment.

We in the GBBA are proud of the fact that in our bargaining we have gone far toward achieving such a relationship. Our union has recognized the problems of the industry and has made contributions toward meeting them. Aware of the tight competition for container fiber glass markets the GBBA has been in the forefront of campaigns to promote sales. The industry also has benefitted from extensive efforts by the union to block or win repeal of legislation which discriminates against glass container uses. For example, some states have sought to prohibit sales of the "one-way, non-returnable" beer bottle, but the union and the industry have been successful in resisting such laws.

Cooperation between the union and the industry has produced benefits for both. The union has won continued gains in wages, working conditions, holidays, vacations and health and pension benefits while, at the same time, assuring maximum protection of the members' job security. The industry, on the other hand, has been assured an enthusiastic, skilled and stable work force maintaining high levels of productivity.

This progress has been realized without a single industry-wide strike.

Primarily, all this has been made possible because of an enlightened philosophy that labor and management must do more than merely meet at the bargaining table. The GBBA and our industry have broadened the collective bargaining con-

"Then, all of a sudden, I discovered I wanted to give my employees a raise without their asking for it . . ."

cept to include day-to-day discussions of problems and plans to promote as a team the interests of both management and worker.

Surely, this is collective bargaining at its best.

To promote such cooperation we first must promote "cooperative thinking." If both union and management will apply such thinking sincerely to their acts and words, cooperative spirit and mutual aid will follow.

Rewards of cooperative spirit are rich. Labor and management tensions are reduced; production is increased; grievances are cut to a minimum; application of work-rules is seldom necessary and, in general, disciplinary action is rare.

Our collective bargaining program is based largely on such a spirit. While we do not claim perfection for the program, we know that it is one of the best examples of effective bargaining to be found anywhere. It is still being improved and will continue to be improved during the years ahead.

The GBBA and its members can take satisfaction in the fact that employment in the glass container and allied industries is the most stable of any industry work force in the U. S. Glass manufacturers have benefitted through increased and uninterrupted production. Labor-management teamwork has been instrumental in helping the glass industry meet and pull ahead of competing products.

Probably the key point in making teamwork function effectively is the union's concern over production and demand.

Toward maintaining that demand, the union spends thousands of dollars annually in advertising its industry's products. This policy has won for the GBBA an accolade from Forbes magazine as "an intelligent union." Said Forbes: "The GBBA has made management's fight for markets a part of its credo. Believing that production jobs can't survive without sales, it has pumped union cash into advertising the industry's products."

GBBA in no way attempts to claim more than its share of credit for the great expansion of the glass container and allied industries. It recognizes full well that the inventive genius of industry is of utmost importance. Since the industry is completely mechanized, speed of the machine is a vital factor. Industry has invested in new machinery which in many instances has doubled or tripled production.

While recognizing the need for high volume production, the union insists that the added effort and skill of members be rewarded.

UNION SECURITY BRINGS INDUSTRIAL PEACE, SAYS BUILDING TRADES LEADER

AFL-CIO News, October 15, 1960

Unions and employers must "learn how to work together" as a matter of national survival, Pres. C. J. Haggerty of the AFL-CIO Building & Construction Trades Dept. declared at an industry meeting in New York.

Haggerty, addressing the New York Building Congress, said employers can best serve their own interests "by learning to work with unions, not against them."

Citing the example of industries "where labor and management have learned to value and enjoy the fruits of cooperation," Haggerty told the employers' group:

"When we examine the special circumstances that have made for industrial harmony in these fields, we find one common factor—peace has come in every instance after the firm establishment of union security.

"It is a matter of good faith. The employer proves his good faith by giving a commitment in writing that he will not attempt to wreck the union or displace it. . . . The union gives assurance of uninterrupted production, of greater productivity, of efforts to promote the business of the employer through all channels available to a labor organization."

The construction industry's "main trouble," Haggerty said, "is destructive competition from non-union employers, from the contractors who underbid by cutting wages and tearing down working conditions."

"As I see it," Haggerty added, "there is only one answer to that kind of unfair competition, and that is organization. For that reason the building and construction trades unions are determined to organize as they never have organized before. We will not be satisfied until all construction—whether in the industrial, public or residential fields—is fully organized in every section of the country."

He called on employers to join in making the building industry "a working model of peaceful, cooperative and mutually beneficial labor-management relations."

OMISSION

The Machinist, January 22, 1959

We give up. We've been holding our breath, waiting for the daily newspaper editorial writers to get around to congratulating labor and management on one of the most peaceful years in labor relations history.

But it's almost three weeks now since Secretary of Labor James P. Mitchell announced the good news that "in terms of industrial peace, 1958 was one of the best peacetime years on record." And we haven't yet seen the first editorial about it.

The 1958 record showed, according to Secretary Mitchell, that "strike idleness, as measured in man-days was about the same as in 1951 and 1954, but lower than any other postwar year except 1957. The number of work stoppages beginning in 1958, estimated at 3,400, was lowest for any year since World War II."

"Perhaps more significant," Mr. Mitchell said, "were the many important industries and establishments in which contracts were negotiated or renegotiated without a work stoppage."

Long ago, we gave up hoping that we could ever make a peacefully negotiated agreement as palatable as strikes to the men who make our daily newspapers. Newspapers live and make their profits on drama and conflict.

But once a year, when the record is as good as 1958, we think more newspapers ought to take the trouble to put the strike headlines in proper perspective. The editors ought to let their readers know that collective bargaining is working well in this country—despite the treatment it gets in many newspapers.

Back on the editorial page, which isn't supposed to need sensationalism, a cheer for the improvement in labor-management relations wouldn't bankrupt any publisher. It might, of course, make it more difficult to convince the American people that unions are ruining the country and need drastic regulation.

We know that in writing this we run a risk. Perhaps there have been editorials praising the 1958 record for industrial peace. If the daily newspaper you buy has published such an editorial, send us a clipping. If it hasn't, perhaps you ought to write a letter to the editor, prodding his conscience. If you're polite enough, he might even print it.

TONY VRABEL, CARNEGIE AWARD HERO APPEARS ON "VOICE OF AMERICA"

John McManigal in The Sentinel (Local 1397, Steelworkers), April 1958

Two years ago Tony Vrabel, a bottom maker in Homestead's 45-inch mill, was awarded the Carnegie medal for saving the life of three men when he pushed their stalled car from the railroad tracks at Amity street with a locomotive bearing down on the car.

As a result of that award Tony appeared on the CBS TV program "On Your Account." Since that initial venture, Tony's voice has been heard throughout the world in an even greater effort.

Realizing the need to tell the people of all nations what it is like to live under this democracy, Tony volunteered to appear on the "Voice of America."

While making six appearances on the "Voice"—for which he has not received one cent of financial reward—Tony has pointedly expressed what unions in America mean to all who labor.

During his latest appearance on the "Voice," an interview with Liston Oak, labor editor of the program, Tony told the world just what trade unionism means to him and millions of other rank-and-filers throughout the United States.

First, Vrabel told of how he went to work in Homestead at the age of 14 and since has completed 33 years service.

Continuing the interview, Oak said, "There must have been considerable changes in the mill in all that time."

Vrabel told Oak and the world, "Yes, there has been a lot of change. I started to work as a messenger boy. In those days we worked six days a week, no time-and-one-half for overtime, no insurance, no paid vacation, no way to settle grievances. We had no seniority rights. We worked only when the boss said

we could work. Without seniority rights we had no guarantee of promotion to the next vacant job. If the boss liked you, he moved you up to a better job, but not on the basis of your right to promotion."

At this point Oak asked Vrabel,

"What has your union accomplished for its members?"

"The union means security," Vrabel replied. Continuing, he explained, "The boss cannot fire me without cause. It gives me financial security, too. With my long years of service I now have an equity in a pension program the union won in 1949 and improved on in the current contract with management. The union will continue to improve our welfare and pension plan, and I can look forward to a fairly prosperous future in retirement.

"If I get hurt, my union-won insurance program protects me, providing medical care and hospitalization and the services of a doctor. It also provides that my family would get an income until I recovered and was able to go back to work. I get a paid vacation of three and one-half weeks.

"That means a lot to me now, because I can spend a lot of time with my boy who is at age when he wants to do things with me.

"Workers who are laid off temporarily get supplemental unemployment benefits in addition to unemployment insurance benefits from the state so that for a whole year, if necessary, the Steelworker who is laid off gets about 65 per cent of his regular wages.

"All these benefits and many others were won for me by the union. So I ask you, is it any wonder that I, like other Steelworkers, support the union enthusiastically?"

1-a | A Case Study in Steel

THE STEEL MILLS AND MINES ARE CLOSING

Steel Labor, July 1959

After ten weeks of collective bargaining sessions between the United Steelworkers of America and the 12 major steel companies, the industry is shutting down its mills and mines.

The steel companies thus bring to a climax the plan which they conspired to impose upon the union and the nation even before negotiations commenced. For selfish reasons of their own, they are forcing a steel shutdown which is not wanted by the Steelworkers or the nation.

The industry must accept full responsibility for the crisis it has precipitated. For the union has done everything within reason to bring about a fair and honorable settlement which would not require increased steel prices.

To this end, the union has made a specific proposal for settlement to enable Steelworkers to make the same rate of economic progress provided for each year under the 1956 agreements. Though this non-inflationary proposal is completely justified by the industry's increased profits and productivity, it fell on deaf ears.

The industry has stood rigidly by its April 10 proposal for a wage freeze and elimination of the cost-of-living clause, and its June 10 proposal for destruction of basic rights and benefits of the workers presently protected by the contracts.

Therefore, on June 25, the union took an unusual step. It requested the President of the United States to appoint a public fact-finding board to determine the facts relative to wages, prices and productivity. We pledged to accept such findings as the basis for negotiation. The steel industry, however, has remained conspicuously silent.

When the President declined to appoint a fact-finding board and suggested an extension of the contracts, the union agreed to a 14-day extension to provide additional time for negotiations. But, the industry persisted in its unyielding attitude.

As a further demonstration of the keen desire of the union to avert a shutdown, the union proposed that the issue raised by the industry—for the first time in mid-June—relating to elimination of local practices, be referred to a joint study committee to be headed by elder statesmen from the industry and the union. The industry gave a blunt answer—No.

After the industry had refused to continue meeting with the union's representatives, the President of the United States proposed that negotiations be revived because there was still ample time to make a settlement prior to the deadline. Our union immediately complied with this request and endorsed the President's view that a speedy settlement was possible.

Again our negotiators met repeatedly with the industry's representatives. But the position of the companies has not changed since the beginning.

During the entire 10-week period of meetings, the industry has not offered anything: not a single penny in wage increases, not a single penny for fringe benefit increases, not a single improvement in any phase of our bargaining agreements.

On the contrary the industry, in the middle of negotiations, sought to turn the clock back by proposing to eliminate a whole series of essential protections of workers' rights. The industry raised this smokescreen because its mock crusade for a wage freeze to stem inflation was exposed for what it was—an effort to retain for itself the spectacular profits resulting from increased productivity.

The steel industry is enjoying the greatest profits and productivity in its history.

The facts show that the industry has never been in a more favorable economic position to grant its employees the reasonable improvements they have earned by their increased output.

Moreover, wage increases are being negotiated, not only in other major industries, but even by the steel companies themselves as employers of coal miners, construction workers and others. Yet the industry insists that Steelworkers must be treated as second-class employees.

We have come to the end of the road, for the first time in more than 20 years of collective bargaining, without a single improvement offered by the companies. Indeed, the companies have insisted on contract language which would eliminate every shred of protection of local working conditions.

The supervisors would be free to abolish spell time, relief arrangements, lunch periods, wash-up time, shift preferences, overtime distribution systems and innumerable other conditions.

This program would also permit reduction of crews even where the equipment and methods are unchanged. Thus, the industry is intent on withdrawing benefits which in many cases date back to the days prior to the organization of our union.

We recognize the new look for what it is—an effort to revert to the days of industrial dictatorship. If the industry leaders succeed, then every Steelworker will be at the mercy of every plant supervisor; our contract will lose its force and our union will be an empty shell.

We do not seek strife but we recognize that there are worse things than strikes, namely the loss of our individual rights, our contract protections and our great union.

Surely, many company leaders must recognize that no one can gain from efforts to reverse the whole labor-management structure developed over more than 20 years.

But if the industry persists in its position and no settlement can be negotiated before the deadline, we have no choice but to reaffirm our honorable tradition: no contract, no work.

'DIDN'T QUIT IN 1937 . . . I'll NEVER QUIT IN 1959'

Steel Labor, August 1959

United Steelworker picket lines throughout the nation are holding tight in the industry-fomented shutdown as federal mediators continue to test new ways to bring peace to the bargaining table.

Their task has been made doubly difficult by heartless steel industry negotiators who have given no indication of abandoning their vicious wreck - and - ruin program directed against their own employees.

In a double-barreled blast, David J. McDonald told audiences at Youngstown, Ohio and at Detroit, Mich. that "they'll never starve us out."

Recalling the dark, dismal days of a few decades ago when millworkers were trying to break their chains of bondage and to become free men, the USW chieftain asserted:

"If we didn't quit in 1937, by the eternal gods we won't quit in 1959."

McDonald lashed out at Roger Blough, board chairman of United States Steel Corp.

"While he and his cohorts wrap

themselves in the American flag in a mock crusade against 'inflation,' the fact is that profits reported so far this year are rolling in at a tremendous three-billion-dollar rate."

The union's president ripped into "feather-bedding" and "loafing on the job" charges raised by the industry.

"There are 44,000 fewer Steelworkers in the industry than there were in 1953 and the reduced work force is turning out 30 per cent more steel," McDonald told the Youngstown-Detroit groups.

"Does this sound like the United Steelworkers are loafing on the job?"

Year after year, McDonald said, the record shows it takes less and less man-hours to produce a ton of finished steel. In 1949, it required 16.3 man-hours. By 1954, this figure was reduced to 15 man-hours and to 13 man-hours by 1956.

The latest figures as of April, 1959, show that it takes but 10.7 man-hours to make the same ton of steel.

"Steel is made by hard-working employees on a continuous eight-hour shift. In order to accommodate the steel-making process, the workers are forced to live with unusual arrangements for eating and for personal relief.

"Such factors are involved as intense heat and the need for rest after prolonged periods of concentrated efforts utilizing the fullest skills and demanding heavy responsibilities.

"In many other industries there are 'hot days' when the men knock off work and go home," McDonald explained.

"In the steel industry, there are 365 hot days every year with the added touch of dust, fumes, and suffocating blasts of gas-laden air. These—plus ear-shattering explosions—and constant squealing and screeching are what the Steelworker is constantly exposed to in the mills.

"There are factors involving safety and health which require so-called 'spell periods' off the job.

"All of these practices were in effect and accepted by the industry long before there was a Steelworkers' union."

McDonald also said there is nothing in the standard wage agreements with the industry which forces it to hire more people than it actually needs.

McDonald pointed out that while remarkable production records are being logged, hundreds of grievances have been filed by union members protesting speed-ups.

"The union has not objected to automation," McDonald declared, "but is vigorously opposed to the automation of individual workers which would enslave human beings in mills and factories."

As McDonald toured picket lines in the Pennsylvania-Ohio-Michigan areas, company negotiators were "going through the motions" of direct bargaining in New York's Roosevelt Hotel.

While the stalemate continued, President Eisenhower continued to reject Congressional pressure for more federal intervention in the shutdown.

He said he still believes that the government should keep hands off.

"Until there is a national emergency discernible . . . I couldn't think of anything more objectionable than to put the federal government constantly in the business of settling these major strikes."

Only a few weeks ago, Chairman Blough, in effect, told the government to "keep hands off" the dangerous situation—created by the industry—which has rocked the nation's economy to its very foundation.

In fewer words, Big Business told the Administration to lay off while it polished off the union with a specially-designed program aimed at wrecking every contract protection gained by the United Steelworkers in almost 22 years of hard bargaining.

This program, which augmented industry's minus-zero offer and the nefarious hold-the-line wage freeze proposition, would have torpedoed seniority and pension rights and would have scuttled vacation plans and other benefits.

While the industry-union stalemate continued, Sen. Stuart Symington (D., Mo.) pressed for his resolution which would put Congress on record as favoring a White House meeting of both sides.

If this top meeting failed, the Symington resolution, signed by more than 25 Senators, would have the President set up a fact-finding board to recommend a contract settlement.

Various sources have pointed out that if Big Steel and the other major producers can hold a while longer—at least until stockpiles start to dwindle, and that seems very soon—

they are going to have to deal with the United Steelworkers in a business-like fashion.

Then, observers theorized, steel will have an excuse for seeking an additional increase in prices to make up anticipated third-quarter "losses."

Meanwhile, U. S. Labor Secretary James P. Mitchell has remained "mum" on his fact-finding inquiry into the steel situation.

McDonald's reference to 1937 was the so-called "Little Steel" strike.

After organizing U. S. Steel Corp., which was then Carnegie-Illinois Steel, the Steel Workers Organizing Committee turned its attention to the other major producers, including Republic Steel.

It was a bloody battle which found the industry resisting every effort to free the men in the mills.

STEAL...

The Machinist, August 6, 1959

We hope the folks who have been swallowing the propaganda about inflation will read the profit report of United States Steel Corp. For the first six months this year, U. S. Steel netted a neat $254,000,000 after taxes. It was the most profitable first half in the company's profitable history.

Even more breath-taking is the fact that this company's profits before taxes are running at the rate of $4,345 per employee—a jump of $1,300 profit per man over 1957. For each man-hour, Big Steel's profit during the first half amounted to $2.28 per employee, a jump of 67 cents over 1957.

The company's 180,000 wage earners were on strike last week. There seemed little doubt that they would have settled happily for a small share of U. S. Steel's increased prosperity—say 15 cents an hour in wages and fringes. That would cost the company $6 a week or $312 a year per employee.

Steel industry propaganda has

made much of the fact that the average wage rate in the industry is $3.11 an hour, before deductions. The annual income of Steelworkers is something else. This the company propaganda doesn't mention. Here are the facts: last year less than one-third of all steel workers earned as much as $6,000. More than one-third—40 per cent—earned less than $4,700. Figured on a full 40-hour week, year round, this would be $2.26 an hour.

A company making $4,345 per year per employee can afford to raise wages $312. The idea that the company would be forced to raise prices to remain comfortably in the black is ridiculous on its face.

All the noisy advertising about "inflation" is smokescreen. The steel industry just doesn't want to share a penny of its new profits with its employees. There's no other interpretation a reasonable man can put on it after reading the profit statement.

YOUR STAKE IN STEEL

The Machinist, November 15, 1959

Every wage earner in the shop, every white collar worker in the office, in fact, everyone who works has a stake in the outcome of the steel strike. The kind of settlement made in steel—whenever it comes—will influence the future of your job, your wages and your union. Here are the facts:

Your Job

The big issue blocking settlement of the steel strike has been the insistence by management that the men give up their share in the control over working rules. That is, over work scheduling, work loads, overtime, shift hours, job classifications and the methods used to determine incentives and evaluate jobs.

Steel management wants to make these decisions without the union having any say whatsoever. Steel management wants to scrap the contract language that has worked for 20 years. Any working rule that protects the employees is called "featherbedding" by management. Management wants people to believe that these rules have no useful purpose, that they hinder the introduction of new methods and new machinery.

The truth is that under these rules, steel workers have increased their production, man for man, by 35 per cent over the last 10 years. Ten years ago, it took more than 16 man-hours to make a ton of steel. Today it takes less than 11 man-hours. But industry isn't satisfied even though profits were highest in history under the old contract. Industry wants to cut payrolls and up profits.

If the industry forces the steel workers to surrender their share of control over working rules, you can expect similar demands in your industry—if you haven't already heard them.

Your Wages

The steel strike is influencing negotiations in many industries. This influence is greater than most of us realize. The Bureau of National Affairs has just reported that fewer wage settlements were announced during the three-month period ending Sept. 30 than during the previous quarter. This is abnormal.

The reason, according to the BNA report, is that many negotiators are waiting to see what will happen in steel. The average negotiated raise for the third quarter was just under 9 cents an hour, a penny less than in the second quarter. In view of the lush profit picture, this drop is attributed by BNA to "the tougher management attitude sparked by the steel makers."

If the steel workers fail to win a just settlement, still more industries can be expected to copy the "get tough" policy. Your chance of getting a fair share of the increasing profits of industry will be smaller than ever.

Your Union

Steel management's insistence on sole control over working rules has kept the steel mills shut until steel inventories in other metal working industries are about gone. Layoffs and hardship are spreading.

Management is encouraging talk about a law to break up the union. They want Congress to make it illegal for union members to seek equal pay for equal work from competing companies. There is also talk about some form of compulsory arbitration. Others suggest more effective kinds of Fact Finding Boards with power to recommend the terms of settlement after hearing both sides and studying the facts. Bills to change the nature of free collective bargaining can be expected when Congress meets again.

If steel labor takes it on the chin, Congress will be a lot tougher. So, our future will depend on whether or not the steel workers can win a fair and equitable settlement.

SUPREME COURT RULING STALLS USW'S FIGHT FOR JUSTICE

Steel Labor, November 1959

The United Steelworkers of America, in compliance with a Taft-Hartley Act injunctive action which had been upheld by the United States Supreme Court, has returned to the task of producing steel to fill the nation's needs.

The back-to-work order was issued Nov. 7 by Pres. David J. McDonald, who said, "we will comply with the law of the land, now as we have always done."

It was apparent that the majority of the 500,000 basic Steelworkers were not happy about being forced back to work after a 116-day siege of endurance and sacrifice in quest of a fair and honorable settlement.

Under Taft-Hartley regulations, USW members will return to work for an 80-day "cooling off" period. Meanwhile, negotiations must continue under direction of the U. S. Mediation and Conciliation Service.

President McDonald, commenting on the situation, had this to say:

"The issues that caused the shutdown still live with us. Eventually, they must be settled by free collective bargaining.

"An injunction cannot alter the fact that the issues still must be confronted by the steel companies which forced this crisis upon the nation.

"We have returned to work in compliance with the law," the USW president said. "But we will not be beaten. There may be a truce enforced by law but there will be no permanent peace."

Supreme Court Justice William O. Douglas cast the only dissenting vote as the court upheld, by an 8-1 vote, the injunctive action which had been set in motion by Federal Judge Herbert P. Sorg at Pittsburgh.

The action brought to a halt, at least temporarily, the longest strike in the history of the industry.

Meanwhile, production at Kaiser Steel moved weeks ahead of the rest of the industry. Edgar F. Kaiser, who broke the united front of the stubborn industry leadership to sign with the Steelworkers union, was praised as a "courageous and enlightened American industrialist."

Detroit Steel and Granite City Steel were other early signers.

FIGHTING MAD LABOR MOVEMENT RALLIES TO AID STEELWORKERS

Southwest Labor (Ark.), November 1959

The labor movement — angered over the Eisenhower Administration use of a Taft-Hartley injunction against 500,000 striking steelworkers—has rallied its strength behind the United Steelworkers of America in anticipation of a renewed showdown fight with the industry when the injunction runs out on Jan. 26, 1960.

Leaders of the AFL-CIO and its Industrial Union Dept. bitterly denounced Eisenhower's intervention on industry's side as "intolerable" and "union busting," and called for swift Congressional repeal of the "slave labor" section of the 12-year-old Taft-Hartley Act to compel unionists to work against their will.

AFL-CIO Pres. George Meany sounded labor's battle cry, calling on the 13.5 million members of the federation to contribute generously to the special Steelworkers' Defense Fund.

In a letter to the officers of affiliated unions and state and local central bodies, Meany said contributions of one hour's pay per month to the fund established by the AFL-CIO General Board in September should continue at an accelerated pace throughout the injunction and "until the hour the strike is won."

The crisis engendered by the Administration's court-approved back-to-work order was the focal point for the IUD's convention here. Both Meany and IUD Pres. Walter P. Reuther warned that the assault on the Steelworkers was part of a war on labor threatening to engulf the nation's railroad workers next.

Reuther reminded the delegates that, far from being an "isolated incident," the steel crisis is "part of a pattern which reflects beyond question the fact that American big business is carrying on a total struggle against the American working people."

He cited as examples the five-year-old Kohler strike; the use of Taft-Hartley's union-busting provisions to break the Rubber Workers strike at O'Sullivan Rubber Co.; the "brutal" use of state police and militia to crush the Textile Workers of America in their strike against the Harriet-Henderson Cotton Mills in Henderson, N. C.; and the "hypocritical propaganda" being used by "the hucksters in Madison Avenue" laying the groundwork for an assault on the rail unions.

Meany attacked the White House use of the injunction compelling steel workers to "work when they don't want to work under the conditions offered" as proof of labor's 12-year-old claim that Taft-Hartley is a "slave labor law."

"How much slavery has got to be in a law before you put a label on it of slavery?" Meany asked to the accompaniment of lusty cheers. "If a law can compel one worker to work against his will, in my books it is a slave labor law.

"How far is it from 80 days to 100 days, to 180 days, and to a law permanently telling a worker he has to work under conditions offered by his employer? This is an intolerable situation. This is a situation that is a threat not only to the American labor movement but to the American way of life. This law must be removed from the statute books."

USWA Pres. David J. McDonald told the IUD the union would press for a settlement during the injunction period, but warned that if no agreement is reached USWA members "will close down the industry and keep it closed until their just desires are met."

Praising the "fantastic" spirit of steel workers, despite the hardships of the long strike, McDonald pledged that "with the continued spirit of the steel workers and the undivided loyalty of the trade union movement, we will win."

Auto Workers Sec.-Treas. Emil Mazey accused Eisenhower of using the injunction as a "political payoff" to steel corporations in return for $214,500 in financial contributions to the Republican presidential campaign in 1956.

High in Mazey's list of contributors to Eisenhower's successful re-election bid was George Allen, a director of Republic Steel, one of the struck companies. Allen was Eisenhower's host on a nine-day golfing vacation in Palm Springs, Calif., just prior to the President's use of Taft-Hartley against the USWA. Also listed were officers of National Steel Corp., including former Treasury Sec. George M. Humphrey, as well as officials of U. S. Steel, Armco, Bethlehem, Inland, and Jones & Laughlin.

The convention hailed as "an historic forward step" the establishment by the AFL-CIO of a central strike fund, saluted the "pooling of resources represented by this step," and pointed out "the need to build this fund so that there shall be immediate and ready financial assistance in emergency situations."

GARMENT TO STEEL: "WE'LL HELP"

The Garment Worker (Pa.), December 1959

A LETTER FROM A MEMBER

"What our shop has done for two families that are hurt by the steel strike. One is a woman and her seven children. I sent a paper around and asked for food for this family and you never saw such a good turnout. Milk, bread, meat, cans—about $75 worth. Some girls gave her money for gas so she could come to work. Another family, the wife was in the hospital and returned to work too soon on account of the steel strike and she had to return to the hospital. I sent a paper around and everyone gave—$47.50 and we only have about 30 employees. Do not mention the names.

"This is only one of many such heartwarming responses. In Lancaster County the workers in one shop collect money and take it to the school to buy lunches for Steelworkers' kids. In Lebanon, a former displaced person, now an ILGWU member, buys a $20 food order for a neighboring family of a steel striker. When offered thanks, donor retorts, 'Of course, I helped. Lots of people helped me when I needed it!' "

Why did our members respond? We interviewed a member who gave what is an awful lot for a garment worker, $5. Here's the conversation:

EDITOR—Not all the girls in the shop gave that much, did they?

MEMBER—No, some wouldn't give at all. They said the Steelworkers made plenty, why should they strike.

E.—They do make more than you.

M.—Yes, but I don't believe any worker ever saves enough to be out of work for several months. Besides, if the Steelworkers make less money, that won't help me.

E.—Do you think they should strike when they are already getting so much?

M.—I know some Steelworkers and they are not striking for money. The Union negotiating committee offered to settle for one year without a wage increase if the companies would just pay the whole cost of the Health, Welfare and Retirement program.

E.—Didn't the companies accept?

M.—No! They wanted to change the work rules. As I heard it explained, it would be like if my employer offered to raise our hourly rate 5 or 10 cents—and then he would set piece rates any which way and we couldn't complain; he would want to put the fastest worker on each job and get rid of some like me who are older and slower. We would never sit still for that!

E.—But there are lots of good causes; lots of people need help. Why pick on just the steelworkers?

M.—Because, I don't feel as if I'm just helping someone else. I'm helping myself. If the corporations break the Steelworkers' Union my boss will be impossible to live with—he's bad enough now. I remember what it was like 20 years ago when the big industries were non-Union.

HELP FOR STEEL FAMILIES

*Catering Industry Employee,
January 1960*

Thanksgiving cheer was served to 1,100 "forgotten strikers" on the picket line at the Phelps Dodge Plant in Laurel Hill, Long Island the Tuesday before Thanksgiving by New York's Joint Executive Board. Shopping bags of food for the dinners of the striking workers and their families were presented to them by Florence Balschak, a member of Local 1 and elected this year as Union Maid-in-Waiting.

Angelo Bottone, Steelworkers' representative, said the plight of the strikers was particularly hard as New York City's Welfare Department refused to give surplus food to the strikers.

NEW CONTRACT ENDS 1959 STEEL STRIKE

The Sentinel (Steelworkers Local 1397), January 1960

The solidarity of the membership of the United Steelworkers during 116 days on the picket line has paid off in a new contract with the nation's steel producers.

Agreement was reached on Jan. 4, 1960—the 58th day of the Taft-Hartley injunction which halted the strike last Nov. 7.

The 30-month agreement preserves on-the-job rights contained in previous contracts and gives Steelworkers an economic package estimated by the industry at 41.34 cents an hour.

The change to a non-contributory insurance program will give workers an immediate 7-cent hourly increase in take-home pay. Effective Dec. 1, 1960, and again on Oct. 1, 1961, workers will receive a basic 7-cent increase. Additional boosts based on job classifications will bring the average raise each time to 8.3 cents hourly.

Each worker retiring after Jan. 1, 1960, is guaranteed a retirement payment of approximately $1,500.

Continuation of cost-of-living provisions can provide an additional maximum raise of 6 cents an hour, depending on the movement of the Consumers' Price Index.

The present Supplementary Unemployment Benefit program is renewed, with certain contributions which were cancelled at the start of the strike reinstated.

The union shop is continued. In "right-to-work" states, where it is illegal, workers are required to pay a service charge to the union which equals the cost of union membership.

Seniority protection is reinforced, with seniority retained for five years instead of the previous two by any worker who is absent because of lay-off or physical disability.

Pres. David J. McDonald jubilantly hailed the agreement which, he said, leaves the union "sound, safe and secure" and assures "peace, pros-perity and lasting happiness" for the long embattled steel workers.

The Union's 171-member Wage Policy Committee, thundering approval of the pact, said that on the key issues of work rules, the Union "emerged completely victorious"—a victory, it added, which was won "not only for the Steelworkers but for all of American labor."

The settlement was announced at a precedent-setting press conference by Labor Sec. James P. Mitchell who credited Vice Pres. Richard Nixon with having brought the sides together.

Mitchell was flanked by the USWA's David J. McDonald and USSteel's R. Conrad Cooper.

The settlement came one week before the workers would have voted in a T-H election on the steel industry's last offer which would have gutted the work rules and given workers 24 cents an hour spread over three years.

Roger M. Blough, chairman of the board of USSteel and regarded as the man who calls the shots for the industry, issued a statement which said in part:

"So far as our company is concerned, it proposes to continue the general level of its prices for the immediate future."

McDonald commended Eisenhower, Nixon and Mitchell for their joint efforts at bringing about the settlement, and Cooper echoed the praise.

Later, Pres. McDonald told of the role of Joseph Kennedy, father of the Massachusetts Senator Kennedy. The union chief related that the elder Mr. Kennedy played a significant role contacting his financial friends on Wall Street to demand a fair settlement of the dispute.

Completely prepaid life, medical and surgical insurance and sickness and accident benefits, without any contribution by the employee—long range goal of the United Steelworkers of America—was finally achieved in the 1960 contract.

The program includes:

Increased life insurance coverage with a range from $4,000 to $6,500. This reflects a $500 increase.

The scale of weekly sick and accident benefits was increased five dollars per week with a range of $53 to $68. The amounts of life insurance and the weekly benefit are based on a scale in ratio to the worker's hourly rate.

Life insurance is to be continued during layoff up to two years. After the first six months of layoff, the employee will be required to pay 60 cents per month per $1,000.

The hospitalization, surgical and related coverages are to be continued during the first six months of layoff for employees with two or more years continuous service at date of layoff.

Pensioners will be afforded conversion rights for hospitalization and surgical coverage upon retirement. The retiree will pay the full premium with the option to check-off premiums from pension checks.

Despite the steel industries' early refusal to consider any changes in the pension program, the Steelworkers gained major improvements in this area.

Each employee retiring under the pension plan after Jan. 1, 1960 (except those who retire under disability or deferred vested pensions) will receive a "special retirement payment" equal to 13 weeks of vacation pay. This is estimated to approximate $1,500.

Workers who retired prior to Jan. 1, 1960 will receive a $5 monthly hike in their pension.

Another boost in pension pay for those retiring after Jan. 1, 1960 was attained through deduction of $80 instead of $85 because of the social security payment.

The regular monthly pension payments will commence with the month following the three months for which such special retirement payment was paid.

Under mutually satisfactory con-ditions, the contract permits early retirement with full pension upon attainment of age 60 with 15 or more years of service.

Employees who have reached the age of 55 and have 20 years of service can also receive a full retirement pension.

If an employee meeting this qualification of age and service is terminated because of permanent shutdown, layoff or sickness, he shall receive a full pension.

The monthly pension payment of employees retiring after Jan. 1, 1960 will be increased through a raise in the benefit credit. The benefit for each year of service commencing on or after Jan. 1, 1960 has been upped to $2.60 per month.

The minimum benefit for each year of service prior to Jan. 1, 1960 was increased to $2.50 per month for employees retiring after Jan. 1, 1960.

The contract also provides an increase in the flat minimum disability pension from $90 to $100 a month.

121. ©1951 Carl Stamwitz

"First, what is your present wage limitation, seniority status, health and welfare benefits, and retirement pension?"

LABOR'S GREAT VICTORY IN STEEL

The Hat Worker, January 15, 1960

The triumph of the Steelworkers Union after its extraordinary trial by combat may well mark a turning point in the industrial and social history of the United States.

For years labor has been subjected to a war of attrition in which the gains of its formative years were torn off by combinations of hostile forces. Now finally, in a test of strength in the basic industry of the country, it proved that it possessed the moral stamina and the economic strength not only to maintain its position intact, but even to throw back the opponents and inflict complete and ignominious defeat on them.

Lined up in alliance with the already all powerful steel corporations were the Republican Adminstration in Washington and its cohorts in Congress. On their side was also the claque that manipulates public opinion in this country, the newspaper, magazine and electronic gallery that raised a din of abuse and hostility against the union.

From its very beginning, the assault on the union was marked by stupendous excursions in duplicity. We recall steel management's claim that it opposed the union because it was fighting inflation. We could think of nothing more cynical or pretentious than this claim, coming as it did from the most profit-greedy, price spiralling factors in the American economy.

Equally hypocritical was the stand the Administration took. For the President to proclaim that he was "neutral" in the steel conflict was, it seems to us, a demonstration of the extent to which the enemies of labor dominated his thinking.

No Chief Executive of our nation, concerned for the welfare of the people, should have remained indifferent to a conflict in which the families of some half-million workers were directly involved and millions of others were indirectly affected.

The Administration discarded its pose of "neutrality" when the union was on the point of winning the strike. It was then that the President invoked the Taft-Hartley Act and the injunction procedure that forced the strikers to return to work on the employers' terms.

And it was on the eve of a Taft-Hartley election that would have shown the complete solidarity of the workers and their readiness to resume the strike that the Administration suddenly discovered that it had sufficient influence and moral force to move for peace.

It was only then that the Secretary of Labor, James Mitchell, a pleasant but non-potent politician, was permitted to intervene in behalf of a settlement. Until then he had been ignored, and shunted aside by the White House.

As the strike was about to be resumed, it was clear that the steel corporations were hurting. The Taft-Hartley injunction had only momentarily staved off a calamitous shortage of steel in the automobile industry. All of steel's customers were faced with ruin if their source of supply was to be cut off once more. They were forced to tell steel management to knock it off; that their plans to emasculate if not destroy the union had backfired.

When the steel owners realized they were licked, they tried to save at least a political brand from the fire. It was at their instance, not that of the union, that Vice President Richard Nixon was brought into the picture.

The settlement shows that Nixon's intervention did not whittle down the terms the union had set as a basis for peace.

We congratulate the Steelworkers Union on its victory. It's an exhilarating triumph for all labor. We commend President McDonald for the skill and courage he demonstrated throughout the long ordeal.

LET'S PRESERVE THE VICTORY

John McManigal in The Sentinel (Steelworkers Local 1397), January 1960

Regardless of what the politicians say, the 30-month contract signed Jan. 4 was won by steelworkers for steelworkers.

Now that a contract—free of the work rules and local working conditions which the industry would have imposed upon us—has been signed, it is up to us to keep the mills free of such conditions.

If we fail, we will not only be selling out ourselves but also the wives, children, mothers and all who stood behind us during our 116 payless days.

Even before management proposed its eight-point scheme to ride roughshod over us, it was attempting to gradually ease those conditions into the plants. Grievances show that:

Low paid workers were being directed to perform duties of skilled workers on higher paid jobs;

Established plant safety rules and conditions were being disregarded in order to further production;

Workers were idle while men from other departments were performing their jobs;

Job vacancies were being filled without being posted or bid;

Workers in some departments were on 32-hour schedules while higher paid workers were receiving 40-hour work;

Foremen were performing duties of hourly personnel although arbitrations have ruled and management contends it only wants foremen to do work during experimental periods, training men, during major breakdowns and critical emergencies.

These are but a few.

If allowed to continue these practices, the company could yell "past practice" when the union protested these moves.

There is only one way we can preserve our victory.

Every worker must read and know the contract.

Know the proper procedure in filing a grievance and, when your rights are abridged or violated, contact your grievanceman. Then, if you have a grievance, file it.

We must not let management weaken us during the next 30 months. We must keep our contract and union strong. For, come June 30, 1962, the industry will be hammering at us again.

We must protect our own as well as our fellow workers' job rights and freedom as American workers, so that they may be passed on to our children as part of our improved American way of life.

If we fail, this new victory is not ours.

STEELWORKERS WILL RETURN DONATIONS

Federation News (Chicago), January 16, 1960

One of the outstanding proofs of labor solidarity behind the Steelworkers was the raising of more than $5,000,000 for the union's strike fund. The contributions, now no longer needed, will be returned by the Steelworkers.

Commenting on the success of the fund-raising campaign, AFL-CIO Pres. George Meany said:

"Fortunately, the Steelworkers did not need that financial support; it didn't get to the point where they were facing starvation, which, of course, was always a possibility.

"The trade union movement responded in a way and to a degree greater than ever before in trade union history. And I say that the machinery for raising the money was just getting into high gear.

"So that to me was of tremendous significance, the gathering together of the trade union movement when there was a real threat to that movement and a threat to the Steelworkers and a threat to the destruction of their union."

COMMUNITY SERVICES AIDED NEEDY, DISTRIBUTED FOOD DURING STRIKE

The Sentinel (Steelworkers Local 1397), December 1959

Throughout the 116 days of the strike one of the busiest committees functioning in Local Union 1397 was the Community Service Committee.

Medical assistance, shoes and clothing, surplus food, information on public assistance, aid to members threatened with eviction, intervention in constable sales and a myriad of other problems were faced by the committee.

During the Local's meeting of Nov. 23, the membership was told that the committee had advised slightly over 1,000 persons on how to obtain public assistance. About 90 per cent of those strikers applying received benefits ranging between $25 and $100 every two weeks.

United Fund agencies also cooperated in giving emergency care. Twelve persons received medicine or nursing care, six obtained glasses and clothing and three individuals were given hospital care.

Emergency aid for eight persons was arranged with the Homestead Salvation Army.

While intervening in threatened evictions, the committee enabled three families unable to meet mortgage payments to remain in their homes. Another five unable to pay their rent were not put on the street after CSC officials talked to the landlord.

There were 16 instances in which the CSC was able to deter constable sales. These proceedings would have put furniture, washers, dryers and sewing machines on the block to the highest bidder.

The committee was also able to make agreements with finance companies which prevented the repossession of five automobiles. In only one case a finance company refused to cooperate with the committee in granting an extension of the payment time.

Approximately 100 persons threatened with loss of gas and/or light were reported to the committee. In all cases where the committee was notified before the gas or power was shut off, the utility company concerned agreed not to cut it off.

Approximately 48 pairs of shoes were given out between July 15 and Nov. 7.

The committee had the burial expenses of a steelworker's wife defrayed. Firth Sterling Local 1000, which was not on strike, furnished flowers.

Surplus food was probably the biggest single undertaking of the committee.

During the September distribution, 2,100 persons were registered, and received government surplus food.

In October, with the addition of union-purchased foodstuffs, the number of persons registered climbed to 5,600.

Registrations climbed again in November with 7,100 local members receiving District 15 purchased foods along with the government surplus commodities.

WIVES, FAMILIES OF STEELWORKERS' HEROES DURING 116 PAYLESS DAYS

The Sentinel (Steelworker Local Union 1397), December 1959

While the American press and entire labor movement were ringing with praises of the steelworkers' solidarity and determination to win the 116-day strike against the steel industry the main supporters and heroes of the strike were to a large extent overlooked.

For, it was the "power-behind-the-throne" that enabled the workers' fight to stand up.

Just as Molly Pitcher joined the fighters for independence during the American Revolution, the mothers, wives, sisters and children of steelworkers stood steadfastly at the sides of the 1959 strikers during the 116-day ordeal.

The role played at the hearthside contributed immeasurably to the steelworkers' staunch determination to protect their gains won over 20 years of union progress.

In a few cases, wives took on jobs as clerks in stores. Some families received aid from relatives unaffected by the strike. But for most, aside from vacation pay due, the only aid aside from loans was surplus food.

Tricks in economics and household management learned during the depression of the 30's and now handed down to daughters and in some cases granddaughters kept a large segment of the steelworkers' families eating nutritious and tasty meals on a limited budget.

Many a steelworker's wife was heard to remark, "I never knew I could make a dollar stretch so far."

Frequent changes in menus were made using the same basic ingredients to give meals some variety.

Many steelworkers and their wives felt the strike would not occur. Others felt it would be a short one. Quite a few heeded the warnings that 1959 would be a "year of decision."

However, regardless of the opinions of early June, all were united in pulling together after the 15-day truce requested by the President expired in July.

Actually, there were few who believed the strike would last until Nov. 8.

At the outset most families continued to follow their usual mealtime menus and social pleasures.

However, as July rolled into August and the time approached when children would have to be readied for school, many changes were made.

Warm clothes, not needed during the summer months, were soon to become a must.

Most women responded to the lack of income by using their skills as homemakers. Purchases of new outfits were kept at a minimum.

Girls' dresses and Junior's pants were lengthened. In quite a few instances children went back to school in shoes with "half soles and heels" rather than the customary new ones.

And then there was the needed dental work, eye examinations and glasses to be bought to protect the children's health. In many cases dentists and opticians gave this service on "tick." However, these bills must eventually be paid.

Again there was the all important utility bills. Water, phone gas and light bills had to be met. In most cases, if contacted properly, the suppliers of these needs were willing to extend credit.

During the summer months many of the children willingly gave up their weekly or semi-weekly movies.

However, the greatest sufferers were the younger married couples and those with large families who were unable to put something aside.

While glad to see paychecks coming in, many of the wives were regretful that the men were returning to work under the injunction rather than a contract negotiated in good faith.

ARTHUR J. GOLDBERG ASKS NEW PEACE METHODS

Steel Labor, November 1959

Obviously the public has a great stake in the steel dispute. When Congress acted to assert the public interest in such conflicts 12 years ago, it fastened, in part at least, on the injunction method. It was the wrong method—one-sided and of no help in settling the underlying dispute. At least one dividend of the long steel conflict has been the growing recognition of this fact by the President and other officials and experts. The injunction provision is based on the assumption that only the union is responsible for big strikes. This is a patently erroneous assumption.

We must seek a better way of asserting the public interest in major management-labor conflicts—a way that will clearly preserve collective bargaining as the fundamental method of solution. When such disputes occur, the White House cannot fail to recognize that it is impossible for government to stand aloof from them. In the present case the President did precisely that, until the unfortunate and unrealistic Taft-Hartley injunction was readied for use in the fourth month of the strike.

It was a sad day when the steel dispute started on the Taft-Hartley route. It did so because the industry has failed completely in its obligation to engage in good-faith collective bargaining. The union has done all within its power to make bargaining work. It offered the industry a reasonable, non-inflationary settlement —one that would not necessitate any price increase in steel. It offered, even before the strike took place, to submit its case to a presidential fact-finding board with the power to make recommendations. It proved, with the Kaiser settlement, its willingness to compromise. President Eisenhower himself stated that this settlement should be a signal for the industry to settle, but the leading companies insist upon a settlement that no self-respecting group of workers could accept.

It is not enough for the President merely to fall back on Taft-Hartley procedures in a big labor dispute. We must provide the executive branch with a variety of methods to assert the public interest in such conflicts. We do not ask a plumber to use the same wrench on every faucet. A wide range of devices would provide flexibility. In the absence of flexibility, collective bargaining becomes frustrated as one party or the other stalls for time—just as management did in the steel dispute (expecting) that the injunction would be used.

What are some of the devices that should be used?

First I would suggest fact-finding by a public body empowered to make recommendations for settlement. The mere entry and functioning of the fair-minded board in the steel dispute helped change the climate of the dispute. Had it been possible for them to make recommendations, it would have helped materially toward settlement.

A second method that we should explore is the use of distinguished citizens as mediators, as has been done in Britain. Visualize how profitably we might use such eminent Americans as Judge Learned Hand, or Adlai Stevenson or the retired Mr. Justice Burton to help conflicting parties find satisfactory solutions to their difficulties.

So far I have been discussing remedies for disputes. There is also a need for thoughtful discussion of principles and long-range policies among all the big groups in the country—business, labor, farmers, consumers and others. We must fashion challenging forums where the big groups of our country can think aloud and exchange viewpoints in the public interest.

It is my fervent hope that out of the travail of the steel strike will come new methods of furthering enlightened labor-management relations in our country.

2 | JUSTICE ON THE JOB

THE HEART OF LABOR-MANAGEMENT RELATIONS

E. L. (Verne) Hageman, president, Commercial Telegraphers,
in Key and Sounder, February 1958

I am convinced that the grievance procedure is the heart of the collective bargaining relationship with the Company.

The negotiation of a contract is only the beginning of the Union's job. The terms of the contract must be put into effect before that contract means anything to the Union members. And after the contract goes into effect, it is the duty of all Union officers, stewards and members to see that the standards established by the contract are maintained.

Our contract with the Company might be compared to a constitution. The bargaining of the contract might be compared with the legislative process. The representatives of the Union and the Company meet and negotiate or legislate. We agree on the laws or rules to be applicable in the telegraph industry. The Union officers and Union members ratify and sign the contract.

The contract shows where the workers in Western Union stand for the contract term. We must live up to the terms of the contract. And we expect and should insist that the Company officials live up to the contract.

It is sometimes difficult for the individual member to decide whether he has a just grievance. If he is in doubt, he should consult with the proper Union stewards and officers, in accordance with his local by-laws and the Western Union Division by-laws.

There are certain general rules governing grievances which must be considered. First, has there been a violation of the contract? In most cases a just grievance will come under a violation of the contract or our agreements.

In such cases it should be shown what specific section or sections of the contract or agreement have been violated. However, there are some grievances which do not seem to be covered by any clause in the contract but which indicate that a member has been treated unfairly. In all cases, if a grievance is filed with the Union, it is extremely important that all the facts are presented.

Unfortunately, the word "grievance" has a bad connotation in the minds of some people, especially in management. Actually, grievance procedure results in a more harmonious atmosphere because the members know that the Union is ready to handle their complaints if they do not receive their rights under the contract.

Most Company officials have finally recognized that the Union is here to stay and that the members have the right to file grievances. But I don't think that most of them realize that our grievance procedure has brought about improved conditions and a better relationship for the Company officials and for employees. The Company officials generally should learn that in many grievances there should be a cooperative effort on the part of both manage-

55

ment and the Union to bring about justice and fair dealing. Oftentimes a grievance settlement is to the mutual advantage of both the Union and the Company if it is considered from a long-range view.

Regardless of the attitude of the Company official, however, a member should see that he gets what's coming to him under the contract. He should have a copy of the contract and read it whenever he has a question about his rights. If he is in doubt, or he is not sure what the contract calls for, he should consult with the proper Union officer in his local.

However, this doesn't mean that a member should be filing baseless grievances or petty gripes. The Union will be less effective if it continually takes up gripes which are not justified grievances. Further-

more, we must continue our good service on grievances and should not clog the grievance machinery with unnecessary complaints.

During 1957, National Vice President Ted Freeman and I appealed 148 grievance cases to the Company at top level. A few of these cases went to arbitration and they cost the Union hundreds of dollars in arbitrator's fees and other expenses, which was in addition to the expense of our legal counsel.

We are not looking for trouble or encouraging it. However, we do insist on our rights and we will fight for them. The AFL-CIO recently put it this way: "To be a trade unionist is to be a self-respecting American citizen who carries into industry the principle of representation as the basis for fair dealing, and the power of organization to win justice."

THE GRIEVANCE PROCEDURE

Milwaukee Labor Press, December 8, 1960

In a recent survey among Milwaukee Labor Press readers the question was asked, what single bargaining function of your union do you think is the most valuable to the individual member?

The results were surprising in that most of the people interviewed did not select the seeking of wage increases or cash fringe benefits as their primary interests.

Instead, those union-won provisions which received the greatest attention were the grievance and seniority procedures.

As one worker put it, "Before the union came into this plant, our jobs were at the mercy or whim of the foremen. We could be fired without notice and without cause, and many times this happened. If a foreman came in with a hangover or took a dislike toward a certain worker, he could deprive that man of his livelihood with a curt, 'You're through!'

"If the worker protested that he was not guilty of any infraction, he was not given a hearing or even the

355.

"I don't see the need of you union shop stewards. . . . I can deal fairly with each employee's silly grievances without you!"

courtesy of being told why he was being discharged.

"With the advent of the union, this is all changed. Now, before a worker can be given his discharge, various steps of the grievance procedure must be exhausted, and the complaint must have a valid reason for its action."

The reaction of this member is typical of the feeling of many others who have found their union membership their best means of job protection. Perhaps no other single provision in the standard union contract means so much to the individual as the grievance procedure.

Before unionism, there was no outlet or means through which a worker could express his dissatisfaction or complaint about unfair treatment or hazardous job conditions. As a result, management had everything its own way and the slightest protest often brought immediate discharge.

The grievance procedure in union contracts has restored a fundamental and necessary concept in human labor, the feeling of individual dignity and the right to be treated as a human being.

This does not, of course, mean that a worker can flaunt necessary rules and regulations. Nor does it mean that he can take advantage of any given situation. But it does mean that he can go to work every morning in the knowledge that he will get fair treatment on the job and that his performance will be rated, not on an employer's capricious whim or personal dislike, but on his genuine and responsible performance of his duties.

The American labor movement has done much for the average worker, but it is probably through the grievance procedure that it has done the most to give the worker a most necessary feeling of security, independence, and dignity.

PREPARATION FOR GRIEVANCE HANDLING

Building Service Local Officers Quarterly, Autumn 1958

The best collective bargaining agreement in the world contains clauses which can be misunderstood, misinterpreted or just not enforced. This is why unions rely on grievance procedure to ensure for all members the benefits specified in the agreement.

Grievances may arise when the contract does not anticipate changes on the job. New evaluation programs, new methods and other developments that alter job conditions can result in differences between workers and management.

More commonly though, the causes of real grievances are related to wages, seniority, discipline and safety.

A worker may feel that he is not getting enough pay for his particular job. He may think his pay has not been figured correctly. When layoffs or promotions come up, he may feel he is not given credit for his seniority. Sometimes, a worker thinks that his supervisor discriminates against him. Or he wants to have unsafe or unsanitary conditions remedied.

The worker's closest contact with his union comes, in many cases, when he needs help in dealing with management. He knows he would not have a chance if he tried to handle the matter himself. Through the grievance procedure the worker receives the support of his union and its resources. He has a channel of communication between himself and management. Otherwise, all communication in industry would go one way—from top management down.

A worker who has a complaint expects and will receive attention from a person empowered to represent him when a grievance arises.

This person may be the business agent, a member of the union's office staff, an elected steward, or some other individual, depending upon the local situation.

In a small establishment, the grievance procedure may be simple.

If a grievance is not settled immediately, the union business agent will be called to resolve the problem with the boss.

In a larger place, the procedure usually includes several steps. A grievance not settled by the fore- and steward may go to the union business agent and the next higher supervisor for a decision. If they fail to solve the problem, the grievance may go to a representative of top management and a union grievance committee. The next stage may be a meeting between a top official of the union and the head of the firm. If all this fails, the dispute may go to an impartial outside arbitrator.

To handle grievances effectively and fairly, many locals have set up stewards' classes.

Well-planned classes may include instruction in human relations, methods of strengthening the union, labor laws, contract provisions, steps in the grievance procedure, and other matters.

A good steward must help his fellow workers learn the benefits of unionism. Active, well-informed and enthusiastic members are an asset to any local. To be effective a steward needs the backing of a strong local. He should learn to present the union's case to unorganized or indifferent workers. If the steward understands the structure and purpose of the labor movement, its history and current activities, he will be better able to educate his fellow workers.

Training in human relations will help the steward know the workers in his unit. It will help him distinguish between the timid worker who is afraid to complain about a grievance when he has one and the chronic griper. The steward must learn to gain the worker's confidence, so that the employee comes to him with a grievance.

A thorough knowledge of the contract that regulates the working life of his fellow unionists is essential to the steward. His training should stress the importance of knowing each worker's duties, wages, and seniority rating, so that the steward can help each employee get the best deal that the contract will allow.

Stewards' training should explain the laws which protect workers' rights to organize and negotiate, and other laws which affect union members, such as those concerning unemployment insurance, social security, safety and health regulations, and accident compensation. If possible, the stewards should have these laws explained by a competent lawyer or other authority.

The steward should also learn how politics affects his welfare and that of all union members. He may find it necessary to persuade his fellow workers to use their vote. Part of his job is to inform members about proposed new laws that will affect them as union members and citizens.

The steward should be acquainted with new developments in his industry which may affect union members and which might lead to grievances.

One possible source of grievances is the introduction of time and motion study systems. Under these plans, some workers may have to do more work for the same rate of pay.

Automation will create problems involving layoffs, job classifications, seniority, and compensation for increased productivity.

A good training program will cover these problems and their possible solutions.

Instruction in accident prevention techniques will help the steward to help the employees. An employee who is asked to work in an unsafe environment has a legitimate grievance.

In some cases, a worker has a personal problem which affects his work and makes him think he has a job-connected grievance when he really doesn't. He may take out his resentments on a fellow worker, for instance. Of course, the steward is not an advice columnist or social worker. Still, he may find it helpful to know about agencies in his area that handle legal, medical, emotional or family problems.

WHEN A BROTHER NEEDS HELP

The Machinist, August 29, 1957

Walter Pleban walked out of Cleveland State Hospital recently to face one of life's hardest problems—getting back on his feet after two years in an institution. Pleban had recovered fully, but the world is not easy on a former mental patient.

Pleban wanted his former job back. Did his fellow workers at Foundry Equipment Co. want him?

They did, but the company didn't, reports Edward M. Webb, business representative for I.A.M. Lodge 2155, Cleveland. The I.A.M. had to take Pleban's case to arbitration before he was returned to his job.

Here's the story as told The Machinist by Webb.

Once before in 1943, after 14 years, Pleban had left a mental hospital. World War II was in doubt then so he stepped into defense work with Foundry Equipment Co., and for the next 11 years he stayed with this company, establishing an exemplary record. He received no reprimands and had few absences. He was a helper in the shear department.

Then in December 1954, Pleban began to feel that someone was trying to kill him.

His condition worsened rapidly and Pleban's brother had him committed to Cleveland State Hospital. Hospital psychiatrists determined that he was suffering from schizophrenia.

During the next year Pleban was depressed, withdrawn and talked little. Then the hospital put him on thorazine, 100 mg. per day. Pleban improved; he went home on 10-day passes; his behavior was excellent, and he participated in social activities.

A year later the psychiatrists decided that Pleban was cured; they placed him on probation, and Dr. Frederick C. Badt, the assistant clinical director, certified that Pleban was quite able to work. Despite 11 years of exemplary service, Foundry Equipment Co. didn't want Pleban back. But his union did.

Three times in three grievance hearings pressed by the union, the company responded: "The company feels no obligation to hire this man."

But the company did have an obligation. Pleban appeared before Horace C. Vokoun, arbitrator, backed up by I.A.M. Lodge 2155.

The union showed that Pleban had maintained his seniority and that the company had never properly discharged him. Vokoun examined the pertinent sections of the contract and agreed.

Pleban got his job back.

In his decision Vokoun pointed out: "Upon latest medical authority, persons with mental disabilities such as are attributed to Mr. Pleban are as likely as those physically ill to effect a recovery that will enable them to resume their places in society."

The hospital staff applauded. Dr. William L. Grover, superintendent of Cleveland Hospital, took the time to write to Walter Balasz, president of Lodge 2155.

"Mr. Webb was very energetic and persistent in his efforts to reinstate Pleban. Beyond this, however, he has taken an active personal interest in Pleban's adjustment and continued treatment at our out-patient clinic.

"We feel that the quality of his work deserves special recognition from the hospital.

"I want to thank you again for your efforts, not only on behalf of Mr. Pleban, but all other patients who may be helped in this way in the future."

GUILD'S JOB PROTECTION MAKES THE DIFFERENCE

Guild Reporter, Sept. 11, 1959

"Although I am temporarily leaving newspaper work for a stint with the U. S. Information Agency, I intend to keep paying my dues regularly to the North Jersey Newspaper Guild," Tom Mulvehill wrote in the August issue of the Guild Bulletin, the local's publication.

"The decision is dictated partially by a sense of guilt," said Mulvehill, until recently a copy reader and rewrite man on the Plainfield Courier-News and more widely known through "See, Here, Private Hargrove."

"In the past," he said, "I have always worked for non-Guild newspapers. The pay was as high as or higher than that paid at Guild-organized papers, as were many fringe benefits. In one instance, when a fellow staffer fell ill for a period of nine months, the publisher paid him right up to the time he returned to work.

"But in every instance, staffers were agreed that the high wages and benefits had been made available because of the publisher's almost fanatical desire to keep his editorial department out of the Guild. So, ironically, the Guild was responsible for getting non-Guildsmen generous benefits, but failed to receive the support of those who had thus benefited.

"Turning to the other side of the coin, I received a liberal education on the Courier-News in what the Guild can accomplish for staffers on a newspaper which has a contract with the Guild. I learned that salaries were raised, fringe benefits gained or expanded and a measure of job security assured.

"In comparing the benefits of working for a Guild or non-Guild shop, the one big difference is outstanding Job Security. On other papers I have seen fine, competent craftsmen dropped from the payroll or reduced in rank without a fair hearing. This, I have discovered, is impossible on a Guild paper.

"All in all, I feel that continuing my dues while I am gone is the most logical move I could make because it will afford me the maximum protection at a minimum cost."

MEMBER RETURNED TO JOB WITH $4,117 BACK PAY

The Machinist, July 28, 1960

American Can Co. has junked a "get tough with the union" policy after an unsuccessful try-out at its Bradley Sun division factory in Maynard, Mass.

Members convinced the company the policy would not work at Maynard, Grand Lodge Rep. Clark H. Goodrich reported last week.

The policy cost the company's Bradley Sun division more than $8,000 before it was scrapped, Goodrich added. Here are the facts:

The trouble started when the management announced a new set of work rules and disciplinary procedures.

First victim was Joseph Van Vorse, member of IAM Lodge 2199.

He was fired for using language a supervisor objected to.

An alert shop committee protested. Management was adamant. The committee took Van Vorse's case to arbitration provided under the IAM contract with the company. Plato Papps, IAM chief counsel, argued the case.

When the facts were in, the arbitrator found the language objected to had been heard around the factory before. Van Vorse was reinstated. Back pay awarded him came to $4,-117. After deductions, he collected $2,548.

The shop committee then persuaded Bradley Sun management to reinstate without loss of seniority seven other victims of the "get tough" policy and rescind suspension of five additional victims.

Over-all cost to the company in back wages came to more than $8,000. Relations at Bradley Sun division are now back to normal.

TEACHERS' LOCAL GETS FIRST PACT

The American Teacher, May 1959

Teachers in Dearborn, Mich. are guaranteed review rights in the first written collective bargaining agreement in this school system's history.

The agreement was reached by the board of education and the Dearborn Federation of Teachers, Local 681.

The review clauses give teachers the privilege of inspecting and commenting on issues having a bearing on their professional status, salaries and conditions of employment.

The bargaining achievement climaxed the presidential year of Wallace B. Smith, now succeeded by Ray Howe who was first vice-president. The two were backed by the work of several committees.

John J. Dunn, editor of the Dearborn Teacher, reported other gains, declaring the year one of the most successful for teachers. Rights and benefits obtained by the Local's personnel policies committee include:

1) Unlimited accumulated sick leave; teachers on tenure receiving 15 days a year.

2) Holiday and religious observance allowances for members of non-Christian faiths.

3) Leave for advanced study after three years instead of five, with automatic return to the position held.

The Federation is seeking two more improvements which the board has approved in principle but not officially recognized. One is better pay for teachers in night and summer school programs, and the other is a guaranteed cost-of-living pay adjustment based on government and industrial forecasts.

This year the board granted a 3½ per cent cost-of-living adjustment, gained through efforts of the Federation's salary committee directed by Fred Long, its veteran chairman.

MINUTES OF GRIEVANCES WITH MANAGEMENT

The Cadillac Steward, June 5, 1959

WEDNESDAY, APRIL 29, 1959

Present for Labor: Messrs. Koller, Hall, Fusco, Eldridge, Lee, Haney, Goins and Hamel. President Lo. 22: J. Wagner.

Present for Management: Messrs. Phillips, Pfeifer, Emery, Oelsner, Gale, Budnik, Peters and Barker.

OLD BUSINESS

1. Employee Grievance No. 479689 —W. O'Key—1603-246.

Management stated the aggrieved employee was assessed a disciplinary layoff for failing to report to the Medical Department promptly after injuring himself. Due to the peculiar circumstances of the case the discipline will be removed from the aggrieved's record and he will be awarded makeup time without prejudice.

The Grievance Committee stated this case may be considered settled without prejudice.

2. Employee Grievance No. 478752 —H. Epperson—1302-21.

Management stated that in view of the aggrieved's good record and the circumstances surrounding the case, the verbal warning will be removed from Epperson's record. However, a re-instruction contact regarding safe work practices will be entered in the aggrieved's injury control record.

The Grievance Committee stated

this case may be closed on that basis.

**3. Group Grievance No. 478073 —
F. Haranczak — 1502-181 — I. Roels— 1502-6009.**

Committee requested this case be referred back to the First Step of the Grievance Procedure.

Management agreed.

NEW BUSINESS

4. Employee Grievance No. 524152 —C. Burton—601-148.

Grievance reads:

"Charge Management with working Record Clerks on packing and carpenters' work. Demand job be placed in proper classification."

(Sgd.) C. Burton.

Committee stated that (non-union) employees classified as record clerks are performing bargaining unit (union) work. Committee contends this work assignment should be confined to bargaining unit employees.

Management stated they would investigate this case.

5. Employee Grievances No. 478754 —J. Weronka—1308-212; No. 478755 —L. Makowski—1308-135; No. 478756 —H. McKinney—1308-285.

All grievances read:

"I charge Dept. 1308 supervision with an unjust and unfair disciplinary action! Demand this be corrected, and pay for all time lost!"

(Sgd.) J. Weronka
(Sgd.) L. Makowski
(Sgd.) H. McKinney

Committee stated the aggrieved employees were assessed a disciplinary layoff for hanging an engine on the conveyor out of sequence. Committee contends these penalties were too severe.

Management stated they would investigate these cases.

6. Employee Grievance No. 462910 —J. Wilson—2307-516.

Grievance reads:

"I charge Management with shortage in pay for week ending 4-19-59. Demand proper adjustment in pay for shortage."

(Sgd.) J. Wilson

Committee stated the aggrieved employee, who is assigned to a continuous seven-day operation worked his regular shift hours Monday through Friday of the week ending April 19, 1959. However, on Saturday of that week he started work at his regular 4:30 P.M. starting time but worked straight through until 9:00 A.M., Sunday, April 19, 1959. He was paid at a time and one-half rate for all of these hours. Committee contends he should have been paid at a double-time rate for his last eight hours worked on Sunday.

Management stated they would investigate this case.

7. Time Waivers.

Committee requested the time limit on the following grievances be waived an additional week:

Zone 1—No. 462512
Zone 2—No. 477905

Management agreed.

WEDNESDAY, MAY 6, 1959

OLD BUSINESS

(See Minutes for April 29, 1959)

1. Employee Grievance No. 524152 —C. Burton—601-148.

Management stated that the work involved was directly related to the preparation of a specification for a standardized container. In Management's opinion, since this type of developmental work has been performed in the past by non-bargaining unit employees, bargaining unit employees were not thereby deprived of work. The grievance is denied.

Committee stated they would take Management's disposition under advisement.

2. Employe Grievances No. 478754 —J. Weronka—1308-212; No. 478755 —L. Makowski—1308-135; No. 478756 —. McKinney—1307-285.

Management stated the aggrieved employees were assessed a one day disciplinary layoff because they failed to hang an engine in sequence on the final assembly conveyor. Investigation shows that had each of these employees followed their job instructions, any one of them could and should have prevented the incident. In Management's opinion the disciplinary penalties assessed were well within the principles of corrective discipline and therefore not too severe. For this reason the grievances are denied.

Committee stated they would take Management's disposition under advisement.

3. Employee Grievance No. 462910 —J. Wilson—2307-516.

.Management contends the aggrieved was properly paid under terms of the National Agreement. Therefore the grievance is denied.

Committee stated this case would be appealed.

UNION LOYALTY PAYS OFF FOR MONTGOMERY WARD EMPLOYEES

Stanley M. Seganish in Retail Clerks Advocate, May 1958

Montgomery Ward's treatment of two workers, Irene Witter Baden and Frank J. Felker, furnishes a concrete example of what the Ward strike and boycott are all about.

Arbitrarily discharged by the company, they would have been powerless as individuals against this mammoth corporation. As members of the Retail Clerks, it was a different story.

Both got their jobs back. In addition, Sister Baden received a check for $2,500 (less tax deductions) and Brother Felker was reimbursed for time lost to the extent of $8,865.

The story of Ward's aggression started on Aug. 17, 1954, when Retail Clerks' Local 1687 won an election in the store in Binghamton, N. Y. Within a week the company fired the two skillful, experienced employees for union activity. Felker had 12 years' experience, Sister Baden had worked for the company intermittently for 12 years and had been employed steadily for four years prior to the successful election.

The local immediately filed unfair labor practice charges protesting this outrageous action. A complaint against Ward's was issued by the NLRB and early in 1955 the charges were aired before an NLRB trial examiner.

The trial examiner found that Ward's was guilty of the charges alleged by the local union, and ordered the company to "cease and desist from interfering with, restraining or coercing its employees." He ordered Ward's to offer the employees their jobs back without loss of rights and to restore all moneys lost to them in pay as a result of the unfair discharges.

The company refused to obey the order, weaseling on the flimsy ground that it was not responsible for the actions of its supervisors.

The full National Labor Relations Board, sitting in Washington, reviewed the case, completely vindicated the Retail Clerks and reaffirmed the trial examiner's orders.

The company still refused to accept its responsibility, and comply with the Board's decision. It tried a further maneuver, appealing to the Courts.

Again it was defeated when the U. S. District Court of Appeals in New York City upheld the NLRB decision and order.

By this time, several years had passed, but the company was not yet ready to obey the order.

Ward's appealed to the U. S. Supreme Court, and again they were rebuffed when the highest tribunal refused to review the proceedings. Nothing in the record seemed to it to warrant such a review.

The order then became effective. The employees were reinstated in their jobs and finally received the checks totaling $9,090.12 net, covering their loss of pay. Three and a half years had passed.

The loyalty of the Retail Clerks

to these two members was finally vindicated. But very few people have the patience, strength and resources to hang on in the face of prolonged company machinations of this sort. That is why the Union is fighting for decent, reasonable, honorable treatment for Ward employees.

It is fighting for the kind of contract that will guarantee that responsible treatment of employees by this corporation will occur on a day-to-day basis.

The right of employees to have a voice in their conditions of work is at the very foundation of the struggle with this corporation.

DIGEST OF SHIP MEETINGS

Seafarers Log, July 1, 1960

CAPT. NICHOLAS SITINAS (Cargo), April 3—Chairman John Kulas; Sec. Joshua M. Lundy. Deck and steward department quarters have been painted. Sink in baker's room will be replaced. Steward department shorthanded but doing a good job. C and B men are reminded to see their department delegate when in doubt and to keep beefs within department. Voted on ship's fund and library. $10 advance at Jibouti. One man missed ship in Ft. Lauderdale. Repair refrigerator in crew messroom. Overtime not equalized in engine department. Crew reminded to flush toilets. Also turn off washing machine. See about having engine department quarters painted. One brother desires welsh rarebits and lamb chops.

June 5—Chairman, John Kulas; Secretary, Joshua M. Lundy. One man hospitalized in Bombay; Union notified. Thanks to delegates for cooperation. $5.60 in ship's fund. Some disputed overtime in engine department—two men short. Will check with chief engineer and captain concerning disputed overtime. Steward department delegate reports one non-union man picked up in Ceuta (US citizen).

NATALIE (Maritime Overseas), June 5—Chairman, N. Magash; Sec. L. W. Pepper. Deck delegate reports one man paid off in Honolulu. Engine delegate reports one man missed ship; one man deported; one man sent home for hospitalization. Some

disputed overtime. Haven't received LOGS regularly. Food in general considered very poor; quality of meat and preparation of food to be taken up with patrolman upon arrival at first port.

STEEL ROVER (Isthmian), June 1—Chairman, J. F. Goude; Secretary, R. A. Sipsey. All beefs to be taken up with department delegates. $58.25 in ship's treasury. No disputed overtime. Engine toilet needs to be repaired. No hot water in cook's room. Hot water in cold water showers.

MAIDEN CREEK (Waterman), May 8—Chairman, Sylvester Zygarowski); Secretary, Johnny P. Baliday. Under new skipper. A great deal of necessary things being done which were ignored for past year. Everything running smoothly. Ship's fund, $11.72. No beefs reported.

FAIRLAND (Sea-Land), June 8—Chairman, R. W. Simpkins; secretary, Charles Goldstein. Ship's delegate reports he talked to chief engineer about ice shortage. Chief okays to pull ice each day. No beefs reported. Crew to get a checker set, steam iron and radio for crew's use from ship's fund. A vote of thanks to steward department for job well done.

DEL SUD (Mississippi), May 8—Chairman, Woodrow Perkins; Secretary, George McFall. Good trip. No beefs reported. Ship's fund, $281; movie fund, $274. Some disputed overtime in engine dept. M/S/C to contact company to try and payoff and sign on the same day. Two men hurt. Rescued crippled yacht at sea. Ship's doctor will have talk on first aid; crew asked to attend.

BIENVILLE (Sea-Land), May 29 —Chairman, F. Sullivan; Sec., D. Gribble. Baker missed ship in Jacksonville. $24 in movie film fund. Motion to see patrolman about clothes dryer as soot goes on clothes when hung on deck.

ATLAS (Cargo & Tankship), April 16—Chairman, A. E. Gourgot; Secretary, S. M. Simos. $17 in ship's fund. Have a TV set. One man got off in Panama, another in ship's hospital. Vote of thanks to crew before for contributing in the purchase of the TV set, also to the captain and steward for taking care of coke machine. Chief cook gave vote of thanks for sending of flowers by crew and officers upon the funeral of cook's sister.

THE CABINS (Texas City Refining), May 13—Chairman, H. G. Sanford; Secretary, Robert Cooper. Delegate reports everything going along on a smooth keel. Expect the patrolman in Texas City this trip so anyone owing dues can pay up. $33.47 in ship's fund. Suggested that steward take up with port steward matter of getting rid of roaches. Also suggestion that more night lunch be put out. Crew reminded to turn off washing machine when not in use. Matter of dirty water for washing to be taken up with chief engineer and if nothing is done to take it up with patrolman.

NORTHWESTERN VICTORY (Victory Carriers), April 2—Chairman, John Risbeck; Secretary, R. V. Haylock. No beefs reported. Take garbage aft. Crew requested to take screws out of pockets before washing clothes. Have messman be more conscientious and try to remember orders.

SHOP STEWARD WINS APOLOGY IN 'SHOVING' INCIDENT

Local 1-S News, December 15, 1959

The management of the Pharmacy Department in Macy's has a long history of supercilious and even contemptuous attitudes toward the men and women who comprise its staff.

Sometimes this hostile attitude impinges upon workers in adjacent departments; recently it spilled over into physical aggression.

Such a case in point was illustrated recently when Mr. Brown, a Pharmacy executive, shoved Vincent Royes, a shop steward in Drugs.

The events which led up to this episode are interesting. Shop steward Royes had observed a Pharmacy clerk doing stockwork—which is forbidden under the Union Contract. Royes went to the Pharmacy to look for the steward in order that an appropriate grievance might be filed.

He was told the Pharmacy steward had not come to work.

In her absence Royes asked Mr. Brown why the clerk was doing stockwork. The executive became nasty, and told steward Royes to get out of the Pharmacy, and write a grievance about it. Mr. Brown thereupon punctuated his remarks with a shove.

Steward Royes was, as a matter of fact, not in the Pharmacy itself, but on its threshhold.

But two main points should be emphasized, one practical and immediate, the other a matter of respect and union principle.

Mr. Brown, a small, rotund gentleman, was surely tempting fate when he poked the chest of steward Royes who is a strapping six-footer. The latter is to be congratulated on his self-discipline as a union representative.

The second point is more far-reaching. No labor-management relationship can survive either the open disdain or physical violence of an executive against a worker.

This principle was evident enough

to the 16th Floor which arranged a meeting between a Labor Relation representative, a union representative, and the immediately interested parties.

At this meeting on December 8, 1959, Mr. Brown duly and properly apologized to Shop Steward Royes.

PROTEST HALTS DELEGATE FIRINGS IN HOTEL

Hotel (New York), October 17, 1960

The sudden firing of two delegates in the Savoy Hilton, in violation of the contract, caused a shopwide protest in the hotel last Thursday.

The contract calls for prior notice and consultation if management is considering action against a delegate. Two banquet delegates, T. Horoskak and Klaus Steinke, were taken off the working list without such notification, and, as a result, workers poured out of every department by the hundreds to demonstrate their resentment. They gathered mainly at the second-floor kitchen and there were about 300 overflowing the area when union officers arrived at the scene about noon.

A quick conference was held between the officers and management spokesmen, and things were placed back on a contractual footing. The two delegates were restored to the payroll, a conference was set on the issue for this Tuesday, and the workers went back to their jobs.

Plaza

The union has complained to the Hotel Association that A. Canovas, a seamstress in this hotel, was denied the July 4 holiday in violation of the contract. Involved in this case is the clause that says an employee shall be paid "if the holiday occurs within 20 working days following the beginning" of a layoff.

Pierre

In this case, also filed with the Hotel Association, our complaint is that Lulu Robbins, a checker, was

denied reinstatement after returning from an illness. The contract says an employee absent for illness "not more than 20 weeks shall be reinstated . . . with all job rights and seniority." Sister Robbins, we point out, was absent less than 20 weeks.

Seaway (Idlewild)

Management had refused to grant vacations to employees after completion of an employment year, and had sought to put them off until next summer. A conference was scheduled at the Hotel Association on the union's charge that this was a violation of the contract, but the matter was settled in direct discussions and the case satisfactorily closed.

Cases Go to Impartial Chairman

Several cases were discussed at the Hotel Association without agreement being reached. As a result the union is carrying them to the office of the Impartial Chairman for resolution. They include the following:

Bolivar

Mae Smith, a maid, was denied full vacation rights due her after more than 15 years of employment. The hotel claims that there was a break in her employment that affects the situation, but the union challenges this.

Ritz Tower

We are demanding reinstatement of Isali Arroyo, a doorman, who was discharged after a tenant's double-parked car was tagged by the police.

It is our contention that he cannot be held responsible for what happened.

Drake

The union, under the terms of the contract, has filed against the hotel for failure of a checkroom concession to comply with the contract's provisions relating to welfare funds and also for its failure to pay several employees for a holiday or grant them vacations.

Hearings Scheduled

The office of the Impartial Chairman has set several cases down for discussion this week, as follows:

THURSDAY: Kimberly — A telephone operator was laid off and her work assigned to a desk clerk, creating a combination job. We are asking reaffirmation of previous rulings that only a telephone operator may handle the telephone job. Chateau Madrid—Denial of contract wage increase to Antonio Terrogrosso, a working chef.

FRIDAY: St. George—Three complaints, involving assignment of house officers as relief watchmen, refusal of the hotel to continue a long-existing practice of giving an hour off on Sundays and holidays to newly hired housekeeping employees, and refusal to pay Roy Merkel, a cook, for the July 4 holiday. Grosvenor—Failure to comply with the arbitrator's order that Angel Suarez be paid as an assistant cook. The hotel had rated him as an apprentice and after losing the case demoted him to potwasher. We charge this amounted to non-compliance with the decision and punishment of worker for demanding his rights.

JOB-SELLING RACKET EXPOSED BY RWDSU IN CHICAGO

RWDSU Record, September 30, 1956

Expert detective work by the Chicago Joint Board of the Retail, Wholesale and Department Store Union has broken wide open a vicious racket in a union plant. The case had all the earmarks of a Hollywood chiller-diller.

Take a bunch of ingredients like a plant foreman who once scabbed during a strike, a number of newly arrived, job-hungry immigrants, and a weasel of a man who speaks the immigrants' language and trades on his countrymen's ignorance, and you have the makings of an ugly racket. The foreman and his stooge turned this situation into a job-selling racket which milked some $8,000 in two years from workers who could ill afford to part with a penny.

It was this flourishing trade in people's misery at a long-time union shop that the Chicago Joint Board of RWDSU broke up after an exhaustive investigation, substantially aided by the Puerto Rican Department of Labor, presently a division of the U.S. Labor Department.

The racket was a simple one. Because of 28 years of service with the company, this foreman was permitted to do the hiring and firing in his department. He hired mainly Spanish-speaking immigrants, referred to him to him by his recruiter and stooge. The stooge, who also served as muscle man and collector, previously extracted pledges from job applicants that they would pay $25 to $40 for a "steady job."

The foreman then put the man on the payroll, but the worker seldom lasted more than a few weeks, never longer than the trial period required before becoming a union member. To keep the money coming in, the foreman kept his turnover of employees pretty high, and the new workers would be fired for "poor performance."

The union had been suspicious of the existence of a racket for some time, and several unsuccessful attempts were made to uncover it. The victims were afraid to give evidence because of threats made to them when they were hired. Twice the union filed complaints with the company, only to be told the charges were unsupported by sufficient facts.

Anthony Vega of the Puerto Rican Labor Department pitched into the case at the union's request, but this effort, too, proved unsuccessful. Radio stations in Puerto Rico were enlisted in the campaign to bust the racket. The stations broadcast messages to locate any victims who had returned to Puerto Rico and who would give information on how the racket worked. But this failed too.

The union then engaged a private investigator, who ran into a wall of fear. He informed the company, however, that a job-selling business was being run in the plant and recommended that the muscle-man-collector be fired. The company refused. The company later explained that it believed the union was "out to get" the two racketeers because they had scabbed.

The break came just a few weeks ago. The operators had slipped up. They fired one of their victims after his probationary period, and the worker was willing to give the union information.

With the help of Vega and Mary Cassaretto, also of the Puerto Rican Labor Department, the union contacted other workers who recruited for the foreman under the threat of physical harm if they refused—and they were willing to talk.

Lie detector tests were used. The Federal Bureau of Investigation became involved when it was learned that forged documents had been used to get recruits across the border from Mexico. Hideouts in Chicago Loop hotels were hired by the union, and cooperating witnesses were lodged there to avoid bodily harm to them.

The climax came when the foreman was confronted with the evidence and charged with being the ringleader. He denied everything at first, threatening to sue the union "because they were only out to get me because I crossed the picket lines during the strike." He was asked to submit to a lie detector test to prove his innocence.

A few days later the leader of this miserable racket confessed fully. He was promptly fired, joining his stooge and partner in crime, who had been fired somewhat earlier.

With the union's case proved, the firm agreed to have membership meetings held in the plant. At these meetings management representatives gave full credit to the union in cleaning up the racket.

Most important, it was made clear to all employees, particularly the Spanish-speaking workers, that their jobs would be steady. There will be no phony layoffs or discharges, and no more fees to get a job at this plant.

410.

"Drop it, man——it's quitting time! That union contract I just signed has an overtime pay clause in it!"

TIME STUDY NOTES
FROM AN 'EXPERT' IN ENGLAND

CWA News, May 1960

We've often felt that some branches of the communications industry carry time and motion studies to ridiculous extremes, but this report from a time study expert on a Philharmonic concert in Manchester, England, is hard to beat. He said:

"For considerable periods the four oboe players had nothing to do. The number should be reduced and the work spread more evenly over the whole of the concert, thus eliminating peaks of activity. All the 12 violins were playing identical notes; this seems unnecessary duplication. The staff of this section should be drastically cut. If a larger volume of sound is required, it could be obtained by electronic apparatus.

"Much effort was absorbed in the playing of demi-semi-quavers; this seems to be unnecessary refinement. It is recommended that all notes should be rounded up to the nearest semi-quaver. If this were done it would be possible to use trainees and lower-grade operatives more extensively.

"No useful purpose is served by repeating on the horns a passage which has already been handled by the strings. It is estimated that if all theme repetitions were eliminated the whole concert-time of two hours could be reduced to 20 minutes and there would be no need for an intermission."

UNION MEN GO TO SCHOOL
TO LEARN SPEEDUP TRICKS

AFL-CIO News, July 30, 1960

The manner in which management uses time studies, wage incentives and job evaluation to reduce legitimate collective bargaining gains was demonstrated to 49 trade union staff memebrs at the 1960 AFL-CIO Industrial Engineering Institutes at the University of Wisconsin's School for Workers.

The unionists — from 14 national and international unions, two federal labor unions, and the field staffs of the national and state AFL-CIO—attended basic and advanced institutes conducted jointly by the AFL-CIO Dept. of Research and the School for Workers.

The basic courses covered time study, wage incentives, job evaluation and wage determination, while the advanced courses were geared to collective bargaining of industrial engineering problems and synthetic work standard systems.

Goal of the annual training program is to provide union staff members with the information needed to effectively represent workers faced with the burgeoning management use of industrial engineering methods and practices.

In issuing the call to the training sessions, AFL-CIO Sec.-Treas. William F. Schnitzler had charged management with "arbitrary and abusive" use of industrial engineering, and said that as a result "wage increases are negated by downgrading jobs, increasing work loads and lowering incentive earnings."

Leading authorities in the industrial engineering field from the trade union movement served on the training staff.

COST OF ARBITRATION COMES HIGH;
UNFAIR CHARGES BY UNIONS SOAR

Federation News (Chicago), January 21, 1959

Unions are piling a large number of grievances against $150-a-day arbitrators.

Unions charge them with setting fees so high that smaller unions no longer can afford to carry disputes to an impartial umpire.

Thousands of grievances go to arbitration each year, usually after union and company officials reach a deadlock.

A grievance can range from a complaint that one worker's vacation pay was miscalculated to charges involving hundreds of employees.

The latest blast at arbitrators' prices came from a union attorney writing anonymously in the Digest published by the AFL-CIO Industrial Union Department.

The attorney said contract disputes of 20 years ago were settled by referring them to a local clergyman, judge, or college professor who made his decision in a matter of hours. He often made no charge for the service.

Today, the union spokesman said, arbitration has become "expensive, protracted and legalistically complicated," with full-time, professional referees.

The attorney said a recent study showed unions paid an average of $1,500 as their share of arbitration costs over a three-year period. He proposed that unions and managements get together to limit fees by reducing the number of long-term contracts, increasing the number of arbitrators and demanding to know the fee in advance. He said one-year contracts would allow more grievances to be settled at the bargaining table.

Meanwhile, labor-management tension which began to build up about a year ago has been sharply reflected by unfair labor practices which have been growing "at steadily record rates."

During the last quarter of 1958 the number of charges filed against employers reached an all-time high while the total number of unfair practices cases reached an all-time high for the fifth consecutive quarter.

The NLRB general counsel also issued 249 complaints—"the greatest number ever issued in any one quarter.

THE LADIES — UNIONS NEED THEM!

Patricia Strandt in Building Service Employee, December 1957

Women, an increasingly important part of the world's working force, are becoming an increasingly important part of the labor movement. This, most labor leaders agree, is good. Women have a real contribution to make to trade unionism. Their viewpoint, often a bit different from that of their husbands, sons, and fathers, is being recognized as a valuable tool in strength-

ening and spreading labor's fight for better working conditions and community welfare.

BSEIU has 187 women in its membership who serve their local unions as elected officers or as business agents. Fifteen of these women are the presidents of their local unions.

Many of the 187 are in BSEIU's smaller locals, but a good number— such as Ruth O. Smith, recording secretary of Local 46 (8,500 members) in Chicago, and New York's Helen Bielak and Nellie Malsky, secretary-treasurer and vice-president respectively of Local 32-J (8,000 members)—are in the biggest.

Some, such as Mrs. Emma King, president of Local 194 in Fairbanks, Alaska, are pioneer unionists in their communities. Others, such as Mrs. Annie L. Kempkes, secretary-treasurer of Local 211 in Northampton, Mass., have devoted many years to their union work. Mrs. Kempkes, at 73, has been a union officer for 14 years.

BSEIU's Department of Research and Education mailed questionaires to all 187 of the International's lady officers and business agents. From the replies we've put together a composite picture of the petticoat unionist.

More likely than not, our composite woman has been a member of a BSEIU union for over seven years, and often she has 15 or more years of union work behind her. She is most likely to be employed in a school or hospital, and to have a somewhat better than grade school education. But she's done a lot of studying after her formal schooling stopped, and some of her sister officers (15 percent) have been to college.

She doesn't mind admitting her age, which is in her fifties more often than not. And she is happily married, though 20 percent are widows, and 10 percent are bachelor girls. Her husband, too, is a union member, and, in a few cases, also a union officer. More than likely he is in a BSEIU union, too, though not always the same local as his wife.

She has two children, on the average, though some of her fellow women officers have as many as six or 10. Most of them are grown and settled as housewives or members of the working middle class, but a fourth of her co-unionists have one or more children still in school.

Her union activity is just a part of this woman's life, although it ranks with her home and family as a basic and significant part. But she belongs to a variety of other groups—lodges, the PTA, civic groups of all kinds. More likely than not she is also an officer in these organizations. And sometimes (12 percent) she is an officer in three or more groups in addition to her union work.

She usually has time for hobbies, too. Fishing and hunting—are you surprised?—is a favorite. She often is a collector, too, and likes to read, sew and garden.

She is a busy woman. She is interested in her own welfare, and her family's, and also in the welfare of her fellow workers—which is why she feels a union is so important. "If we could only get more people interested in unions," she wishes. "If we could show labor and management and the public how necessary unions are!"

Sometimes her interest in unions is a long-standing one (Says Mrs. Bessie Hughes, Local 290, Pullman, Wash.: "It was through my husband that I became interested in union activity. We had Union for every meal!"

And Mrs. Ralph Klock, Local 383, Reading, Pa.: "My deceased father was a 100 per cent Union Man" and sometimes it was not until she began to see what a union could do for her own working situation that she became enthusiastic.

She wants, very much, to be a good union officer and to help people. She sees people as individuals, and her job often as that of peacemaker.

She believes that labor's most pressing current problem is the so-called "right-to-work" movement.

BSEIU's women, judging from this sample, are remarkably clear-sighted. Their interest in unions is genuine and their sincerity and warm concern for people gives an added dimension to union affairs.

RESPONSIBILITIES OF A UNION SHOP STEWARD

The Electrical Workers' Journal, December 1959

You're not just John Jones, union member, anymore. You're John Jones, shop steward. Maybe they call you "committeeman" or "representative" or "grievance chairman." Whatever the title, you've been selected to be the leader of the union in your department and to see that members get fair treatment on the job. That's an honor.

It's also a responsibility. The members are depending on you to settle grievances for them and to help with their problems. The union relies on you to enforce the contract and keep the members informed about union activities.

Perhaps you're wondering just what you've let yourself in for. Are you supposed to be a genius like Einstein or a magician like Houdini? Of course not. You will earn the respect of both members and management if you are willing to work at the job and learn as you go along. And you have a right to that respect. For as a conscientious IBEW steward, you are doing a most important job.

No matter how strong the IBEW or your local union may be, they must depend tremendously on you, the shop steward. It's easy to see why. The steward is on the spot every day to see that the employer lives up to the contract. The international officers and representatives can't do this job. Neither can the staff (if your local has such) at the local union office. You are there and they have to depend on you.

Most workers judge the union by their steward. Too often they don't go to the union meetings; they have infrequent contact with the union officers. When they think of the union, they think of the steward and the kind of job he does.

When a steward is fair and helpful and settles their grievances promptly, the workers feel that the union is working for them. (But never present a grievance just to "get a mem-

ber off your back!" Make sure it has merit before accepting it, and if it doesn't, carefully explain to him why it doesn't.) If they are enthusiastic about union ideas and programs, the members will take greater interest and be more active! When the steward does a good job of enforcing the contract they respect his judgment on other union matters. Therefore, you can make the union alive and effective. The steward holds the key to a strong local union!

There are, then, two parts to a steward's job. Your foremost responsibility is to protect the workers' rights in the shop. This means settling grievances and watching for violations of the contract and labor laws. Secondly, it's up to you to strengthen the union and build support for its programs among the workers you represent.

These two jobs aren't really separate. When you settle grievances justly, you strengthen the union. And if you and the other union leaders don't have support from the workers to begin with, it will be hard to get fair grievance settlements from the foreman—or a better contract from top management. So let's now take a closer look at how you can take the lead in building a stronger, more effective union.

Did you ever think of yourself as a moulder of public opinion like the radio commentator and newspaper writer? Well, you certainly have the opportunity to be. The members expect you to have more information about the union than they do; and when you do, they respect your judgment. They will listen to your opinions on union affairs and departmental problems. They may not always agree, but much of what you say will sink in.

A steward can build support for the union because he can talk to the members every day—at lunch, during a smoke, and often on the job. The union counts on you to carry the word about union activities to the members and to encourage them to take part.

Of course you can't tell the members anything you don't know yourself. A steward should attend union meetings regularly. Make it a point to read your international publications, and many other trade union publications such as the AFL-CIO News, the American Federationist, and your local union paper, if one is published.

On departmental problems a steward has to have the backing of the workers he represents. When you are fighting a tough grievance, the wholehearted support of all the workers will often persuade the company to see it your way. If a worker is afraid to fight his grievance through, moral support from his fellow workers will give him courage. Let your members know what's going on in your department, shop or plant, and get them to stick together.

It's important to be a *democratic* leader rather than a dictator. You'll soon find yourself without any support if you try to tell the members what to do. Tell them what you think, and always explain why. You must have a mind of your own, but you've got to be ready to change it, too.

Every time a new person comes to work in the department you are seeing a potential union member. Maybe he'll be an enthusiastic member; maybe he'll be a griper. You can get him off to a good start if you show a friendly interest in him as soon as he comes in the department. Introduce yourself and offer to help with any problems he may have. Tell him about the union. He'll appreciate your welcome.

Unless your bargaining unit has a union shop contract, it's up to the steward to get a new worker to join the union. One of the most convincing approaches is to explain the benefits the Union has brought to the workers since your shop was organized—wages, vacations, pensions, job security and seniority protections, etc. When you've convinced him in a friendly manner how much better off he is because of the union—and will be by joining the union—SIGN HIM UP!

Where there's a union shop clause, the worker joins the union automatically after a certain number of days. Just joining doesn't make him an active, informed, loyal member though. If you want him to back up the union, it's just as important to sell him on the union too.

There has been so much propaganda against the union shop that some workers don't understand the reasons for trade unions' continuous fight for it. The union's thinking on this question is very simple. Everybody benefits from the union, because under the Taft-Hartley Act it is the bargaining agent for all workers in the unit—members and non-members alike—when a majority of the workers vote for the union. What could be more democratic? They all get the raises negotiated by the union; they all have the protection of the contract and the right to use the grievance procedure. Therefore, it's only fair for everyone to belong to the union and share in its work and expenses.

Of course, members should support the union by attending union meetings and finding out the union problems. The membership meeting is the place where the members have their say on union business. It's easier to sit home and watch TV, though, so it takes work on the steward's part to get members out to meetings.

You can remind them beforehand, and tell them what's coming up. If they don't come, tell them about the meeting the next day so they know they've missed something.

You will never get all the members to all the meetings, but a steward's job is easier when there is a group of active members who know the score and back him up.

It's especially important for a new member to see for himself that it pays to be a union member, and that the union is a democratic organization which he can be proud to belong to.

You can help your members—and strengthen the union—if you let them know what services and opportunities the union offers them outside the plant. Perhaps your local has a Credit Union. Or a Blood Bank. Maybe you sponsor picnics. Or Christmas parties for the kids. Whatever community services are available, make sure your members know about them.

Often workers need help on problems that come up outside the plant. A member may be having difficulty with a claim for unemployment compensation or hospitalization insurance. Perhaps a woman can't find a day nursery for her child. These out-of-plant problems are just as impor-

tant to the worker as a grievance. Often they look to the shop steward for help.

In your work as a steward you will hear a lot about COPE—the Committee on Political Education. This is the arm of the AFL-CIO which works to elect good candidates to office at all levels of government.

Political education is the union's answer to a lot of the worries that bother workers. Why can't I get a house at a decent price? Why is unemployment compensation so low? Why don't they build more schools and hospitals? Problems like these worry everyone who wants a happy, healthy life for himself and his family. The people we put in office on Election Day, in the city, the state, and in Washington, make vital decisions about the way we live.

A TRIBUTE TO SOME UNSUNG HEROES

*Anthony E. Matz, union president, in Firemen and Oilers Journal,
February 1958*

On the rails they're known as local chairmen and committeemen.

In the commercial power plants they're known as shop stewards.

In our book, and in the book of many other international union officers, these local chairmen and shop stewards play an absolutely vital role in the life of any union. If it is true that no chain is stronger than its weakest link, it is certain that no international union is stronger than its shop stewards and committeemen. They are operating on the real "grass roots" level of unionism, and it takes a man of various talents to be a successful shop steward.

This international union is fortunate to have more than its fair share of effective shop stewards and local chairmen.

Particularly on the rails, with the large number of layoffs that have occurred recently, it takes a real man to stand up under the pressures and strains of the local chairman's job. When a member receives a fur-

lough notice, his first contact generally is with the local chairman. When the local chairman already has seen numerous friends and acquaintances laid off, it takes a real standup guy to stay in there pitching to keep the morale and spirit of the local high.

A valued friend of ours, writing on this subject in his own union publication, asked "Why do union members seek or accept this job of few rewards and staggering obligations?" Answering his own question, our friend stated, "Many see steward's duties as an opportunity to serve the union cause that they know is right and just. Others find it a way to exercise their knack for leadership. Quite a few stewards are 'drafted' for their jobs by fellow union members who recognize unusual talents which can benefit the entire membership.

"Virtually all top officers in the labor movement began as shop stewards. This fact encourages many young men and women to accept steward service as the possible beginning of a career as a trade union leader."

All this is true. And it is also true that the steward or local chairman must provide strong leadership and, at the same time, make friends for himself and the union. He should have the diplomacy of an ambassador and the stern determination of a top sergeant. The first responsibility of the shop steward, of course, is the effective day-to-day handling of grievances that arise when members feel their rights have not been properly protected. The effective steward endeavors to see to it that complaints are settled amicably and fairly before reaching the stage of a formal grievance.

The shop steward's and shop committeeman's world is one of the finest training places we know of for a man to mature in. Tact, level-headedness, leadership and a pleasing personality are just a few of the qualities that are called for. In addition, the shop steward, or committeeman, has to be an informed individual. He must be informed on Railroad Retirement or Social Security, as the case may be, as well as on the union contract and job requirements. As he gains experience on the job, he finds that his usefulness often increases.

A GOOD UNION MAN

East Bay Labor Journal
(Oakland, Calif.), October 16, 1959

M. D. Cicinato, who died October 3 as the result of an accident on the job the day before, was the kind of a union man we like to hear about.

He had been a member of the Brotherhood of Carpenters for 51 years, and nearly all that time of Millmen's Local 550 here. He had been president of the local, and at the time of his death was recording secretary.

It is men like these, alert over the years to the interest of their union, holding various offices which are not full-time but which take much of the time others devote to amusement. working day by day at their craft to the very day of their death—indeed it is men like these who keep the union spirit alive, close to members' hearts.

We have come into a time of complexities and technicalities, forms to fill out, hearings to attend, law to understand, economics to grapple with, negotiations to wear out the participants, when it is essential that there be full-time paid officers who slowly become professionals, technicians able to meet the much higher paid full-time professionals of the corporations and firms and courts and agencies with which the modern union must deal. Some of these men attain high and deserved office in unions without ever having worked at the trade which is the basis of the union.

Inevitably even the most conscientious full-time paid officer gets a little away from the members: he is so busy serving them that he can't be as well acquainted with them as he'd like to be.

But the salt of the earth in a union, the holders of the line for the rank and file, the men who are there to be counted when the time comes, are men like Brother Cicinato, who carried his card for more than half a century, loved what that card stood for, and served his union on committees and part-time offices all the while that he was serving sticker and shaper or other machines in the mill.

If unionism ever dies it will be because all the men like Brother Cicinato have died, and nothing is left but an army of generals and a mass of indifferentists incapable of becoming first class privates, corporals, and sergeants. May that day never come!

2-a | The Runaways

HANDS ACROSS

Justice, July 15, 1960

The principle for which 1,200 garment workers struck at the four Virginia plants of the Kenrose Co. has been won. It is that a company which has grown and prospered on the labor of its devoted, productive employees cannot turn its back on them and open an overseas plant, with complete disregard for the impact of ensuing imports on the earnings of its workers.

From the start of the lengthy negotiations, the ILGWU conceded that the location of plants was management's prerogative. But this union insisted that workers also have prerogatives. Chief among these is their right to work through their unions — Kenrose was unionized by the ILGWU 17 years ago at the start of its growth—to increase the security of jobs and earnings by which they support their families.

A good deal of our union's history can be told in terms of what we have called the "out-of-town." This is the geographic periphery around the metropolitan centers where the garment industry was originally located. As bargain-hunting employers fled unionization and as union organizers caught up with them, "out-of-town" areas became increasingly distant, melting into each other.

In our own time, through organization and legislation, low-wage bait for runaway employers has been less enticing. A quarter of a century ago, federal legislation firmly established the idea of a floor below which not even free enterprise could depress wages.

Today, bargain hunters scroung-ing for cheap, desperate labor have pushed their horizons beyond "out-of-town" to greener profit fields out of the country. Indeed, recent trade press reports tell of the bitterness of Japanese export producers. As substandard as their wage rates are, they now have their own "out-of-town" problem with Hong Kong where wages are even more depressed.

There are as yet no parallels in international commerce for the wage and hour safeguards in interstate commerce. The terrible gap between our wage levels and those of some nations exporting to us creates a profit windfall that reflects neither management nor productivity superiority.

In our economy prices are set as high as possible, the only condition being that they must be just low enough to beat the competitors, if there are any. Profit windfalls from overseas production for domestic sales are of such dimensions that even when small portions of them are returned to the consumer in the form of competitively lower prices the huge bulk remains with the bargain-hunter.

With weak or no trade union organization, the overseas workers get little benefit in the form of higher living standards from their production for export. The U. S. producer, using that labor to produce for domestic sales, can therefore undermine domestic industries.

The Kenrose settlement is neither punitive nor protective; it is ethical. The firm has not been stopped from

76

producing in Ireland or importing into the U. S. Its Irish workers will sew and the company will reap the windfalls. But Kenrose must henceforth set aside a portion of that windfall to indemnify its Virginia workers should their earnings decline because of its Irish imports. If there is no decline, as stipulated, in the covered period, the company pays nothing, recoups the money.

As with so many other principles for which the ILGWU has fought, this one is concerned with responsibility; the union's responsibility for the job security of its members, and management's responsibility to the workers and the community that depend upon it for their welfare, and which provide the skills and energy without which neither garments nor profits can be made.

THE BLOOMFIELD STORY

Ozzie Bartelli in IUE AFL-CIO News, March 30, 1959

Bloomfield, N. J.—GE is closed and 700 workers are out in the street.

GE's determination to kill that plant and punish these loyal workers and members of Local 442 became an established fact on March 16, 1959, two weeks before the "scheduled" closing of the Bloomfield, N. J. plant.

The 700 workers were the last of a work force which numbered 2200 in 1954 when the company was solemnly pledging an employment increase ot 3000 as it implemented a $6,500,000 renovation modernization and expansion program.

But what the company called an expansion program turned out to be installment of automation equipment, and moving out of production causing the cut-back in jobs from that date until the last blow was dealt out with the wholesale slaughtering of jobs on March 16.

Reading a mimeographed memorandum to the hourly workers reporting to work at 8 o'clock Monday morning March 16, the company turned Bloomfield into "Gloomfield" as it falsely claimed that "a handful of Local 442 officials" protesting the plant-closing notice had made it "impossible to continue" factory operations.

Company officials were referring to a week-end "chain-down, sit-in" by 16 employees who chained themselves together and to fixtures on the third floor of the plant in protest against the scheduled closing of the air-conditioning plant by April 1. The workers were pleading for a "real right to work" and effected their "sit-in" after working hours Friday, March 13 through Saturday and Sunday, which were non-production days.

The chain of events leading to full disclosure of GE's penurious soul include:

1. Company cut-back in employment to 1200 by 1955 despite repeated promises of plans to increase the work force from 2200 to 3000 with completion of the $6,500,000 renovation program in 1954.

2. Transfer of home heating, cooling, furnace machinery and other units to Trenton, Bridgeport, Conn., and Tyler, Texas by 1957 with resultant loss of about 700 jobs despite further false promises that planned moving out of units would not cause a reduction of jobs in Bloomfield.

3. Cut-back to about 650 by late 1958 with the moving out of the Weatherton units, model shop work and laboratory work.

4. Reduction of jobs to approximately 400 within the 10 weeks of 1959 prior to final closing as the marketing, engineering, finance section, and water coolers work was dropped following announcement that even the industrial and commercial airconditioning was being ended.

Against all this the union had

been protesting, as the company loftily promised "increased employment" or desperately pleaded with the union to "trust us to do what's right for all concerned."

The workers and the union brought their protest of seasonal work and weekly layoff stubs and other GE tactics to the community. Religious, business and civic leaders of Bloomfield became interested in the workers' struggle. The union also won the help of New Jersey Congressmen and Senators

Union action to ward-off the company death-blow to the Bloomfield plant included:

• Grass roots meetings, with the latest held April 26, 1958 by District 4.

• Formation of a citizen's committee of Bloomfield clergymen and civic leaders, headed by Mayor Donald Scott, in July 1958.

• A bus cavalcade and demonstration by GE workers on Nov. 18 protesting GE policies and "Operation Turn-Out" in Bloomfield.

• A Dec. 20 protest march by the children of Bloomfield workers spotlighting the doom being imposed on the community by GE.

• A Dec. 30 citizens' committee conference with GE-Bloomfield officials. (The meeting authorized formation of a committee including the New Jersey Governor, two Senators, three Congressmen and religious, business and civic leaders, to study the Bloomfield problem.)

• A meeting with Defense Department officials on the possibility of channelling defense work to the plant.

• Exposure of GE's "cat and mouse" game through the uncovering of a company diary for 1959 listing all GE locations minus Bloomfield.

• A "chained sit-in" when it became obvious that GE had unconscionably been going through the motions of a defense contracts "survey" when it had no intention of accepting defense work if made available.

• Union solidarity in the form of help from Operating Engineers Local 825.

When the company enforced its cold-blooded retaliation against the workers with a premature shutdown of production at 8:20 A.M., four of the workers led by Local 442 Pres. Charles Ziegler, grimly decided to continue their courageous hold-out for "work" at Bloomfield-GE.

IUE Secretary-Treasurer Al Hartnett denounced the company with an excoriating accusation that the shutdown was "a brutal, transparent reprisal against workers who are fighting for the real right to work."

Management tried to minimize Hartnett's expose of GE's heartless methods by calling a make-shift press conference where company officials C. A. Salmonsen, plant manager, and H. W. Pierce, community relations manager, issued a post-fact, left-handed claim that the "demonstrations" and "harassment" rendered operations impossible.

They ignored the fact that the "sit-in" had originally been carried out only during non-working hours of the weekend and that their decision to terminate operations had been taken in GE's New York headquarters long before the start of Monday morning production, as evidenced by the reading of a mimeographed notice of plant shutdown.

News reporters, radio and television cameramen reporting the plight of the protesting workers fighting to save their jobs and against the economic homocide GE was imposing on the community which housed this company since 1892, continued to focus public attention directly on the facts GE wanted to keep from public view.

It was noted that "GE's exodus from Bloomfield, will rob the community of over $3,717,000 in personal income and inflict a loss of $2,268,-000 in retail sales."

Before being struck down by the dictatorial company whose decentralization time-table is steadily creating more and larger pockets of misery and economic despair throughout the country, Bloomfield workers succeeded in focusing the nation's attention on the "pocketbook citizenship" of the giant GE.

In fact, the union has been protesting the shrinkage of jobs through every device at its command. In 1957 oversized buttons declaring "We Want More Jobs Brought Into GE - Bloomfield" were distributed throughout the area.

The union capsized every GE "moonlight escape" scheme. At the Newark GE Grass Roots meeting, the fantastic profit-hungry GE assertion that it lost money on the Bloomfield operation was revealed as nothing more than crocodile tears.

Because the estimated profit harvest of $50,000,000 in 1957 fell short by $15,000,000 as the company reaped "only" $35,000,000 in profits in Bloomfield alone, GE officials were bemoaning the difference as a "loss."

The union's campaign to save jobs and shield the community from the subsequent economic shock swung into high gear when a citizens' committee of clergy, business and civic leaders was formed under direction of Bloomfield Mayor Donald Scott.

On June 30, 1958, the committee asked Ralph Cordiner, GE board chairman, for a conference since local management evaded repeated union requests.

Cordiner "passed the buck" by suggesting that the committee get in touch with Salmonsen.

In a hypocritical reply to a letter from Cong. Peter W. Rodino, (D., N. J.), Salmonsen maintained "there has been no management announcement to move our present manufacturing operations from Bloomfield, nor any decision to that effect." A copy of the letter went to Cong. Hugh Addonizio (D., N. J.).

Finally on Aug. 7, a bigwig from GE met with the committee.

"Trust us" the GE spokesman said as he pledged GE would "do its best" to locate a new department in Bloomfield. He denied that a final decision had been reached to abandon Bloomfield vowing the company would live up to its "moral responsibilities' and "do right by the employees and the community."

Singer of the GE siren song "Trust Us" was James H. Goss, GE vice president, accompanied by Salmonsen and Pierce.

Ziegler reminded Goss of GE press statements saying: "This we owe to our employees — good jobs and steady employment; to the community—good and reasonable corporate citizenship."

In November the workers sacrificed a day's pay and thronged right ups to the company's N. Y. doorstep in a mass demonstration against the heartless "job-slaughter" being committed by GE. The bus cavalcade was followed in December by a children's protest march in Bloomfield.

On Dec. 5 the ax fell. Pierce and Salmonsen announced GE was deserting the community after 67 years of exploiting it.

Meanwhile the union had unveiled GE's "cat and mouse" game when the 1959 GE diary came out, listing all GE locations except Bloomfield. The diary was printed Oct. 1. Considering the work involved in its preparation, it must have been prepared in August 1958 or earlier.

In short, GE was piously saying "no decision has been made" long after the fate of Bloomfield had been sealed.

But the union didn't waver in its determination to save the jobs. On Dec. 30, at another citizens' committee conference, Salmonsen and Pierce were questioned on GE's stampede to the low-wage hinterlands.

Stammering and evasive was Pierce. When this GE expert on poor relations piously solicited help in solving the Bloomfield situation, Hartnett deftly cornered him with an offer to "help" if in fact GE was honest in its "hope to attract someone from our own company or an outsider if it comes to that. We ask for help."

Pinned down by Hartnett, Pierce

had to admit that the only moving the company was interested in was out of—not into—Bloomfield.

The committee GE referred to included: Gov. Robert H. Meyner; Sen. Clifford Case and Harrison A. Williams; Cong. Pete Rodino, Hugh Addonizio, and Florence Dwyer; Mayor Leo P. Carlin, Newark; City Councilman James Callaghan, Newark; State Senator Donald Fox and Assemblyman Richard Lynch, Essex county; Rev. Eugene F. X. Sullivan, of East Orange Holy Name Church; Rev. Joseph A. Doyle, of St. Thomas the Apostle Church; Rev. C. Lincoln McGee, of Montclair Presbyterian Church and Moderator of the Newark Presbytery; Rabbi Sabokin, of Temple Menorah; Frank Terlazzi, businessman; and Charles Ziegler, Local 442 president.

Rev. McGee said the closing "reveals the inhuman aspect of giant organizations in their attempt to keep profits at the highest level. This dehumanization factor has caused great hardship in the lives of many families. Unwillingly workers become victims of depression unable to meet their basic needs.

"This condition destroys human personality, family home structure and prevents children from doing their best in school situations. We must stop this movement that is de-stroying democratic foundations. Machines were made for man, not man for machines."

On Feb. 6, 1959, a conference was arranged with the Defense Department at the Pentagon, Washington, D. C. At the last minute GE officials announced they would not attend unless the union withdrew.

The union withdrew since its principal interest was the good of the workers.

The meeting was held with Cecil Milne, assistant secretary of defense for supply and logistics, and N. J. Senators Case and Williams; N. J. Congressmen Rodino and Wallhauser. Congressman Addonizio was unable to attend but was listed.

The Defense Department agreed to conduct a "survey" for possible channeling of defense work, but GE managed to see that this never materialized.

GE did, however, close the plant and contrive to commit the "economic murder" of 700 productive employees ranging in age upward to 58. Losing their jobs are also some younger workers who may find other work at 38 years of age but their fate is the "loss" of some 20 years seniority with a company so obsessed with profits that it hasn't yet learned the difference between "goods" and "good."

'RUNAWAY' MANUFACTURER FORCED TO RETURN; REOPENS CLOTHING PLANT IN NEW YORK

The Advance, November 1960

A men's clothing manufacturer who staged a "runaway" from New York City to Mississippi has been forced to cease operations and resume production in New York under terms similar to those existing before he pulled out.

The precedent-setting case involves Jack Meilman, a manufacturer of men's suits and coats, and the N. Y. Joint Board of the Amalgamated Clothing Workers of America.

In May 1960, Meilman surreptitiously moved all of his equipment and unfinished garments from New York City to a non-union plant in Coffeeville, Miss., thus throwing out of work, without notice, some 300 employees, all members of the ACWA Joint Board.

The Joint Board, charging a violation of its union agreement with Meilman, immediately began arbitration proceedings before Prof. Herman A. Gray of New York University, temporary impartial arbiter for the men's clothing industry in New York.

Prof. Gray found that the "runaway" had in fact violated the agreement, which prohibits a manufacturer from moving his plant or production without union consent, and which prohibits any employer from becoming directly interested in any non-union enterprise. He directed Meilman to return his plant to New York and pay the union over $200,-000 for losses suffered by its members.

Meilman appealed the decision to the courts without success. New York State Supreme Court Justice Arthur G. Klein finally confirmed the arbitrator's award in August. Meilman finally gave up the fight, agreed to close his plant in Mississippi and re-open in New York.

Under terms of a new agreement all work in the Coffeeville plant will be transferred to New York, all machinery in the Coffeeville shop disposed of, and the lease of the southern plant was to be assigned.

The union released Meilman from payment of the $200,000 in damages if he complies with the other provisions of the arbitrator's award. He must, however, give two weeks' vacation pay to each employee in his New York plant at the time he closed it. This amounted to an estimated $35,000 to $40,000.

Louis Hollander and Vincent Lacapria, co-managers of the ACWA Joint Board, hailed the settlement as vindicating the union's contention that an employer has certain responsibilities to his employees, plus an obligation to abide by his union contract.

To bring the plant back, Hollander said the union employed every legal means, including litigation proceedings, an educational campaign among retailers, union pickets and informational materials passed out in front of retail stores handling his products.

REMINGTON RAND EXPORTING 1,500 JOBS

The Machinist, September 11, 1960

More than 1,500 IAM members at Elmira, N. Y., men and women who build the famous Remington typewriters, are scheduled to be laid off soon.

Remington Rand, a division of the giant Sperry Rand Corp., is transferring all work on portable and standard typewriters to plants overseas. Only the Remington electric typewriter will be built in the U. S. hereafter.

Although the company has not said precisely where the work will go, it is now manufacturing standard and portable models in plants in Scotland, England and Italy. In all, Remington Rand has more than 30 plants abroad.

Lester B. Elliott, shop chairman, and Nicholas Liberatore, president of IAM Lodge 826, reported the facts to The Machinist last week after a meeting with management. Here are more details from their report:

The company called in the nine-member IAM shop committee as well as Justin J. Donahue, business representative for IAM District 58, including Lodge 826.

The management informed the union members of the move and announced that portable manufacturing at Elmira is scheduled to halt by November. Production of the standard model will cease soon after the first of year.

Asked why the move was necessary, company officials said costs were too high and they couldn't meet foreign competition. A union committee pointed out that their competition was mainly from Remington Rand plants abroad. Layoffs have already begun. They will continue gradually until production of the standard and portable models is closed out.

Some employees will be transferred to work on the electric typewriter, but the number is not expected to be large. The union officers conmmented:

"The company vaguely discussed possible new work but it is evident there is nothing of any consquence on the horizon that will take care of the hundreds of people who will lose their jobs.

"By the time the full impact of the shutdown of both models occurs we estimate that in excess of 1,500 people will be laid off.

"It is difficult to determine the full impact of the free trade program because during the past several years the steadily increasing foreign imports have been gradually reducing domestic production.

"Taking a conservative view on the overall basis of the past ten years, we believe that between 2,500 and 3,500 jobs will have been lost when this shutdown is concluded.

"Even if the company were to provide new work to absorb all of these people, we believe it morally wrong for an American-based company to curtail or terminate its U. S. production in a move to a foreign country and then reimport its products for sale in this country."

LATEST RUNAWAY PARTY LINE: 'WE TREAT THE NATIVES WELL'

Seafarers Log, July 1, 1960

"Panama and Liberia Place Prime Importance On Safety At Sea."

If you don't believe it, the American Committee for Flags of Necessity, a public relations front for runaway ship operators, is ready to convince all comers that this and other equally dubious statements are the gospel.

The assertion regarding Panama and Liberia's non-existent "safety at sea" machinery is contained in a glossy, expensive booklet which the committee has sent to all newspaper editors. Featured in the booklet are the joys of living on and working for runaway ships operated principally by major American oil companies.

The literature readily admits that these are American-owned ships built by American companies, operating in American trade, but registered under the flags of Panama, Honduras and Liberia to avoid payment of American wages to the crews who operate the vessels.

Carefully evaded in the booklet are dollar-and-cent figures on run-

away wages as compared to the wages of seamen on American-flag, American-owned ships; the fact that runaway-flag ships pay no taxes on their earnings to Uncle Sam, or to Liberia and Panama for that matter; and the fact that the seamen involved, hired all over the world, are totally-lacking in representation, job security or enforcement machinery for whatever shipboard conditions exist.

The implication conveyed by the booklet is that of a benevolent, smiling shipowner dispensing the benefits of food, clothing and shelter to the "starving natives out of the bush."

"If you have any further questions," the covering blurb advises editors, "please don't hesitate to write or phone (long distance phone calls will be accepted collect)."

The stepped-up propaganda campaign of the runaways is seen as reflecting their increasing concern with the inroads of the International Maritime Workers Union among runaway crew members, as well as their increasing difficulties in hanging on to special tax privileges at home.

Also of concern to the runaways are cases pending in the courts and in the National Labor Relations Board on the rights of US unions to organize US-based ships. In general, the unions have been arguing that a ship based in the US is much the same as a shoreside business and should be subject to US labor law.

The runaways' brochure helps substantiate the union's claims when it boasts that their ships are subject to American Bureau of Shipping inspection. In the SS Florida case, the National Labor Relations Board held in effect, that ships which participate in US commerce and subject

themselves to US agency inspection cannot claim exemption from US labor law.

The basic concern of the runaways is that the seamen aboard these American ships should be kept isolated from union organization. The runaways will go to any extreme to keep their seamen from being contacted by US unions.

Obviously, if these seamen got the idea they were entitled to American wages, "morale" would take a steep nose-dive — particularly in cases where ships are manned by Asian seamen who "sign articles of agreement prescribed by their governments." Wage scales on Asian flag ships start at around $30 per month.

LABOR SEEKS TO REDUCE GAP IN FREE WORLD WAGES

UAW Solidarity, May 1959

An effort to work out a "feasible" method of raising wages of workers in foreign industries that now enjoy a competitive advantage—one based largely on lower wage scales—over American manufacturers, will be started in the coming months inside the International Metalworkers' Federation, according to UAW Pres. Walter P. Reuther, who also heads the automotive division of IMF.

Reuther, fresh from a tour of Europe, where he conferred with heads of state as well as the leadership of several free trade unions, told reporters on his arrival in Detroit the "free world must work together to promote freer trade" but not at the expense of European workers.

He suggested imposition of a "penalty" to be assessed by the U. S. government against those firms that refused to raise wages thus attempting to maintain a competitive advantage over American firms by "sweating their workers."

Currently, he said, workers in low wage countries are paying the price of the competitive edge their industries have over American producers.

"All workers," he said, "must be

able to share in the fruits of our advancing technology."

"We want to maximize the flow of goods among the nations of the free world," Reuther said, "but at the same time we must deal realistically with the problem faced by competing industries in foreign countries which have gained an advantage over American firms by paying lower wages to their workers . . ."

Reuther made it clear he was referring only to those industries whose "technology was as advanced" as that in the United States.

The basic goal of his plan, he said, was "to raise wages in other countries," thus forestalling a retreat to a protectionist philosophy.

"Unless we solve this problem," he said, "the free world will find itself veering toward "high tariffs and isolationism."

Reuther rejected the notion that wages must be equal as among the various European nations and the United States but said there should be established a "reasonable relationship" between wage levels.

3 | ORGANIZING

IN ONE WORD, ORGANIZE

Anthony E. Matz, union president,
in Firemen and Oilers Journal, January 1958

In the new year we might re-examine some of the basic principles of organized labor which can serve to guide us. Of paramount importance is unity for strength. Labor organized to gain collective strength to enable workers to meet their employers on an equal footing. Instead of taking what is doled out because of weakness we can now bargain for a rightful share on the basis of collective strength.

But our strength in any individual plant as a unit is not always the whole story. We are sometimes held back in various areas by lack of organization in non-union plants where workers receive sub-standard wages. If we raise the wages of these people we help our own cause as well as theirs. This gives us a basic principle and constant objective to guide us in the new year; organize the unorganized.

Years ago it often meant great personal sacrifice and even danger to organize and, in some cases, even to join a labor organization. Yet the leaders of that time worked toward what they knew was right for all working men, union organization.

But newer generations have swelled the ranks of labor, and many have known little but prosperous times. Many union members accept their membership passively and do little to advance the cause of the movement. Some even harbor the thought that they would have received the benefits they are now getting without their unions. These attitudes are a danger to the welfare of every working man for they tend to weaken his organization. If we all still subscribe to the old maxim of shorter hours and better pay and working conditions, we should try to do at least a little something to strengthen our unions and our own bargaining positions. That little something is organizing.

Every one of us comes in contact with many people in our daily lives. We are bound to meet some of the nation's millions of unorganized workers whose working conditions hold us all back. All we have to do is talk union and what the union has done to improve our wages and conditions through the years. Get the unorganized thinking union. It has helped you; get him to see where it can help him.

Call the attention of your local officers, local chairman, or shop steward to the unorganized plants in your area. Your representatives can then notify International Headquarters of the locations so investigation and determination of proper representation can be made.

Many international and national unions bear the word Brotherhood somewhere in their titles indicating the fraternal bond between its members. This fraternal bond was an important aspect of union activity that has been gradually falling into disuse in an atmosphere of impersonal concern toward the organizations. We must all remember that we are joined together for the mutual benefit of all, to help and assist our brothers wherever necessary.

With growth an increasing burden falls upon the shop steward and local chairman to maintain this fraternal bond. His is the daily contact with the membership and periodic contact with the Union's representatives. It is his good faith and hard work that provides the membership with the feeling of fraternity or brotherly love; especially when we have a problem. Your support and assistance, when needed by your shop steward and local officers, can be your contribution to the fraternal bond and success of your organization.

ILGWU POSTS REWARD IN 3rd ATTACK ON ORGANIZERS

AFL-CIO News, March 7, 1959

For the third time in as many weeks, staff investigators of the McClellan special Senate committee are probing a new case involving the beating of a union official.

The latest instance flared in Tenafly, N. J., where Sol Greene, assistant general manager of the Joint Dress Council of the Ladies' Garment Workers, was attacked by a gang of thugs who beat him with lead pipes and glass bottles on a darkened street near his home.

Greene has been leading a strike against 11 dress manufacturers in the Greater New York area who refused to accept an industry-wide settlement, including wage boosts and a union label campaign, won by the ILGWU in a week-long strike in February 1958.

The union immediately posted a $10,000 reward for apprehension and conviction of the hoodlums, charging that the attack was an attempt by the unorganized firms to "intimidate" the ILGWU and force it to give up the organizing drive.

McClellan committee investigators, meanwhile, were pressing their investigation into two other instances of anti-labor violence, both of them in North Carolina.

The committee assigned Investigator Harold Ranstad to Henderson, N. C., where Boyd E. Payton, vice president and regional director of the Textile Workers Union, was brutally beaten Feb. 24.

Since the attack on Payton, violence has broken out repeatedly in that community, where 1,200 TWUA members have been on strike for 15 weeks at Harriet-Henderson Cotton Mills.

The situation was made increasingly tense by the company's plans to reopen the mill with strikebreakers. Gov. Luther Hodges—himself a textile magnate—dispatched a detachment of the North Carolina Highway Patrol to Henderson to "preserve order" as the first scabs reported for work.

Originally 44 highway patrolmen were assigned to the community but as strife raged between pickets and strikebreakers, the number of club-wielding patrolmen increased to 135.

After he completes his investigation in Henderson, Ranstad is scheduled to visit Franklin, N. C., scene of an attack Feb. 11 on Hosiery Workers' Organizer Robert D. Beame who was conducting an organizing drive at the Franklin Hosiery Co., a subsidiary of Burlington Mills.

Beame, who has already told his story to the McClellan committee staff and to the Federal Bureau of Investigation, indicated mill supervisors may have recruited the mob which assaulted him, stole his signed authorization cards and forced him out of town and over the state line.

In New York, ILGWU Pres. David Dubinsky called on retailers to refuse to buy dresses from what he said were the "racketeer" firms Greene was trying to organize at the time he was attacked.

"Those dresses," said Dubinsky, "are stained not only with the sweat of exploited workers but with the blood of union organizers."

The ILGWU published advertisements in the New York Times, the Women's Wear Daily, a prominent industry publication, asking retailers to respect the union label as "a symbol of decency, fair employment standards, stabilized and dignified management-labor relations and the American way of life."

SCENE: FARM LABOR OFFICE
TIME: DARK OF MORNING

Kay Black in The Valley Union (Calif.), June 19, 1959

At 3:30 A.M. the streets of Stockton are peaceful and serene. They look made for poets walking and cats seeking companionship and lovers taking it lazy on the way home.

But stroll a few blocks west from the center of town, to the vicinity of the Farm Labor Office, and there you will find a regiment of early risers—the anxious, job-hungry Waiting Men who cheat sleep rather than miss one chance at the day's offerings when the squeaking buses of the labor contractors begin arriving.

The crowd under the mustard street lights, fogged with old peat dust, is not belligerent, not fretful or antagonistic. It has a quality of resignation, and also a quality of hope and anticipation and even liveliness in the knots of young men who laugh and spin on their heels and joke in the cold dark.

With Delmer Berg and Norman Smith of the Agricultural Workers Organizing Committee I went among them in old jeans, unnoticed. Presently we came on Raul, talking earnestly in Spanish to an elderly gentleman who listened without expression, then broke into eager response, much gesticulation and head-nodding. As Raul spotted us and moved on, the elderly man called in Spanish to three or four of the men leaning against the building and began his explanation.

We were there to meet the reporter and the photographer from the San Francisco paper who wanted to do a story on the first steps to a decent life for these forgotten people of one of the most prosperous areas of prosperous America.

Before they came the contractors' buses had begun to slide up. They parked along the side streets, or sometimes double-parked. The contractors opened the doors, got out and began to call their offerings:

"Need forty today! Forty to work in the beets. Eighty-five cents an hour." "Can use 60 cherry pickers. Loaded trees. Dollar a bucket." "Boysenberry pickers wanted at this bus. Very easy work." "Cherries! Cherries! Get you a partner and pick cherries for $1.25 a bucket!"

Some buses filled up fast. Some gathered in a few and the contractor made an extra effort by walking through the crowd and calling his wares. One seized me by the arm and looked sharply in my face. "Where you from?" "Stanislaus." "Oh, well, ever done any hoeing?" "Yep." "Better come down with me today. Nothing to it. No weeds at all in that field—just carry the hoe 'n down the rows and collect 85 cents an hour."

Delmer gave an experienced snicker when I told him about this. "You notice he hasn't got many," he said, "The word gets around—bet it's a killer of a job."

By five o'clock the sky was graying and the seedy street was showing its neglected face. The Delta breeze came up sharp and chill and the lightly - dressed ones huddled against the buildings while a very few dashed in and out of a tiny cafe with paper cups of hot coffee splashing in their haste.

The Labor Office was open by this time. Now and again, a brassy loudspeaker repeated a request we had already from some prowling contractor: "Cherries for $1.25 a bucket. Need 50 cherry-pickers at this good rate."

"Uh, huh," said Delmer, "Trees probably big, scrawny, with few cherries and you got to move the ladder all day long."

There were women in the crowd now, I noticed, and a silent, serious cripple or two. An old man, with purple, quivering lips said earnestly to a much younger one leaning on a bus: "I'm a good cherry picker. Just get me the right partner for the ladder. I go fast on the low ones, and I can carry. You got a partner today?"

Delmer was busy "organizing." I sidled up and listened. ". . . no other way I can see for things to get any better," he was saying. "Been following the crops all my life. Where did we get? Just the right to have the minimum wage turned down, no insurance, and no decent treatment." The two fellows in old Army pants and tattered jackets to whom he spoke both nodded.

"We're floaters," said one. "How're you gonna manage for us?"

"You could have a traveling card. Turn it in at a local office when you hit a town. Pick it up when you left."

"I'll buy that," said the other one. "How much and where do we get it?"

Delmer told them. We moved on to another knot of sober looking workers. Delmer began the story. The ones who were doubtful or not interested moved away; one or two ran out as some job was called that sounded good. Always a few stayed and listened and asked how to get to 805 East Weber, union headquarters.

The spirit came over me, too, and when Delmer climbed on the bumper of a loaded truck, board seats down, its slides and boxes in middle full, I climbed up, too. We picked a couple of intelligent looking dark young fellows and began the story.

Then the driver tooted. The bus began to move. A young guy leaned out as we jumped off. "Where did you say to go?" he called. "I'll get me some friends today and we'll get in to that place. That Union is for us, for sure!"

Norman Smith came over to us and said, "I think it's about time for breakfast." The young reporter and photographer were behind him.

Delmer and I looked at each other, and around. The crowd had thinned down to a mere trickle even though there were some buses still not full. Those left looked at us, not unkindly, and in the gray light some even smiled a little. It was a great crowd, a really courageous regiment, and I felt both humble and excited. There is something in such a human-to-human operation that cuts all the non-essentials down to size.

∽

"Long ago we stated the reason for labor organizations. We said that they were organized out of the necessities of the situation; that a single employee was helpless in dealing with an employer; that he was dependent ordinarily on his daily wage for the maintenance of himself and his family; that if the employer refused to pay him the wages he thought fair, he was nevertheless unable to leave the employ and resist arbitrary and unfair treatment; that union was essential to give laborers the opportunity to deal on an equality with their employer . . ."

—*U. S. Supreme Court, in declaring the Wagner Act constitutional.*

FARM UNIONISTS ASK ACTION NOW

The Valley Union (Calif.), March 20, 1959

Once upon a time there was a Native Son of the Golden West, aged 8, who helped his family keep the wolf from the door by milking cows at dawn and drudging at such farm work as his size permitted.

When he grew up he did not become President—he became a hired hand—but he went to Washington just the same.

Delmer Berg, who helps promote the National Agricultural Workers Union, AFL-CIO, in the Stanislaus, Calif. area, promised the Valley Union an interview about his trip to testify at the hearings of the National Advisory Committee on Farm Labor last month. Berg was one of three farm workers who described the substandard wage and working conditions in American "farm factories."

But when we went to interview Delmer, he modestly had called in other expert witnesses—a dozen men and women who work in valley fields and Ernesto Galarza, their champion, field general and hero.

Galarza for 10 years has been a dedicated man—combining belief in ultimate justice with intense unflagging vitality against big - grower propaganda, public apathy and the hunger-driven fright of workers who dare not lose one single day's wage even at peon pay.

Now, as secretary-treasurer of the NAWU, he speaks with renewed confidence and zest; for the importation of Mexican nationals has aroused native field hands by the thousand to the cause of union organization.

As they have become more desperate, and vocal, they have found friends to help carry their cause to the public; top leaders in the AFL-CIO, the Farm Advisory Committee, the National Catholic Welfare Conference, and especially, says Galarza, "the wonderful labor press."

Two questions we put to the group in the neat living room of the small South Modesto house. Will farm workers join and support a union? What should organized labor, right in our area, do to help?

The immediate, desperate, need they unanimously agreed, is to persuade Governor Brown to replace the head of the California State Farm Placement Service, so that Public Law 78 will be fairly enforced. Galarza stated that plenty of evidence has been collected to show that this man has ignored the law in favor of the corporation farms. P. L. 78 provides that qualified domestic workers in search of farm jobs have priority over imported Mexican, or other, nationals.

Next move is to notify your State Senators and Assemblymen that you want a minimum wage bill which covers farm workers, without exception. As the bill is set for hearings before the Burton committee on March 19, fast action is needed to indicate popular support. Sending of local delegates to the hearings is very effective.

Galarza said, "Don't be talked down by the old malarkey that farm workers must be exempt because women and children can't earn a man's wage. Women and children would not be in the fields if the family bread-winner received enough for his labors to keep them at home and in school. Sixty years ago, 11-year-olds worked in factories. They got out when union organization fattened Pop's paycheck."

Small business men and small farmers are becoming sympathetic to the plight of the exploited domestic farm worker, those present said. Many neighborhood businesses face failure because of the drop in purchasing power of the farm-hand income. Small farmers, who cannot contract for Mexican nationals, are seeing that they cannot compete in the market with mammoth, low-cost, corporate field operations. They can be won as allies by patient explanation.

Other regulations are needed, such as representation of the Agricultural Workers Union on the board of the Farm Placement Service, a strict rule of seniority listing when jobs are filled, and provision of insurance and compensation for farm workers.

Will these people support a union? Yes, said their representatives, if the union is explained carefully to them and they understand that the union will not move until it is strong enough to be effective. The success of the Imperial Valley Packinghouse Workers strike is spreading like wildfire and speeding up the numbers of agricultural workers asking about union membership.

AFL-CIO Sec.-Treas. William F. Schnitzler, at the Washington hearings, called the treatment of farm workers "the most shocking story of our times; "and pledged that the labor movement will throw its weight behind ending this human exploitation.

ORGANIZATION OF 'WHITE COLLARS' CALLS FOR NEW APPROACHES

James W. Goodsell in AFL-CIO News, December 27, 1958

How do we organize white collar workers? This is no idle question. It may prove to be a life-or-death question for the American labor movement.

If we don't, unions will represent a dwindling minority of American workers, and the influence of unions for economic and social progress will gradually fade away.

This is much more easily said than done. The fact is, we don't know how to organize white collar workers. Many an old-time organizer has tried it, with all the skill and dedication at his command, only to come away defeated and shaking his head in genuine puzzlement.

There are many reasons why white collar organizing is different. Some of them are:

1. Most white collar workers are women. Many of them work only to supplement their husband's incomes. Many believe that their work is temporary—until they marry . . . until their husband gets a raise . . . until the house is paid for.

2. Most white collar workers are snobs. The word "labor" offends their self-esteem. They identify themselves with the customer and the employer —not with their fellow worker. They are glad to accept a title, a pat on the head or a Christmas bonus in lieu of decent wages and working conditions.

3. Most white collar workers are not highly skilled. This gives them a feeling of job insecurity. They feel (sometimes correctly) that they would be fired and blacklisted for engaging in union activity.

4. Most white collar workers have no idea what a union is, what a union can do for them. They don't even know that such "glamorous" white collar workers as newspaper reporters, airline pilots, movie and TV actors have strong and effective unions.

5. Employers of white collar workers are smart. They are fully aware of all these peculiarities of their employees, and they play upon them as Heifetz plays a violin. But most unions have not yet tumbled to the fact that white collar workers are a different breed of cats.

So what conclusions can we draw? For the purposes of this editorial, just four:

FIRST, that the 20th Century will leave the labor movement behind unless we learn to organize the white collar worker. We must do it even if we feel that the white collar worker (in his blind ignorance of his own self-interest) doesn't deserve the benefits of unionism.

SECOND, that the old organizing techniques won't work. This is a job for psychologists, for innovators, for daring pioneers.

THIRD, that the white collar worker will demand a new type of union—a union tailored to meet his dual need for security and self-esteem.

FOURTH, that the effort will fail unless it has the all-out understanding and support of the older, stronger unions.

EMPLOYERS TURN TO 'SNOB APPEAL' TO BLOCK WHITE COLLAR DRIVE

John W. Livingston, AFL-CIO director of organization, in AFL-CIO News, August 10, 1957

It is my conviction that the next great advance in organization will be among white collar workers.

In the first place, it is among white collar workers that the greatest need and potential exist. These workers have lost whatever advantage they once held, economically. They lack any effective protection against arbitrary management decisions affecting their security and well-being.

Even the prestige they once felt was theirs by reason of occupational proximity to management is fast dwindling. As a business magazine put it, "the white collar is no longer the badge of respectability."

Second, organized labor knows that not only the needs of these workers but labor's own self-interest demands that white collar workers be brought within the fold of the trade union family. Any bloc of unorganized workers constitutes a threat to the established labor movement.

Third, changing techniques in industry are creating a new white-collar, blue-collar balance. For the first time white collar workers in America numerically exceed other workers—and statistical predictions indicate an increasing change in the ratio, to the numerical advantage of the white collar force.

Fourth, white collar workers themselves are becoming more aware of the necessity for, and desirability of, organization.

Finally, our movement is equipped to assist white collar workers in their organizing endeavors as at no previous time.

Management and those agencies which serve management interests are not unaware of these facts. National business associations have called special conferences at which unionization of white collar workers has been discussed.

Management recognizes that white collar workers are more responsive to unionization today than at any previous time. It will intensify efforts to stave off the union drive.

Professionals have been hired by companies to conduct studies of their white collar workers to determine what conditions exist, and what attudes prevail which, if unchanged, will induce those workers to become union members.

These alleged experts have now reached some tentative conclusions. They advise attention to the prestige factor — "play up the professional angle" the experts advise—in a frank, cynical snob-appeal campaign.

At best, the snob campaign will prove a mere delaying tactic here and there. White collar workers are no less capable of analyzing their situation than their supervisors.

BOSSES GIVEN SCHEMES TO KILL 'WHITE COLLAR' ORGANIZING DRIVE

Labor, December 27, 1958

Some of the traps in the Taft-Hartley Act that enable many employers to block union organization are high-lighted in a pair of unusual business documents received by LABOR. The documents were put out by Prentice-Hall, Inc., which publishes a confidential weekly "Labor Report" that's widely sold to employers throughout the nation.

The new Prentice-Hall documents are a letter and sales-pitch sent out by the firm to employers of white-collar workers. These documents seek to scare the employers by declaring:

"The biggest unionizing drive in labor history is heading for your white collar workers. For your successful counter-attack we offer 'How to Meet the Critical Problem of White Collar Organizing'."

The latter is a booklet offered to employers who subscribe to Prentice-Hall's weekly "Labor Report." The sales-pitch goes on to say that Prentice-Hall's staff of editors and lawyers is "now ready to send you the vital information you need."

For example, under the heading "Banning Union Literature," the sales-pitch has this to say: "Generally speaking, you cannot ban distribution of union literature by non-employees. But do you know of a court-approved setup that will permit you to enforce a company rule against ALL types of distribution "

Under the heading "Predicting 'Bad Times' Under Union Rule," Prentice-Hall tells the employers: "If you believe unionization will have a deteriorating effect on working conditions and pay rates, you are free to tell your employees so. But be almighty careful you don't threaten to use your economic power to make your predictions come true. There are safe, legal ways to put the idea across and make it burn in."

Under the heading "Captive Audi-ence," comes this significant lure to employers: "Do you know the rule that permits you to assemble employees during working hours to discuss unions with them while denying the same privilege to the unions?"

With the aid of these and other similar dodges provided by Taft-Hartley, Prentice-Hall indicates, the organizing challenge of unions among white collar workers "can be met, definitely and triumphantly."

However, the document also makes this significant statement: "Employers cannot shut their eyes to the fact that the success of organized labor in obtaining substantial wage and security benefits for factory workers is a strong propaganda weapon in the hands of the unions."

130.   ©1951 CARL STAMWITZ

"I'm really a non-union white collar worker by trade—I'm just doing this to earn a living!"

WHY TEACHERS ORGANIZE

Charles Cogen, president, (New York) United Federation of Teachers,
AFL-CIO in RWDSU Record, May 8, 1960

First let me state why most teachers are still, unfortunately, not organized within the labor movement. They consider themselves professionals, for whom unionization is not in good taste.

To many of us, on the other hand, union organization is a must. We are not only professionals—more important, we are workers. As such we have the same basic strivings as other workers throughout the land.

Salaries are only part of the picture and, as many studies have shown, they are not necessarily the major cause of dissatisfaction. Working conditions are perhaps even more important. To the average layman it may seem strange to talk about "working conditions" in a school, with its academic atmosphere.

Take the matter of class size. Crowd 40 or more varied adolescents into a class which should have only 20 to 30 students. In many instances put in more students than there are seats. The sum total is a bad learning situation for the children, and, for the teacher, a disciplinary as well as a difficult teaching problem.

Things would be bad enough if the teacher only had to teach under these unfavorable conditions. But a job analysis shows him to serve also as clerk, health officer, guidance counsellor, banker, charity solicitor, patrolman, and a number of other sidelines of equal irrelevancy to his supposed job of teaching.

During the official period and other parts of the day, the teacher runs a ten-ring circus—checking attendance, filling out various records, selling tickets for school affairs, collecting savings for thrift accounts, soliciting funds for sundry charities, checking Johnny's physical condition, etc., etc., while trying to maintain a calm and orderly atmosphere throughout. Is there any doubt that teachers need to organize in order to bring teaching back into the classroom?

Related to this non-teaching burden is the problem of after-school or extra-curricular activities. I am not referring to the regular school work that the teacher takes home with him — lesson planning, marking of homework and of examinations, report cards, and the like.

I mean such things as conducting after-school clubs and teams, chaperoning evening dances, collecting money and tickets and acting as ushers at school concerts and athletic events, and taking children on trips. These are all worthwhile educational activities. But why should the teacher be required to give of his own time without overtime pay?

Talk about impinging on the teacher's time! You would hardly believe this, but many teachers do not even have a work-free lunch period! These are some of the conditions that the organized teachers are seeking to end.

More important even than salaries and working conditions is the authoritarian atmosphere that pervades most school systems. Teacher A gets a heavy class load while teacher B has it easy because he "plays ball" with the principal. Time schedules are changed with or without reason. "Free" time is taken away when a teacher is required to cover another teacher's class. Sick leave pay may be arbitrarily denied.

Only in school systems where strong teacher organizations have a functioning grievance machinery is there any assurance that teachers will be treated like free human beings.

A union man is an independent man. He has his rights on his job, as well as his duties, and he can insist on them. For the teacher, as for any other worker, unionization provides status and dignity. For this we organize.

ENGINEERS ARE WORKING PEOPLE

Russell M. Stephens, president,
American Federation of Technical Engineers, in Engineers Outlook, April 1957

The engineer of today is a part of the work force, the same as the machinist, the sheet metal worker or other highly skilled craftsmen. In most instances he punches a time clock on arrival at his office and upon departing for the day. Why then should the engineer not receive compensation for extra hours worked as do his fellow employees working in the skilled trades?

In America today over 90 per cent of technically trained persons are employed on a salary basis, regardless of the skill, knowledge and experience they may possess.

This condition is the result of the transition of industry from single ownership to the corporate type of collective ownership. It has created the employee-engineer.

No longer do the vast majority of engineers work as independent contractors for one person or a small group of people. The engineer is but one of a large group employed by a large company.

Engineers, architects, chemists, bacteriologists and all technicians are, in fact, subject to the same economic conditions as any other employees, regardless of the degrees of skill they may have.

A young engineer cannot look forward to spending four or five years in a company's employment and then entering the practice. His employment focuses his attention now on the specialty his employer wants him to pursue. His employment becomes the means of earning his livelihood for the rest of his life.

To his corporate employer the engineer becomes a number who clocks in at starting time and who clocks out at quitting time. The corporation has no feelings nor can it know the engineer and his problems.

Under a collective bargaining agreement negotiated by the American Federation of Technical Engineers, minimum standards are assured, patent rights are protected, classification descriptions are developed by both sides and the standard work day and work week are firmly established, with premium pay provisions for work beyond the standard hours.

Rewards for individual merit and efficiency are established, discrimination is eliminated, the rights of free expression and assembly are guaranteed, bilateral discussions on health, safety and sanitation are inaugurated, vacation leave, personal leave and sick leave are guaranteed by contract, and many other conditions of employment are spelled out in detail, to the advantage of both the employee and management.

The AFTE does not resort to strike action until every possible peaceful means has been exhausted for the settling of disputes, including federal and state mediation. Neither do we strike until after a secret ballot has been taken, and then only after the international president has been furnished with all the facts involved and, after a very close study, has issued strike sanction to the local. Our organization's strike record over the years is testimony to our successful settlement of disputes by peaceful methods.

In the salary area our practice is to establish a minimum rate for each classification, with regular and definite adjustments provided for ability to perform the job of a given classification with greater efficiency and productivity as a result of experience.

Regular periodic merit reviews are given to each employee in the bargaining unit for the purpose of determining and rewarding the so-called "rare bird" for his exceptional talents. While many employers insist on establishing a maximum salary for each classification, the AFTE does not believe in setting pay maximums.

20-MONTH BATTLE GOING STRONG AGAINST MIAMI'S LUXURY HOTELS

Willard Shelton in AFL-CIO News, Dec. 15, 1956

Twenty months after the Hotel Workers' Local 255 struck the luxury hotels of Miami Beach, nearly 5,000 union members are still seeking a basic contract with more than 100 of the multi-million-dollar hostelries.

It is a strange "strike." The local has been enjoined, by Dade County judges, from maintaining picket lines. It has been enjoined from publicizing a list of 'unfair" hotels that have pointblank refused to bargain.

The local is caught in a no-man's-land of legal non-jurisdiction in all efforts to prove its majority and its right to bargain for the workers.

The National Labor Relations Board refused to order a representation election, holding that it had no jurisdiction. And Florida state law is grossly insufficient; it establishes no machinery through which a union may prove its majority.

Strike "headquarters," where strikers were fed three meals a day for months and where picket and social activities were coordinated, now serves principally as the place from which job assignments are channeled.

"For a long time we were the best-looking, healthiest strikers in the world," says one waitress who walked off her job at a hotel on April 13, 1955. "We were sun-tanned from the picket lines and the best-fed workers in the country. Chefs described by the hotels as the best in the world prepared our meals and we had a capacity crowd every night."

The Dade County injunctions against the union have been sweeping and drastic. One judge ruled that the existence of a picket line implied "psychological violence." Another held that the union could not picket because it had not given sufficient notice and "time" before striking.

The local has sent many of the strikers back to work even at hotels on the "unfair" list of the parent international. Partly this was to enable them to vote in an NLRB representation election in case one should be ordered; partly it is because the drastic injunctions robbed the local of its power to exert picket-line pressure.

The contrast between the wealth and power of the hotels and the penurious wages paid their workers is startling. During the "season"— the lush December-through-April period—the poorest bedrooms begin at $35 a day. Accommodations are more likely to run to $45 or $50 or more a day.

The hotels pay their chambermaids $5 a day, their housemen $6 or $7, their waitresses $2.50, their bellmen from $25 to $50 a month. Waitresses and bellmen are supposed to "make it up" in tips—but the tips can be scanty during the long months outside the "season" even for the skeleton crews who keep their jobs.

The international has poured more than $2 million into supporting the fight for recognition by Local 255. And despite all handicaps, the local has continued to grow in membership and to maintain a high morale.

A total of 13 hotels and one big motel have signed contracts with the local. Intl. Pres. Ed. S. Miller and General Counsel J. W. Brown have engaged in lengthy negotiations for a master contract with scores of hotels in the Miami Beach Hotel Association.

The hotels that have signed contracts apply to the local for qualified personnel. Union members, even in the "unfair" hotels, notify the local when jobs are available.

The Florida Federation of Labor will hold its 1957 convention in Miami Beach, where its delegates "can sleep in union beds and eat in union restaurants."

Advertisements published in New York and other northern newspapers warned the public that the "beach" workers were grossly underpaid and were fighting for recognition of their union.

"One of our problems," says a spokesman for the local, "is that many hotels here are not run by hotel men who recognize the value of stable labor relations and a stable staff of workers.

"Another is that so many retired people come here and women can take jobs as housemaids without any special training: they have made beds, after all, all their lives."

As the new "season" opens, Local 255 remains confident that its fight for recognition and decent wages and working conditions will end in victory.

The local, despite court prohibitions on legitimate strike activities, has proved its capacity to live and grow.

"When we struck the Saxony Hotel, a few of the housemaids had their first 'day off' in months," a union member said. "They had worked seven days a week, Saturdays and Sundays included, with no overtime benefits. They spent the 'day off' on the picket line."

"What we want is job security, a day off once in a while, to be treated as human beings.

"We were ladies and gentlemen on the picket lines. We turned the other cheek under provocations and we went into court with clean hands. It didn't do us any good; we are still enjoined.

"But we are going to win."

(The hotel strike in Miami ended in victory with a 10-year master agreement which provided for union recognition—the major objective of the 21-month walkout. Also established were bargaining committees to negotiate on wages, working conditions and benefits never before enjoyed by the Miami Beach hotel workers. In addition, arbitration committees were set up to settle disputes which might arise.)

SIXGUN BOSS LAW ON THE MISSISSIPPI — ANOTHER STRANGE CASE OF NLRB JUSTICE

NMU Pilot, February 27, 1958

You're a union organizer. You get a letter from the crew of a river boat asking you to sign them up so they can improve their wages and working conditions. You mail pledge cards. Eight of the nine-man crew sign the pledge cards and return them along with a request that you come aboard to hold a meeting.

You meet with the crew and are hashing out their problems in the galley over a cup of coffee when the boat captain, who also happens to be the owner, comes charging in like a wildman and orders you off the boat. He slugs a crew member with a flash light and challenges all and sundry to a knife fight. Dissuaded from the use of cold steel, he threatens to shoot up the "whole shebang" with a shotgun.

You try to quiet him down and get him to listen to reason, only to have him chase you with a meat cleaver. The crew piles off the boat even though the captain offers some of them a raise in pay to stay on.

A picket line is thrown around the boat. The captain returns next day with a gang of relatives armed to the teeth with shotguns and revolvers.

Soon after a shooting spree ensues. The unarmed pickets run for their lives. A revolver slug catches you in the arm and puts you in the hospital.

At this point the law enforcement agencies, including the National Labor Relations Board, step in. The wheels of justice turn and the NLRB comes up with one of the most cock-eyed rulings in labor history; to wit, that you, the unarmed union organizer who was shot down by the captain, are "guilty of violence."

In addition, the NLRB hands down an equally astounding injunction to restrain the union from what the government agency describes as "coercing" the men on the boat to join the union. All this in face of the acknowledged fact that the men had invited the union to come in and had voluntarily joined in picketing the boat.

The case of the Banta Towing Company vs. the Rivers Joint Organizing Committee marks a shameful milestone in the anti-labor road travelled by the NLRB under the Eisenhower Administration. It exposed for all to see the extent to which Eisenhower appointees to the NLRB are committed to the destruction of decent and normal union practices guaranteed by law and how they give employers a blank check to disrupt union organizing among the workers.

The Taft-Hartley Law forbids an employer to: "Interfere with, restrain, or coerce employees in the exercise of the right to organize and bargain collectively. . . ."

On the other hand, Taft-Hartley similarly forbids a labor union to: "Restrain or coerce employees in the exercise of their right to organize and bargain collectively or to refrain from any and all such activities. . . ."

In the Banta case the NLRB was faced with the question of deciding whether the union had forced the men on the river boat into union activity against their will, or whether the boat owner had interfered with the men's right to organize.

Flying in the face of all the evidence—the signed pledge cards and the crew's willingness to join in picketing their employer's boat—the NLRB ruled that the union organizers had "restrained and coerced" the boat crew and were thus in violation of the Taft-Hartley Act. In making this decision the Board overruled the findings of its field examiner,

Thomas S. Wilson, who reported that the union organizers were not to blame for unfair labor practices.

The trial examiner, moreover, strongly recommended to the Board that the charges be dismissed. In a rare move, he strongly criticized the St. Louis Regional Director for his failure to issue a complaint against the company. Incredibly, the NLRB, ignoring the fact that the trial examiner was the one person who actually heard the witnesses testifying, reversed him and found against the Union.

The highlights of that trial examiner's report, revealed that:

• Despite the fact that the employer had violated the Federal Anti-strike-breaking Act by bringing in a new crew from another State, no NLRB charge was ever made against him.

• While the complaint was ostensibly issued to protect the rights of the employees, not one single employee was called to give testimony.

Last month, NMU attorneys filed for a reversal of the NLRB decision in the Seventh U.S. Court of Appeal.

The union's appeal move is just one of a tremendous number of law suits forced upon the unions by the NLRB's refusal to enforce the nation's labor laws as written by Congress.

During the court term in 1957, the Supreme Court had a heavier load of labor cases than in any past term since the enactment of the Taft-Hartley Act. More than a hundred labor decisions were presented to the court for review last year. A significant number of the NLRB's decisions have been reversed by the courts after long and expensive legal battles by labor.

Meanwhile, however, four long years have passed and the river men on the Banta boats continue to work under sub-standard wages and working conditions without union protection.

(Note: The NLRB decision was ultimately reversed by a Federal court.)

LADIES' AUXILIARIES HELPED BUILD UAW

United Automobile Worker, September 1956

The plant manager stopped in his tracks when he heard the pickets singing—soprano and alto.

With a puzzled look, he walked around the corner with his hired bully boys at his heels to crash the line. They had brass knucks and clubs—and a lot of beef.

They found the line was manned—by women.

That incident was repeated at plant after plant in the early days as quickly-formed UAW Auxiliaries helped their men with their struggle for justice.

In the crucial strikes, the chips-down organizing drives, in nearly every historic struggle, the gals were there. They kept soup kitchens going around the clock, tended each others' kids so families wouldn't be neglected, passed out literature, formed protest committees and even took a hand at keeping the picket lines intact.

The history of the UAW Auxiliaries is as old and as colorful as the history of the Union itself. And, like the Union, the Auxiliaries' activities have made great changes with the times.

Back in 1936 and 1937, when the Union was struggling for existence, hundreds of heroic women organized Auxiliaries. Their "Emergency Brigades" were famous in their time. They were as respected as the "Flying Squadrons."

Managements, expecting to out-maneuver "disorganized ragtag and bobtail groups," found the women's ranks jelling with amazing speed. Where yesterday a bunch of fearful, disorganized workers were in the plants, a tightly-knit determined Union was in its place. The women dumbfounded them.

Their "Emergency Brigades" were set up with military precision. Each Brigade had a "general" and five

"captains." Each captain had 10 "lieutenants." That made it possible to call together thousands of Union women at a moment's notice.

Their uniform consisted of colored berets and arm bands with "EB" on them. Each group had its own color. Flint was red; Lansing, white; Detroit, green; Ohio, blue.

When the call came to their colors, they mobilized fast. Old-timers will never forget the parade of 7,000 women and children, strikers' families, during the historic Flint sit-downs. It helped crack the might of General Motors.

Call the rolls of the historic struggles — Kelsey-Hayes, Chrysler, Hudson, American Brass, Ford and all the rest—and you name the places where the Auxiliaries helped carry the day.

Managements, hoping to exploit woman's natural desire for security, found the Auxiliaries more than their match. The Auxiliary members understood full well that the early fight was for a better way of life, for a better chance for kids, for the common hopes and dreams of people everywhere. Ideas taken for granted now were revolutionary then. Auxiliary members helped persuade thousands that the biggest chunk of "right" was on the side of the Union.

The Auxiliary members never were nickel unionists. From the beginning they wanted more than just money in the contract. They wanted to build the kind of world in which their kids would never have to know the poverty and the fear and the insecurity that had plagued the lives of too many of them.

They mobilized for the great struggles still confronting the Union. They had a major part in the great demonstration in front of Briggs Stadium which helped bring the Union to Briggs. They helped in the historic

Ford organizing drive. After the battle of the overpass, they quickly formed leaflet teams to show Harry Bennett and his servicemen that Ford might couldn't buffalo them.

After the war, they tackled the price line with a frenzy. When soaring prices began to make mockery of many Union gains, thousands demonstrated in Detroit's Cadillac Square. The rally was duplicated all over the country. In Kenosha, 3,000 turned out. They formed a huge delegation to Washington to let the White House know just where they stood on the matter.

In ever-growing numbers, they became a part of community organizations devoted to solving community problems. The blood drives, March of Dimes and Red Feather campaigns always have had Auxiliary support.

During every Union emergency, the Auxiliaries always gain in membership and activity.

In Sheboygan, Wisconsin, where workers face about as tough a management as exists any place, the largest Auxiliary in the Union keeps the boycott going. The gals made a host of boycott material. They keep themselves in business by selling it to unions and union members to spread the message. They have their own speakers' bureau, man picket lines during meetings and take an active part in politics.

Today, confronted by broad social problems which require political solution, the Auxiliaries are taking an ever more active part in political activity. Their motivation is basically the same as it was during the days of the "Emergency Brigades." They want to build a world which is a lot better for raising families.

CHARTER 5,000 ISSUED

William C. Doherty, president, National Assn. of Letter Carriers, in Postal Record, May 1959

Every time an organization issues a charter to a new affiliate it indicates progress, greater numerical strength and increased effectiveness of the parent body. A charter also is a good barometer for measuring the acceptance or rejection of an organization by its potential membership, especially when membership is wholly a voluntary decision.

These reflections are in the nature of a preface to the announcement that we issued charter number 5000 during the past month. It was forwarded in response to the request of the carriers at South Hamilton, Mass. Everyone identified with the National Association of Letter Carriers joins in expressing a warm, fraternal greeting to this newest affiliate.

To temper the enthusiasm engendered by the issuance of this particular charter, it should be noted that many eligible carriers are not yet members of the NALC.

In studies made of motivations that prompt workers to join unions it was found that 60 per cent join simply because they were asked to do so. Another 22 per cent require persuasion of one kind or other. In other words, the overwhelming bulk of union membership potential is to be found in these two groups.

These same studies indicate that only 3 per cent of eligible union members can be expected to persist in their refusal to affiliate. The remaining 15 per cent are "union-minded" and seek out the organization representing their interests.

All letter carriers have the same interests. They belong together. If the carrier working next to you is not a member, ask him to join the NALC.

HOW MUCH DOES IT COST *NOT* TO BELONG TO A UNION?

The Voice of 770 (Retail Clerks, Los Angeles), September 1959

You are a member of Local 770. You are a clerk. If you have been working at your trade for fifteen years, you are from $21,938 to $27,292 richer than your counterpart who worked in a non-union department store for the same period!

This fact is only part of the fascinating discoveries made by Local 770's Research Department in comparing the real incomes of union and non-union clerks in Los Angeles.

Let the employer try to spread the myth that "union dues and assessments eat up any wage gains." The hard, cold facts—the things which have happened to us—tell a dramatically different story.

Let's start the story in 1945, when many Local 770 members joined. If you joined in that year, your total initiation fees and dues—from that day to this—amounted to $872.50. That's what it has cost you in actual dollars and cents to invest in your union. That's what's on one side of the ledger sheet. Now let's see what's on the credit side.

For one thing, you have had job security. You have had wage increases. You have received fringe benefits which have an actual dollars and cents value.

In wage increases alone, food clerks received $32,774 in this fifteen-year period. Drug Clerks received $27,428, and pharmacists an incredible $51,196! This does not include any overtime; nor any fringe benefits at all.

But, you say the cost of living has gone up. Indeed it has; it has gone up nearly 90 per cent since 1945. But if you were a Local 770 member all that time, your pay alone has increased from 325 to 500 per cent.

Now let's talk about the money value of fringe benefits in those 15 years. Statisticians have calculated the dollar value of your pension, health plan, extra holidays, longer vacations, etc. If you were a food clerk, these benefits are worth $5,853. To pharmacists they are worth $4,260. To drug clerks they are worth $3,974. Remember, this is in addition to the increases in pay, and does not take into consideration the Union's militant handling of grievances which has saved the jobs of hundreds of members and brought in nearly half a million dollars in wage claims in the same period.

Thus, with your pay increases and the value of fringe benefits, you are thousands of dollars ahead because you've been a member of Local 770. Exactly how much? For food clerks it amounts to a total of $38,628; for drug clerks, $31,402; for pharmacists, $55,456!

Now let's see how the non-union clerk has done in the same period. We are talking about people in department stores doing much the same kind of work as our clerk members.

During the 15-year period, the pay of non-union clerks has also increased. It had to increase; the very fact that they were working in the same city as Local 770 members made it necessary for employers to pay them more money. But how much more?

The record shows that the increase averaged $9,464 during the same period—about one third the increase in pay that Local 770 members have received!

Now what of fringe benefits for these non-union clerks? They are insignificant compared to union fringe benefits. Where a health plan exists, the employee pays either all of the cost or a large proportion. Very few have pension plans of any kind. They do not have the kind of holiday, sick leave, jury duty, night premium and other special benefits which Local 770 members enjoy.

Summing up, if you are a non-union department store clerk, it has cost you from $21,000 to $27,000 not to belong to the union during the last 15 years. And the total bill for dues and initiation fee during that entire period would have amounted to only $872!

What has the money meant for our members? It has meant homes of their own. It has meant education for their children. It has meant health security. It has meant peace of mind.

So far we have talked about money; now let's consider something equally precious. Local 770 fights for its members. They always have a friend in need, a friend in court. In one court case, food clerk members won many millions of dollars in disputed night premiums only because the union fought the case through to the Supreme Court.

Who fights for the non-union clerk? No one.

Union clerks have pensions, cannot be cast off like an old shoe when their working days are over. But non-union clerks are often given the shoe (a pink slip at Christmastime; perhaps a store service pin) after years of devoted work.

The future is assured for members of Local 770. Contracts negotiated this year guarantee an expanding standard of living for the next five years, at least.

Younger members of Local 770 might reflect about how lucky they are to reap this harvest of benefits sown by older members. Most of our older members already know this story. We want to tell it to the whole world in the cold, hard facts presented in this publication!

OVER 250,000 VOTED 'UNION' DURING 12-MONTH PERIOD

AFL-CIO News, September 3, 1960

More than a quarter of a million unorganized workers voted "union" during the 1959-1960 fiscal year, to set a new high for any fiscal year since the national AFL-CIO merger in December 1955, an analysis of National Labor Relations Board figures indicates.

The mounting vote in favor of trade unionism was hailed by John W. Livingston, director of the AFL-CIO Dept. of Organization, who declared that "despite three years of an intensive anti-union campaign, the majority of workers in this country still desire union organization."

The rebound in the number of workers who won union bargaining rights during the last fiscal year came in the face of efforts by the National Association of Manufacturers, the U.S. Chamber of Commerce and other business groups to use McClellan committee disclosures as a weapon against union organizing.

It also came despite last year's action by a conservative Republican-southern Democratic coalition in Congress to forge new restrictions on trade union activity through enactment of the Landrum-Griffin Act.

In the fiscal year which closed June 30 there were 6,380 labor NLRB-conducted representation elections, an eight-year high.

During the fiscal year, 179,364 workers joined AFL-CIO unions via the representation election route. This was the highest for any complete fiscal year since merger. The balance voted for unaffiliated unions.

Livingston said that during the second quarter of 1960 there was a "substantial decrease" in the number of persons in units involved in elections which pitted AFL-CIO unions against each other. There were only 6,200 workers involved in such elections involving two or more AFL-CIO affiliates.

JUST A SINGLE STEP

William L. McFetridge, recently retired president, BSEIU,
in Building Service Employee, August 1956

"The Longest Journey Begins With a Single Step."—Chinese Proverb

When we talk about organizing the unorganized, adding new members or carrying on organizational activities, it is easy to forget the old Chinese proverb. The bigness of the job, the greatness of the challenge, the urgency of the need lead us to talk with big words about big programs.

But if we forget that even a march across a continent must begin with but a single step, we are likely to plan much, do little. For even a great coast-to-coast drive for new members of our Building Service Employees' International Union starts with single steps. The International Union's campaign rests upon local union efforts. The local union's efforts depend upon individual members' support. And individual member efforts begin with something less than getting a non-member to sign on the dotted line.

No small part of a successful union organization drive comes from the members thinking, talking and explaining trade unionism to others. When you talk about the newspaper headlines with your neighbors, tell them of your union's stand on the issues of the day. When the wife and her card-playing friends are at the house, tell them about your union's fight for better wages and working conditions. When you are with your old cronies at a club or pub, tell them about the things your Union has done to improve conditions in our industry.

In this way, you develop your own skill at explaining the union movement to others. You help make your community union-minded. And you make it more likely that, when you do talk to the unorganized worker in the next building or next block, you will be able to interest him in union membership.

If this sounds like some "new" idea borrowed from a public relations textbook or organizers' handbook, just think back to the days when the organized labor movement got its start. Every possible influence was lined up against the right of workers to organize. All the fledgling labor movement had was a membership that lived unionism, that talked it up and made converts by the sheer force of enthusiasm.

So, as we go about building stronger BSEIU units, let's start the journey with the single step—of telling others of the things our Union has done and can do.

404.
CARL STANSWITZ

"If you'd join the union, you wouldn't have that feeling that the whole world is against you."

3-a | The Changing South

'OLD SOUTH' FADING AS INDUSTRIALIZATION BUILDS BASE FOR UNIONISM AND PROSPERITY

Electrical Workers' Journal, July 1959

In ancient Rome, there was a temple to the god, Janus, who had two opposite faces. "Forward I look, and backward," Longfellow once quoted Janus as saying.

Our own Southland, as the god of old, has presented two opposite faces to the world, keeping the past alive, even while looking on a changing and turbulent present.

The complexities of modern life are today altering the visage of our Southland before our very eyes.

As we look at the South wrestling with the school integration problem —which has taken up most of the news and attention—we find this agricultural area living through an industrial boom.

Industry is literally pouring money into the South, opening plants (for awhile it was almost at the rate of three a day) at a tremendous rate. In 1958, the nation experienced a recession, but Southern industry boomed.

According to one report, in 11 Southern states, eight per cent more new plants were established last year than even in the boom year of 1957. Virginia alone got 64 new plants last year, while Georgia got 169 new plants in 1958. Florida claimed 201 new factories, Texas, 257.

All of this is good news for working men and women of the sunny Southland. However, there are shadows and clouds in the picture too.

The AFL-CIO Industrial Union Department warns in a recent publication: "The area (the South) is still a major bastion of the open shop and sweated industry . . . and despite great changes in recent years, the problem of race relations is yet to be solved.

"Labor has yet to complete the organization of the South and, until this is accomplished, there will not be full economic and political citizenship for hundreds of thousands of workers in the Southland and elsewhere in the nation . . .

"The new industrialization of the South," the report continues, "has in part, therefore, gone forward on the basis of an unfair wage competition with the rest of the nation. This has meant lower living standards for millions. A continuation of this situation threatens the welfare of all."

The report states further: "Industry has come to the South to stay, seeking to take advantage of the region and its people. To attract Northern capital, many Southern communities have joined with employers in a shameful competition that has had depressive effects upon whole industries.

"Not the least of the concessions pledged to Northern employers has been a virtual guarantee against the organization of their workforces. To make good their pledges, public officials have joined with anti-union employers in creating an atmosphere reminiscent of the open-shop North half a century ago."

Existing on a plantation and then a farm economy, the Southland has stepped up its industrialization during and since World War II. Today, with great added impetus it is emerging as a great industrial center.

The union fight in the South has been long, going back to the earliest days of our nation. It has been hard fought, sometimes violent and bloody, with workers pitted against great odds in their bid for a decent way of life.

Anti-union employers through the years in the South have run the gamut from the old days of hiring hoodlums and "vigilantes" to terrorize strikers, to branding unions as "alien" and even to suspending workers or using racist propaganda to divide workers among themselves, thus leaving them easy prey to the will of the plant owner.

Then, of course, came the national Taft-Hartley legislation, followed up by state "right-to-work" laws put on the books of such states as Arkansas, Georgia, Virginia and others, to further block union activity.

Today, while progress in organization and collective bargaining gains is being made slowly but surely in many previously anti-union towns of our Southland, an impasse or worse is reached in many others.

Just recently a six-month old strike of textile workers in one community was climaxed when National Guardsmen were called out.

Our own IBEW has more than 300 local unions distributed throughout the 11 Southern states. Our organizers in the South are working long and hard to bring unionization to electrical workers in every part of the relatively newly-industrialized South.

In Birmingham, Alabama alone, in that city of titan steel mills, the IBEW has six local unions. Over in Montgomery, a city right out of the old South, its streets showing fine ante-bellum mansions, its fringes spreading out into cotton fields, the IBEW has three local unions.

IBEW representatives write in constantly of Southern organizing efforts. They write in with news of victories won at cable companies, at electronics plants, at utilities or electrical manufacturing plants, and so on. They write in too of attempts made and elections lost and of the hard fights involved. (One city even tried to impose an exorbitant fee on any organizer within its limits.)

And other AFL-CIO unions are expending efforts to organize the newly-industrialized and traditionally anti-union Southland, looking towards a fuller life for all working people.

Today we must bring our picture of the South into focus with reality. We must picture modern farm equipment where before were many farmhands, for an agriculture geared to modern times plays a tremendous role in the southern way of life. We must see the industrialization that has come late to the Sunny South. The picture of sleepy southern towns must give way to one of giant textile mills, tremendous food processing plants, thousands of assembly lines, vast steel mills and teeming ports.

In our picture we see thousands of workers in blue collars working in shiny new plants. We realize that the fight is on to lay waste the old ideas of "open shop" and "sweated industry" and to bring wages and working conditions "into line with those of the industrial North" for the benefit and future prosperity of the South.

The old taboos of sectionalism must crumble away and the great race problem must be solved before the South can reach its full promise.

Though labor has a great fight left to win against such odds as "right-to-work" laws, traditional antipathy to unions, and the evils of run-away shops, it can still look steadfastly ahead to a unionized South. It can look forward to a time when organized southern labor and industry, mutually benefitting each other can walk together into a bright, prosperous future.

The new face of our Southland is emerging. The old image is fading, as if having seen the end of an era.

UAW GROWTH SPELLS PROGRESS IN SOUTH

Ray Martin in UAW Solidarity, November 1957

The South is getting to know the UAW.

You don't have to look hard for signs of UAW progress against southern holdouts opposing economic prosperity and social understanding, two achievements that result from UAW organization.

An "outstanding" contract has been won for UAW members at Martin Aircraft's Orlando, Fla., plant— a plant that recently voted over-whelmingly for the UAW and which soon will employ nearly 6,000.

In Atlanta and Memphis, office workers and technicians now in the UAW are showing more enthusiasm than ever in organizational work among area salaried workers whose history has been non-union.

Douglas Aircraft office workers and technicians at Charlotte, N. C., are leaning heavily toward the UAW in advance of an up-coming NLRB vote.

At the Ford glass plant in Nashville, Tenn., only one vote was cast against the UAW in an NLRB election. That plant will soon employ upwards of 6,000 also.

A late-spring UAW Local 1155 settlement at Hayes Aircraft, Birmingham, Ala., pushed wages and working conditions up to the point where "it was like an alarm clock to thousands in non-union plants," as Region 8 Director E. T. Michael put it.

Another roadsign along the way: the pending NLRB vote at Ford's Lister Hill, Ala., plant. A resounding UAW victory there, said Michael, "will jolt the anti-labor Southern industrialists right down to their cotton socks."

As UAW membership strength spreads in the South, Michael said the union is:

1. Adding to the security of workers outside the South—making it less profitable for runaway plants to desert their responsibilities.

2. Building a broader economic base for southern workers' families so that their increased purchasing power can attract more industry.

3. Strengthening democratic trade unionism to the point where it can influence social thinking.

"As the UAW lifts the South economically, it musters the grass roots support necessary to lift it socially so that both economic and social justice is possible," said Michael.

The 35-year-old Michael's office is in Baltimore. He's seldom found there, though, because of widespread UAW activity.

He pointed to a large map on his office wall. His finger moved from Mississippi to Alabama, from Georgia to South Carolina, from Tennessee to North Carolina, from Virginia to Delaware and Maryland, then down quickly to Florida.

"Our success in Florida has the South talking," he said. "Workers in the depressed South now can see significant, almost unbelievable economic standards among workers, made possible by collective bargaining.

Runaway plants from the North do a double injustice to workers, said Michael.

They dump their veteran workers in the North, creating unemployment, and seek to consolidate themselves in the South "to perpetuate social and economic injustice."

Economically, said Michael, the South is no better off if its industrial growth is based on irresponsible management. And he has the figures to back up his statements.

For example, after years of luring runaway plants, Mississippi workers earn $55.20 for a 40-hour week as against $99.04 in Michigan and $93.51 in California. The Mississippi figure is not the best or worst for the South.

Average income per person in Mississippi is still only $815 a year—as against $1,831 in Michigan and $1,899 in California.

"It's a long, long jump from the Mississippi-Georgia level to the Michigan-California level," said Mi-

chael, "but until that gap is narrowed, millions of families in the South will remain economic victims of industry. And their low economic status will hold down the level of prosperity for all Americans."

ROCK HILL, S. C.: WHERE 5,000 TWUA MEMBERS HAVE BUILT A UNION WAY OF LIFE

Irene Pave in Textile Labor, February 1958

In Rock Hill, South Carolina, which lies 350 miles south of the Mason-Dixon Line, 5,000 workers belong to the Textile Workers Union of America, AFL-CIO.

First, workers at Rock Hill Printing and Finishing Co. formed Local 710. Then they helped to organize the Gold-Tex Fabric mill. Then Gold-Tex Local 929 pitched in with 710 to organize the Celriver plant of the Celanese Corp. Then Celriver Local 1093 joined 710 and 925 in organizing American Thread Co. Local 1386.

Together they made Rock Hill Printing and Finishing Co. the highest-paying dye house in the South . . . built two union halls that are the social centers of Rock Hill . . . worked for civic causes with such energy that, according to a Celanese official, "the outstanding success of the last few United Fund drives has been due to the union."

Not that it's all been peaches and cream. TWUA has lost campaigns as well as won them. Mills have closed. A United Southern Employees Association grinds out quit-the-union propaganda.

But add up the victories, subtract the defeats, keep in mind the constant harassments of running a union in the South and you're still left with the remarkable statistic: 5,000 workers belong to TWUA in Rock Hill.

The first 900 joined 14 years ago when a Rock Hill Printing Co. official brushed off a request for a raise with the remark that only unionized plants could receive raise authorization from the War Labor Board.

A committee immediately drove 30

miles to the TWUA office in Charlotte, N. C., returned with a stack of union cards and signed up the plant.

Reid Roach, Local 710's first president and current recording secretary, has seen his hourly pay rise from 20 cents in 1931 to $1.61 today. But that wasn't all he talked about when he visited friends employed at other mills or described "What the Union Means to Me" over the radio during the Celriver organizing campaign.

A tall man who grows chrysanthemums, keeps a cow and thinks before he speaks, Roach remembers he said something like this:

"A union means protection. It gives a man a say-so in his working conditions. If the company increases workloads, the union can fight to cut them down. Maybe the best it'll get is a compromise, but a worker in a non-union shop gets nothing. He takes the stretch-out or quits.

"The same with grievances. The company pays no attention to complaints in a non-union shop. It's got to pay attention when the union takes them up through the grievance procedure.

"And the union protects your seniority, a great thing. There's no seniority in a non-union shop. The foremen's kinfolk get the good jobs."

As befits an elder of the First Presbyterian Church, Roach admits honestly that it was partly self-interest that sent the Rock Hill dyers out to organize.

"We wanted to help others, yes. But that wasn't all of it. We knew we couldn't live by ourselves. We knew the more members we'd get, the stronger we'd all be."

Under the direction of TWUA staff men, they stood at mill gates when the shifts changed, passed out leaflets, called on workers after hours.

They said, "We are your kinfolk, your neighbors, not the outsiders the company talks about. We do the same kind of job you do. We know how a union works because that's the way it works for us."

The Gold-Tex plant went TWUA in 1948, Celriver in 1949 and American Thread in nearby Clover in 1955.

There were also setbacks, some of them heartbreakers.

But the organizing went on, and goes on.

So do the meetings and the stewards' classes—of No. 1 importance from the beginning, when a Catholic priest, the Rev. Maurice Berthiaume, enrolled the first Local 710 members in his labor relations school. Today stewards from all four locals attend Berthiaume's classes.

The Red Cross bloodmobile drives also go on, and the United Fund campaigns (at Celriver each foreman and steward form a UF team), the credit union (largest in South Carolina), the college scholarships given annually to two children of union members—all the activities that make up the TWUA way of life in Rock Hill.

Since 1954 these activities, like almost everything else worthwhile in Rock Hill, have centered on the handsome union hall built by the 2,800 members of Local 710. Last year the 1,500-member Local 1093 put up its own building and began sharing the role of host to Rock Hill.

For all comers the rule is the same: no charge, this is a community service, just clean up before you leave.

In each building there's a comfortable lounge with TV, a spacious auditorium with a stage, a fully-equipped kitchen, a meeting room and a couple of offices.

The lounge is also an off-and-on

inspection station where members turn up their heels to prove they're not O'Sullivan's. On one well-remembered occasion a textile worker discovered he was wearing shoes heeled by strikebreakers, ripped off the O'Sullivan's with his bare hands and hobbled off to the shoemaker to buy union-made heels.

"When the dye house was on strike in 1956, union men in places like Massachusetts and New York picketed stores that carried goods produced by Lowenstein, the chain that owns Rock Hill. They've never forgotten that here," Berthiaume explains.

Typical events that have taken place in the union halls are a meeting of the Four Square Gospel Church Ladies' Sunday School class, a high school graduation party, a stork shower, a Safety Council meeting, a National Guard dinner, a meeting to organize a new ball club, a Youth Crusade, a rock and roll show. . . .

Local 1093's datebook also records shift dances, a Celanese beauty contest and bingo games sponsored by the Celanese Recreation Association, which draws its membership from both production workers and supervisory staff. There's mutual respect between union and management at Celriver, where the personnel man, Ben Sands, says, "When TWUA agrees to something, we know we can count on it."

The bulletin boards in the union halls show the same spread of interests: copies of proposed textile laws, notes from members, leaflets about the Kohler and O'Sullivan boycotts, newspaper clippings—and on the Local 710 board, a list.

Here's the story behind that list:

In March, 1955 the local founded TWUA's Southern Dyers Conference, which set up wage goals and circularized the industry—successfully. When the conference tried again in 1956, the Rock Hill Printing Co. forced Local 710 into a 15-week strike. Settlement included an "unofficial" promise of a 10-cent raise. The raise came through shortly afterwards and was followed, as before, by raises throughout the industry.

It was also followed by a full-scale anti-union campaign.

Instructions on how to quit TWUA (under South Carolina's right-to-work law, a worker may withdraw his checkoff authorization on the anniversary of the day he signed it or on the anniversary of the contract) appeared on the Rock Hill Company's bulletin board. As each worker's anniversary approached, supervisors called him in for a "heart-to-heart" chat. A newly-formed United South-ern Employees Association began issuing anti-union literature.

A flying visit from Bill Gordon, TWUA's dyeing director, persuaded the company to take down the notices and drop the chats. But the USEA campaign continues full blast and Local 710 regards itself as still on the firing line.

That's what the list in Local 710's union hall is all about. It names the workers who left TWUA. Their former union brothers are asked to talk to them, to help them understand why they need their union— why everyone, 350 miles north or 350 miles south of the Mason-Dixon Line, needs his union.

ORGANIZER LICENSE UNCONSTITUTIONAL, SUPREME COURT RULES IN BAXLEY CASE

Justice, January 15, 1958

The U. S. Supreme Court, in a case involving the garment workers, ruled on Jan. 13 that a city ordinance requiring the licensing of union organizers is unconstitutional. The case of ILGWU organizer Staub v. the City of Baxley, Georgia, was appealed by the ILGWU to the Supreme Court. It was argued before the court on Nov. 18 and 19, 1957 by the union's general counsel, Morris P. Glushien, joined by attorneys Bernard Dunau and Ed Pearce.

The court agreed with the ILGWU by a vote of 7 to 2. The decision was written and read by Associate Justice Charles E. Whittaker.

The Court held that the Baxley ordinance requiring a license fee of $2,000 from union organizers is invalid because it is a restraint and abridgment of the right of free speech guaranteed by the Constitution of the United States. The majority decision was based on constitutional objections to the ordinance.

Associate Justices Felix Frankfurter and Tom C. Clark dissented on certain procedural grounds.

Informed of the decision, ILGWU Pres. Dubinsky declared:

"We are, of course, pleased by the decision. Many communities, especially in the South, have used the device of requiring union organizers to be licensed in order to keep unions out of their midst and wages at a low level.

"This decision by the U. S. Supreme Court eliminates an interference with organizing, and thus clears the way for greater union efforts to raise wage and work standards in the South."

The majority opinion of the Court declared, in part:

"It will be noted that Appellant [union representative] was not accused of any act against the peace, good order or dignity of the community, or any particular thing she said in soliciting employees of the manufacturing company to join the union. She was simply charged and convicted for 'soliciting members for an organization without a permit.' This solicitation, as shown by the evidence, consisted solely of speaking to those employees in their private homes about joining the union."

ED BLAIR, AFTER BRUSH WITH DEATH, SET TO RENEW HIS ORGANIZING JOB

AFL-CIO News, August 18, 1956

Back from his brush with death, Ed Blair is ready to take up once more the organizing job to which he dedicated his life a score of years ago.

In the Amalgamated Clothing Workers they call him Durable Ed Blair, this big, solid fellow who has been cursed, reviled, pistol-whipped and nearly slain while bringing the message of unionism to his native Southland.

He is heading for the Carolinas next while still recovering from the shooting that nearly cost him his life last Jan. 16 on a street in Columbus, Miss. At Doctor Hospital in Columbus where Blair spent three months and underwent several operations they still marvel at the courage that aided his fight to live.

They marvel too at the way union people rallied to help his fight, flooding in with more offers to donate blood than the hospital had ever known before. Helping people had been Blair's work, now people were helping him.

"I had 60 blood transfusions before I was out of danger," Ed recalls now, "and they were given by Amalgamated people, by Bricklayers, Carpenters, Communications Workers, people from the IUE and lots of others."

The events of that January morning happened so fast that Ed's recollection of them is blurred. Members of the Electrical Workers had gone on strike that day against a plant of the American Bosch Arma Corp. Ed knew many of the strikers; some of them had worked previously in a clothing plant he helped to organize. Good union man that he is, he went to the picket line to give what help he could.

James T. Miller of Ethelsville, Ala., 20 miles distant, headed for the same picket line that morning. With him was his wife. Miller crashed his car through the IUE picket line to get his wife into the plant to work. He narrowly missed hitting several pickets driving into the plant and was coming out at the same high speed until he was stopped by a more solid line of pickets.

Miller brandished a rifle and Jesse Rye, IUE local president, was forced to let him pass. A short distance down the block Miller's car was slowed by an approaching station wagon. Blair, too, was approaching on foot.

Too late he heard a shouted warning that Miller had a rifle. Miller leaped from his car, firing as he did. Blair dropped in the street, one slug having ripped through his liver, severing an artery, and passing completely through him and inflicting a wound on his right arm.

Miller fled to his home across the state line where he was later arrested and is now under indictment by a Lowndes County grand jury.

For Blair, it was not his first encounter with violence. He was in Lafolette, Tenn., in March 1943 when a band of thugs invaded the hotel room he shared with Franz Daniel, now assistant to AFL-CIO Organizing Director John W. Livingston.

The thugs pistol-whipped the pair who were trying to organize a clothing plant and one of them shot at Daniel. The slug was stopped by a wallet in Daniel's pocket.

Blair is proud of the organizing record he and others have made in the South against formidable odds. "The Amalgamated has built 11 locals with 5,000 members in Mississippi alone since 1948," Blair said. "But there are thousands more to be organized and I'm anxious to get back on the job."

4 | APPRENTICESHIP AND VOCATIONAL TRAINING

THERE IS NO SUBSTITUTE FOR SKILL

The Carpenter, February 1957

It is not often that this journal can see eye-to-eye with literature published by the National Association of Manufacturers. In fact, we have often criticized the efforts of NAM to swamp our schools with pro-management propaganda which plays down or ignores completely the part labor contributes in making our economy the productive miracle it is.

Recently, however, NAM released a new "educational aid" booklet which does a better job of properly evaluating the role of skilled craftsmanship in today's industry. The pamphlet stresses the fact that the skilled craftsman is the "anchor man" on today's technological team. Without his skills and know-how, the theoretical advances of scientists could never be translated into effective, productive techniques to make living easier and better for all the people.

In the chapter entitled "Opportunities in Atomic Energy," it notes that "from three to six skilled craftsmen are needed for every scientist and engineer of the atomic team." Wood craftsmen, core makers, plumbers, steamfitters, welders, mechanics, glass blowers and electronics specialists are needed to transform into working models the mechanisms scientists and engineers dream up in their laboratories and on their drawing boards. Without an adequate supply of skilled workers to back them up, the scientists and engineers would soon be slowed down to a crawl.

"There is no shortcut to acquiring a skill," the pamphlet emphasizes. "You can't acquire it simply by reading textbooks or listening to lectures. It takes aptitude, courage, ambition, months of study, on-the-job training and related technical instruction."

All these things organized labor has pointed out repeatedly. That is why an apprenticeship training system second to none exists in the United States and Canada today. Unions such as our Brotherhood have devoted much time and energy to pushing apprenticeship training. Without their persistent efforts for better apprenticeship training over the years, the supply of skilled mechanics today might well be an insurmountable bottleneck to further progress.

True craftsmanship is worth all the sacrifice, time and study it demands during learning years. To make this point, the pamphlet quotes Dr. James Bryant Conant, former president of Harvard University. Dr. Conant recently said: "In the whole range of scientific and technological activities, there is no substitute for a first-rate man. Ten second-rate men cannot replace him."

Opportunities open to truly skilled men are increasing rather than decreasing, for all the automation and electronic advances that are taking place. Nothing will reverse that trend. The man who knows the theory as well as the mechanical side of his trade is going to be in demand regardless of how many half-mechanics are walking the streets.

What is happening in a Pennsylvania electronics plant may be a foretaste of what is coming. This particular plant, which long has been plagued by a shortage of graduate engineers, last year turned to its skilled craftsmen for an answer to its manpower problems.

Instead of turning over all its problems to the engineering department, the firm now takes many of them directly to its skilled craftsmen.

"Look, fellows," it says, "we want a gadget to do this and this, but it must fit in a space of such and such a size."

The woodworkers, metal workers, tinsmiths, etc., take it from there. In a few weeks they come up with a working model. The model is then turned over to the engineering department for refining. In this way the firm gets a great deal more mileage out of its technical staff. It can do this because it has a full crew of really skilled craftsmen.

Dr. Conant probably summed it all up when he said that 10 second-rate men cannot replace one first-class man.

APPRENTICESHIP TODAY

*James A. Brownlow, president, AFL-CIO Metal Trades Department,
in the AFL-CIO American Federationist, December 1959*

We have read and heard a good deal about the state of our apprenticeship programs, how we are not training enough apprentices to replace the skilled workers who retire, die or move into other occupations.

We are told that not enough apprentice are being employed and, of those who are employed, less than half complete their apprenticeships and become journeymen.

This condition varies among the different crafts. Some have a better record than others. All have a great deal to do to bring the ranks of the craftsmen up to the numerical level needed to support a rapidly expanding population. Not only must the number of craftsmen correspond to population growth; it is also essential that training for craftsmanship be conducted so as to prepare the skilled workers for easy adjustment to the innovations constantly developing in their trades.

In January, 1958, there were 186,-408 apprentices registered in all trades, while at the end of the year this number had dropped to 177,695. These apprenticeship registration figures do not reveal the number of apprentices who may have been furloughed or temporarily suspended from training, but who are still counted as a part of the registered apprentices on the active list.

Yet the demand for skilled workers in our labor force continues to increase. Our recognized apprentice programs are failing to turn out anywhere near the number of fully skilled journeymen who are needed each year to offset even the number of skilled workers who leave the labor force each year through death or retirement, let alone to meet the demand for the additional skilled workers which scientific and industrial development requires.

Several government attempts have been made to recognize the need of a balanced, regulated apprentice training program. At the solicitation of management and labor, Congress passed the law establishing a Federal Apprenticeship Bureau within the Department of Labor in August 1937. This is commonly known as the Fitzgerald Act.

Today the Federal Bureau of Apprenticeship is composed of some 500 employees, most of whom are craftsmen affiliated with the many unions of the apprenticeable trades and who have devoted their abilities to their crafts and to the effective dissemination of information designed to assist labor and management in developing meaningful apprenticeship programs.

The essence of this apprenticeship system is the cooperation of labor and management; in each of the trades there are joint apprenticeship committees. The participation of the federal government and of the states is confined primarily to promoting apprenticeship, formulating joint apprenticeship committees, and giving these joint committees the benefit of the wide experiences of the federal or state apprenticeship representative.

Even in the face of this activity we are falling far short of our goal.

The number of completions and cancellations has been exceeding the number of new registrations. There were over 28,000 cancellations in 1958 and just short of 30,000 completions, while our total new registrations were slightly over 49,000.

These statistics deal only with registered apprentice employment, with state apprenticeship agencies, or the Bureau of Apprenticeship and Training. They do not tell all the story, for not all apprentices are registered.

There is an urgent need for more comprehensive information on the extent to which we, as a nation, are meeting our demands for skilled labor through apprenticeship training programs.

It is encouraging to note that international unions have continued their efforts to extend and improve their apprenticeship programs and that these efforts have not slackened during the recession in employment occurring during the last many months.

Unions are giving increased attention to the development of the technical knowledge and skills of their journeymen. If a journeyman is to keep up with the demands for increased knowledge and new skills coming with the rapidly changing industrial picture, it is imperative that he have an opportunity to acquire the further training and knowledge.

Journeymen who are called on to play an important part in apprentices' training should themselves be fully competent in all phases of their craft, including new and improved techniques and developments as they come into use.

The problems inherent in journeyman training differ substantially from those of apprenticeship training; the journeyman must be sufficiently concerned with the need to broaden his knowledge that he will be willing to give of his time for such purpose.

A journeyman must realize that the taking of additional training courses is no reflection on him or on the apprenticeship program which he completed. The rapid changes occurring in techniques, processes, materials, etc., are bringing changes to crafts which the best apprentice training program of a decade ago could not anticipate and train for.

One successful method of arousing the interest of journeymen in further training courses is carrying out sound, updated apprenticeship programs in their areas and establishments. When the skilled journeymen see that the apprentices are acquiring knowledge and skill which they don't have, they are frequently encouraged to request courses which will give them the same knowledge and technical information.

Surveys of apprentices who have completed training demonstrate that job training is the weak spot in apprentice training. Some former apprentices indicate that they are not given a sufficient variety of work experience. Some indicate that the journeymen to whom they were assigned were not good instructors. They indicate that the urge for production may have kept them on jobs in which they had developed a high productivity—at the expense of having adequate opportunity to work at other jobs relating to their trade.

These complaints suggest that steps need to be taken by joint apprenticeship committees, by apprentice supervisors and, above all, by management. Such complaints would not arise if those responsible for the operation of the apprenticeship program checked the apprentices' job training at least once a month, and had the authority to move the apprentices to different operations in accordance with the established training schedule.

The writer has long recognized a problem with which we have been confronted. That is, whether with the change in industrial processes, we can continue to limit our training in the old, traditional way; whether there has been such a crossing-over or mixing of craft skills that it is almost impossible to follow the legendary jurisdictional practices of the respective unions.

We do not wish to be misunderstood. We are not now advocating that a diversity of operations be made a part of a formal apprenticeship of any particular craft, but it is a subject which is going to require the attention of both management and unions alike. We believe management would much prefer the retraining of already skilled craftsmen, even at journeymen's rates, to meet new technological developments, rather than to start in an apprenticeship of a new and indefinable trade. This problem increasingly requires the attention of all concerned.

The writer further believes that the day is rapidly approaching when the classroom and technical training requirements of the apprentice can no longer be taught after hours, after the day's work has been completed. Apprentices must spend a full workday at vocational school at their regular pay.

The day is past when the entering apprentice has only completed elementary school and is from 14 to 16 years of age. Today in most instances entering apprentices must be high school graduates, or at least have had high school training and not be under 18 years of age. Compulsory military service has had its effect, increasing the age and responsibility of the average apprentice.

Many apprentices are married and have families. It is unfair to the apprentice, following his day's work, to compel him to take related classroom training after the regular workday is ended. He is tired and lacks the enthusiasm which he would have at the start of a day.

Experience has proven that the length of the apprenticeship served at present, as determined by labor and management, is not long enough and should be increased, rather than reduced. Only in this way can we hope to turn out fully skilled journeymen who are capable of coping with the technological developments of their trades.

Apprentice training is costly to the employer. It is, however, an investment upon which American industry can expect a full return. It is not wise that this investment be dissipated in partially training workers who cannot become competent journeymen upon fulfillment of shortened apprenticeships, as some have proposed.

Much has been said about the limitations placed by some unions and management on the number of apprentices in certain occupations. It must not be forgotten that the apprentice is hired as a learner and works as a learner. As such he is entitled to continuity of employment during his apprenticeship and to some reasonable assurance that upon completion of his term there will be a job for him at his trade.

There is an additional obligation upon industry. That is to accept apprentice training programs and apprentices and not depend upon other industries or plants to bear the burden of training craftsmen, only to have them pirated away by some company which has shirked its responsibility to train its own skilled craftsmen.

The whole complex subject of apprenticeship skills and their development is one which needs the full attention of labor and management, and the cooperation of federal and state governments.

JOB TRAINING FOR THE SIXTIES

Russ Allen in IUD Digest, Winter 1960

Training for skilled tradesmen and technicians in American industry will wear a different aspect in the 1960's. Though the need for such training has always been present, it will be different in several crucial aspects:

● The educational and skill requirements for the traditional trades will be raised.

● There will be an added technical factor demanding more education in science and mathematics, and more practice in applying theoretical knowledge to job problems.

● There will be a much greater demand for technical jobs that are not directly related to the traditional skilled trades.

On the latter point, U. S. Labor Department figures for 1957 show 575,000 technicians employed in industry, as compared with 8,500,000 skilled workers in 1958. In the next 10 years the number of professional and technical workers is expected to rise by 40 per cent, or almost twice as much percentagewise as the number of skilled workers.

Buried in these cold figures are some powerful warnings. A boy who is good with his hands and not much interested in "book learning" could, in the past, drop out of school and learn a trade. No longer. Not only are the skill requirements higher, but most companies will not touch a boy for skilled job training or an apprenticeship without a high school diploma.

Present estimates are that in the 1960's three out of 10 workers will get jobs without graduating from high school, as compared with four out of 10 today. With higher entry requirements for skilled trades, these 30 per cent are fated to be barred forever from the top skilled occupations. That's lesson number one.

Lesson number two is that present skilled workers will, in many cases, have to upgrade their skills if they are not to be displaced or barred from top-rated jobs.

If the electrician is to become an electronic technician, he must learn to use engineering handbooks, oscilliscopes, signal generators, and the slide rule—as well as basic hand tools. The "tools of the trade" are changing, and the skills must adapt to the new tools.

If the machinist wants to become a tool designer, he has to add to his knowledge of machine shop practice a grasp of drafting, shop mathematics and the characteristics of the metals he works with.

The union must be the agent that makes these opportunities available to its members if it is to keep up with the dizzy pace that American industry is setting.

The traditional in-service method of training has been the formal apprenticeship program leading to journeyman status. This is the tried-and-true method and is still the best way yet devised of transmitting skill and trade knowledge from the master of his craft to the learner.

Sad to say, there is mounting evidence today—attested to by union after union—that management is fobbing off its responsibility to train its own skilled workers.

Evidence of the failure of companies to meet their obligations in skill training is provided in a recent U. S. Department of Labor study of the tool-and-die industry. Three salient facts were uncovered:

1. Only 60 per cent of the apprentices needed to replace journeymen lost through death and retirement are being trained by the industry.

2. Over 43 per cent of the firms were unable to hire enough craftsmen that met their hiring standards.

3. Most significant of all, only 57 per cent of the shops have apprentice training programs.

The responsibility of the union to press hard for the establishment of apprentice training programs is clear. Management must not be permitted to abdicate, but neither can it be permitted to write its own ticket with company training programs that fail to recognize the public and union responsibility involved.

Not all of the problems can be laid at management's doorstep. Even when formal programs have been adopted, many workers will not relinquish short-run earnings opportunities to work at apprentice rates and build for the future. They feel that through normal upgrading and high semi-skilled rates they will do all right without all the bother of going back to school. In such instances, the union has a tough and thankless job showing these workers where their real self-interest lies.

In the vocational education provided in high schools there is also much room for improvement. Too often there is a woeful lack of intelligent counseling. The vocational program becomes a side-track for slow learners and discipline problems rather than a creative experience for those with manual skills.

Somewhere along the line the educators must be educated. They must work more closely with both industry and labor so that the education prepares students for real up-to-date jobs that exist in industry today, preferably in the immediate area.

Although the percentage of technicians will increase more in the next decade than that of skilled workers, we will still need 11,000,000 skilled workers as compared with 8,500,000 today.

The number of unskilled workers will remain about the same in the next decade, which means their proportion of the total work-force will be reduced. If these new workers do not have a skill, they will not find jobs.

Educators make a distinction between vocational and technical education. Many of the skills of the technician relate closely to those of traditional trades. Examples are the electronics technician and tool designer mentioned earlier.

But other types of technicians are not related to skilled trades but rather to professions, such as the "engineering aide" and the "laboratory assistant." Then there are the new jobs spawned by computer technology, such as "data processor" or "linear programmer."

All of these technical jobs have one characteristic in common that distinguishes them from skilled manual occupations: their jobs depend not so much on manual skill as upon application of technical knowledge to practical shop problems. For example, when an instrument technician assembles and connects a panel control board in an automated plant, he relies less on the skill of his hands than on his technical knowledge.

This means that in training for the technical job, more emphasis must be placed on applied mathematical and scientific knowledge than on manipulative skills repeated over and over. This calls for more hours in the classroom and less on-the-job training.

Technical education is now being provided in a limited number of technical high schools, in community colleges and in some junior colleges, and in both public and private technical institutes beyond the high school.

The cost of private technical institutes is high. Not only are there substantial tuition fees but high living costs are frequently entailed. Though important, private institutes are by no means an answer to the general problem.

Once again we return to public assumption of a public responsibility. The federal government has assumed a limited responsibility in its program under Title VIII of the National Defense Education Act of 1958. This title provides federal funds for technical training only, where it can be shown that the need for such training exists for defense-related occupations. It remains to be seen how sticky the federal government will be in defining "defense-related" occupations, but the program is important not so much for its scope as for its recognition of a federal obligation.

Initially, the unions had their differences with the Office of Education over the definition of "technician." This word at first was so construed as to eliminate the possibility of extension training for skilled journeymen who wished to upgrade their skills. The definition has since been liberalized to make such training possible.

Funds are available to states on a matching basis, with both state and local funds counting for matching purposes. However, even matching funds from the states are hard to come by these days, with a universal stringency in state budgets. This program has run for two years, and has two more years to go.

The impression should not be left that facilities for technical education are readily available. Good technical high schools are few and far between, and many community and junior colleges have very limited facilities. Even those available can only be utilized by unions which seize the initiative and apply with their companies for these services.

The union that is alert to its responsibilities can, in effect, make its own opportunities where they do not exist now. If it wants to get re-training facilities for workers displaced or about to be displaced by technology, it should canvass the local facilities first and then apply to the state office of vocational education for assistance.

If it wants similar opportunities for union members already in skilled trades to learn technical skills, it should follow the same procedure.

Vocational education as it exists today is the stepchild of secondary schools, and the teacher is in many cases little more than a policeman without a badge. The students who are slotted into these courses immediately bear the brand of inferiority, regardless of their merit.

In part this is a cruel result of the American cult of success, of which the college degree is the preeminent symbol. This is a form of discrimination so widely practiced and so universally accepted that few voices are raised to protest its injustice.

Significantly, President Emeritus James Conant of Harvard University, in his study of American high schools, had warm praise for vocational education.

Vocational and technical education must be raised to a coordinate position in American secondary education with the college preparatory courses. It must be made generally available, without stigma, to students in the hinterlands as well as in the major industrial cities. The addition of subject matter in science and mathematics, provided it has clear relevance to the real world and to industry, may catch the imagination of some of the brighter students who drop out of high school out of sheer boredom.

Some dropouts will always occur because of financial pressures and lack of mental equipment, but every means must be made to prevent them if possible.

Not only the school drop-outs are at stake. Each year 60 per cent of high school graduates enter the labor market directly, most of them without any semblance of job skills or any knowledge of what it means to work, to say nothing of working with their hands.

This is not to say that the schools must be a training ground for commerce and industry. Far from it. But they must recognize their responsibility to all of the nation's children and not merely those who are headed for college.

The problems of job training are both economic and political. It comes down to how much we are willing to spend as a society for the training and education of the coming generations. And how much we spend is determined by government at all levels.

JOB SECURITY THROUGH TRAINING

The Electrical Workers' Journal, January 1959

Even though the use of electricity has become common-place, it remains one of the truly great marvels of our age, and one of its indispensable elements.

Modern industry is supported by an electrical framework. Today, one of every 20 employed persons is in some branch of the electrical industry and related services. In just the last dozen years the electronics industry has grown from a two-billion-a-year level to more than 13 billion.

And every day we are finding new ways to use electricity. It is making possible developments never dreamed of a few short years ago. Through electronics, a whole new world has been opened to us.

The transistor is only about 10 years old, but look at the advances it has made possible. Nucleonics, cybernetics, thermoelectrics, atomic power: these are terms that forecast even greater changes in the future.

This rapid acceleration in technological progress has a special meaning for IBEW members, whose jobs are directly concerned with the growing electrical and electronics industry. It points up the urgent need for our members to prepare themselves for new methods, new materials, new kinds of jobs that are replacing the old.

Of the many challenging aspects of technological changes, the most significant are human ones, such as developing the newer skills needed.

Training actually is the second step in meeting this problem. First there must be a desire for it.

There are good dollars-and-cents reasons why our members must concentrate on skill improvement. With rapid developments in automation and other technological changes, old skills can become obsolete very quickly. Education and training today cannot stop with the completion of an apprenticeship course.

Experts tell us one of the significant trends of the next few years will be an increase in the skill level of the labor force. The number of skilled workers will increase at a faster rate than the labor force as a whole during the next decade, largely because of the growing need for workers who can build install, operate, maintain, and repair increasingly complicated machinery and equipment.

As the demand for skill goes up, the demand for non-skilled workers will go down. Improved productivity through automation or other technological change makes the unskilled worker less needed. Add to this the expected growth in the labor force (an estimated increase of 10½ million by 1965 over 1955. Industry cannot absorb all these people as non-skilled employees.

The 1958 recession demonstrated this trend. Many companies learned they can get along without some of the employees let off during early 1958. Many of those not being re-hired are the unskilled or semi-skilled workers. The companies are able to maintain or even improve productivity with new equipment and a smaller but more highly-skilled work force. So skill improvement for the IBEW member is very definitely a matter of job security.

Some of our members inevitably are displaced because of technological change or other reason, and the IBEW has fought and is fighting for job security provisions to protect those workers. But, in the long run, the best kind of job protection is training which qualifies a man to keep himself in a productive capacity no matter how fast or how technical the change.

There is another side to this matter which is important not only to the worker and to the IBEW, but to our nation as well.

Scientists say that the free world and the slave world are about equal in material resources. Our advan-

"Missing Piece"

Hope

The horse I ride is minus shoes;
  My hawk no talons bear.
The tools I use are ancient now
  Since missiles pierce the air.
Taft-Hartley act is getting old;
  Its sins are lingering still.
However there's a booster now
  The Landrum-Griffin Bill.

Why do we plasterers have to share
  In guilt we did not shape?
We did not ask for drywall
  Nor premix perfotape.
May Providence relieve our strain
  And eliminate each fear;
Then we'll have "dibs" upon the moon
  And "dot it out" next year.

—JACK JORDAN, Bricklayers Local 12, Oakland, Calif.

tage is the superior skill of our craftsmen.

U. S. Commissioner of Education Lawrence G. Derthick is among those who have emphasized the need.

He has pointed out that we face unparalleled demands in the years ahead for skilled workers and technicians, that unless we have the fullest development of the nation's manpower through education and training, we will not realize the brilliant potentiality of our country.

According to Derthick, job security through proper training may well be a significant factor in our future prosperity. He said, "The maintenance of highly-developed craft skills . . . is essential to our very survival in today's technical world."

APPRENTICESHIP . . . TOMORROW'S INSURANCE!

Joseph J. Delaney, general president, Operating Engineers,
in The International Operating Engineer, February 1959

During our mid-winter meeting early this month few topics excited as much interest and discussion as did the subject of apprenticeship training. Following the comments and observations of our people, I would like to indicate some pertinent observations advanced in two days of open forum discussions.

1. The work of the operating engineers is a skilled craft. To operate the complex machines installed in our institutional buildings, hotels, commercial buildings, office buildings, power houses, plants and other structures requires skill of a high order on the part of a well trained corps of stationary engineers.

Likewise it takes great skill and training for hoisting and portable men to be able to operate their varied machines with the skill and safety the job requires.

We have been called a "service" trade. To those familiar with the skills and training needed in our work, the word "service" is far short of describing our responsibilities.

We must remember that we cannot lay claim to be men of professional — as distinct from service — status unless we do have a program of training. This means not only practical, on-the-job training for our future engineers, but training in book work and the theory of the operation of our machines. It means a thorough knowledge of the way our machines work, why they work, and ways and means of keeping them in proper working order.

2. We are living in a rapidly growing, changing economy. The demands for skilled operators in the industrial age will increase, not decrease. We are entering an age in which more and more work will depend on machines, many of them automatic or automated.

The increasing work of automation can and should mean more work for operating engineers, not less. Even in construction, mechanization is increasing. More work is being done by power methods and tools, and less work by manual methods. As power tools increase both in construction and in manufacture the needs for our type of skills and our type of well-trained manpower increases.

If we are to hold our own, we have to have a flow of skilled manpower filling the vacancies which occur through attrition, retirement, deaths, etc. The demands ahead in road and highway work, in factories and production work are tremendous. We are faced with a great challenge.

3. A new reason for developing a sound training program has emerged under the regulations and rulings of the National Labor Relations Board. The Board has indicated that ours is not a professional or a skilled craft,

but a "service" calling. It has been ruled that we are "service" because, claims the Board, we have no national, uniform, intensive training program!

We have long been proud of our craft and there is not time nor space to develop a refutation of the rulings of the Board in this issue. I would like to note that we are faced with a hard, harsh, legal reality. We are virtually told that we are in danger of losing our craft status unless we have a national uniform training program. We have virtually been told by the NLRB "Get yourself a good training program or else . . . !" The answer to that should be obvious.

Another sound reason for a strong national training program, and this applies with special force to the hoisting and portable phase of our jurisdiction: machines are getting bigger and more costly.

Our men are called upon to man machines which run not into $10,000 but in many tens of thousands and well over a hundred thousand dollars. No employer in his right mind is going to entrust this heavy and expensive equipment to an operator without adequate training.

We recognize that training is not solely our responsibility. Our employers and our industry must share it. We have evidence that our industry is willing to share and to help out. How that help can most effectively be given is a matter yet to be worked out, but it must be worked out in the mutual need of our employers and our members.

A great deal of sound and effective ground work has been laid in fulfilling the basic needs for a great apprenticeship program. We have many able, dedicated operating engineers in both the stationary and the hoisting and portable field. We have the practical and theoretical knowledge to meet the needs of a program. Our job is to coordinate, to plan and weld into one great usable and useful program our many skills and knowledge in this training field.

A sound apprenticeship program today is life insurance for our union tomorrow. With a good program we will survive and grow. Without one we are endangering our very life.

PURDUE RECORD BREAKERS

Plumbers' Journal, September 1959

All previous records were broken at the United Association's sixth annual international apprentice contest held at Purdue University Aug. 10-14, 1959.

"This has been our greatest success so far," announced General President Peter T. Schoemann. His appraisal was universally shared by more than 600 union officials, industry leaders and instructors who attended the award ceremonies in the university theater.

The distinguished audience broke out into sustained applause as the 97 apprentice contestants marched into the theater and filed into their reserved seats in the front rows to hear the announcement of the results of their labors in the classrooms and shops of Purdue.

Here were the cream of the crop of the fifth-year apprentices in the United States and Canada—all of them winners of state-wide and provincial contests in their home areas. They had worked at top speed and under terrific tension for five days at their appointed projects, not only for personal reward but for the honor of their local union. Now the moment of decision was at hand.

Heretofore the contest was confined to plumber apprentices and pipe fitter apprentices. This year a third category was added—sprinkler fitters.

Each of the apprentices was called up to the platform by Pres. Schoemann, introduced to the audience and handed a certificate. Then Dr. H. S. Belman, head of the Industrial

Education staff at Purdue, presented certificates to the 327 instructors— the largest number ever enrolled— who had taken a week's course at the university in the most modern teaching methods.

At this point, Pres. Schoemann reached into his pocket for sealed envelopes containing the coded numbers of the winners, who were then identified by name from a master list. As each winner was announced, the contestant came to the platform and was handed a check written on the spot by Secretary-Treasurer William C. O'Neill. The decisions of the impartial judges had been kept a top secret, and not even the officers of the United Association knew the results until the envelopes were opened in plain sight of the audience.

When the cheers and the picture-taking had subsided, Pres. Schoemann proceeded to the next order of business—the award of plaques to the local unions which had produced the winners.

More prizes came next—from representatives of seven industry associations to those apprentices who had shown outstanding skill in special projects.

Opening the award ceremonies was the showing of an AFL-CIO film, "Americans at Work," hailing the educational program conducted by the United Association. The film, which is being shown over more than 100 television stations throughout the nation, captivated the audience.

Pres. Schoemann then made a few opening remarks. He said that the Purdue program this year obviously has been the U. A.'s greatest success so far. This success, he emphasized, would not have been possible without the active assistance of industry leaders and employers.

It is usual to achieve such a high degree of labor-management cooperation, the U. A.'s general president pointed out, in these days when strife is spreading in many industries and when pressure is being exerted upon Congress to enact anti-labor legislation.

Pres. Schoemann expressed his appreciation to the large group of instructors who had come to Purdue from all over the Continent to learn the latest and most effective teaching methods.

Turning to the apprentices, he told them "your real job is just beginning." He asked them to remember that they had received educational advantages far and beyond those available to the "old-timers" in the trade, and concluded:

"We look to you to carry on—to discharge whatever tasks are assigned to you with honor and ability, to uphold the high principles of your union and to take full advantage of the good things, the fine training, you have received."

Secretary-Treasurer O'Neill, emphasized that the United Association has become more than a trade union.

"Today it is also an educational institution," he said.

The United Association has 28,000 apprentices enrolled in 760 local unions in the United States and Canada, Mr. O'Neill disclosed. In addition to thousands of local agreements, the United Association also has national agreements with the six major employer associations, he said.

George E. Davis, director of Adult Education at Purdue, recalled that when the late U. A. General President Martin P. Durkin selected Purdue as the site for the annual apprentice contest, university officials had no idea it would grow to its present size.

One of the big hits of the week's program at Purdue was the first distribution of a new book published by the National Joint Pipefitter Apprenticeship Committee — a complete manual of all the mathematical, scientific and mechanical courses which form the curriculum of apprentices. This is the first time any trade union has undertaken and completed such a monumental task. The book, which has about 500 large pages, many containing color illustrations and charts, is the product of six years of preparation. It was hailed at Purdue as a boon not only to the young men learning the trade but to journeymen as well.

The International Training Fund, through which the United Association generates labor-management support of its educational program, has now granted a total of $725,900 to 85 local joint apprenticeship committees for the improvement of their training facilities and operations.

Meeting at Purdue University during the apprentice contest, the ITF Trustees approved eight new applications. These involved grants of $90,000 for the purchase of new training equipment and materials, for visual training aids, supplement-ing the salaries of instructors and for the purchase of textbooks.

The ITF was created March 1, 1956 by agreement between the United Association and the National Constructors Association. It is the first national trust of this character in the collective history of America.

Under the terms of the agreement now prevailing, each signatory employer contributes two - and - a - half cents for each hour's work performed by journeymen and apprentices on his payroll.

The money thus raised is administered by a Joint Board of Trustees composed of five representatives of the U. A. and five of the National Constructors Association. The first grants were made only a year ago.

BRICKLAYER APPRENTICE CHAMPION CROWNED IN SAN FRANCISCO

The Bricklayer, Mason and Plasterer, June 1959

The country's outstanding bricklayer apprentices gathered in San Francisco last month to compete for the title of National Bricklayer Apprentice Champion for 1959.

When the final brick was laid on the fourth day of the contest, held in conjunction with the AFL-CIO Union Industries Show, the three San Francisco judges went into a huddle and selected Donald Zimmer of Local 45, Buffalo, New York as the 1959 champion. Like champions from past contests, Zimmer received $500 in cash and the Belden Trophy, presented annually by the Structural Clay Products Institute, national association of brick and structural tile manufacturers.

Finishing second, third and fourth, respectively, were Charles Maurice of Fort Worth, Texas; Alfonso Zanni of Waukegan, Ill., and Kenneth Smith of Fresno, California.

The annual competition, eleventh to be sponsored by the B. M. and P. I. U., attracted thousands of San Franciscans and many from other sections of the Bay area.

At a dinner tendered by the Inter-national for the apprentices on the night preceding the start of the contest, many noted Californians and other distinguished guests were present to tell what a fine thing they thought the annual apprentice contests were. Representing the International at the dinner, and at the contest which followed, were Secretary John J. Murphy, Treasurer Thomas F. Murphy, and First Vice President William R. Connors.

Although the field of entries was comparatively small this year, it was very fast, and the three San Francisco judges, all journeymen members of Local 7, had to take very close readings throughout the elimination rounds of the contest. The four boys who reached the finals, Zimmer, Maurice, Zanni and Smith, were as finely trained a group as ever appeared in a national contest. There were 27 contestants this year, as against an average of 40 in past years. The smaller number this year does not indicate diminished interest in the contest, but rather reflects the fact that the trip to San Francisco from the east coast is a costly one for some of the smaller locals and sponsors.

The daily elimination rounds commenced early in the afternoon, and each morning at 11 o'clock the apprentices were thoroughly briefed in the procedures that were to be followed.

San Francisco, famous for its year-round "air conditioning," provided ideal working conditions for the apprentices, permitting the boys to function at peak efficiency.

The 1959 champion, Donald Zimmer, is 19 years old and lives with his parents in Buffalo. He is a graduate of McKinley High School, and is attending night sessions at Erie Technical Institute, Buffalo, taking engineering courses. His father works for Civil Defense, and there are five other brothers, none of whom is a bricklayer. Zimmer's sponsor at the contest was Daniel J. Higgins, chairman of the Buffalo apprenticeship committee.

Speaking informatively over a public address system to the crowds outside the enclosure in which the apprentice carried out their work assignments, were Treasurer Thomas F. Murphy and William F. Roark. Their talks focused attention on the B. M. and P. I. U.'s program of training skilled journeymen bricklayers. It was pointed out to the crowds that the young men competing in the contest were among 14,000 between 17 and 24 who are engaged in bricklayer apprentice training in the United States. It also was pointed out that the apprentice studies 144 hours in related classroom instruction in blueprint reading, the use of tools, mathematics, mortars and cost estimating.

A considerable volume of literature also was distributed at the contest, including thousands of copies of a pamphlet titled "How Many Bricks a Day?" published by the Allied Masonry Council. This frank discussion of bricklayer production points up the fact that production is up today, due in part to the bricklayer's "whole bag of new tools and tricks." The pamphlet also pointed out the differences involved in constructing old-style load-bearing walls that were often three and four feet thick, with only one-ninth of the brick exposed, and in constructing today's masonry curtain walls.

Prior to announcing the winners, the International sponsored a strictly informal bricklaying contest between two models from the Union Industries Show. A three-piece Dixieland band also helped to pull the crowds to watch the proceedings and see Don Zimmer crowned as the 1959 champion.

Int'l Treasurer Thomas F. Murphy presided at these ceremonies, and again regaled the crowd with his observations on the bricklaying abilities of the two models. For their part, the models appeared to enjoy slapping mortar on bricks. Lending them a helping hand was Vincent Guise, secretary of the California State Conference of Bricklayers, who appeared to enjoy the assignment.

For the opening of the Union Industries Show on May 1, which also was the starting day of the apprenticeship contest, a full complement of government and labor leaders was present, including California Governor Edmund G. "Pat" Brown and AFL-CIO Secretary-Treasurer William F. Schnitzler. Joseph Lewis, secretary of the AFL-CIO Union Label and Service Trades Dept., presided at the opening day ceremonies.

Secretary-Treasurer Schnitzler of the AFL-CIO said in his remarks that the show was "living proof that here in America, operating under the free enterprise system, labor and management can work together, live together and share together the wealth that they produce together."

Schnitzler told the large crowd that the union label, shop-card and service button are more than "a mere advertising gimmick." They represented, he said, "an organized effort by the trade union movement to provide a solid and substantial market for the products and services of cooperating employers."

THE ITU UPDATES ITS APPRENTICE TRAINING PROGRAM

The Typographical Journal, July 1960

Legislation was enacted last year at the ITU convention at Philadelphia which paved the way for launching a credit system of apprentice training. This method is based on competency in each classification of work and displaces the time element followed for so many years.

Under the old system, at the end of a six-year apprenticeship, apprentices were transferred to journeyman status—competent or not. Applicants for journeyman membership now must be fully qualified, having acquired not less than the minimum of credits, before being eligible for transfer.

This is a drastic departure from a long-established policy on apprentice training, but the major overhaul in the setup has accomplished, in part, what the new approach was intended to produce.

It is designed to reactivate dormant apprentice and joint apprentice committees; stimulate interest in apprentice training; minimize the need for accepting related trades applicants; supply the employer with more and better trained ITU personnel and attempt to equalize the percentage of ITU-trained apprentices transferred to journeyman status as opposed to the percentage of journeymen lost to the trade through retirements, deaths and other pursuits.

If we are to obtain, maintain and recapture jurisdiction over work which is rightfully ours, our members must be occupationally competent.

This is essential to the welfare of the individual as well as to the security and economic well-being of the organization.

Our apprentice-training programs must be kept in tune with the technological developments in the printing and publishing industry.

In establishing a training center in Indianapolis, and through those set up on a local level, we have advanced rapidly in scientific and technical know-how. We must continue to increase our knowledge.

How well we will realize the potential of this advance in terms of the well-being of our members, depends in large measure on how effectively our members as individuals are able to use the new tools.

It is vitally important to the ITU that we recognize our manpower capacities and develop them well. We must improve our competence, present and prospective.

The apprentice is going to play a mighty important role in carrying out the traditions and principles of the ITU in the future. Make him a part of the organization of which he is a part.

Emphasis on the need for, and more responsibility on the part of, a joint apprentice committee are of prime importance if the multiple purpose of the program is to be accomplished.

We are opposed to spelling out a training program in a contract. By so doing, the committee is frequently handcuffed, so to speak, because of the time element.

In eliminating a spelled-out program in a contract the committee has more latitude in establishing different programs in different shops, even setting up different programs for different apprentices when advisable. The program decided upon need not necessarily be incorporated in the contract.

When including a program in a contract the following is suggested:

The training program of printer apprentices shall include thorough training under journeymen on all phases of floor work such as hand composition, makeup, markup, imposition and proofreading. Where paste-makeup is used or where training on paste-makeup is available it shall be taught during the first five years of apprenticeship.

In addition, at least one year of the training program must be devoted to training on one or more of the following: Linecasting machines, monotype keyboard and caster, teletypesetter tape perforator, or phototypesetting keyboard.

In the above language you will note that it does not specify the length of time to be devoted to any particular classification. We are trying to discard language that states the apprentice must be employed on a certain type work during the eighth six weeks or the ninth six weeks, etc.

We believe that in advancing an apprentice consistent with his aptitude, ability and initiative, more alert young men will be attracted to the trade and competent, qualified journeymen produced.

The credit system can accomplish both purposes of upgrading procedure. Upgrading serves two purposes: first, to place the apprentice in a higher wage bracket as a financial reward for applying himself; second, to shorten the apprenticeship period.

If an apprentice is advanced in his training as soon as he proves him-

self in a particular phase, he will be automatically shortening his time through application of his talents. If each advance carried an automatic wage increase the end result would be the same as upgrading.

When an apprentice completes the ITU Course of Lessons in Printing and is judged competent in five work classifications under the credit system, he is eligible to sign a certificate of transfer.

Transferring apprentices to the journeyman roll requires a covering letter, accompanying the certificate of transfer, listing the five or more classifications in which the apprentice is competent.

The certificate of transfer eliminates the period of waiting for an apprentice to be obligated as a journeyman at a union meeting.

Apprentices are obligated as members of the union when they become registered. Re-obligation as journeymen is unnecessary. Therefore, transfer of the apprentice to journeyman status can be effected at any time.

Upon signing the transfer the apprentice assumes all obligations and responsibilities of journeyman membership and his continuous membership starts with date on transfer.

5 | SAFETY

LABOR'S STAKE IN SAFETY

Al J. Hayes, I. A. M. president, in The Machinist, November 7, 1957

We all profess to agree that human life is not cheap; that man is not something to be sacrificed to a machine. And yet these ethical principles are not always applied in day to day life nor are they self-enforcing.

On the whole, the story of factory employment in the nineteenth century—and through the early years of the twentieth century—was a pretty ghastly one. It did not seem to matter how many men, women and children were killed or crippled in the course of a day. There were always more waiting at the gates the next morning—driven by raw poverty to plead for a chance to take the place of the injured and dead.

Change—when it came—was not the result of any regeneration of moral and ethical conviction on the part of employers as a whole. It came rather because society as a whole was thoroughly revolted. It came because the American people were finally shocked enough to try to correct a condition that had prevailed—and grown worse—for a period of one hundred years.

And so we finally got factory laws and workmen's compensation — and an organized effort to make the mines, factories and mills of America safer places in which to work. But of all the types of legislation that were aimed at this objective, I think that workmen's compensation was the key. Because until employers were made directly and financially responsible for the results of workers' ac-

cidents, they had no economic reason to try to prevent accidents.

It is my opinion that our industrial safety program throughout the nation rests entirely on how good and how effective our workmen's compensation and our occupational disease laws are.

There are, of course, many good economic rationalizations for industrial safety. Industrial accidents add all kinds of direct and indirect costs to production. There is the cost of hiring and training a new employee, the cost of damaged equipment, the time lost by other employees when an accident occurs. I have heard all these justifications.

But I say that it wasn't until accident prevention was reinforced with workmen's compensation and occupational disease legislation that employers really became safety conscious.

This nation has tried to deal with a national problem by having forty-eight separate, conflicting—and in a sense — *competing* state statutes. There is no doubt that workmen's compensation is one of the kinds of labor legislation that various states use to compete with one another to attract industry.

In fact, whenever trade unions go to the state legislatures to try to get improvement or expansion of existing laws, we are invariably met with employer counter-arguments. These are to the effect that any improvement in coverage or benefits will shove industry into the waiting and sympathetic arms of states

125

more concerned with payrolls—than with the people on those payrolls.

Certainly the health and safety of the nation's work force should not be a pawn in any state's bid for new industry. But they are under a system that allows Mississippi or Arkansas or Georgia to compete for industry by offering low workmen's compensation benefits and a minimum of safety regulation at the plant level. Why should an employer pay $45 a week for a temporary total disability in Illinois—when he can go to Arkansas and pay $25 a week for the same injury?

The lack of a strong equitable workmen's compensation system leads, quite naturally, to a corresponding lack of interest in enforcement of safety codes and regulations. In many states the Bureau of Factory Inspection — by whatever name it goes under — is little more than a sop to the conscience of the state legislature. In fact, the inspection service in such states is not only understaffed, but underpaid, untrained, and on the whole, technically unqualified to do a competent job in a field that needs a high degree of competency.

And the situation in occupational disease coverage is much worse. Almost none of the ways by which man makes a living is completely free of some hazard to physical or mental health.

The risk of occupational disease grows greater every day as industrial processes become more and more dependent upon and saturated with toxic fumes, vapors, gases, acids and alkalies. Every day thousands of workers are being exposed to everything from arsenic to mercury poisoning, from sulphuric acid to chromium poisoning.

Thousands of workers have no physical or legal protection whatsoever against the chemicals and poisons that are slowly killing them. In fact, many are not even aware of the risk they are running. They will find out when it is too late. And in many states they have no right to

compensation under the occupational disease law.

I recently read a statement to the effect that "the scope of occupational disease is vast almost beyond calculation" and "it comes, in fact, unpleasantly close to being the major public health problem of our time."

If that is so—and I for one am inclined to believe it—it is a tragic commentary on our time and on the ethics of a business community that has done so little about it.

I am not exaggerating when I say that industry has taken a "head-in-the-sand" attitude up to now. It has tried to cover up occupational diseases rather than to isolate, prevent and care for them.

There has been very little research—either governmental or private—in the field. The Public Health Service, for example, spends less than one cent for each worker each year, on the prevention of occupational diseases. And the National Institute of Health, which has made hundreds of research grants during the past three or four years, has made less than half a dozen in the field of occupational health.

There is an iron curtain of secrecy around this whole subject. Not only does industry, with few exceptions, fail to support and subsidize research in occupational diseases, but men who have tried to do independent research find that it is virtually impossible to get facts, information, or cooperation from the people in industry.

Worse still, if a research project does tend to show a correlation between employment and disease, the authors find it almost impossible to get their work published or distributed. The result is a deplorable lack of information about occupational disease. And we are years behind other countries in this respect. In fact, only recently one of the experts in this field informed me that research in pneumoconiosis in this country is fully twenty-five years behind that of Great Britain.

I can only assume that industry, with a few exceptions, actively op-poses objective research and free interchange of information on occupational diseases because it is more afraid of the possibility of paying compensation benefits than it is that workers will die from lack of proper information and adequate precaution.

Let me give a few examples. There is some medical evidence that the chemicals used in the dye industry and in the manufacture of synthetic rubber cause or contribute to cancer of the bladder. One of these —amine—is so dangerous that it has been outlawed for all industrial uses in Britain since 1951. But efforts to prove and to publicize and restrict the dangers of this deadly acid have hit a stone wall of stubborn resistance in this country. Many of the companies concerned not only have refused to try to find out if amine does, in fact, contribute to cancer of the bladder, but have strongly resisted independent research.

In another large industry the incidence of lung cancer is very high. According to unpublished research reports there are strong indications that the dust inhalation from the basic product contributes to this condition. Here again, the industry has been traditionally reluctant to cooperate in a full-scale scientific study of this curious correlation. The reluctance to do research in health hazards recurs in industry after industry.

Even worse, I think, is the fact that when workers succumb to some horrible disease, we are treated to the spectacle of company doctors who testify that the disease couldn't possibly have been caused by their employment.

I know that doctors are supposed to be above reproach in our society and, indeed many of them are. But as a labor official I know too many cases in which company doctors testified against workers and for management in occupational disease cases even though they knew their testimony was biased and unobjective, to say the least.

We cannot help but wonder wheth-er the lust for profits has made many men forget the real purpose of life. Is it production and profit— or the well-being of the individual? If there is conflict between the two do we sacrifice production and profit —or the well-being of the individual?

The ethical answer is obvious. But reaching the logical, ethical conclusion is more difficult.

We could make a start by enacting comprehensive federal workmen's compensation and occupational disease legislation to replace the chaos that results from having forty-eight different state systems. But I have no hopes for such a constructive approach in the foreseeable future. I am afraid the insurance lobby, and the employer groups that profit from weak administration are too strong for us at this time. So we'll just have to make that one of our long range objectives.

But there are some things we can do right now. We can try, for example, to have programs set up in the National Institute of Health and in the Public Health Service which would recognize the importance of occupational disease — and which put the research effort in this nation on a par with that of other civilized industrial nations.

If we cannot get decent factory inspection from the states then we in the labor movement must resort to self-help. Already many unions are thinking in terms of collective bargaining clauses to require the employer to adopt safety standards set by the American Standards Association as the minimum acceptable in the shop.

We are also prepared to bargain for more supplemental injury benefits when the compensation provided by state laws is not adequate to sustain a worker and his family. Although our efforts will directly benefit only the seventeen million organized workers, perhaps they will release new pressures that will eventually result in improved legislation benefitting all workers.

A DEAF EAR

Trainman News, March 9, 1959

Accidents on the railroads of the nation are on the upswing. The frightening result is that a greater number of passengers on the trains and railroad workers are being killed or injured in these mishaps.

Last year, 61 passengers lost their lives in accidents on the railroads and 1,642 other passengers suffered injuries, according to the Interstate Commerce Commission. The total in 1957 was 15 killed and 1,617 injured.

In 1958, the ICC report shows, 187 railroad workers had their lives snuffed out in accidents on the silvery ribbons and 12,899 others were injured. The figures add up to 13,086 "rails" who were killed or incurred injuries on the job.

Looking back to 1957, there were 196 "rails" killed and 12,252 injured —a total of 12,448.

The ICC figures show a substantial — and disturbing — rise in the number of accidents on the railroads in 1958 as compared with 1957.

Who is to blame?

The railroads, says BRT National Legislative Representative Harry See, who heads the Committee on Safety of the Railway Labor Executives' Association.

For more than two years, the association has urged rail management to join hands with rail labor in an endeavor to tackle the rail accident problem, but to no avail.

Tired of management's aloofness and disinterest, the 23 rail labor unions which comprise RLEA set out last fall and named their own Committee on Safety.

Railroad workers have long reported from all sectors of the nation that managements are ignoring rail safety practices. The truth of the matter shows up in the ICC figures concerning deaths and injuries on the railroads.

At every opportunity, the railroads attempt to undermine and abolish Full Crew Laws in the various states. These laws, won by the Brotherhood of Railroad Trainmen and other rail labor unions—with the railroads offering all opposition possible—deliver a great measure of safety to raiload operations.

During the recent recession months, the carriers lopped off thousands of employees, including many whose jobs were directly connected with safety on the rails. With the upturn in traffic as business conditions improved, the railroads in many instances did not recall these workers.

It's no surprise to "rails" that accidents are on the rise on the railroads today. They have had a front row seat to see what has been happening. Meanwhile, railroad management turns a deaf ear and walks away.

THE NO. 1 KILLER OF COAL MINERS

United Mine Workers Journal, June 1, 1960

Further grim evidence of the necessity for amending the Federal Coal Mine Safety Act is provided in the official Bureau of Mines fatality statistics for April, 1960.

The No. 1 killer of coal miners— roof falls—snuffed out the lives of 17 men in that month. Of the total there were ten men who lost their

lives in so-called Title I mines, those employing 14 or less men. That represents close to 60 per cent of the roof-fall deaths for the month.

These small mines, which are not subject to closure orders by Federal coal mine inspectors, had nearly as many roof deaths in April alone as they had in the first three months of 1960, the Bureau report disclosed.

The UMWA has opposed the exemption of these mines from mandatory safety provisions of the Federal law ever since the law was enacted in 1952. The Union has fought now for eight years to make the operators of these so-called small mines subject to the same safety rules as the Title II mines that employ 15 or more men.

Although these small mines produce only about 12 per cent of the underground coal they consistently kill nearly one-third of the men whose lives are lost each year in coal mine accidents.

Rock and coal falls claimed 11 lives in Title I mines in the first three months of the year. The ten deaths in April—six in two disasters that occurred the same day in Maryland and Kentucky—pushed the roof fall toll in small mines to 21 for four months.

There are 66 fatalities caused by falls of roof, rib and face in American coal mines in the January-April period this year.

The U. S. Senate already has acted on the UMWA-backed amendment to the Safety Act that would subject the Title I mines to closure orders by Federal inspectors. The Senate voted 80-4 to improve the law.

The vital safety legislation is now bottled up in the House of Representatives labor subcommittee on safety and compensation.

There is no excuse for further delay. The Senate has acted, the facts are in and the needless deaths continue in the small mines.

ICE COVERS DETROIT; 29 LETTER CARRIERS INJURED IN ONE DAY

Postal Record, March 1959

Rain and freezing weather have kept Detroit letter carriers on ice since the first of December. The *Detroit Times* quoted James H. Rademacher, Jr., president of Branch One as stating that "160 carriers had been hurt in falls on icy sidewalks and porches since Dec. 1, the worst record of injuries in the history of the Detroit post office."

Rademacher declared that of the 160 carriers injured since Dec. 1, 32 had suffered fractures, six with broken legs. There were 29 injuries in one single day.

The dangerous nature of a letter carrier's work is well illustrated by what has happened in Detroit. A few years ago we had a similar streak of weather in St. Louis, where many injuries occurred in a short space of time.

The hazards of a letter carrier's duties should be considered when the pay of letter carriers is under consideration. Trying to balance a sack of mail and keep control of a handful of mail while walking on sheer ice is a chore for an acrobat.

FACTORY DIN SPLITTING MORE WORKERS' EARS

Hollace Ransdell in AFL-CIO News, June 23, 1956

It's a noisy world we live in, and every day it's growing noisier—on the streets, at home, in the air—but most of all in the factories.

In big and small plants across the nation, industrial workers have long had to endure what seems a terrific roar to anybody coming into one of them from outside.

Workers have been putting up with the racket without protest, as something that couldn't be helped, or that you finally get used to.

But if you ask them what they

mind most about their work, many will say—the noise.

There are upward of 400 noisy trades and occupations where there is danger of ear damage.

Not only is the loud noise in a boiler shop, shipyard, jet aircraft plant, forge shop and other job places likely to harm the hearing, but injury can also be caused by less loud but higher frequency noises, such as the whir of textile machinery and the high speed ringing sounds of a saw in a lumber mill, among many others.

The boilermaker's trade has the longest and worst record of deafening workers. Boilermaker's deafness was long accepted as practically inevitable after years on the job and was even taken as a kind of proof of experience at the trade.

The Boilermakers since the late 40's have been active in pressing for improvements in state workmen's compensation laws involving occu-pational deafness and have fought many a struggle in the courts to win compensation for its members suffering from job-induced loss of hearing.

* * *

"It used to be that the paper maker could be identified by the fingers missing from one or both hands." said Pres. Paul L. Phillips of the Paper Makers at a labor-management safety conference.

'Today he can be recognized by his hearing aid," Phillips told the group. "This has become a serious problem, and it grows progressively worse as more and more machines runs faster and faster."

"Industrial noise is perhaps the most serious environmental health problem confronting American industry today," Dr. Charles F. Shook, medical director, Owens-Illinois Glass Co., told a recent round-table discussion on noise in industry held by the National Industrial Conference Board.

24 KILLED — WHY?

Justice, April 1, 1958

This time there was no miracle. This time they died. This time 24 human beings, 18 of them members of the ILGWU, lost their lives in a tragic fire on March 19, at the Monarch underwear shop on New York's lower Broadway.

Five months ago, an explosion rocked West 36th Street, in the heart of New York's garment center. A chemical button-spray device had blown up. Fire Commissioner Edward F. Cavanagh, standing in the midst of the smoldering rubble, told the editor of JUSTICE: "It is a miracle that no one was killed." We warned editorially at that time that miracles are not enough, that the safety and lives of garment workers must not be dependent on luck.

Now the city is stunned, shocked. There are calls for action. But what kind of action?

We must know how these tragedies happen—and why—before we can take effective steps to prevent their repetition.

The tragedy at 623 Broadway was the fourth of its kind in little over a year.

On Jan. 24, 1957, in New Haven, in a state noted as the home of insurance companies, an 85-year-old wooden structure went up in flames. Fifteen workers in garment shops lost their lives. The building had been inspected shortly before the fire. It had been found safe—although it had no fire-sprinklers. It had been found safe—even though its fire escape was faulty, with a jammed drop ladder that caused the death of many. And the law did not require fire drills.

On Oct. 29, 1957, the boom of an explosion shattered West 36th Street. The spray plant and its equipment had been approved as meeting the requirements of law. Dazed workers fearful of riding the elevators, not knowing any other means of egress, huddled in the darkened staircase until rescued by firemen. The miracle was that none died.

On Nov. 13, 1957, another explosion and flash fire occurred in an inspected and approved spray plant in Brooklyn. This time there was a casualty.

On March 19, 1958, 24 died in the Monarch underwear shop, 47 years to the week after 146 garment workers died in the historic Triangle Shirtwaist Co. fire only six blocks away.

WHY DID THEY DIE?

Why had not violations—structural or otherwise — been found in the building that became their flaming sepulchre?

Why was a clean bill of health given to a wooden-floored loft, laid out like a wind tunnel, with an 8 x 10 x 10 foot oven in a 77-year old structure and with an entire shop of garment workers on the floor above—where all the casualties occurred—who never knew how close they were to sudden death during their working hours?

Why was there no fire-retarding ceiling, let alone a wall, to stop the flames from eating upward from the third floor to the roof?

Why does the state law exempt New York City from holding fire drills in such structures if the city, in turn, does not make them compulsory?

Why was there no sprinkler system on any of the floors, no chemical fire extinguishers, only pails of water, on the floor with the oven?

Why were there no fire escapes so that a heroic employer, keeping his employees — for a time — from panicking, was compelled to smash windows from whose ledges workers hung until rescued?

Why didn't the approved stairway door on the third floor close and keep the approved stairwell from filling up with the choking smoke that drove workers back? Why, if it is true that workers could have come down those stairs, did not their rescuers come up them?

Why are not explosives and highly combustible materials banned from city loft buildings? Why don't precautionary signs warn against them and point out emergency exits, in several languages and in pictographs, understandable by all?

Forty-seven years ago, New York City Fire Chief Edward F. Croker stood among the bodies of those who had leaped eight and nine stories from the fire in the Triangle shop to death on the sidewalk below. He choked with tears of anger.

He had warned of the imminence of that tragedy. He had asked that fire-sprinkler systems be installed in all commercial and industrial enterprises, even in fireproof buildings. But only days before the Triangle conflagration, he had been castigated for this at a rally of real estate owners. He had asked for fire escapes—and had been laughed down by cocksure builders and architects. He had asked for fire drills—and the answer had come roaring back at him that this would be a waste of time.

Forty-seven years later, the editor of this newspaper stood in a chilling rain as darkness came on at the corner of Mercer and Houston Streets, saw brave firemen face a hell, fought back his own tears as he watched them, weary and begrimed, lower charred bodies of garment workers, in wicker baskets, out of the gaping windows of the Monarch underwear shop.

What difference have these 47 years made?

Now, as then, there were no sprinklers. Now, as then, there were no fire drills, no fire escapes. If there had been these things, the tragedy would have been avoided. Now, as then, the dead lay smashed on the sidewalk.

Buildings may be fireproofed—but not human beings, and not the stuff they work on to earn their daily bread. The Triangle fire, as Chief Croker stressed almost half a century ago, occurred in a fireproof structure that suffered only small damage.

Obviously, there are faults in safety laws which put the stamp of approval on conditions under which lives have been lost. There can be only approval for Fire Commissioner Cavanagh's tightened-up inspection campaign and for Mayor Wagner's legislative proposals. But faulty laws, even with the finest enforcement, can be as costly as the best laws with poor enforcement.

As after the Triangle fire, the city is now awake to the danger which can at any moment flare up into tragedy again. There is need to act quickly, decisively and without compromise where the choice is between property and profits, on the one hand, and life itself on the other.

SHOP FIRES DOWN 18%; DRILLS MANDATORY

Justice, October 15, 1959

Proof of the effectiveness of the Garment Workers' Shop Fire Warden program and its further extension were announced last week. In a special report to the ILGWU, the New York Fire Department declared that the number of fires in women's garment shops in New York City had been reduced by 18 per cent. The ILGWU, at the same time, called upon its affiliates to write mandatory shop fire drills into all new union agreements.

The Report from the Fire Department covered the year ending August, 1959, corresponding to the first year of the operation of the ILGWU warden program. As compared to the year ending August, 1958, the number of garment shop fires had been cut by 17.7 per cent. In the same comparison the number of general structural fires in the city had risen by 9.3 per cent.

"This is positive proof of the effectiveness of the industrial fire warden program," New York Fire Commissioner Edward F. Cavanagh, Jr., declared. "Thanks to the splendid cooperation given our department by the ILGWU we have been able to make this remarkable improvement even in an industry handling combustible materials under crowded conditions."

A letter to all affiliates from General Secretary-Treasurer Louis Stulberg points out that the ILGWU convention last May authorized the General Executive Board "to expand and effectuate the machinery of fire wardens in our industry."

In line with this authorization, the GEB directed the General Office to inform all affiliates of the future inclusion in contracts of a fire drill provision. Suggested provisions are:

"A volunteer shop fire warden selected from among the employees shall be authorized to inspect the work premises for safety purposes as recommended by the local fire department, to make form reports where these are called for and to work with the employer and the local fire department for the removal of safety hazards.

"Semi-annual shop fire drills are to be held (preferably in March and September) in which workers are to leave the building or move into safety areas or fire towers as recommended by the local fire department. Workers hired in the period between drills are to be instructed as to the location of all means of egress from the shop."

The ILGWU shop fire warden program was developed cooperatively with the New York Fire Department following the tragic fire at the Monarch Undergarment shop at 623 Broadway in New York.

Under the shop warden plan inspections are made twice a year. The results are filed with the Fire Commissioner and made the basis of immediate shop inspections by the Department where hazards have been found. Cooperative efforts are made with employers to remove the hazards.

LABOR SEEKS TO PREVENT ACCIDENTS

P. L. (Roy) Siemiller, I.A.M. vice president, in The Machinist, June 19, 1958

Labor's interests in accident prevention are practically as broad as the whole area of human activity in which accidents occur. We believe that safety is not divisible, that the prevention of accidents everywhere— on the streets and highways, in the schools and in the air as well as at the work place — is an inter-related job. In teaching and promoting safety we can't stop at the factory gate.

An important example of the wide range of labor's interest in accident prevention is the legislative program for safety and industrial health which was adopted by the AFL-CIO convention last December.

• Press for a law to create a Fed-

eral Accident Prevention Bureau to establish, through tri-partite boards, national safety standards.

• Call upon the states to approve flexible safety codes that keep pace with technological changes and are adaptable to different industries and individual factories.

• Cooperate in all community and national efforts to control off - job hazards, especially in the field of traffic safety.

• Maintain Federal control over the hazards created by atomic energy.

• Demand Government funds for safety research, inspection and enforcement.

HOW LABOR CAN HELP MAKE SHOP JOBS SAFER

Paul L. Phillips, president of the United Papermakers and Paperworkers, in United Paper, October 31, 1959

It is the individual worker who has the most at stake in the field of reducing industrial accidents, for it is the individual on the job who has at stake his life, his sight, his hearing and his health. But it is the union which must get through the complacent "It can't happen to me" attitude of the individual worker and create a desire by the group as a whole for a positive program. Moreover, once a joint safety program is underway, the union must see to it that the goal is kept in proper focus, so that the safety program is not allowed to slow down.

The union is a human institution concerned with human welfare, and because it has the power to bring workers to a status of equality with their employers, it is the union's job to preserve proper priorities in safety programs.

Top priority, of course, must go to human needs. The union cannot allow the safety program to be neutralized by management making pro-

ductive efficiency a matter of prime consideration. By the same token, the union cannot allow its own internal petty politics to sabotage the effectiveness of a safety program.

Let me be specific on this last point, because I think it does deserve attention from trade unionists. It is easy for us to spank management, but it is equally important that we take some of our own bad boys out to the woodshed for an occasional paddling.

Let's take the case where a union negotiates with management and gets the company to agree to spend money on safety equipment. Because the union was persuasive or perhaps because an accident occurred, management gets the equipment and makes it mandatory that employees use it.

Well, it always happens that we have a few assorted characters in the ranks who choose to ignore these protective devices or who refuse to wear the safety gear. There will be discipline, and then there will be loud protests from the disciplined workers.

When they are disciplined, it often happens that some union official will storm to the defense of the offenders, demanding grievance processing, arbitration in some cases.

I think we've got to put a stop to that kind of irresponsibility—and I'm talking about us in the labor movement. We've got enough good causes to fight for, rather than wasting our energy and ammunition fighting for the privilege of permitting members to kill and mutilate themselves and their fellow workers.

Let's get every conceivable safety device we can into our mills and plants, let's educate employees in their use, and then let's help enforce reasonable regulations to put those safety devices to work.

THE UNION CONTRACT AND SAFETY

George Brown in AFL-CIO American Federationist, June 1960

Every year since shortly after the end of World War II nearly 2 million American workers have suffered on-the-job injuries serious enough to keep them from their daily employment.

For about 14,000 of them each year injury means working days are over, for their injuries are fatal. In addition, about 85,000 are permanently disabled. There is tragic economic loss too—some $2 billion a year alone for the workers, almost countless millions of man-days in production.

Last year was not better than usual. In fact, it was a little worse than 1958, a reflection at least in part of recovery from the sharp drop in employment that marked the recession and resulted in a lowering of the "exposure rate." Preliminary estimates of the Bureau of Labor Statistics are that 1,970,000 workers suffered injuries in 1959 serious enough to keep them from their jobs for at least one day after the day they were hurt. In 1958 there were 1,820,000 such injuries. The preliminary industrial accident rate for 1959 was 11.9 for each one million employee manhours worked, an increase of one full point over 1958.

The trade union movement regards these grim figures with the seriousness they deserve. After all, it doesn't profit a union much to win good wages and pensions for a member if he isn't going to be around to enjoy them.

The 1959 AFL-CIO convention "put a union label on safety" by directing its Committee on Safety and Occupational Health, headed by Vice Pres. Richard F. Walsh, to establish an AFL-CIO trade union safety movement.

It is "dedicated to the principle of cooperation between labor and management so that progress shall be achieved by positive prevention of accidental death and injuries rather than through tragedy."

Delegates to the committee's first conference requested a survey to find out just how many contracts have safety clauses, and what they cover. The first fruits of the study are now available.

The 50 cooperating international unions submitted approximately 7,000 contracts to the committee for examination. Nearly two-thirds of them contained safety clauses. By comparison, a somewhat similar study in 1956 showed that an estimated 50 to 60 per cent of all union contracts had safety clauses.

While some affiliates in the sample had safety clauses in all their agreements, there were others with only a rare safety proviso.

There is a need for a major effort in collective bargaining to stimulate every affiliate to work toward the 100 per cent goal of "safety by contract" wherever it is practical. This goal is within reach, thanks to the past efforts of individual unions. Safety and occupational health are as much a part of the contract as wages, hours and other working conditions.

Of all the contracts submitted which had safety clauses, 40 per cent gave union members an active role on safety committees. Of course, what an "active role" means has many interpretations. It can mean that the safety committee has equal labor and management representation; it can mean several management representatives and just one lone union representative; or it can mean several committees, related though separate, with one made up exclusively of worker representatives.

Only about 15 per cent of the contracts with safety clauses granted equal joint participation on safety committees to labor and management.

Here again the different individual unions had varying records. A few showed equal and joint representation in all their contracts, but the typical union had it in less than 25 per cent of its agreements.

This finding gives a hollow ring to the pleading of many managements for "cooperation" between labor and management in the safety and occupational health area. There is no denying that management has a "right" to provide safe and healthful working places for wage earners. Equally so, no one can deny the "right" of union members whose lives and limbs are in jeopardy to take active steps to insure their safety on the job.

Common sense dictates that labor and management have a joint duty to achieve the goal. The means to that end is the joint and equal labor-management safety committee.

Two facts are clear. Joint committees are in daily use; they are no mere theory of the labor movement. Secondly, the trade union movement is faced with the practical problem of making truly joint committees universal. It cannot be

given the duty of "cooperating" with management without being given the right to participate equally.

Specific provisions making the grievance machinery available for safety problems were found in 97 per cent of the contracts with safety clauses. Where such provisos were missing, the right to use the grievance setup for this purpose was established by common practice.

All unions believe their bargaining relationships include safety matters. "Safety by contract" is a practical approach of trade unionism.

This use of the grievance machinery, both regular and special, is an effective answer to critics of labor's role in safety. But nowhere in the safety clauses submitted is there any indication that a member cannot be disciplined for just cause, subject to the grievance machinery.

Where safety is made a part of the collective bargaining machinery it is no less enforceable than any other part of the contract. In fact, a clearly written safety clause which includes explicit procedures for handling safety grievances removes any doubt as to its enforceability.

The survey demonstrated clearly that turning over the responsibility for safety to the state through legislation is not a satisfactory answer for labor unions.

At best, safety laws set up minimum requirements only, and they leave administration in the hands of government employees rather than management and labor. Safety legislation of course is a form of protection for unorganized workers and therefore is necessary. But in matters of life and death—and safety means just that—trade unions have demonstrated by this survey that they prefer to rely primarily upon the voluntary actions of management and labor to provide the essential safeguards against disabling injury or death.

Nevertheless, the fact remains that just as the United States needs minimum wage laws to protect all wage earners, so it needs safety and occupational health legislation.

TEXAS PAYS 'BONUS IN BLOOD' FOR LACK OF SAFETY CODE

Texas State AFL-CIO News, September 1958

Texas' death rate from industrial accidents is far higher than the national average because of the state's lack of an industrial safety law, the Texas State AFL-CIO has charged. The facts were presented in a study filed with the Industrial and Occupational Safety Study Commission which is expected to make recommendations to the next legislature.

"It would appear that while the nation as a whole has been taking steps to reduce industrial fatalities, the inaction which characterizes Texas policy has resulted in a situation which is worsening," the labor report stated.

The detailed study noted:

1. The annual industrial fatality rate for Texas is considerably higher than that for the U. S. as a whole, varying from 20 to 100 per cent higher during the last seven years.

2. While the industrial fatality rate for the nation as a whole has been declining steadily over these seven years, the Texas fatality rate exhibits no such tendency.

3. Thus, the gap between the two fatality rates has been widening over these years.

In 1957, the 763 Texans killed in industrial accidents were 167 more than would have died if Texas had been as safe as the national average.

The report described these "excess deaths" as an "unsavory bonus in blood" paid for Texas' failure to enact an industrial safety law.

In contrast, it was pointed out that Missouri is over 60 per cent safer than the national average, Illinois and New Jersey 50 per cent better, Michigan and Wisconsin 40 per cent safer, New York 20 per cent, California 15 per cent, and Pennsylvania 10 per cent. All states except Texas have industrial safety laws, it was pointed out.

"There is definite correlation between low fatality rates and legislative concern," the report continued. "Texas ranks 10th in industrial size and 32nd in effort (to improve industrial safety)."

WORKMEN'S COMPENSATION LAWS NEGLECT REHABILITATION NEEDS

AFL-CIO News (PAI), May 14, 1960

Probably six million persons of working age today have serious disabilities which create difficulties in getting proper jobs, according to estimates by the Bureau of Labor Statistics.

The magnitude of this problem has too frequently been overlooked.

In 1954 the Rehabilitation Committee of the Association of Industrial Accident Boards and Commissions ripped into the states for their failure to up-date archaic aspects of workmen's compensation, saying:

"Workmen's compensation has long been looked to as the program with primary responsibility for protecting the welfare of injured workers; it is now often accused of being one of the institutional barriers to successful rehabilitation."

In the years since this statement appeared little progress has been made.

A frontal assault on the problem took place recently when a group of experts met at a conference called by the National Institute on Rehabilitation and Labor Health Services.

The primary purpose was to establish a program whereby labor and consumer-sponsored health programs could be brought into closer working relationship to help meet the problem of disability.

In their studies the technicians concluded that workmen's compensation, far from helping injured and disabled workers rehabilitate themselves, actually serves to defeat the avowed objects of rehabilitation. Here are some of the ways this happens:

• Victims of occupational disease or injuries are often given a lump sum settlement, usually closing the case, without proper attention having been given to the use of full, retroactive medical and rehabilitation services which could have enabled them to return to useful work.

• Injured workers sometimes have stiff and useless hands, atrophied muscles and other conditions which could have been prevented if they had been given other physical treatment in the early part of medical care.

• Injured workers often suffer from traumatic neuroses and are unable to work. This could have been prevented if they had received early counseling before being overcome with feelings of discouragement and fear as to the future.

• Injured workers are frequently discharged from hospitals as "cured" but are unable to work thereafter, and nothing is being done for them.

There are today more than 60,000 men and women from the ranks of organized labor serving on boards and committees of public and voluntary community health and welfare organizations.

The plan is that these and other community service workers be familiarized with the many rehabilitation facilities and programs so that workers may fully utilize them.

In addition, of course, the growing medical and welfare programs of unions are expected to be geared more closely with rehabilitation agencies. Labor has assumed a major role in the work of the President's Committee for Aid to the Handicapped. In several states unions are represented on state vocational rehabilitation agencies.

All told, though, there is great need for a vast, coordinated program involving labor, government and rehabilitation agencies.

WORKMEN'S COMPENSATION CRIPPLED IN STATE ATTACKS

AFL-CIO News, September 27, 1958

For less than an added two cents per manhour worked, American society could provide a full workman's compensation program instead of the present hodgepodge that fails to meet the needs of men and women injured on the job.

The extra two cents would furnish medical care for as long as needed, provide all the rehabilitation possible, and allow cash benefits large enough to give an injured worker a reasonable standard of living, explains the current issue of Labor's Economic Review published by the AFL-CIO Dept. of Research.

The Review spells out the reasons why the bright promise of protection, envisioned in 1908 when Pres. Theodore Roosevelt asked Congress to give federal employees protection in case of death or injury while at work, has become something less than reality.

"Only three out of four workers are protected by workmen's compensation against the hazards of injury on the job.

"State legislatures have applied numerous exemptions; have failed to recognize the hazards of industrial disease; have bowed to the pressures of the agricultural industry; have de-

clared certain industries non-hazard-
ous; and in many states have made
coverage voluntary.

"State administrative rulings and
court decisions have often narrowed
the area of statutory protection by
interpretation.

"When these various exclusions of
coverage are joined together, more
than 15 million workers for one reason or another are unprotected by
insurance against a job-sustained injury."

The amount of money that can be
spent to give an injured worker
proper medical care is often re-
stricted, and only 13 states provide
adequate rehabilitation programs.

The benefits an injured worker is
entitled to are often substandard.
Most states provide from 60 to 66⅔
per cent of the wage loss during a
temporary but total disability — and
then set maximums which make these
percentages impossible.

Permanent total disability benefits
—the amounts due workers who can
no longer work — are hedged in by
limits either in total amount or length
of payment, it continues, and permanent partial disability — such as the
loss of an eye or an arm—"bring bargain prices for an employee in today's
workmen's compensation market."

Financing is inadequate, state administration is too often inefficient
and costly, the Review says.

Pointing out that legislatures "have
failed to fit their programs to the
needs of injured workers," it calls
for enactment of the program adopted
at the 1957 AFL-CIO convention.

This includes compulsory full coverage, weekly indemnity payments
equal to at least two-thirds of average wages, a revised appeal procedure, insurance through a state fund
and enactment of a federal minimum
standards program.

'UNNEEDED' FIREMAN AVERTS TRAIN WRECK

AFL-CIO News, July 2, 1960

Portland, Ore.—A diesel locomotive fireman, whose job would be
abolished by the Association of
American Railroads as "featherbedding," has been proposed for a union
safety award for stopping a speeding passenger train when the engineer keeled over with a fatal heart
attack.

R. M. Berland, a member of the Locomotive Firemen & Enginemen, was
calling signals in the cab of a Union
Pacific express approaching Portland
at 70 miles an hour when Engineer
John E. Muck failed to repeat the
signal.

When Berland saw the engineer
slumped down in his seat, he moved
from his post on the left side of the
cab and applied the brakes to stop
the train. Berland called other crew
members who summoned an ambulance.

They found the engineer's foot
resting on the so-called "dead man's

pedal," a device intended to stop the
train when an engineer is stricken.
It did not work in this case, Berland
said.

Engineer Muck was taken to St.
Vincent Hospital and was pronounc-
ed dead shortly after arrival.

The train's route into Portland
was a steep down-grade from the
point where the engineer was strick-
en. Berland said that, had the engineer been alone in the cab, the train
would have continued at increasing
speed and probably would have left
the track at a curve near Providence
Hospital.

"This is not the first time," he
said, "that the dead man's pedal has
failed to work. I believe this demonstrates why diesel locomotives need
a fireman in the cab. Railroads
claim the fireman is superfluous."

Berland's name was to be submitted for BLF&E's monthly and
annual safety awards.

6 | PRODUCTIVITY AND TECHNOLOGY

ADJUSTMENT TO TECHNOLOGICAL CHANGE

AFL-CIO Collective Bargaining Report, April-May 1958

Unions in the United States are not opposed to and do not stand in the way of technological improvement. They well recognize that technological advance and the resulting productivity are needed to enable improvement in standards of living.

They typically cooperate with and, indeed, frequently encourage and stimulate management efforts to improve technology. This is well reflected in the fact that, although billions of dollars of new equipment is installed each year, there is barely a handful of claims or complaints of union opposition.

At the same time, unions want to see to it that workers get wage increases to provide them with a fair share of the benefits of increased productivity.

Unions are also greatly concerned about the manner in which technological change is introduced. They want joint management-union consideration of possible adverse effects on workers, and they want efforts taken to meet affected workers' problems on a mutually satisfactory basis.

The union concern about the manner in which technological change is introduced is sometimes mistaken for resistance to the change, when in fact it is not. If a union has not been informed and consulted about a major change, or if it finds that worker problems have not been taken into account, it may quite understandably be critical and resentful of the procedure, and seek corrective steps, even though it does not object to the technological change itself.

Unions believe that management has a positive responsibility to soften any blow of new technology on its workers. The workers should not be forced to carry all of the sacrifice or burden of adjustment. Measures needed to aid affected workers should be considered as properly a part of the cost of the introduction of new machines. To put it another way, management should devote some of the savings to be gained from introduction of new equipment to the easing of adverse effects on workers.

There is no one set of steps or "protections" equally helpful or desirable for all situations. The measures to be emphasized and the details of needed adjustments will necessarily vary with the individual situation.

In addition to the various "protections," it is important to emphasize the significance of the economic climate. The extent to which new labor-saving equipment may mean layoff of workers depends a great deal on the economic situation at the time.

In an expanding economy or industry, in which new equipment is needed to fill demand from a growing market, employment may not have to be cut back. But if business is stable or declining, new labor-saving equipment may replace rather than supplement workers.

Also, the difficulty which laid-off workers would have in finding employment elsewhere depends on the prosperity of the economy. An expanding economy will offer job opportunities elsewhere.

The employment effects of new technology are of course by no means confined to an individual plant or operation or the time of the installation. New equipment installed at one company may not displace workers there, but may indirectly lead to lay-offs at competing, less efficient companies elsewhere. New equipment may also reduce the need for future hiring.

In short, the ease of adjustment to technological change is closely linked to broad economic questions which cannot be met through collective bargaining alone. What is needed are the basic public and private economic and social policies which will assure that technological advance goes hand-in-hand with a steadily expanding economy.

AUTOMATION

32B, February 1959

Automation. What is it? A monster? A new technology that is geared to the pace of the atomic age? A blessing for the industrial giants of America, or a curse for millions of working people who earn their daily bread through their labor?

Nothing in the history of labor from ancient times to the present has captured the interest and concern of so many people. More than any other industrial development in modern times automation holds the secret that may change the lives of countless millions for better or for worse. So rapid has been its development that its full significance is still not understood. To make matters worse, relatively little has been done on national, state and city levels to understand automation and to resolve the many problems it has created.

When automation first appeared on the national scene, organized labor was assured that there would be a need for more maintenance workers, more planners, more white collar workers and that the total work force in factories would rise rather than decline. Time has disproved this claim.

In 1953, the nation's mills and factories employed some 17,238,000 persons. By 1955, with production higher than ever, total employment in manufacturing amounted to 16,557,-000 workers. While there has been a tremendous surge in plant and capital investment since 1955, in 1948 there were as many manufacturing workers as there were in 1958, ten years later.

Here are some statistics that indicate to what extent automation has affected certain industries:

● A million coal miners of ten years ago have been replaced by machinery, and some 200,000 are now working part time and producing more coal.

● In 1939 and 1940, more than 45,000 sheet metal and tin workers were replaced by 4,400 workers in one strip mill.

● Because of "canned music" of every description, the total number of musicians employed today out of some 260,000 union members throughout the nation amount to about 25 per cent.

● The total number of members of the Brotherhood of Sleeping Car Porters has dwindled from 16,000 to 8,000 members since World War II.

● Although the numbers of office employees in the nation has increased steadily since 1949, thousands of office workers are losing their jobs because of robot machines which can perform the operations of hundreds of clerks.

● The steel industry has more than doubled its capacity in the last few years utilizing a reduced number of employees.

● The tin can industry now produces with fewer employees more beer cans alone than the total produced of all types of cans a few years ago.

● The automobile industry has enough capacity for triple the country's demand and requires fewer employees.

• A few years ago, 750 employees produced paper cups, cottage cheese buckets and other items at a certain paper plant. Today, 250 employees make a larger number of these items.

• Huge machinery used in thruway building and construction jobs is taking the place of literally thousands of laborers by performing as many as half a dozen operations.

AUTOMATION SEEN AS BOON IF HARNESSED PROPERLY, SAY EXPERTS

Trainman News, February 18, 1957

Automation, a fearful word among workers up to this point because of its connotation to them of resultant unemployment as technological changes take place in industry, can and must be a boon to us all if harnessed properly.

It can bring untold rewards to the people if, for one thing, organized labor is vigilant and steps forward to see that the benefits of automation are used to the advantage of workers and all other segments of the citizenry.

More than 400 attending the two-day Joint Labor Conference on "Automation—A World Challenge to Labor" in Hotel Carter here Feb. 9 and 10 heard labor leaders, representatives of industry and university professors spell out the benefits that can be reaped from automation. They also stressed the action that must be taken to insure these benefits.

The conference was sponsored by the Cleveland Joint Labor Conference Committee, comprising representatives of AFL-CIO and rail labor unions, in conjunction with American Labor Education Service.

"Our job, it seems to me," declared Joseph A. Beirne, president, Communications Workers of America, in the opening address of the parley, "is to maintain our vigorous, healthy economic situation so that we can move forward without fear and without strife to enrich as many lives as we can with the wonders which these new machines have made possible."

"We should not lose sight of the fact," he continued, "that automation doesn't only create problems but helps solve many of them also. Let's understand that automation is our friend if harnessed properly."

He said that changes in one plant's operations "can adversely affect employment in a whole series of plants where operations depend upon the first plant's production. When this first plant automates, it may in fact take over the operations of many subsidiary or auxiliary plants which depend upon it for existence."

Declaring that the time is here to get down to specifics in automation, the Communications Workers' chieftain said that reduced work weeks and earlier retirements are among the things that must come unless work is obtained for all in industry.

In bringing out the facts about automation, said Beirne, "we don't want to frighten anyone; we want to prepare them for reality."

"Wherever possible," asserted Beirne, "we should be discussing not only the broad over-all, but also the day-to-day, on-the-job problems created by automation and using our best efforts to solve them in a fundamentally decent and rapid manner."

Dr. Lawrence B. Cohen, professor of engineering, Columbia University, told the hundreds in attendance that the sights of unions must be focused on the entire problem and the changes that are to come about.

Trade unions must keep in mind, he continued, that whatever employers have put into use so far is only the beginning of much more which is in the offing.

Dr. Cohen said he feels that unions are going to help more than they will hinder as automation progresses, pointing out that the pressure for better wages make it feasible and that every step by unions to improve conditions will improve the situation as technology is introduced.

The Columbia professor pointed out that while the machine is old, the self-correcting and self-regulating feature of machinery is new today.

He noted that the people who are creating automation are those who are going to use it, and, that should be kept in mind at all times, said Dr. Cohen.

"Automation is just a label—and let's not get scared over that word," declared Martin H. Miller, assistant to Trainmen Pres. W. P. Kennedy.

He said that rail labor unions "have a lot of thinking and planning to do" with respect to automation in the railroad industry.

"The railroad worker of today and tomorrow," asserted BRT'er Miller, "must be more alert so that automation is automated in the direction of human benefits and not dollars for stockholders alone."

Locomotive Firemen and Engineers' Vice Pres. Homer Ellis called attention to the drop in rail employment from 1,600,000 to one million in the past decade.

Deputy Pres. Legge discussed the technological changes being effected on the silvery ribbons, such as the use of TV in yard operations, automatic humps and greater dieselization.

"We have to live with it—and it can be our friend if we meet the situation head-on and set out to protect ourselves," declared Legge.

He criticized the railroads for failing "to tell the story of the industry to the public. They have failed miserably."

Locomotive Firemen and Engineers' Asst. Pres. Sam Phillips declared that management and labor must sit down and talk over the problems in the rail industry.

Other panel groups covered automation in communications; electrical, machine, machine tool and metal industry; service trades and food processing, and office workers.

At a luncheon conference the first day, E. R. White, Machinists' vice president, said that "organized labor of today, unlike the movement of years ago, does not, nor will it oppose technological changes which will contribute toward a higher standard of living for the working people. This, however, does not alleviate our concern for probable economic dislocations which may occur."

Continued White:

"Our ability to meet 'changes' and our ability to foster that society which encourages and permits 'change' will determine how rapidly we will reap the benefits which can result from automation."

"We must continue to insist on a fair distribution of the fruits of productivity — for without this insistence we will fail to fulfill an inherent obligation to our free enterprise economy," declared White.

"We of organized labor," said the IAM vice president, "must better mold our organizations to react at a rate of speed just as rapidly as technological changes occur. The need to become more flexible withsacrificing that which we have gained in the past is the challenge before use today.

"From past experience, I can assure you that we will meet that challenge."

"We are wondering what there is on the planning boards and in the blueprints for the people we represent," declared Trainmen General Secretary and Treasurer Weil, chairman, in opening a round table discussion.

Nat Goldfinger, of the AFL-CIO Research Dept., called attention to the problems of automation and noted the possibility of large-scale unemployment; the possibility that the economy will not produce enough jobs for those entering the labor field; the possibility of an increase in the number of distressed communities, and the possibility of economic concentration with big companies having the advantage.

He said that labor should be notified plenty of time in advance when changes are planned so that the problems arising can be worked out properly between labor and management.

The problems in the plant cannot be settled in Washington, New York, etc., he said. "A major part of the answer to the problems will be worked out locally," Goldfinger declared.

Phillips asserted that automation is much like what has happened in the past under different names.

He discussed the trends to automation on the railroads throughout history — the unifications, mergers, etc., the technological changes of the 30's and the present day changes.

"Management and labor have the responsibility to sit down and find answers to the problems that will arise," said Phillips. "Answers should be found by those who have created them."

Assistant Vice Pres. Hursh of the Pennsylvania Railroad lauded the high caliber of labor's spokesmen who participated in the two-day conference.

Relative to the issues which arise in automation, he said:

"I have no misgivings that we cannot sit down and work out this problem to the benefit of all."

Wentz of Ohio Bell told of improved service to the public through automation in the telephone industry and he said employment has increased.

Ninety-six per cent of Ohio Bell's phones are dial operated, he pointed out.

Bergen of Standard Oil said that the only trouble he could see in automation is "that old enemy: fear."

A French team studying automation in the auto industry, and representatives of the labor movements in England and Italy attended the two-day meetings.

WHITE COLLAR AUTOMATION CAUSING BIG DISPLACEMENT

IUD Bulletin, August 1960

For every job that office automation adds, it eliminates five others, a recent survey has revealed.

The survey, made by Ida Russakoff Hoos, in preparation for her Ph.D., is reported in the current issue of the Harvard Business Review.

Dr. Hoos spent two years surveying the impact of office automation in the San Francisco area. Included in the survey are large and small firms, banks, insurance companies, manufacturers, processors and distributors.

In one firm employing a total clerical force of 3,196, centralization of operations on a computer in San Francisco has been in progress for two years.

"With only two accounting operations on EDP (electronic data processing), 286 jobs have already been dropped from the payroll, and it is estimated that 982, or about one-third of the workers, are being affected," Dr. Hoos found.

The researcher also found that automation has created a new job elite. These are the programmers and analysts. The problem, however, was that there were only a handful of such jobs, and the qualifications are highly variable.

Accounting, bookkeeping, filing and ledger clerks—the "backbone of the clerical force"—and their supervisors are hardest hit by automation.

Contrary to the stories about automation's skill requirements in the front office, the new method has brought about a different kind of drudgery. Dr. Hoos found that the fastest growing category of office worker in the automated office setup is the key-punch operator.

"Workers I have interviewed consider their previous jobs more interesting," she observed.

Automation is encouraging recentralization of record keeping and this also is causing problems. Dr. Hoos reported that since most clerical workers are women, they are less mobile than almost any other occupational category and least likely to be able to transfer even when transfer is offered.

Other side effects of the new office technique include stagnation in the middle management layers, since EDP takes over certain decision areas formerly at that level. It also has made time-and-motion studies "a standard procedure in the office, with output clocked and errors counted."

AUTOMATION'S IMPACT

CWA News (Communication Workers), August 1959

Since the end of World War II there have been some highly significant changes in the relation between Bell System profits, number of telephones in service, and employment.

Since 1945 we have seen the number of Bell System phones go up 144 per cent while employment over this 13-year period went up only 53 per cent. Last year's net profits, after taxes, were over five and one-half times what they were in 1945.

An even more significant fact is that, last year, employment actually dropped—by 67,000 while the number of Bell System phones in service rose by two and one-half million.

CWA's research department points out that "tremendous increases" in demand for phone service are necessary if high levels of employment are to be maintained.

Last year, for example, the number of local telephone calls handled by the Bell System increased 4.4 per cent while long distance calls rose by 5.3 per cent. Research points out that the company handled this increase and installed an additional 2½ million telephones, with an 8½ per cent reduction in employment.

CWA's goals of longer vacations, a shorter work-week, shorter tours, earlier pensions, and other work-spreading practices are becoming increasingly realistic in view of the impact of automation. In addition they have become economic and social imperatives if we are to cushion the impact of technological change.

The worker is becoming increasingly important as a consumer. Machines can be used to make automobiles, refrigerators, and dial telephones. But the machine is a poor customer for these products.

543.

"My last boss was always yakkin' at us to show more 'Get-up-and-go'... So I got up and went!"

2 NEW TA AUTOMATONS MAKE BIG INROADS IN TRANSIT JOB

TWU Express (Transport Workers), June-July 1958

NEW YORK—Automation continues to make its inroads on Transit Authority jobs.

This month the TA introduced a "Cyclone" cleaner which automatically cleans a bus in two minutes. Presently, the hand operation can do only 40 buses in an eight-hour shift.

The automatic cleaner operates like a giant-sized vacuum cleaner. Its intake is fastened tight to the front door of the bus. All the windows except the rear two are closed. When the two five-horsepower engines of this automatic dirt-eater are turned on, 'whoosh,' out blows the dirt and trash in the bus.

Cost of this new mechanical job-eating monster is $4,000. How many jobs will be gobbled up? No one knows until the TA decides the extent of its use. At present there is only one at the Crosstown Depot in Brooklyn. But if the machine performs as it is advertised, who knows?

This would be bad enough. But the TA had more "good news" for its workers.

This month it installed two more "standard wheel-truing machines." Previously installed in the Coney Island shop, this new marvel swallows up 40 jobs at a clip.

It's impossible to stop progress. But, TWU has alleviated much of the suffering that such mechanical improvement too often causes to individual workers.

The no-discharge agreement which TWU wrested from the TA several years ago has protected all workers. There have been no firings because of the excess in titles created by automation, new techniques or service cuts.

Men thus displaced are able to get other jobs in the TA without loss in pay. Attrition in the form of retirements, deaths, resignations, etc., are painlessly absorbing the shock of technological progress in the city's transit system.

LAYOFFS, SHORT CHECKS CONTINUE AT GUIDE

The Lampmaker (UAW Local 663 in Anderson, Indiana), February 27, 1959

"What 't' hell's the matter out at Guide Lamp — only working four days a week and still laying off?" That's the question being asked.

"Remy's is workin' six days a week and ten hours a day." This usually follows the question.

Rosy newspaper reports about area of square feet expansion at Guide Lamp and other juggled figures can't cover up for the real facts. Our production people at Guide are being hurt. Layoffs for people with many years of seniority, four-day weeks, and more and more short days.

"We're out of stock. Go ring out and come back tomorrow." This is the excuse given in many instances. In one situation people were sent home because of a leaky water valve. The pipe fitters had it fixed fifteen minutes after the people had rung out.

While production workers suffer short days, short work weeks, short pay checks and layoffs the overhead salaried people still jam offices, and step on each others heels as they move around those increased "square feet of work area."

GM Tech boys, GM Tech graduates, Purdue engineers, salaried observers, time study boys, foremen, supervisors, superintendents, factory managers, technicians and a host of other non-productive personnel make up an army supported by the automated production worker.

"Looks like every time they eliminate a production worker they promote a new boss or hire a new engineer," a buffer commented.

Management has automated many workers out of the plant to "cut the cost of production to meet competition in the market place." This is the argument. But the displaced worker is replaced by a top salary engineer or overhead foreman. And costs go up.

We are still maintaining much of the overhead of technicians promoted foremen, engineers, et cetera, as well as filling all the additional office space built during the peak '55 and '56 years.

We're not advocating a wholesale layoff of white collar workers or supervision. But Guide should face the facts. It's that guy at a buffing wheel or girl on the assembly line that actually has to exert the physical energy to pay for the white collar parade that marches down the aisles of the plant. It is the guy hammering away at a punch press who is paying his own wages plus that of the observer, time study man, the engineer and the boss breathing down his back.

The big question is: With all this tremendous pool of brain power, why can't we come up with something to maintain full production or at least a forty-hour week?

Suggestions and automation have cut the number of production workers to the core. A smaller band of production workers is carrying an increasing load of overhead. It's up to the "brains" to start producing now.

AUTOMATION: LONELY, NERVE-RACKING JOBS

Jerry Dale in UAW Solidarity, December 1957

"On my old job, I controlled the machine. On my present job, the machine controls me."

This was one of the opinions expressed in a survey of worker attitudes toward automation conducted by a member of the Michigan State University department of sociology and anthropology.

William A. Faunce, a graduate student and recipient of a scholarship set up by the Square D unit of UAW Amalgamated Local 351, Detroit, interviewed 125 workers in four large machining departments of one of the most highly automated auto plants in Detroit.

Their main complaint, according to Faunce, is that automation makes them lonely on the job and isolates them from fellow-workers.

"Machine noise, increased distances between work stations and the need for closer attention to work is decreasing the social exchanges between workers," Faunce explained.

Other complaints include increased tension because of faster production; too much supervision from foremen; the closer and more constant attention required by complicated machinery; frequent breakdowns and costliness of mistakes; lack of identification with the work; and a decline in conversation.

To the question, "Are you able to talk very often to the men around while you are working?", only 45% of those doing automated work answered yes, compared to 80% who answered in the affirmative concerning their conversational habits while on previous non-automated work.

Only 18% said they had some form of contact every few minutes while on automated work, compared to almost 40% who reported some form of "social interaction" on their old job.

Only 13% reported making more friends on their new (automated) job, while 47% said they had made more friends on their old (non-automated) job. While 40% said there was no difference, these were either working with the same people on both jobs or were the type who have "no difficulty making friends any place."

"Almost 2½ times as many workers reported that they used to get together socially off the job more often with friends from their old job than they do now with friends from their present job, but approximately half reported no difference, with most of these indicating that they didn't get together socially with friends from either job," Faunce's survey reports.

Supervision in the automated department is closer and the worker's relationship to the foreman has worsened, the survey discloses. Faunce quotes one worker as saying:

"It was better on the old job— nobody breathing down your neck . . . Over here it's altogether different, just push, push all the time. They never say hello . . . treat you like a machine. They used to be friendly. Now they seem to be under a strain. The foremen at the new plant have too much to do and too much responsibility and they get tired and cranky. They'll die of a heart attack yet."

The same worker said his depart-

ment used to have 134 men with one foreman and one assistant foreman. Now they have 100 men with five foremen.

Speaking of lack of identification, Faunce says in his survey:

"The worker on the automated line is alienated in the sense that he no longer has control over the machine and work pace, machining skills previously acquired are no longer needed, and it becomes increasingly difficult to identify what the transfer machine does as his work."

Concerning the nervous tension workers experience on automated machines, Faunce cites this quote:

"I pushed a wrong button and stuff flew all over. I was lucky (not getting hurt) but it cost the company $13,000 to fix the machine."

Those workers who said they preferred working on automated machines cited the smaller physical effort required and the decreased need for handling materials. Some regarded the job as involving more responsibility, and said it was more interesting and more challenging.

Their previous work included handling cylinder blocks, crankshafts and other heavy engine parts. This is one aspect most disliked in non-automated work.

NCPC CONDUCTS COAL JUNKET

Justin McCarthy in United Mine Workers Journal, July 1, 1960

The National Coal Policy Conference's recent two-day press tour of modern mechanized coal mining facilities in Indiana, West Kentucky and Illinois was, for lack of a better description, breathtaking.

If there had been any doubt about the health of America's basic coal industry among the more than a score of hard-to-convince newsmen who made the trip it was quickly dispelled by the immensity of what they saw.

Everything was big; some of the modern equipment was literally the biggest. Everything was efficient; some of it the most efficient. And

the coal kept coming, all the time. Every second it was gouged out of the earth in a continuous, assembly-line operation, black and rich with all its wealth of power and heat and chemicals. And the millions and millions of tons more of it were laying there ready to be scooped up or gouged out of the earth. The reporters saw it all.

We saw huge shovels nearly 20 stories high bite into the earth to remove as much as 100 tons of overburden from the coal veins in one scoop.

We saw the Kolbe Wheel Excavator, a 2,100-ton towering giant of steel, quietly—because it is operated by coal-produced electricity — going about its business of chewing away at 146 feet of overburden above three coal beds at the Fidelity Mine of the United Electric Coal Companies near Pinckneyville, Ill.

We saw electrically-operated conveyor belts rolling steadily and quietly along with their burden of freshly mined black diamonds.

We saw five-story high coal preparation plants churning and shaking, whishing and stirring, rattling and hissing as the raw coal was broken, shaken through screens, washed, dried and rushed along to railroad cars or fat, brown river barges. One of these has a raw coal capacity of 800 tons an hour.

We saw 100-ton coal trucks emptying their precious cargoes into hoppers. We saw a 50-ton all-aluminum truck that could handle an extra ten tons of coal load, thanks to the comparatively light weight of the metal.

We saw underground mines with automatic miners chewing away at as much as nine feet of coal face and shoving ton after ton of coal onto belts and into shuttle cars.

We saw thousands of acres of stripped Illinois coal land reclaimed for fruit orchards, for cattle grazing, for man-made lakes, for forests —all at a profit to the coal company.

We saw bright new industries springing up along the rivers in the rich heart of industrial America, powered by the electricity made available to them in such abundance by the millions and millions of tons of low-priced coal.

We saw a lumbering drag line scooping up ton after ton of earth and rock so that smaller, electrically powered shovels could bite into the coal that lay underneath.

We felt and heard the rumble of cardox explosions in the East Diamond Mine of the West Kentucky Coal Co.

We participated in the formal dedication of Illinois' newest major deep shaft coal mine near Benton, the No. 21 Mine of the Old Ben Coal Corp. of Chicago—a mine that taps a reserve of 100 million recoverable tons of low-sulphur coking coal, 670 feet down in the rich Illinois earth.

Back of all of these mechanized operations, we saw the working men of the American coal industry, proud men, smart men, efficient men—but men of modesty. There wasn't a phony among them.

There is a spirit among these men of coal that can, perhaps be explained best by an example.

The example is D. W. Buchanan, Sr., chairman of the board of the Old Ben Coal Corp. Down through the years Old Ben has had good relations with the UMWA because of Buchanan and the other practical coal men who worked with him in the company. He was asked by the West Frankfort reporter about the "troubles" between the UMWA and the operators in days gone by.

"I saw a lot of that," Buchanan said. "We never had any trouble because we always believed in collective bargaining and knew how to talk to the men."

In the early days, Buchanan said: "A man who could load six tons a day was doing real good. By comparison, our mine No. 9 back in 1917 was mining 4,000 tons a day with 1,200 men. Now we mine 10,000 tons a day at No. 9 with 375 men."

One of "the men" with whom we talked briefly was John R. Smith of UMWA Local Union 1124, District 12. With great pride, Brother Smith was busily operating a Goodman continuous miner 670 feet underground in Old Ben's new Mine No. 21 when the press party and other guests visited his working place.

Recently developed Bureau of Mines 1,000-watt safety lamps glared down on Smith and his monstrous machine. Cameras clicked and flashbulbs flared as he gently touched the levers that maneuvered the multi-tonned automatic miner's jaws into the more than eight feet of coal face.

"How long have you been a coal

miner?" we asked later. "Oh, I've been working in the mines for Old Ben since 1926," Smith replied, a broad grin cracking through the layer of coal dust on his rugged face.

It's men like Buchanan and Smith, practical mining men—it's these men who have made the American coal industry the most productive and modern in the world today.

Another coal miner once said: "You know, there is an under-standing and a bond and fraternity among mining men all over the world. Our industry is an industry apart, with specialized problems. The average man engaged in the mining industry, whether he is on management's side or labor's side, is a rather extraordinary personality."

The man who said that is an example of the "extraordinary personality" of the men of the coal industry. His name is John L. Lewis.

SPEEDUP IN INDUSTRY

Hat Worker, June 15, 1960

The productivity of factory workers—one of the key issues in modern collective bargaining is continuing its climb as revealed in preliminary statistics for the first quarter of 1960.

A study of Government figures by Press Associates, Inc., shows that productivity during the first three months of the year was 4 per cent higher than during the first quarter of 1959.

While the Government's figures on productivity mean strengthening of labor's hand against efforts to blame high wages for unjustified price boosts, the figures also have a dark side for they reflect a cutback in the factory labor force at the same time that production itself has been increasing.

The 1960 first quarter productivity figures came as somewhat of a shock to government statisticians who last year predicted that there would be a fairly good increase in jobs on the theory that there would be a moderate increase in production accompanied by only a small increase in productivity.

Instead, the increase in production has been less than what was expected while at the same time there has been a considerable increase in productivity, with a resultant relative loss in jobs.

Here is the story as told in the first quarter 1960 statistics as compared with the first quarter 1959 statistics:

Factory production — up 9 per cent.

Total factory payrolls — up only 3.9 per cent.

Factory production and maintenance payrolls — up only 3.3 per cent.

The meaning?

More production by relatively fewer workers for a gain in productivity surpassing what had been predicted for the year thus far.

The importance of productivity advances from the labor viewpoint was recently analyzed by Nat Goldfinger, assistant director of research for the AFL-CIO, at a recent meeting of the National Industrial Conference Board.

"Productivity will obviously be a factor in collective bargaining in the period ahead and it may be a factor of growing importance," Goldfinger said.

Pointing out that a rise in output per hour represents important economic gains, he said that union members expected a fair share of those gains at the same time taking into consideration other factors such as profits, rises in the cost of living and the desire to eliminate substandard wages and working conditions.

OUTPUT SHOWS PAY BOOST DUE

Trainmen News, November 30, 1959

Are members of the Brotherhood of Railroad Trainmen, currently asking a 14 per cent increase, and members of other rail labor unions who are seeking pay boosts in negotiations with U. S. railroads, entitled to increases?

Railroad management won't admit it—the industry's chief executives prefer to spread simple, downright lies about loyal rail workers—but actually the rail labor unions' wage demands in the negotiations now are modest in view of what rail employees are producing for the industry through their increased productivity.

In the past two decades, since 1940 to be exact, the productivity of rail labor has risen 95 per cent.

That is "featherbedding?"

While rail labor's productivity has been on a steady upswing, the real purchasing power of rail labor's pay has been skidding.

Facts of the matter reveal that rail labor's pay in real purchasing power for every 100 revenue ton miles per service hour slumped from 108.5 cents worth (in 1958 dollars) in 1940 to 89.3 cents worth in 1958.

Percentage-wise, BRT'ers and other rail workers were receiving 17½ per cent less in 1958 than in 1940 in real grocery money and rent money for each 100 revenue ton miles per service hour.

It makes you think, doesn't it?

It makes you realize just how big are the untruths which railroad management is circulating today and how absurd the rail propaganda becomes when it is face to face with the facts.

Management of railroad industry should smarten up.

Railroad workers are due the wage increases they seek — their increased productivity is evidence enough.

For once, why doesn't rail management level up and give the public the truth?

LIFE MAGAZINE WALLOPED ON 'FEATHERBED' CLAIMS

Labor, September 5, 1959

For Life magazine, the railroad side on the issue of "featherbedding" is still the only side it will publish. That's apparent from a new exchange of correspondence between A. E. Lyon, executive secretary of the Railway Labor Executives' Association, and the editors of Life.

Back in its June 1, 1959, issue Life carried a big scare editorial in which it made the unqualified statement that "obsolete work rules" of the "operating Brotherhoods" cost U. S. railroads "an unnecessary $500 million or more a year." On other points also, Life merely "rubber-stamped" the propaganda of the carriers, with no mention of the labor side.

Some weeks later Lyon sent a sharp letter to Life, giving a detailed refutation of the magazine's charges and pointing out that they were taken "straight out of the propaganda manual of the American railroads." Not a word of Lyon's answer appeared on Life's pages.

Later, Page d'Aulney wrote to Lyon as spokesman "of the editors." In this reply, d'Aulney made some significant admissions, on the one hand, and trotted out some figures, on the other hand, purporting to substantiate Life's claims.

Lyon responded with a hard-hitting rebuttal. First, he cited an analysis made by E. L. Oliver, prominent economist, which demolished the carrier "featherbedding" claims, point by point. Also, Lyon stressed that "the carriers have made no reply" to Oliver's analysis because "it is based on the railroads' own selected cases and they know that refutation is impossible."

Then Lyon commented on a major admission made by d'Aulney for Life's editors—namely, that "the $500 million estimated cost of featherbedding is determined not from Interstate Commerce Commission figures, but from railroad figures."

"That, indeed, was the point of my earlier protest that your editorial was biased," Lyon told d'Aulney. "The simple fact is that this figure of the railroads is pure hokum, derived by such questionable accounting practices as including vacations and holidays and other so-called premium payments common in every other industry under a column headed 'time paid for, but not worked.'"

Lyon also said he was "glad to note" d'Aulney's assertion that "the carriers themselves admit the duties of the fireman are essential under certain conditions and on certain runs." In other words, the carriers say firemen are needed on passenger trains, but not on freight, on the theory that the latter are less hazardous.

Lyon followed with a powerful "sockdolager"—that is, with the disclosure that insurance companies fix the classification of enginemen in freight and yard service as a "higher risk" in setting rates.

Turning then to Life's claim that the "rate of return" of the railroads was "inadequate" in 1958 and that "railroad profits are low" compared with other industries, Lyon said bluntly: "I respectfully suggest you don't know what you're talking about."

"First, you have applied the rate base which the carriers use for propaganda purposes, but which has never been accepted for any other use," Lyon asserted. "The Interstate Commerce Commission itself has never accepted it in its rate and fare cases."

Lyon pointed out that comparison with other industries is "misleading" because of the relatively high fixed investment in roadway and equipment on the railroads. Many industries use "the margin on sales" for comparisons.

On such a basis, the railroads would show a profit margin of 6.3 per cent in 1958, compared with 2.7 per cent on airlines, 1 per cent for traction and bus companies, and 5.2 per cent for all manufacturing industries.

"You will note that the railroads, even in the bad year of 1958, were well above the average for all manufacturing industries," Lyon said.

Lyon gave a similar refutation of Life's claims that hourly wages of railroad workers have gone up faster than those in other industries. He showed these wages have actually lagged—and, moreover, that productivity of rail workers has risen much greater than that of workers in other industries.

As for d'Aulney's assertion that the carriers, "because of obsolete work rules have gotten no benefit from the advancing productivity of their workers," Lyon suggested that "you take your eyes off the railroads' press release long enough to check on their earnings."

"The railroads have never had it so good," he said. "In the last 10 years their net income has been higher and more stable than ever before in history."

Lyon presented figures showing that in every period since 1900 many more miles of railroad were under receivership than in 1958. Mileage under receivership ran as high as 27 per cent in 1935 and 30 per cent in 1940, but in 1958 this had fallen to an all-time low of nearly 44/100 of 1 per cent.

"The generally improved financial health of the railroad industry," Lyon said in conclusion, "has followed from a number of factors, but the efficiency of railroad labor was one of the most essential. The service supplied by railroad workers is the only product the carriers have to sell. The continuing record of their employees' productivity improvement is the strongest and surest element in the railroads' outlook."

IAM AUTOMATION PLAN AIMS TO SAVE JOBS, BUYING POWER

AFL-CIO News, September 3, 1960

An eight-point plan, geared to protect the million members of the Machinists from mass unemployment as a result of automation, has been voted by the IAM Executive Council.

The council declared in a special automation report that unless the increase in production and consumption keeps pace with the rapidly increasing output per man-hour, not only will those coming into the labor force be unable to find jobs, but those already at work will be displaced.

"Increased productivity without increased overall demand is a clear-cut formula for recession and unemployment," the report warned.

The IAM bargaining program of safeguards against automation, based on a year-long study, will be presented by Pres. Al J. Hayes to the 1,500 delegates attending the union's 1960 convention.

The union's formula calls for:

• Advance notice and consultation whenever employers plan major automation moves.

• The right to transfer to jobs in other plants, with adequate moving allowances which would also cover living expenses, and losses resulting from the sale of homes.

• Training for new jobs, or for old jobs which have not been eliminated, at full pay and no expense to the worker.

• Preservation of previous rates of pay of workers who have been downgraded, and the maintenance of a substantial part of the income of those who have been laid off, either through Supplemental Unemployment Benefits, severance payments or some other device.

• Provision for early retirement with assurance of an adequate pension.

• Continuance of insurance coverage and other fringe benefits during periods of layoff.

• Negotiation of new job classifications and pay scales wherever automation has increased skill requirements or responsibility, or has imposed additional demands on workers.

• An equitable distribution of gains resulting from greater productivity through a general wage increase, more leisure time, or in "some other socially desirable fashion."

At the same time, the IAM executive council recommended that the union press its demands for a shorter workweek or a reduction in the workday "as rapidly as the needs and resources of the nation permit."

The Machinists' study, on which the eight-point program was based, disclosed that automation is responsible in great part for the tremendous shift from blue-collar to white-collar occupations, both in the U. S. and Canada.

The report cited the Boeing Airplane Co., where the ratio of white-collar to blue-collar workers has changed from three-to-one in favor of blue-collar workers 15 years ago to the present three-to-two ratio in favor of white-collar workers.

"The fact is," the IAM report declared, "that the U. S. has become the first industrial country in the world in which the working class as traditionally conceived is no longer the major element in the labor force."

Here is a digest of the IAM's findings in key areas:

Changing jobs—Due to the rapid introduction of automation, many now employed as production workers will have to transfer to other occupations, and in many cases to other sectors of the economy.

In a number of cases, the adjustment may be "exceedingly difficult." Older workers will find it hard to adjust to the new kinds of jobs and minority groups may find their entry into white-collar occupations "even more difficult than their entry into blue-collar" jobs.

Hourly wages vs. weekly salary— As work becomes more and more a joint effort and more machine paced, the possibility exists that group incentives will replace individual incentive systems, and workers may be paid on a weekly salary basis as it becomes more difficult to isolate, measure and pay for small segments of individual effort.

Need for automation—Labor has not called for any moratorium on technological change, knowing that there are "tremendous unmet needs in America," and that the nation needs to grow in order to cope with the Soviet challenge.

At the same time, businessmen "cannot be allowed to be carried away by the possibilities of cost reduction and to forget social problems and personal hardships to which rapid technological change gives rise."

WE MUST EMBRACE AND MASTER NEW THINGS

Thomas E. Dunwody, president, Printing Pressman, in
The American Pressman, March 1959

There are two avenues open to man when change confronts him. He may resist the change, refuse to acknowledge it, continuing in his old ways until the world no longer has need of his task or skill. Thus he loses his income, his security and even an element of his pride. Or he may accept the challenge of the new thing that represents change. With a willingness born of the experience of others he will embrace it and master it, confident that by so doing he will thus enhance his job security and contribute something of value to the industry upon which he is dependent.

It is well nigh impossible to understand the thinking of a man who resists change because he fears it may destroy his job. For every pony express rider there are thousands of mail carriers operating from motorized vehicles. For every blacksmith there are thousands of garage men and filling station attendants. For every stage coach driver, streetcar motorman and river boat captain there are thousands of bus drivers, airline pilots, and a veritable army of truckers. For every job, for every task, for every skill displaced by technological advancement there have been thousands upon thousands of new jobs and tasks and skills created. Displacement of men by machines is a myth.

So it is within the vast empire of the graphic arts. For every compositor who once set type by hand, there are thousands today operating hot metal type casting machines, setting more type, working shorter hours and being paid more money. For every bookbinder who once gathered signatures by hand, there are thousands today who are filling the jobs created by the demand for books by the millions.

For every pressman, industry no longer needs to hand feed its printing presses, there are now thousands upon thousands of printing pressmen, setting and operating mechanical paper feeding devices and the automatic presses to which they are attached. They, and others like them who have embraced and mastered new things are "out in front" so to speak, while the ones who refused to accept technological advancement, declined to acquire new skills, deemed it unnecessary to learn new machines or methods are left behind with a lower pay scale, less consideration when promotions are considered and are the first to be let out in search of new employment.

But it is not enough that our International Union believe in and proclaim a willingness and a necessity to embrace and master new things in the printing industry. It is almost mandatory that our membership support this philosophy by their actions. To put it more simply, they must practice what we preach.

Our membership, individually and collectively will gain nothing of lasting value from resistance to change. They will endanger their position if they are unwilling to master new machines, employ new techniques, learn new skills, expand their craftsmanship and adapt themselves to changes in the industry.

Neither by thought, word nor action, can they delay for long the technological advancement that is bound to come in the various fields of the graphic arts. We may be assured that jobs in the printing industry will be done. If our members do not do the new jobs then somebody will be found who will do them. It behooves each one of us to see that they are done by members of the Printing Pressmen's Union.

Our members must establish a record of willingness to accept and master new things.

"Tramp! Clank! Tramp!"

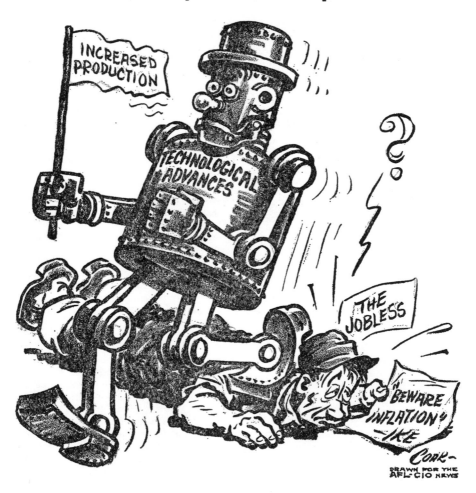

7 | UNEMPLOYMENT

UNEMPLOYMENT

Labor's Economic Review, July 1960

The nation now has a half-trillion dollar economy ($500,000,000,000).

Yet, one aspect of the economy is casting a dark shadow over this picture. This is the continued persistence of high unemployment.

Over the past few years, the problem has become serious. In the future it may become even more critical as the postwar "babies" start out to hunt for jobs.

In the U. S. unemployment is considerably higher than in any other industrialized country in the world.

The 1958 recession produced the most serious unemployment problem of the postwar period as the number of jobless reached more than 5 million (over 7 per cent of the labor force). Two years after the recession, the unemployment rate has dropped only to 5 per cent.

It should be noted that the unemployment figures do not take into account the time lost by those workers who would like full-time work but are only working part-time.

Moreover, the high rate of unemployment has undoubtedly kept many people at home or in school who would otherwise be interested in finding a job.

The highest rates of unemployment occur among younger single workers, among Negroes and other non-white groups, and among laborers who would like full-time work industries as construction, agriculture, mining and manufacturing.

A relatively high rate of unemployment is expected among younger workers looking for jobs for the first time.

Among older workers, too, unemployment has increased. Although the increase among men 45 years of age and older is about average, a substantially larger proportion today are forced to remain idle for long periods of time looking for work.

This country rightly prides itself on the dynamic character of its economy. New products and new industries are constantly being developed. There are no restrictions forcing corporations to locate in particular areas, or preventing them from shifting their operations to new locations.

Yet the social costs of such change have generally been ignored. The textile company closing down its plant at Lawrence, Mass., pays little attention to the unemployment it leaves behind. There is no way that that corporation can be made to bear the social cost for which it has been responsible.

While new enterprises are constantly springing up, the workers who have been displaced, are generally not the ones with the skills in demand by the newer industries. Moreover, the new enterprise may not locate in the same general area as the old, while lifetime ties to their community, as well as the costs of moving, naturally make workers and their families reluctant to move.

The result is that workers made idle often have to undergo a prolonged period of unemployment. Even when they find new work, they are not likely to receive their previous level of pay.

The unemployment situation is serious. In the next recession it can easily reach as high as 8 per cent of the civilian labor force.

In the next few years, an increasing number of young people will be entering the labor force. The number of those reaching the age of 18 will jump from 2.6 million this year to 3.8 million in 1965. It will still be difficult for them to find suitable employment.

The test of our economy is not only whether it can generate jobs for a growing number of young people, but also whether it can find work for those who have lost their jobs and who may not be as highly training or qualified as some younger job-seekers.

'A PLAGUE THAT ROBS A NATION . . .'

Harold C. Crotty, union president, in Brotherhood of Maintenance of Way Employee Journal, April 1959

Unemployment is a plague that robs a nation of its vitality, striking down young and old until community after community is gripped by economic paralysis. Men become frightened by its very thought for they know it can mean desolation, debt and despair.

Where unemployment travels it leaves its mark, and often strikes without warning, catching its victims unprepared. They cannot escape for there is no way to turn. Christian men, distraught with the sight of their suffering families, have been driven to crimes such as theft and even worse to secure the necessities of life.

During April last year more than five million men and women were walking the streets in search of employment; and at the present time, this figure stands at 4.7 million.

In commenting on the necessity of immediate action by the federal government to provide some measure of relief for the unemployed, President Eisenhower remarked: "But I beg of you, let's don't be trapped into expenditures that have no useful purpose except to hand out something—that have no useful purpose except that of helping a man exist for the moment."

This statement by the President was made to the National Food Conference on February 24, 1958. On October 21, 1952, when speaking as a candidate and pleading for the votes of the people, he said: ". . . if there is any sign on the horizon of a recession or an economic collapse, the full power of the government (will be) instantly marshalled, instantly concentrated and localized, to prevent that kind of catastrophe in this country . . ."

With the administration assuming such a "wait and see" attitude, what do the people have to look forward to? Refusal to recognize the present inflation has cost the average family of four a total of $256 the past eighteen months. In the past year, over a million people have joined the labor force; and if employment remains at the 1957 level, none of them will be able to find jobs.

Countless thousands have been compelled to accept relief and many have lost their homes. Must we accept this lethargy by the President as being in accord with his assistant who announced in Detroit late in 1956 that "the right to suffer is one of the joys of a free economy just as the right to prosper is?"

If unemployment must become a permanent and integral part of our economy, we have no alternative other than to adopt broader and more comprehensive insurance laws. The protection provided by such laws, together with an increase in the purchasing power of those actively employed would contribute substantially to a healthier economic picture.

BEHIND JOBLESS STATISTICS ARE HEARTBREAK STORIES LIKE THESE

Bernard Stern in Toledo Union Journal, April 10, 1959

The faceless mass of unemployment statistics came to life Tuesday.

Some 500 unemployed in Toledo and Northwestern Ohio — a small fraction of the many thousands of jobless workers in this area — climbed aboard a special train in Toledo to carry a message to Washington.

They were men and women of all backgrounds and ages with families to support, brought together by a common purpose—to petition their government for help . . . to make jobs available so they could support themselves and their families in decency and dignity.

There was a serious air of purpose on this train, but it wasn't somber. Many were heartsick with the anxiety that comes from being out of work for long periods and are unable to understand why there aren't any jobs for them. There was a feeling of discouragement among some, but no despair.

Through it all there was a feeling of hope that by coming to Washington they might be able to do something to help themselves and others like them.

For the most part those aboard the jobless special from Toledo were factory workers. But there was a good representation from other fields. There were truck drivers and laborers, a seaman and a railroad worker, some building tradesmen and some skilled workers.

If anything stood out it was the comparative youth of those on board. An estimate made of the average age would be in the middle 30's. While there were many middle-aged and oldsters aboard, there were many more in the 20's or early 30's. The majority were out of work a year and longer and they were anxious for action—any kind of action.

As the train pounded its way through the farmlands of Ohio, past the rubber center of Akron, and steel mills in Youngstown and Pittsburgh and along the Allegheny Ridge to the nation's capital, these were the heartbreak stories they told:

Charles L. Winegardner, an IUE member from Lima, felt he was near the end of the line. Thirty-seven years old, married with four children, he has been off work from the Westinghouse plant since February, 1958, although he had more than 10 years' seniority. The plant itself is down from a normal employment of 3,000 to 1,100.

He had exhausted his 26 weeks of unemployment compensation benefits and another 11 weeks of extended temporary compensation. Now he was $3,000 in debt and kept going by loans on his furniture and car and as a door-to-door cosmetic salesman.

Charles Mastin, 23, of Swanton, was bewildered. Married with two children, ages two years and 11 months, this was his first bout with unemployment. A member of the Operating Engineers Union, he had been laid off since the first of the year.

His hope that warmer weather would bring more jobs was fading and he came to lend his voice for government action.

From Excello plants in Bluffton and Lima came Gwynn Coon, 25, Richard Judy, 30, and Dan Campbell, also 30.

Coon, an assembler with 19 months' seniority, has been laid off since February 1958. He has two children.

Judy has been off work for 19 months, and has three children.

Campbell had not worked since last October. But he felt far better off because he was single with no family to support. All felt the government could do much more than it had done.

Another young factory worker was Vaughn Grant, 25, from Toledo. A press operator, he had been laid off since Christmas of 1957. Married, with two children, he was swamped with doctor and hospital bills.

He had found a job with a greenhouse at $1.25 an hour, a little more than half his regular pay, but left it to go back to Prestole on a promise of six months' work. It lasted only six weeks. He owed bills on his furniture and appliances and had moved to a $35-a-month apartment to pare expenses.

From Port Clinton came Mrs. Haroldean Lessentine who left her four children in the care of friends. She had been out of work from Standard Products since December, 1957.

Her husband, Oren, 33, lost his job when the Lakeside and Marblehead Railroad went out of business

three years ago, and he had worked only intermittently until last August when he found a job with Ford Motors in Sandusky.

An older worker in poor circumstances was Homer E. Jones, 47. A laborer with a contractor, he had not had a regular job since Dec. 16, 1955. To get by, he had sold his car, his tools and was now living with his wife in a furnished room.

Unable to find a job since last May was Dan Liesk, 35. He was an able seaman but there were no jobs with half the Great Lakes fleet still tied up.

There were hundreds of other stories of misery and heartbreak caused by unemployment. But none of them was bitter. All they wanted was a job and they were doing the little they could by coming to Washington to let their government know that behind those jobless statistics there were people—them.

TALE OF TWO CITIES

Burt Beck in Textile Labor, January 1958

This is a story of economic disaster in one American community. It happens to be about the twin towns of Biddeford and Saco, in Maine, but it could be about any one of the hundreds of textile towns, mining villages or farm machinery and ordnance centers that have been left stranded when their prime industries gradually or suddenly collapsed.

The twin cities sit astride the Saco River, and the historic falls of that river provide the power that initiated the area's industrial development more than three centuries ago. One of the prime industries was cotton textiles.

When Admiral Perry sailed to Japan in 1854 to open the doors of that country to foreign trade, he carried, as samples of America's finest products, textiles made in Biddeford. From this famous textile area poured uncounted millions of yards of textile fabrics, to all corners of the world.

Textile machinery, shoes, ships, sewing machines, machine guns, bricks, nails, airplane parts, men's collars — all of these have been turned out by the skilled craftsmen of Biddeford and Saco.

Today the area is rapidly becoming a deserted village. A typical headline in the Biddeford Journal proclaims:

UNEMPLOYMENT IN
BIDDEFORD-SACO
AREA TAKES JUMP

Michael Schoonjans, TWUA's international representative in the Biddeford-Saco area, is understandably concerned about the situation. To Mike, the unemployment figures are not statistics; behind each number is an unemployed worker, in most cases the chief breadwinner of the family.

"A few years ago," said Mike, "we had 7,000 members in the Biddeford-Saco Joint Board. Today, we have less than 3,500. The decline in textile manufacturing also hits all the other workers in town."

For concrete evidence of this, it took only a visit to the Biddeford office of the Maine Employment Security commission and a talk with manager Francis M. Coughlin.

The last week for which he had figures was the week ending Dec. 14, 1957. The report showed that there were 1,252 claims for unemployment benefits, and what was even more alarming, 561 people had already exhausted their benefits.

Unemployment in Biddeford-Saco has not increased gradually. Only a few years ago, practically the entire labor force was employed. In 1953, a survey of 10 of the larger employers showed that 9,616 men and women had gainful employment. By 1956 the figure was down to 7,836 but the bottom reallly dropped out in 1957, when unemployment rose 22.2 per cent. The Bates Mill had closed up and over 1,400 jobs were lost. One of the large shoe companies shut its doors and another 325 jobs went down the drain. These plants did not move away; they shut up shop. Only one new industry has moved in — a cabinet manufacturer employing 30 workers.

Biddeford and Saco, instead of the bustling communities they were until recently, have started to take on the characteristics of a "ghost town." You see as many men as women on the business streets — and mostly middle-aged and older men and women. The younger people have left to find jobs elsewhere.

Arthur Maxwell, president of one of the largest banks in the area, is confident about the future. He thinks that the bottom has been reached, and although it may take a few years, things will pick up.

"If some sort of plan can be drafted to redevelop depressed areas, we can come through this with flying colors. It will take hard work," he maintained, "and we'll need help in attracting other industry, but we can do it."

Most of the civic authorities share Maxwell's cautious optimism. The mayor of Saco, Peter A. Garland, is of the opinion that something must be done along the line of encouraging new industry.

"We've laid the groundwork by starting an industrial development committee," he declared. "Now we need help. We're contacting certain manufacturers, but until these things bear fruit, some of the assistance contained in the area redevelopment bill would give us a terrific boost."

The outgoing mayor of Biddeford, Albert C. Lambert, and Carl Swanson, secretary of the Biddeford Industrial Development Commission, were also confident that the Biddeford-Saco area could make a comeback.

"We've got the skilled man-power," said Mayor Lambert, "and we've got wonderful industrial sites. All we need now is—industry."

While the outlook, according to the officials, has its bright side, the current picture is bleak.

Item: Many mid-town stores held their year-end sales prior to Christmas, instead of after the holiday season, as was the usual custom.

Item: For the first time in quite a few years the Community Chest drive will fall short.

Item: Breaking and entering, especially into food stores, has now become a fairly common notation on official police records.

Item: City welfare aid doubled from July to November, and many more cases were expected by the overseer of the poor, Mrs. Annette Gagne.

"Right now, nothing short of area redevelopment assistance, as proposed by Senator Douglas, will help us and other depressed sections," is the way Mike Schoonjans summed up the situation. "There are a lot of people here who are too young to die and not old enough for social security. They want to work, and this sort of program could provide the work for them."

ARE YOU 'JOB-DEAD' AT 40?

Robert W. Hansen in Service Employee, April 1958

It's mighty hard to find a purchaser interested in buying a 1918 Model automobile, and it's getting mighty hard to find an employer interested in hiring a 1918 Model human being.

Just so, more and more employers, especially the larger corporations, aren't hiring people born 40 years ago. More than half of the job openings listed with employment offices in cities included in a recent survey contained maximum hiring ages, with age 40 the most usual top limit.

Actually, the older auto and the older worker are both victims of "planned obsolescence," the practice of making things or considering them in such a way that they are outmoded after a certain period of use or time.

While there may be waste of human energy and economic resources in the practice of 'planned obsolescence," it's hard to visualize our industrial economy functioning well on a "patch it up and make it last" approach. Some artificial stimulation of consumer demand with new designs and new models is more than a gimmick dreamed up on Madison Avenue.

Nowadays, more and more employers apply this practice of "planned obsolescence" to the field of employment policies.

Personnel men, particularly those in large corporations where hiring policies tend to be impersonal and inflexible, have read their company's advertisements so long that they have come to believe that what they have taught consumers to do—trade in the old model for a new one—applies to their workers.

More and more individuals and more and more organizations are responding to the problem of the older worker, by challenging the analogy between manufactured products and human beings. Labor is not a commodity, and people are not products.

Not only is the analogy between men and machines false, but the basic assumption that a younger worker is a more desirable or productive employee is a false one. It is no pitting of young vs. old, but rather an insistence upon the right of both groups to be treated on an individual basis. Surveys—and there have been hundreds of them — have established that older workers can match the pace of younger workers.

Very recently the government's Bureau of Labor Statistics studied the job performance of production workers in 15 shoe factories and 11 household furniture plants for 1956 and 1957.

The findings? As reported in the bureau's Monthly Labor Review, the survey showed that average output of men and women workers did not vary significantly on an age group basis and that "individual evaluation of a worker is far more important than any general ideas concerning the relationship between age and productivity."

This study and many others show the older worker doing more than holding his own. Studies by the Bureau of Labor Statistics reveal that mature workers have 20 per cent better attendance records than their more youthful co-workers . . . that workers over 45 had 2.5 per cent fewer disabling injuries and 25 per cent fewer non-disabling injuries than those under 45 . . . that 72 per cent of the mature workers were either equal to or more efficient than the younger group . . . that the average output per man-hour of piece rate workers remained stable through age 54 . . . that "there is no basis in fact for the misconceptions of prohibitive extra costs of private pension plans and insurance benefits for older workers during employment."

Census Bureau surveys long ago revealed that the wage earner's periods of unemployment last longer as he passes age 40. By the fifteenth week of unemployment, one and one-half times as many workers over 45 compared to those under 45 are still unemployed. When unemployment mounts, it is the worker over 40 who is hit the hardest.

Since impersonal statistics so often mask individual hardships, listen to August Schnell, a small, white-haired man who, up until about a month ago, was a general floor inspector at the A. O. Smith Corporation in Milwaukee. Then he was laid off.

Schnell had been laid off before, but, even in the depression of the 1930's, he had been able to hustle a job somewhere. Now he is in his mid-fifties and, as he told labor reporter John Pomfrey of the *Milwaukee Journal*, "You can't find a dog-gone thing."

August Schnell's main problem is his age. Nobody has told him outright that he is too old to work, but he knows what they mean.

"They ask you how old you are," he said, "You tell them and they sort of hesitate. Then they start talking about something else, so as not to bother you. It kind of hurts."

Economically, job discrimination based on age hurts not only the individual affected, but also industry and the national economy. In fact, the nation suffers the loss of a tremendous productive capacity. This involves the value of the purchasing power that would be earned, as well as the reservoir of skill and experience that this nation cannot afford to lose. This economic loss is aggravated because the economy must be taxed to provide assistance for those who are arbitrarily refused employment because of unfair and unsound hiring practices.

Socially, job discrimination strikes at the family, the basic unit of our society. Most mature workers are heads of families. Job discrimination cuts off family income, denying the chance to provide for wife and little ones.

Morally, job discrimination based on age cuts the deepest of all. It is an affront to the dignity of the person. As BSEIU Research Director Anthony G. Weinlein told a midwest Eagles conference last month, "Besides the financial loss he suffers, the victim of age discrimination is given the feeling that he is useless —exactly at the time when he is at the height of his powers." A worker can stand many things — sickness, hardship, disappointments. But the one thing he cannot stand is the knowledge that he is not wanted, that he has been labelled "too old" and cast onto a junkheap.

Introducing one of several Congressional bills, aimed at outlawing job discrimination based on age, the late U. S. Senator Richard Neuberger, had this to say:

"Discrimination based on age is, in my opinion, as reprehensible as discrimination which originates in racial or religious bigotry."

Yet the want ads of every American newspaper boldly assert the group exclusion of older workers. See the advertisements that read: "MACHINISTS. Experience in all phases of set-up on planers, millers, shapers. Must be under 40." Sometimes the ads state an age limit far less than 40 years—35 or even 30! Why have we failed for so long to see these arbitrary exclusions as wrong and unfair as discrimination on any other basis? Why so few to challenge these job barriers, insisting that economic institutions should serve man and that the human person is the beginning, the center, and the end of all economic activity?

Well, better late than never, and now is the time to join a great moral crusade, convincing employers and general public alike that it is economically wasteful, socially harmful, and morally wrong to deny a man or woman a job because he or she happens to be a 1918 Model instead of a 1938 Model.

HOW TO MEET THE PROBLEM OF UNEMPLOYMENT

Labor's Economic Review, July 1960

Unemployment problems are obviously related closely to a host of other economic issues facing the economy as a whole. Yet there are certain steps that can be taken to help meet the specific problem of unemployment.

1. Give the Unemployment Issue the Attention It Deserves. Unemployment makes headlines during a recession. It makes headlines during a political campaign if the competing candidates are spending their time in a state like West Virginia which has been plagued with this problem. Yet, both government officials and community leaders have tried to minimize its importance.

2. Considering Public Policies. Give Greater Recognition to Their Impact on Unemployment. In the past few years the prevailing question in considering public policies seemed to be, "Will this cause infla-

"This is the only place that will have us after we're 40 years old."

tion?" Posing the problem in this manner has led to a series of restrictionist policies affecting monetary and fiscal policy, taxation, and government expenditures. A far better test for public policy would be "Will this accelerate economic growth and put unemployed people to work?"

3. Strengthen the Role of Unemployment Insurance. Of the 3.7 million now unemployed, half are not drawing benefits, largely because they have not worked in covered employment, or have exhausted benefit rights.

Construction workers have a special problem because they cannot add up "base year" earnings from different states and must have sufficient earnings in one state to qualify.

Agricultural workers are excluded entirely, as are seasonal workers in many states. Some states deny benefits to those over 65 years old even if they are actively searching for work.

Changing technology and geographical displacement of industry have lengthened the duration of unemployment beyond the provisions of state laws. Most state laws limit the unemployed to 26 weeks of benefits, but there are now over 500,000 who have been unemployed 27 weeks or longer. Clearly benefits should be available for a longer period of time —up to 39 weeks if a weekly review of each individual case shows that no jobs are immediately available. Along with broader coverage and longer duration of benefits, there is urgent need to raise the weekly benefits substantially.

4. Meet the Special Problems of Depressed Areas. Communities hard-hit by persistent unemployment have simply been unable to climb back on the path to prosperity. Only if the federal government lends its support will these communities be able to get back on their feet.

Legislation to assist such distressed areas has been debated in Congress since 1953. On two occasions Congress has enacted legislation providing a specific federal program including technical assistance, loans for industrial purposes, grants for community facilities, a more intensive vocational training program, and allowances to unemployed workers while undergoing training. Each time such legislation has passed the Congress, it has been vetoed by the President and his veto has been upheld.

5. Devise a New Type of Training Program. The U. S. spends an esti-mated $18 billion on education to prepare young people to take jobs in industry. Such expenditures, including federal grants to states for vocational education, have become an accepted part of the federal government's responsibility.

Today, the need for training is much broader. The introduction of new technology has left many middle-age and older individuals without jobs. For them, finding work is far more difficult, and the burden of unemployment far more onerous than for a young person who has received greater educational and technical training.

"You Can Say That Again!"

COMMUNITY SERVICES SETS
PROGRAM TO AID JOBLESS

AFL-CIO News, June 14, 1958

Here is the basic 10-point program for aiding the unemployed prepared by AFL-CIO Community Services for its recent Washington conference:

• Informing the jobless worker that the labor movement has a plan to help with personal problems.

• Establishing a system whereby union counsellors are on duty at union headquarters.

• Protection of unemployment compensation claims by acquainting workers with the procedure for filing, and in some instances, setting up auxiliary branches of unemployment compensation offices at union halls.

• Explaining how jobless workers can obtain supplemental unemployment benefits where available under union contracts.

• Finding public welfare sources of food, shelter, clothing and medical care where compensation is exhausted, checks are delayed, or claims are disallowed or the amount is too small.

• Getting welfare officials to relax usual eligibility requirements that frequently involve virtual pauperism in order to provide temporary assistance.

• Informing union members of arrangements made to protect medical and hospitalization coverage during a layoff.

• Setting up a program to distribute surplus foods to augment unemployment benefits and public assistance.

• Securing secondary assistance from voluntary agencies, which labor supports to the tune of more than $150 million annually, in cases where residence requirements or other restrictions disqualify families from public assistance.

• Prevailing on private agencies to lend staff members to Public Welfare Departments to enable such public agencies to carry the larger case load resulting from the recession.

SUB PLANS EMPHASIZED TO STABILIZE JOBS

AFL-CIO News, December 8, 1956

The guaranteed annual wage or supplemental unemployment benefits are now a major goal because they are the only fields in which labor unions had not already taken steps to aid workers in times of adversity.

Elliot Bredhoff, associate general counsel of the Steelworkers, told the University of Tennessee's conference on collective bargaining trends in Knoxville that union pleas for aid in providing for jobless workers long fell on deaf ears "but will find a more ready response from management today."

The principle of private supple-

mentation is now well established, he said.

Unions through negotiation have applied the principle of group insurance, with the risk and costs spread over the largest number.

Industry has moved toward this view, he said, and plans now in effect and contemplated will have an impact on the employment picture and help to sustain the economy.

In states where supplementation is banned by law, Bredhoff promised, unions will find other methods of providing assistance.

JOBLESS PAY PLAN SET UP BY PLUMBERS

AFL-CIO News, June 2, 1956

A new type of "guaranteed wage" unemployment benefit has been negotiated here between Plumbers and Pipefitters Local 159 and union contractors in Richmond, Calif.

The Local 159 plan provides that the employers will pay 25 cents per manhour worked into a special individual bank account in the name of the employee working.

After one year, an unemployed worker may draw upon his account to supplement his unemployment insurance up to the maximum of $100 a week. If disabled, the employee may use the bank account to supplement his disability insurance up to the $100 weekly figure.

Funds in the employee's individual account will always be his—to use in event of unemployment or disability or to go to his heirs in event of death.

No payments are to be made in a strike situation, but the funds may be drawn during a lockout. The accounts will draw the usual bank interest.

A HAPPY THIRD BIRTHDAY FOR SUB— $105 MILLION IN BENEFITS FOR JOBLESS

UAW Solidarity, July 1959

Only three years old, but already a lusty and growing force in gaining economic security for workers.

That's the story of the UAW-negotiated supplemental unemployment benefit plans which in June marked the third anniversary of the first payments. Benefits began in June 1956 under SUB agreements negotiated in 1955.

In three short years, SUB plans have:

1. Paid out more than $105 million to unemployed UAW members.

2. Stimulated effective political and legislative action to bring about integration of SUB and state unemployment compensation benefits in states where integration was resisted by reactionary employer groups.

3. Added impetus to improvements in many state Unemployment Compensation laws.

4. Been significantly improved in 1958-'59 negotiations, particularly with Studebaker-Packard and Allis-Chalmers.

5. Proven that SUB offers a realistic, practical new force to increase the security of workers and help to stabilize the nation's economy.

Of the $105 million in SUB payments during the three-year period, Big Three auto SUB plans alone paid out more than $62.7 million to jobless workers. Big Three SUB funds have received contributions of almost $182 million; their balances as of June totalled nearly $124 million.

SUB funds came through the relatively heavy drains of the 1958 recession in excellent financial shape, bearing out UAW predictions that employer contributions to the funds would be more than adequate to meet both current and improved benefit programs.

UAW achieved another important milestone on the road to effective employment security during the past three years with the integration of SUB with state UC benefits in virtually all states.

This gain was realized despite bitter opposition from reactionary employer groups which lobbied for anti-SUB legislation or sought state rulings that SUB payments were "wages" which would bar or reduce benefits to workers receiving SUB.

Action to bar SUB integration with state UC either by legislative or administrative steps was successful in only four states—Ohio, Indiana, Virginia and North Carolina. A total of 39 other states (including Hawaii) and the District of Columbia permitted SUB integration, while the issue did not arise at all in seven states where there are no plants covered by SUB.

Ohio and Indiana enacted legislation permitting SUB-UC integration, despite strenuous opposition of reactionary employer groups, after effective political action by the UAW and other labor and liberal groups.

California, where a lower court decision overturned a pro-SUB ruling made by the then-attorney-general, now Gov. Edmund G. (Pat) Brown, the 1959 legislature enacted legislation nailing down the right of jobless workers to get both SUB and UC benefits.

Only Virginia and North Carolina still bar SUB-UC integration and alternate benefit programs are in effect there.

UAW-negotiated SUB plans have helped to give marked impetus to the improvement of state UC laws. Required to meet full cost of maintaining SUB plans to supplement inadequate state UC benefits, employers have noticeably slackened resistance to improved UC laws in the past three years.

New separation payments, providing a maximum of 1,200 hours' (30 weeks' pay) in a lump sum to workers laid off permanently as a result of transfers of operations, plant closings or other causes, also will come out of SUB funds.

Significant improvements were made in 1958 in the standard SUB agreements negotiated with the Big Three. In addition, important breakthroughs were made this year in key provisions of SUB plans, including those at Studebaker-Packard and Allis-Chalmers.

For example, at Allis-Chalmers, benefits for workers with children are higher than 65 per cent of the weekly after-tax pay. Maximum benefits are $50 a week if UC is also received, and $75 a week if UC is not received.

Although these recently negotiated plans contain significant improvement, they do not mark the full measure of economic security against layoffs and short workweeks which workers, like other groups in American society, have a right to expect.

Improvements in benefit amounts, duration, and eligibility must still be made in order to reach the goals of stabilizing employment, maintaining income security for workers and helping to insulate our economy against spiralling recession.

INADEQUATE JOBLESS BENEFITS CAUSING MILLIONS TO SUFFER

AFL-CIO News, April 26, 1958

Millions of jobless Americans and families are "suffering severely and needlessly" because of the inadequacies of the unemployment insurance laws.

In addition, business is "losing customers" who can't afford to maintain purchases on the low weekly benefits currently in effect, says Labor's Economic Review published by the AFL-CIO Dept. of Research.

The AFL-CIO has called for emergency action to increase benefits and extend their duration, protect the jobless not covered by the unemployment compensation system and provide general assistance to those in dire need.

But beyond the immediate emergency, says the Review, the need is for an improved federal-state system with new federal minimum standards geared to the current American economy.

Benefits are too low because of maximums or ceilings imposed by the states, with the typical maximum at $32 a week. One-half of the states permit less than $32, one-half more, with an overall range of from $25 to $45 in the 41 states that do not make provision for additional benefits for dependents.

The Review declares that about one-half of all workers who receive benefits have their weekly amounts held down by state maximums.

Present state laws on duration of benefits are based on past employment and earnings with the result that for the nation as a whole during 1957 the average was 20.5 weeks of benefits at the time of exhaustion.

The Review concludes, "Employers have succeeded in getting tax rates cut by two-thirds and in reducing average benefits to about one-third of average weekly earnings. This benefit average in relation to earnings is only three quarters of what it was 20 years ago when the proportion was 43 percent.

"The typical maximum benefit permitted today is only 44 percent of average weekly wages in the states as compared with 65 percent in 1939."

The Kennedy-McCarthy bill, strongly supported by the AFL-CIO, would create new federal standards so that the benefits available to each worker would not be less than 50 percent of his regular earnings and give the nation an average benefit of more than $40 rather than the $30 now in effect.

The bill would provide also benefit duration of 39 weeks, extend coverage and eliminate some present disqualification procedures.

ACT NOW TO AVOID SLUMP, CONGRESS TOLD

UAW Solidarity, March 1960

Declaring that the present recovery is only a "short term" one, UAW Pres. Walter P. Reuther has presented a 16-point program for economic growth to Congress.

The program recommended measures to avert a slowdown during the second half of this year and counter-recessionary measures to be adopted now for use at the first sign of an economic decline.

"The factors necessary for continued full production, full employment and steady growth in our economy simply are not present," Reuther said.

"For the second time within the brief lifetime of the present Administration we are moving out of a recession into a 'recovery' that is not a true recovery at all, with the signs clearly portending that unless there are vigorous and immediate changes made in our national economic policies, we shall soon be staggering into a third recession," he said.

Highlights of Reuther's proposals follow:

• Balanced economic growth of 5 per cent a year and full employment should be established as the goal of national economic policy.

• A halt in the Administration's "tight-money" policy.

• Need, and not necessarily budget balancing, should be the criterion for defense and public service programs.

• Overhaul of the tax structure to eliminate tax loopholes for the wealthy and to give the small income family a break.

• Enactment of necessary programs in housing, education, health, slum clearance and development of natural resources to meet the needs of a growing population.

• Examination of the national defense effort in terms of today's needs.

• Boosting of consumer buying power.

• Improvement of the minimum wage act and the unemployment insurance program.

• Adequate help for the depressed areas.

• Improvement in trade relations.

• Continued investigation into the price structure to expose monopolistic price fixing.

II

Serving
The Family
And Nation

EDITORS' NOTE

Labor's organized activities long ago moved beyond the shop or factory. Union programs do not end with the closing bell or the quitting whistle. In the 1960's working people expect their unions to do something about living conditions as well as working conditions.

Today unions are represented on the boards of United Funds or Community Chests in most communities.

Unions are actively teaching wage earners how to spend their hard earned money more wisely.

Union health and welfare plans have become the biggest single factor enabling working people to finance medical and hospital costs.

Supplementary pensions to make up for the inadequacy of the Social Security system are part of the union contract in a steadily growing number of industries.

Better public schools, better housing have long been part of the community programs of most labor organizations.

The chapters in this section of *Labor's Story* reflect labor's growing concern with the health of their communities, and growing awareness of labor's community responsibilties. In most communities, the labor press has become a source of strength for progress and reform, a channel for education on good citizenship, as these sections prove.

8 | COMMUNITY SERVICES

LABOR NO LONGER A CHARITY CASE

Voice of the Cement, Lime, Gypsum and Allied Workers, May 1960

There was a time when the laboring "class" was the recipient of charity and the wellspring of the poor and the maimed. Today, however, labor—particularly organized labor—is farther up the ladder of economic security, and it is usually either the non-union family or the unfortunates of all strata of society who receive the benefits of community welfare programs.

Unions have become increasingly concerned with the life of union men and women beyond the plant gates, with their homes and their clothing and their food, with their hospitals and their schools and their parks, with their roads and their playgrounds and their jails, with the places where they work.

All this has become a union responsibility to be discharged through community organization, in concert with other groups of citizens.

Labor's community services program perceives that the union is also a community organization; that the union member is also a citizen; that the union leader is also a community leader. The fact is that one can no more separate the community services program from the union than one can separate the union from the community.

More than 75,000 men and women from labor unions across the continent currently serve on boards and committees of voluntary community welfare agencies. More than 40,000 men and women from labor's ranks have completed voluntary eight-week union counseling courses sponsored by the AFL-CIO—courses in such subjects as health services, public assistance, child and family services, recreational facilities, social security, workmen's compensation, unemployment compensation, and similar community-provided welfare services.

In major cities across the country, more than 125 labor representatives currently are on the staffs of community health and welfare organizations, providing an effective day-to-day liaison between the agencies and labor.

For decades each labor union handled its own community service program independently. When a needy case was reported, the local union pitched in financially and manually to assist the unfortunate. When a family was left destitute after its home burned, the labor union contributed time and money to rebuild a new home. At Christmas, baskets were prepared and distributed to the destitute.

At the time of the AFL-CIO merger it was decided to combine the varied efforts of the 135 affiliated organizations. An AFL-CIO Community Services Committee was established to coordinate the work.

Leo Perlis was appointed as director of all AFL-CIO Community Service Activities.

Perlis explains the duties of his organization as follows:

"The major purpose of the program—reflecting one of the basic objectives of the AFL-CIO as a whole—is to work for a community which is more representative of the people and which is more responsive to the people's needs. The community services program, therefore, is designed to encourage first-class citizenship and more than adequate health, welfare and recreation facilities and services.

"The active participation of AFL-CIO affiliates and trade union members in the affairs of their communities is the tangible expression of labor's consistent refusal to become a socially separatist movement. It is in labor's community services work, perhaps more than in any other area, that the class struggle is most visibly rejected.

"It is here where you find men and women of labor, management, the professions, the clergy and citizens generally working together for the common good of the total community. It is in this voluntary association of free men and women from all walks of life and from all shades of political opinion and economic background that our flexible democratic society expresses its very heart and soul."

Early in 1958, Community Services set in motion six priority programs, each designed to meet an important public need or establish a new service in the community.

Unemployment relief headed the list. The Community Service Activities staff and volunteers in many cities launched programs of assistance to unemployed unionists and their families. Ways were found to expedite and extend unemployment benefits and public assistance, establish or expand surplus food distribu-

tion, and to set up special facilities to meet the immediate needs of the jobless.

Full use of the Salk polio vaccine was the second priority program. CSA's manpower was responsible in many communities for reducing the cost of inoculations and stimulating mass inoculation programs.

Community Services used its program machinery in an effort to provide more adequate medical care to greater numbers of people through increased consumer and labor representation on hospital boards and committees.

Fourth in priority was the national program for fluoridation of water. CSA spearheaded education campaigns in communities where tooth decay is still allowed to go unchecked despite the proven effectiveness of water fluoridation.

The critical shortage of trained social workers became a direct concern of CSA, with the organization promoting a program for United Funds and Community Chests to set aside one percent of all funds raised in annual campaigns for scholarships in the social welfare field.

CSA designated community health education as its final priority program for 1958.

Last year, the CSA added other projects: consumer counseling to aid workers and their families in ways to get the most for their hard-earned money, retirement planning to assist the elderly and retired worker, and the creation of a national health fund.

VOLUNTARY SERVICE HAS NO EQUAL — BEIRNE

AFL-CIO Community Services Chairman Joseph A. Beirne in
AFL-CIO News, November 10, 1956

One of the chief distinctions marking the difference between a free society and a dictatorship is the existence of voluntary social services freely and generously supported, and democratically administered by the

citizens of the community. There are no Community Chests in the Iron Curtain countries.

When we support and serve the Red Cross, the Family Service Society, the Visiting Nurses, the various religious social services, the Boy and Girl Scouts, the YMCA and YWCA, and the settlement houses we are supporting one of the bulwarks of a democratic community.

This is not to say that government does not have a responsibility in the area of social welfare. It is a basic function of a free society to assume responsibility in such large areas as public assistance, financial aid to dependent children, to give assistance to the needy aged, the blind and the totally and permanently disabled. But this is also to say that we must not permit government to assume direction in matters of personal or family concern.

CORONET TELLS TRADE UNIONS' ROLE IN COMMUNITY SERVICE

AFL-CIO News, May 3, 1958

In times of disaster or need, labor unions have been among the first to volunteer their manpower and money to perform unselfish feats of public service.

In an article titled "Labor's Labor of Love," May Coronet reveals that union members are breathing a thousand forms of life into unionism's slogan: "What's good for the community is good for labor!"

Union members, says Coronet, are spearheading drives to combat juvenile delinquency, to provide employment opportunties for handicapped persons, to foster public understanding and awareness of such diseases as diabetes and alcoholism. All over the country, in fact, alert community-conscious unionists are finding imaginative ways to help in times of need.

Millions of dollars are collected by union members for special charities outside the scope of joint community campaigns. Union contributions to heart, cancer, TB, polio and other drives are huge, and some unions have their own special charities.

For example, May Coronet cites three local unions in San Jose, Calif., which, last fall, contributed a total of $4,500 for the down payment on a new school for retarded children. In Harlingen, Tex., unionists donated nearly $20,000 for the construction of a home for neglected and dependent girls.

Unionists volunteered their time and effort without pay during floods in New England and Yuba City, Calif.; the tornadoes in Flint, Mich., and Dallas, Tex., and in other emergencies.

Women in unions, reveals May Coronet, have their record of community service as well. In Miami, Fla., over 300 union women donate their time each year to the United Cerebral Palsy Telethon.

DONATIONS POUR IN TO SAVE INA HANNA'S LIFE

Toledo Union Journal, August 29, 1958

Ina Hanna, whose heart is dying a little every day, lies in her dimly-lit house trailer these days and rejoices in her newly-rediscovered secret.

She has learned what many of us desperately wish we knew—that her friends will stand by her when she needs them most.

Only last week, Ina had to forego a delicate operation to free her heart valves of calcium deposits which exorably are choking her heart to death.

The operation had been scheduled in a Cleveland hospital, and the UAW City-Wide Charity Fund had made arrangements to have 31 donors on hand to supply blood during the exhausting surgery.

But the tiny Buddies Unit member had to call it off because she was broke, unable to make the $400 down payment required in advance by the surgeon and hospital.

Thanks to many friends she didn't know she had, Ina is a little closer to living again.

Small donations, ranging from dimes to ten-spots, have come in from fellow union members, most of whom preferred to remain anonymous.

Workers at the Champion Spark Plug plant, whom Ina served while working at the Buddies canteen there, have filled a box with their donations.

Blanche Brown, who works at the canteen, reported that Champion workers quickly filled a box with $67.23 for Ina.

When Mrs. Brown removed the box, some Champion workers protested that they hadn't had a chance to contribute. The box went back, wtih a Journal clipping about Ina pasted on it. By Friday, $50 more was in it, Mrs. Brown said.

Contributions have come into the Ina Hanna Fund from Standard Oil workers, from Libbey-Owens-Ford Glass workers and from Willys Unit members.

The total is rapidly nearing $200, reports Thelma Haworth, chairman of the Buddies unit. If contributions keep up, Ina may have her operation in several weeks. It must be then, for soon she will be too weak to undergo the exhausting surgery.

A letter, signed only "A Retiree," was forwarded with $1, "from a retired Champion worker who knows what hard times are."

The letter said:

"May the good God bless and help you through your troubles and at last save you, is the earnest prayer of a Journal reader.

"This dollar isn't much, but if each union member would see fit to do the same, your problems would be solved."

But while so many generous hearts have responded to her need, Ina now has found another problem added to her burden.

Her weekly sick benefit of $30 expired this week.

Since her illness forced her off her job at the Champion canteen early this year, Ina not only has managed to live on her $30 weekly benefit, but she has scrimped hard enough to save nearly $100 from it, to go toward her life-giving operation.

Now the 26 weeks of benefits, provided for under the UAW contract at Buddies Lunch System have ended. Ina must face the problem of staying alive until the time comes for the operation which may restore her to health and to her job.

The City-County Relief Dept. undoubtedly will help on that problem, Jack Thompson, the AFL-CIO welfare director in Toledo, said.

But no help seems to be available from any Toledo agency for Ina's operation, he added.

The city's Central Hospital Bureau, for example, would help pay Ina's bill if she were to undergo the surgery at a Toledo hospital. The agency cannot help pay the bill if it is incurred in an out-of-town hospital, Mr. Thompson was told.

Unfortunately, Ina cannot have the operation in a Toledo hospital. Her doctor advised her to have the surgery performed in the Cleveland hospital because it has specialized facilities for such surgery, greatly improving her chance for recovery.

So Ina lies in her dimly-lit house trailer on Dorr St. and rejoices in her new-found friends. No matter what the future holds for her, she is confident that she will have help.

The Union has a heart, she knows because the Union is people, and people will help each other if they are given the chance.

COMMUNITY SERVICES AND GUIDANCE
AVAILABLE TO UNION MEMBERS

Local 1-S News, January 15, 1960

New York is a giant city, so large and complex that the individual sometimes feels lost, especially when he may have personal problems which are not in his power to solve.

He may need the special guidance of a social worker, or the "expertize" of a community agency specialist. Guidance to help work out individual difficulties may be available, but first a person must know where to look . . . whom to contact . . . what to ask . . . to tap the skills and facilities of the vast structure of social and community service organizations in New York.

The labor movement throughout the nation has been learning how to build these bridges of communication between worker and agency, and Local 1-S can rightfully claim to have been one of the first.

On every Wednesday night throughout the year, except during the summer months, a Local 1-S Counselor is on hand to consult with any union member about any problem on which he needs help.

The sessions are conducted privately of course, and without charge, by Louis Levine, secretary of the New York AFL-CIO Community Services Committe, and a labor representative at the Greater New York Fund.

The basic form of the Wednesday night interview is simple. Lou asks the member to state all the facts relating to the problems, and may ask various questions to get the whole story. That starts the ball rolling.

Sometimes the problem is an easy one, and the Community Services Counselor may make a recommendation on the spot. Otherwise, the union member is referred to one of the 425 agencies affiliated with the Greater New York Fund, or to another source of aid or expert information.

The member is usually notified within 24 hours or asked to call Lou Levine for additional information or action of some kind. Fully one-third of Local 1-S member problems center on the inadequacy of housing, Lou Levine reports, and he may make an appointment for the member to file an application for a housing project.

Many emergency situations have been resolved through the Local 1-S Community Service referrals. In one case, a member's wife was recuperating from surgery, and someone was needed to look after her and two youngsters while he was working. In this case, a trained home-maker was provided for five weeks by Catholic Charities. Under such circumstances, the home-maker is paid what the worker can afford. The worker pays nothing if he can afford nothing.

In another case husband-wife problems and conflicts had reached a point where the family was in danger of being torn apart. The family, which included a mother-in-law and two children, was living in three rooms. The husband was threatening to leave the family. Through Local 1-S referral, a family counseling expert has been providing guidance in exploring emotional difficulties which require understanding, patience and therapy. In such situations, a skilled and sympathetic social worker can help a great deal.

In another case, a member who had been operated on for cancer needed longtime nursing home care and bed rest. The member had no money saved at all. Through the Local 1-S referral service, admission to a nursing home was arranged, with the Department of Welfare paying the cost. The period of nursing home care is expected to last about a year.

Consider now another area of union service: legal counseling.

There's hardly anything a person does anymore but there's a law involved. Work in Macy's . . . there's a law called the union contract, and you see your union representative about it. If you have a personal legal problem . . . well, you can see your union Legal Counselor about that!

In the latter case, attorney Edith Lowenstein is at the Union Office every Wednesday evening. She is there to provide legal counsel on all the problems which may arise in daily life: trouble with a landlord, sharp practices in installment selling, accidents other than Workmen's Compensation cases, wills, estates, person's rights under the law, etc.

In one recent case, a Union member was overcharged $55 a month in rent. He came down to the weekly counseling session and, in time, the union attorney instituted action in court. After trial, the landlord had to pay the union member triple damages for the willful overcharge.

Moreover, the City Rent Commission reduced the rent because of fail-ure to paint and to supply heat and hot water. Today, the Union member and his family still live in the same apartment but they're paying the registered rental.

Through this case, the union lawyer helped the Rental Commission to expose a flourishing racket, and greatly benefitted many other people.

In another case, a young woman member went to a dance studio and signed up for a number of lessons. A male teacher paid considerable personal attention to her, inducing her to sign up for a dance course beyond her financial means. She consulted the union lawyer at the counseling session. Legal pressure was brought to bear. As a result, the case was disposed of for exactly the amount of money she had already spent.

All counseling and referrals are, of course, completely without charge. Subsequent legal action, however, may entail modest fees.

"Melting Pot"

SEAMAN

COUNCIL 33 HELPS BUILD CITIZENS

The Public Employee, October 1959

This is the story of how the city of Philadelphia and AFSCME District Council 33 have successfully joined forces to make good citizens of boys who may become tempted to run afoul of the law.

The city's Welfare Department recognized the fact that recreational programs aren't enough to keep teen-agers occupied during the summer months and after school hours.

After much soul searching the city officials decided on a "works program" known as the Philadelphia Youth Conservation Corps to keep youngsters with active minds and limited opportunity from going astray.

Council 33 started playing a leading role in YCC after a consultation with Mayor Richardson Dilworth made clear that the jobs of none of its members who work in Fairmount Park would be sacrificed. The corps works in the park, ditching low lying areas to remove standing water that breeds mosquitos.

As a result of the program, Philadelphians already enjoy several newly-cleared picnic areas in the park that are easily accessible to roads and parking areas. These had been unuseable previously.

Members of Council 33 locals are in charge of five groups of 10 boys each. The boys are chosen from all areas of the city with some of them from depressed areas. Grouping of the boys by age has kept the boys from the same neighborhoods from ganging together. This has produced some cross-town friendships and has broadened many of the boys' horizons.

The jobs they have been doing are no cinch. They had plenty of blisters to contend with at the outset. They were bitten by mosquitos, wasps and bees. Quite a few got cases of poison ivy. But they stuck it out and liked it.

The boys are learning the use and care of tools and good work habits. Some of them have become proficient axemen, capable of chopping down a six-inch diameter tree in a few minutes. The amount of pay each boy receives is based on his group leader's evaluation of his work.

Inasmuch as members of all racial, religious and ethnic groups are eligible for the corps, the boys whose ages ranges from 14 through 17 are learning a basic lesson of democracy —tolerance of and respect for the other fellow and his ideas.

542 CHILDREN CLOTHED!

Amplifier (Local 1048, IBEW in Indianapolis), January 1960

You came through again! This year Local 1048, IBEW, was able to clothe 542 needy children at Christmas time! Your cooperation and sharing made this possible. Beginning the middle of December union members picked up the children from the "Times" Clothe-a-Child headquarters and took them to Block's for outfitting. Earlier a Committee from your union met to compile a representative "shopping list,"

and then invited a number of stores in the city to submit bids on the clothing for the children. This year, as in 1958, Block's Department Store offered the best arrangements and price.

In this yearly undertaking, Local 1048 cooperates with the "Times" annual drive. The "Times" has the facilities for investigating applications for clothing, and we rely upon their recommendations in this field.

The department store agreed to stay open on several evenings to accomodate our shoppers, and at the appointed hours, the "Times" had ready for us the number of children we requested—ranging from twenty or thirty to several hundred at a time. Our members picked up the children and the happy shopping began. This year we averaged $24 per child, clothing each with a complete outfit "from the skin out."

Final Clothe-a-Child reports indicate that you folks have contributed over $13,000 to the Clothe-a-Child Fund this year!

LETTER FROM HAWAII

Wally Miyazono in Postal Record, April 1959

Previously, I haven't breathed a word to any one of you, for I wasn't sure just how our first venture in the way of a community service project would develop. But now it can be told:

The Honolulu Mailman's March, ringing door bells for the Heart Fund, was an overwhelming success.

The Heart Sunday was designated the 15th of February, and the march commenced at 8 A. M. for a 4-hour "skirmish" against heart disease toward an objective of going beyond a $1,000 per hour rate. This fund, added to the grand total received by the Heart Association through other means, will in the very near future finance and bring to Honolulu a complete medical research program and surgical unit such as the heart-lung machine so that no longer our patients, especially the youngsters, will have to travel the thousands of lonely, painful and costly miles to California or elsewhere on the mainland for open-heart surgery and treatment of heart disease.

The success of the March can be attributed to the determined, willing cooperation by the letter carriers, by mean of TV and radio appearances, and publicity through our local dailies.

In any campaign, there is always someone outstanding. The honor goes to Mrs. Ruby Yuen, who prepared refreshments for the letter carriers who marched on Heart Sunday.

ARIZONA WORKERS GIVE AID TO HANDICAPPED

AFL-CIO News, May 18, 1959

PHOENIX, ARIZ.—Because organized workers in Arizona were willing voluntarily to give up an hour's pay a year, physically handicapped children and adults will be given a new lease on life and be prepared to make their own way as useful members of the community.

Members of AFL-CIO unions have pledged themselves to raise the $100-000 needed to take advantage of a matching federal grant of Hill-Burton Act funds to Arizona. The result is a new total rehabilitation center at the Samuel Gompers Memorial Clinic, built by Arizona workers in 1953.

The $200,000 addition encompasses 15,000 square feet of space and gives the Maricopa County Society for Crippled Children and Adults, which supports the clinic, a total of more than 22,000 square feet.

The addition has expanded the clinic's pre-vocational testing, which is one of the important elements of total restoration of the handicapped. Woodworking equipment, for instance, is used to test work tolerances as well as to get a line on the abilities of those undergoing treatment.

Three private treatment areas have been set up in the physical therapy department for use as needed. A new conference room will be used for extension courses in special education given by Arizona State University, and as a seminar room for specialists.

The handicapped who are helped through the memorial clinic to achieve the dignity of labor and become self-supporting are not the only ones to benefit from the program.

There is an economic advantage to the community, too. A recent survey, according to the Easter seal committee, shows that the handicapped person who is given the advantage of total rehabilitation through medically-oriented team service returns $10 to the community in his complete restoration to useful living for every $1 spent on his rehabilitation.

AMALGAMATED BANK OF NEW YORK CELEBRATES 35 YEARS OF PUBLIC SERVICE

The Advance, May 1, 1958

The Amalgamated Bank of New York, the first labor bank to be established in New York City and one of the first labor banks in the United States, marked its thirty-fifth year of operation in April, 1958.

Owned and operated by the Amalgamated Clothing Workers of America, the Amalgamated Bank was established in 1923 to provide banking services primarily for working men and women, the small business man and community organizations.

At this bank, the workers, the small businessman, secretaries, professionals and housewives are treated, not as banking statistics, but individuals whose financial problems require and receive sympathetic attention.

The traditional chill of banking institutions is not present in the Amalgamated bank where the worker feels comfortable, assured that this is indeed his bank.

A pioneering institution, the Amalgamated Bank was the first commercial bank in New York City to make small personal loans at reasonable

bank rates—and introduced the convenient monthly payment system.

While today the small loan service is accepted procedure in most banks, the Amalgamated Bank of New York continues to lead the banking world with the lowest interest rate for personal loans. To date over 127,000 people have borrowed in excess of $47,000,000.

Another "first" in banking services was the Amalgamated Bank's introduction of low-cost services that require no minimum balance.

From modest beginnings, with an original capital structure of $275,000, the Amalgamated bank has grown into a large and sound institution with a present capital and reserve of over $92,000,000.

Today, the Amalgamated bank's clients range from the self-employed and wage-earners in all walks of life to large publishing, industrial, financial, insurance, textile and apparel companies, and of course, labor unions. Today, more than 15,000 people transact business with the Amalgamated bank.

ᘒ

In Columbus, Ohio, state officials boasted of a new $12,000,000 prison they were opening for 2500 convicts. Chief features of the new pokey, they disclosed, would be pastel walls, window bars that look like lattice-work, piped in music, and private cells for most of the criminals. Said a stunned Ohio AFL-CIO official, "Good God! the surroundings in that hoosegow are 10 times more congenial than in most Ohio factories!"   —LES FINNEGAN

LABOR RUSHES RELIEF FOR VICTIMS OF VICIOUS HURRICANE AUDREY

Gene Zack in AFL-CIO News, July 13, 1957

LAKE CHARLES, LA. — Amid the chaos and ruin spread by hurricane Audrey throughout southern Louisiana, organized labor rolled up its sleeves to tackle the grim job of bringing relief to the storm's victims. Within a matter of hours after the hurricane's fury spread death and destruction over the coastal towns of Lake Charles, Cameron, Creole and Grand Chenier, the AFL-CIO— through its Community Service Activities—began mobilizing its forces to assist in the emergency relief program.

AFL-CIO members in hurricane-ravaged Lake Charles were among the first to respond to calls for help in the disaster, according to Kenneth Kramer, CSA labor liaison staff man with the American Red Cross who had been rushed into the stricken area.

Members of all 28 locals affiliated with the Lake Charles Labor Council turned quickly to the major jobs of rescuing survivors, searching through rubble and flooded bayous for bodies, digging out debris in the communities buffeted by the wind and inundated by the accompanying tidal wave, and aiding in the grim task of burying more than 150 unknown dead.

Over 150 members of Carpenters' Local 953, assisted by other volunteers from other AFL-CIO locals, worked in round-the-clock shifts fashioning the rough, pine boxes to be used for burial.

Lake Charles local unions raised a fund among their own members to pay for the lumber used in the coffins, and the Operating Engineers donated men and secured equipment used for opening and closing the graves for the mass burials of the dead.

Three of the AFL-CIO mobile canteens—labor's gift to the American Red Cross—are operating here on Louisiana's hurricane-wrecked coast, serving together for the first time since leaving their factory last January.

From totally destroyed Grand Chenier, down the debris-filled roads to Creole and on into tragic Cameron, where hundreds perished under Audrey's battering, the three sturdy red and white vehicles carry fresh water, food and coffee to the volunteers restoring the essentials of life to this hard hit area.

Kramer, who directed labor participation in the relief operations here, reported from the disaster scene that the rehabilitation work would be impossible without the labor canteens on the job.

"Thousands and thousands of decaying bodies of dead cattle fill the swamps; masses of insects and the constant threat of pestilence hang with the odor of death over the whole region."

It was estimated the death toll would exceed 500, principally because the area was crowded with hundreds of migrant workers a large number of whom are unaccounted for.

The mobile canteens are being manned by AFL-CIO volunteers from the building trades unions, and are kept supplied from Red Cross field kitchens operating in Cameron, as they make their circuit of the ravaged gulf coast area.

To bolster the volunteer work of organized labor from Cameron, AFL-CIO Reg. Dir. E. H. Williams and Pres. Victor Bussie of the Louisiana State Labor Council AFL-CIO made a first-hand inspection of the disaster area. They found trade unionists from the area working with the Defense Agency and Red Cross in the relief operations.

UNION LABOR REBUILDS 10 NEW HOMES WITHIN MONTH; RED CROSS ESTIMATES VOLUNTEERS SAVED AGENCY $25,000

The Laborer, September 1957

AFL-CIO building tradesmen last month in a series of "building bees" on weekends completed about one dozen homes to replace houses wrecked by Hurricane Audrey and the tidal wave which struck the Lake Charles, La., area June 27.

The volunteer effort of 150-250 building tradesmen from craft unions of Louisiana and Texas was praised as a "magnificent performance" and "a lasting monument to the spirit of unselfish cooperation" by Don Stout, Red Cross director for the Hurricane Audrey disaster relief operations program.

The volunteer workers joined in a mighty effort to mobilize skills and manpower to work on weekends to build five new houses each weekend working from early Saturday until late Sunday. Five home were put up the first weekend, August 3-4.

The building bee was a practical demonstration by unionists of how organized labor comes to the aid of the disaster-wracked areas in time of need. The American Red Cross is providing the building materials and the union men the skill and manpower. The building operations are planned by the Red Cross and the building trade unions.

A union man is assigned as foreman of a team of 30 to 35 workmen for each house. Jurisdictional lines are completely obliterated by the enthusiastic workmen. The only objective: to build the houses as quickly as possible.

The workmen come to the site by buses and planes and live in tents provided by the National Guard. Air Force cooks prepare meals and everything possible is done to make the operation as smooth as possible in the interest of expediting the work. Operations at the outset began at Creole, Cameron and Grand Chenier, La.

The job, while fast, has not been easy. Workmen had to fight a blazing sun as well as flies and mosquitos. The workmen involved asked no fee for their work — the job turned out was their way of contributing to the relief of a seriously and tragically affected community. Each man was given a special appreciation certificate on behalf of the Red Cross ". . . for services as a volunteer builder of homes of victims of Hurricane Audrey under the program of the Louisiana Building Trades Council and Louisiana Labor Council, AFL-CIO."

PRESS COMMENTS FAVORABLY ON THE HILLMAN FOUNDATION

The Advance, July 15, 1958

Through the years, many newspapers have commented favorably about the work and ideals of the Sidney Hillman Foundation. In recent months, several daily papers have published editorials, as follows:

Milwaukee (Wis.) Journal: As or-

ganized labor's power grows, so do its responsibilities to the society of which it is a vital part.

"Some unions have claimed their rights, but shirked their duties. Many, however, have demonstrated a praiseworthy concern with broad social objectives above immediate self-interest.

"One such union is the Amalgamated Clothing Workers of America (AFL-CIO).

"The Amalgamated's officers, with the advice of a number of public-spirited citizens, run the Sidney Hillman Foundation, established in the memory of the Amalgamated's late president.

"The foundation recently reported on its first 10 years.

"It has given $205,380 in grants to support projects in such fields as education and medical research. Scholarships worth $183,000 have been awarded through 22 institutions (including $50 to Marquetté university medical school) to 350 students. The Foundation has sponsored lectures at 22 institutions."

Rochester (N. Y.) Democrat Chronicle: "The biennial convention of the Amalgamated Clothing Workers, which has been going on at Atlantic City, reminds this department to remark on a bit of openhanded ACW-connected philanthropy that benefits everybody.

"Of course the convention itself is of great interest in Rochester where there are close to 13,000 ACW members.

"One of the Foundation's grants in Rochester has been to the University of Rochester. The university used the grant most recently to underwrite the highly successful lecture series staged by the university's Non-Western Civilizations Program. The lectures were open to the public, and presented the thoughts of some of the finest minds on the university faculty."

PAST COMMUNITY SERVICE HELPED STRIKERS AT LIMA

John D. Mitchell in The Guild Reporter, June 10, 1960

A Guild local that never had more than 67 members spearheaded a community attack that has fought the multi-million dollar Freedom Newspapers chain to a standstill in Lima, Ohio.

The Freedom Newspapers of R. C. Hoiles had a long and successful anti-labor, union-breaking history. The Hoiles management had a year to prepare for removing the unions from the Lima News plant. And yet the unions, with the Guild in the vanguard, "hit the bricks" in a move that culminated in the establishment of the competing Lima Citizens, Lima's No. 1 paper in circulation and advertising since its first issue appeared July 1, 1957.

How did a Guild local with its membership down to 45 at the showdown successfully strike the Lima News? In the light of stepped-up anti-union activity by other news-

paper managements, all Guild locals might consider one aspect of the answer:

Lima Local 166 had an outstanding long-term community service program going for it.

It was partly a formal program and partly a result of strictly individual activity on the part of Guild members, but the end result was that the Lima Guild had a large backlog of community good will on which to draw.

Much of that good will came from other organized labor groups, political parties, the Community Chest board, the YMCA, business men, service clubs, and cultural organizations.

The local was extremely active in such community labor groups as the Allen County Allied Labor Council. This also involved helping organized labor in Lima achieve responsible participation and representation in the Community Chest organization and on the community hospital governing board.

Several members were active in organized politics, both Democratic and Republican.

A partial catalogue of individual memberships would include the city's two country clubs, the Elks, the Sons of the American Revolution, the Daughters of the American Revolution, the Optimist Club, Torch Club, the Junior League, the Lima Art Association (a Guild member was its first president), Order of the Eastern Star (a Guild member was a grand worthy matron), the American Association of University Women, Lima Friends of Music (a Guild member was on the board of directors), and the Allen County Sports Car Club (a Guild member organized it).

In the city's religious communities, a Guildsman was a prominent member of Trinity Methodist Church, others were officers in the First Presbyterian Church, one was a lay leader in the organization of a new Roman Catholic parish, another was an organizer and charter member of the local Unitarian Fellowship.

When the showdown came, the local had a maximum audience—and a receptive one—for its story. It also meant the usual management argument that the union members were either radicals or innocent victims of exploitation by labor bosses fell on generally sterile ground: too many people knew Guild members as effective members of the community.

THE WAYNE CITY STORY: The Impact of a New ILGWU Contract on "Our Town"

Justice, August 15, 1959

This is our town — Wayne City. Two roads through the flat, southern Illinois farm country meet here. There's a street of stores, the school, the churches, the garment factory— and our homes. Population—750. Or no, it must be 753 now. We've had three new babies lately; one of them, Verna Irwin's little Sue Ann, is an ILG baby.

Like ILGWU members in the big cities, we have been negotiating for the 35-hour week, a higher minimum, better pay, pensions, the union label —and getting them! We've got a new contract that we're proud of, and it's not just important to us, it's important to everybody in Wayne City.

"Wayne City will greatly benefit by this new contract," our weekly paper, the *Wayne City Journal*, said. "More dollars will be circulated and spent here. Working mothers will have more time to spend with their families. Workers will have more leisure time to participate in civic activities in the community."

Sure, an improved contract in St. Louis or Los Angeles or New York has the same meaning, but in a town our size, where our plant is the only industry and the 70 people who work in it are almost a tenth of all the people living here, it's easier to see just what the new conditions mean to the community.

Proprietors of Wayne City stores can see what the new contract means. Take Roe Garner who runs one of our two groceries. He doesn't have to read the contract. He can see it in action when his sister-in-law, Leona Garner, comes in after work to buy her groceries. She heaps that basket higher these days because her paycheck is bigger, and Roe knows that's the kind of thing that keeps his cash register ringing. Leona's little girl, Sybil, and her grandson, Billy, are all for a full grocery basket too, especially jam and cookies.

Mrs. Carl Thomason gets a taste of the new contract too, when Beulah Rost and her son, David, come in to buy some new furniture. Beulah knows that she's not just doing better now, but also that there's going to be another raise during the life of the agreement, so she feels secure about making some big purchases.

Mrs. Thomason's husband, Carl, is our Mayor. This is what he says about us: "We feel that there are no better people to be found. They are neighbors, friends and customers of those who are in business in Wayne City."

We don't want to give you the idea that it was always like this. When we first joined the ILGWU, a lot of people here were suspicious of the union; they thought it was an "outside" organization. They were afraid the company would move out to get away from the union. But that was 16 years ago. Now they know *we're* the union in Wayne City and they know us as relatives, friends, neighbors, members of the same church or club.

Take for instance what our volunteer firemen did recently. They have a building that's much bigger than what they need for the fire engine, and they heard we had outgrown our old meeting place. To fix up a place for union meetings, which would also be used for other community groups and activities, they are making over the firehouse.

"King" Chase, who has the hardware store in town, and is president of the Fire Protection Board, took our president, Carrie Hagel, over to look at the place before they started to work on it.

"We are happy to be of assistance to the ladies," Mr. Chase said. "They are doing an important job for all the folks working in the garment plant here, and we consider them a very worthwhile organization in our community. They should have a nice place to meet and conduct their business."

Even the kids, though they may not understand the "whereases," know that Mama's union got her a shorter work day, and that means she has more time for them.

Shorter hours at work mean more time and energy for community activities, too, and Louise is one of those ILG'ers who works to better the community as well as to improve conditions in the factory. She is president of the Monday Evening Woman's Club, which sponsors Cub Scouts for our boys, and collects for the polio, heart and cancer funds.

High spot in the year for the Sanders family is Bonnie's two-week paid vacation. They'll spend it where the fishing is good, if David has anything to say about it. More of us than ever before are getting vacations this year, because the new contract gives some vacation to every worker who has been on the job eight months or more, and those who have worked for the firm five years get two weeks.

Lydia Shreve was so happy the new contract provided retirement pensions that she took her twins out for ice cream, and promised them they'll see a lot more of Grandma when she retires. Lydia is our delegate to the district council. She is not ready to retire yet, but it gives here a feeling of security to know it's going to be possible.

The retirement pensions mean something to the community too. They mean that our older people instead of being a burden to the community, are a real asset.

Sometimes we kind of take our union for granted, but when we stop to think about what it would be like to work without a union, then we really appreciate our shop committee. You know how it is in a non-union shop. If anything goes wrong, you gripe about it, stew over it, and since you can't do anything about it you take it out on each other, which just makes matters worse.

Since we have our union, we can take complaints up in an orderly way and get something done about them. That's democracy in the factory, and though it often means money in our pockets, it has a value that can't be figured in dollars and cents.

URW HELPS BUILD BETTER BEDFORD, VA.

William Abbott in United Rubber Worker, January 1960

"This is a good union area. Nobody's ever said a word against the rubber workers' union, and the textile union has a high reputation here."

The man must have realized my surprise for I had identified myself as a union staff member. He also let me know emphatically he didn't like strikes and other industrial unpleasantness.

He was conservative, and his friends were conservative. In fact, some had accused him of being "pro-labor" for printing both sides of the only strike in the town's history, which involved a dress factory. He was Keith Harvey, publisher of the Bedford Va., Bulletin.

However, citizens of all shades of opinion are apparently proud of the peaceful and adult way labor relations have been carried on for the most part, and there is a story in this general attitude.

For Bedford is deep Virginia, and in 1959, the only labor stories coming out of the South were those of violence and bitter class war.

Here, however, was an example, perhaps a typical one, of labor doing right well in a small, rural Southern community.

Area merchants recently contributed generously to help make an all-Bedford labor picnic a whopping success.

Certainly URW Local 240 played a prominent role, for it was the biggest union in the county.

To its inhabitants, Bedford is the best way of life in the best of possible worlds. Some travel, look around the country, and then return home, eternally grateful to their parents for having the good sense to bring them to birth in this mountain grandeur.

It is rural, and it is steadfastly conservative. The town closes down tight before ten. Living is home-centered; only the teen-agers romp. Southern politeness is mixed with mountain candor; there is a glowing charm of sincerity about the people.

Politics are Chamber of Commerce and Byrd machine; most candidates for office are unopposed. They are all Democrats, of course.

But it is a good union town. Six local unions with members from all over the county almost equal the population of Bedford itself.

The largest local union is the URW Rubatex Local 240 with 475 members out of 500 production workers.

The union shop is outlawed in Virginia. But these unionists don't often speak of themselves as rubber workers, paper workers, or textile workers; they're union people. Advancing all unions is their cause.

Local 240 is about as typical a local union as one could find. It has never had a full-blown strike. While it took two efforts to organize the plant, according to former president Robert Smith, once the union won, the company decided it could live with the situation.

The reasons for organization were also typical. "It wasn't so much the wages," said Smith, "it was not knowing where you stood, no grievance procedure. If you complained, the foreman told you to get out if you didn't like it here. He said there were plenty of others to take your job."

Fed up, rubber workers organized in 1942.

"I feel the union has benefitted the company," added Smith. He pointed out that before the union, workers were demoralized; they didn't care what sort of job they did. But since the union came in production has kept rolling, the plant has expanded, and the workers have a much better spirit.

WHOLE TOWN HAILS UNION FOR MERRIMAC DEED

The Hat Worker, Feburary 15, 1960

The entire town of Amesbury, Mass., marked the first anniversary of the new Merrimac Hat Company on Feb. 2, 1960, the first anniversary of the re-opening of the plant under union auspices.

The year before, the doors of the Merrimac plant opened after having been shut for several months. The first contingent of workers returned to their jobs, to begin a novel attempt at industrial resuscitation. At stake were the jobs of the Merrimac workers and the prosperity of the town of Amesbury.

Exactly one year later the experiment had been proved successful. Merrimac was again producing hats, Amesbury was on the economic upgrade, and all the regular Merrimac workers were back on the payroll. In addition, the first collective agreement with the new firm had brought gains to the workers, the stockholders had received dividends of four per cent, a Merrimac scholarship fund had been established for Amesbury students, and even management conditions had been improved.

Merrimac had earned the toasts of townspeople, civic leaders, labor and industry. Their congratulations were rounded up in a special issue of the Amesbury Daily News, published Feb. 2, 1960, which contained a five-page section devoted exclusively to Merrimac. On the front page, Merrimac hatters were shown at work.

The special issue reported the full story of the Merrimac experiment, headlining it "Hats Off to Merrimac Hat Firm!" The community newspaper congratulated the Merrimac Hat Company "on completing a successful first year under union ownership," and tendered thanks to Vice Pres. Cynewski, "who set the ball rolling in the dark days of 1958 when it looked as if company would be liquidated."

Senator John F. Kennedy called the management of Merrimac "one of the path-breaking industrial innovations in Massachusetts." He credited the company and the union with doing much "to improve the economic climate in Amesbury and to serve as an inspiring example to all of New England."

Pres. Alex Rose wrote, "Our Merrimac experiment may well become one of the most fruitful industrial innovations of our times. Its growing implications are worthy of thorough and imaginative exploration. . . . Merrimac, as an embodiment of industry's responsibility to the community welfare, is still an exception. But its success should indicate that this kind of responsibility can go hand in hand with efficient and profitable business. . . ."

9 | CONSUMERS

LIVING—A LA CARTE

Justice, June 1, 1958

More and more, Americans are living from hand to mouth.

"We expected food consumption expenditures would rise to about $79 billion in 1958 from $75 billion in 1957," says Paul S. Willis, president of the Grocery Manufacturers of America. "It appears the industry is running ahead of that prediction," adds Mr. Willis. The food industry is "the brightest spot in the economy at this time," says he.

Running it a close second are the medical profession and the landlords. Food, rent and medical care are essentials. They can neither be delayed nor denied. They take the prime share of the pay envelope.

Against them the consumer has no defense. The family budgeting the pay envelope for the coming week must first set aside for such standing charges as loans and installment payments. Then it must provide for the triple-threat food-medical-rent or mortgage costs.

With what little is left, it makes other purchases in a fast diminishing order of priority. Many purchases must now be passed up. "You can quite reasonably say, for example, that the food stores' fine gains are robbing other retailers," says Business Week magazine.

Under these circumstances, it is ironic for members of the present Administration in Washington to consider cures for this situation in terms of greater windfalls for corporations. Tax relief is being denied to the nation's consumers, who have insufficient power to purchase what is already produced. Yet rapid-depreciation tax schemes for new corporate plant and production facilities, which many believe are the cause of our present production-purchase imbalance, are being urged.

An Administration surrounded by Big Business brains seems unable to think in non-corporate terms of the plight of millions of American families feeling the pinch of total or partial unemployment.

Addressing the mobilized managers of American industry last month, President Eisenhower conceded that the "American people believe in good wages." But the assembly cheered him rousingly as he warned that the "American people are going to be looking over the shoulders of those sitting at every [wage] bargaining table."

The cheers burst forth because the President was pointing to the new cure for the recession. That is "flexibility."

Make no mistake! It is flexibility in *wages* that Big Business masterminds are talking up. At this turn in our economic history, they hold it is good sense to keep wages down while using tax windfalls to encourage corporations to build for producing more.

The Administration's gravest error in this respect is its refusal to recognize that the nation's biggest and most numerous consumers are precisely its wage earners and their families.

HIGH LOCAL LIVING COSTS NOT CAUSED BY HIGH WAGES

Sidney Margolius in The Paper Worker, October 1960

The U. S. Bureau of Labor Statistics is trying to discourage people from comparing its latest estimate of modest living costs for a family with actual average wages. The BLS staff has argued in its publications that (1) the budget was made out for a mature worker in his late thirties who, the BLS feels, probably earns more than the average; and (2) this is not a "minimum" budget since you could live on less.

As of last October, the BLS "modest but adequate" budget for a family of four cost $117 a week in a typical city, including taxes, compared to average industrial wages of approximately $89.

The government bureau argues: "A family could live quite satisfactorily on less income than is represented by this budget. . . . They could, for example, give up their automobile. . . . They might also refrain from buying new furniture or a TV set or a radio, etc."

Well, if that budget is not the minimum it's not far from it. The meat allowance would permit you about 1½ pounds of meat or fish for supper for four people and another ½ pound for lunch. The budget also allows just 3½ eggs a day for four people, and that includes baking. Of course Papa could give up the three cans of beer a week allowed him by this budget.

Papa can buy one topcoat every five years, one wool suit every four years, a lightweight suit every five years, one pair of dungarees a year, a hat every two years. Mama does slightly better on the Government budget. She's allowed a coat every two years and three-fifths of a hat every year, rain or shine.

No doubt you also can answer easily enough the argument that this 38-year-old worker probably earns more than the average. The fact is, in real life most workers earning the average wage don't earn it 52 weeks a year every year. For one thing there's been a recession about every four years with numerous lay-offs. Also, the mature worker often has more than the two children on which this budget standard is based.

Having thus established, to our satisfaction at least, that a comparison of living costs with average wages is valid, we've done it. Kate Papert, former New York Labor Department official, has worked out for this department a comparison of the budget costs and average earnings in 20 cities. The figures in the chart hit you right in the eye. They show:

1—In only two cities, Detroit and Houston, are manufacturing wages approximately equal to living costs. In most U. S. cities, wages run $7 to $42 a week less than local living costs; and most typically, are about $20 below this modest living standard.

2—There is little relationship between the level of wages and of living costs in the various cities. This contradicts the general belief that high wages make high living costs.

For example, wages in Boston are far below those in Minneapolis, which we selected as typical in both living costs and wages. But living costs in Boston are among the highest in the country. Detroit has the highest wages, but is only moderate in living costs. Houston and Cleveland have relatively high wages, but only moderate to medium living costs. Scranton, Pa., has the lowest wages on the list, 30 per cent below typical Minneapolis. But its living costs are only eight per cent less.

Low wages in the South do not mean proportionately low living costs, even though the BLS allowed a little lower budget standard for the South (providing less for meat and clothing). There's a gap of $25

"Simple?"

UNION FAMILIES MAKE MORE MONEY

New York Union Label News, January 1961

The 1959 median income for union families was $5,773, compared to a median of $4,339 for non-union families! More than 75 per cent of union members earn between $3,000 and $7,500 a year. Union families tend to have larger bank savings than non-union families and, on the average, more union families own their own home than non-union families! It is obvious that it pays to belong to a union . . .

*   *   *

The right to wear union buttons was upheld in a recent NLRB case involving the Hotel and Restaurant Union and Bartenders International Union. "The right of employees to wear union insignia at work has long been established and recognized as a reasonable and legitimate form of union activity" the trial examiner stated. May we just add that the display of union labels, shop cards and service buttons is not just a right but a privilege. An employer, as well as employees, should be proud of the standards of employment signified by the hallmarks of organized labor.

a week between living costs and wages in Atlanta.

Nor are living costs necessarily lower in small cities, as employers sometimes maintain. Costs are higher than New York and Philadelphia in such moderate-size cities as Cincinnati, Minneapolis, Portland, Ore., and Seattle.

In fact, Miss Papert points out, while there is a great difference in wages in various parts of the country, the difference in living costs is comparatively small.

"If you omit the cities with the lowest and highest wages, the range in wages is 29 per cent," she reports. "In comparison, if you omit Houston with the lowest budget costs, and Chicago and Seattle, with the highest, the range in budget costs in the remaining 17 cities is about 12 per cent."

3—In the seven months since the budget was priced in October, wage-earners in some cities have done better in catching up on living costs than in others.

On average, the cost of the budget has gone up about $1 a week while wages have gone up about $2. Wages have gone up especially in Houston (now $105.47); Baltimore ($96.22); Cincinnati ($99.92); Washington ($98.80); Cleveland ($108.99); Pittsburgh ($111.56); Portland ($98.36); St. Louis ($99.14); San Francisco ($107.36); Seattle ($101.14). They've dropped a bit in Minneapolis, Atlanta, Detroit, Kansas City and Scranton. The other cities are the same or a little higher.

In general, unionized wage-earners made greater gains than non-union this year in catching up on living costs. Almost four-fifths of the workers who got general pay increases this year were covered by union contracts, although such union-represented workers comprise only two-thirds of the nation's production workers.

BURIED IN BILLS? HANG ON — HELP'S COMING!

Catering Industry Employee, September 1959

Not long ago Chicago papers reported the deaths of an immigrant couple who died in a tragic finale to their mistaken effort to seize the American dream of plenty. Buying on the easy installment plan, they had been overwhelmed as their debts mounted beyond hope of control or liquidation.

Had they been members of a union with a credit union, or with a program of consumer counselling, they might still be alive, enjoying the freedom they reached these shores to share.

The American dream, for these unhappy consumers, had turned into an ugly nightmare of despair.

But millions of us know the taste of their despair. And more millions, every day, join the multitude on the dreary treadmill of Nothing Down And A Few Pennies A Day, heedless of the oldest battle cry of all: Let the buyer beware!

But help is on the way for the consumer lucky enough to belong to a union. Recently launched plans by AFL-CIO's Community Services Committee foretell many ways in which workers may gain through their unions not only better wages, but help in spending them to yield the most.

Since time began the buyer has been at the mercy of predatory traders. Bent on buying cheap and selling dear, these worthies used short weight, shoddy goods and false claims as standard practices. Things reached such a state that government had to take a hand. Scales were tested, honest labelling laws were passed, and here and there flagrant fraud would send a salesman to jail.

With mass production and modern ways of inspecting goods and testing claims, the worst of such abuses were checked. But mass production, by its very nature, forced a search for profitable ways to move a torrent of things from factory to family. The result: mass merchandising.

Mass merchandising, in turn, came up with three highly effective techniques for making it easy to buy what you don't need, sometimes can't use, and often have trouble paying for:

- Installment credit.
- Planned obsolescence.
- High pressure selling.

To use these weapons in the lively competition for access to your pocketbook, mass merchandising then put in the field a well-trained, well-staffed army to persuade you to buy.

Officers of this army are corporation presidents, vice presidents in charge of sales and advertising, ad agency executives, chain store magnates and those who lend the nation's money.

In key staff jobs are psychologists, designers, packaging experts, sales engineers, market researchers and merchandising specialists.

And the front-line fighters are legions of salesmen, their eyes fixed firmly on the main chance.

These highly trained competitors for what's in your pocketbook are backed to the hilt by one thing the Russians didn't invent: modern advertising and its handmaiden, market research.

Millions of carefully-planned impressions daily exhort you to enjoy anything from Wheaties to a world cruise. TV and radio commercials clutter the airwaves. Skywriting and billboards mar the out-of-doors. Four-color magazine spreads, newspaper displays, taxi tires, truck panels and the left-field fence—all scream! No surface is spared, no medium barred.

Market research has reached such a point that the experts have learned to sell us, not a new Buick, but improved standing in the neighborhood. It has given us coupons, box tops and trading stamps. It has discovered we'll buy more soap if it's displayed at eye level. It has proved we'll spend more for red widgets than for yellow, and that we'll pay $10.95 for an item worth $5.98 if the sign says, simply: SALE!

Armed with easy credit; offering goods intended to wear out early or be out of style before they do; trained in both the craft and guile of the "soft sell" and the hammer blows of the "hard sell"; and backed by this saturation of advertising, the salesman sallies forth each day to meet his quota—or lose his job. In self-defense he picks the first target he sees—and it's you.

But the besieged consumer need not stand alone.

AFL-CIO is now beginning to mobilize a number of allies to help the wage earner defend his pocketbook, his standard of living, and his peace of mind.

As Leo Perlis, director of our Community Services Activities program says, the reason for AFL-CIO's interest is easy to understand:

"Too often money won at the bargaining table gets lost at the checkout counter or on the used car lot."

Those losses are often preventable. And, since a union's job is chiefly helping workers to win a better standard of living, what's more natural than that unions should seek ways to turn those losses into savings?

In essence, the Community Services Committee plans for the consumer the same kind of service it has long made available to people with personal problems: it will bring together the worker and those who can help him.

On the consumer front are many such agencies, some private, some public. Here are a few of them:

The Credit Union National Association. CUNA is a non-profit center which helps set up credit unions, where workers may save money at good interest rates, and borrow money at low interest rates.

Many credit unions offer counseling help to borrowers in shopping for a "best buy" in cars or other major purchases.

Consumer's Union. This is a pioneer, non-profit testing center which publishes a monthly magazine, *Consumers Reports,* and an annual buying guide. Both are devoted to impartial performance reports on all kinds of advertised products. CU's technical experts, by comparing products, are able to recommend as "best buys" those which give the best results for the money. Their reports often reveal wide differences in quality, price and performance which are not apparent to the shopper.

Better Business Bureau. Generally supported by retail merchants and other business men, BBB is to be found in most cities. The Bureau is specially alert in detecting fraudulent operations by the sell-and-run artists who move from town to town with high-pressure door-to-door sales schemes. It is also quick to move into action when consumers report unethical business practices by firms in the community.

The Federal Trade Commission, and the *Food and Drug Administration* are two federal agencies with responsibilities for consumer protection. Through CSC's national network of staff and community committees, the cases these agencies should investigate can be channeled for appropriate action.

The FTC has broad authority to police advertising claims, and to prosecute for fraud those who promise what they don't deliver.

In a famous instance, sparked by the International Association of Machinists, FTC forced mail order health insurance companies to abandon fraudulent sales practices and claims.

FDA, on the other hand, is charged with tracking down cases of mislabeling and adulteration of foods and medicines. Both publish "cease and desist' orders which seldom see the light of day in the daily press, where advertising revenues sometimes govern editorial content.

By drawing upon such sources for help, the CSC's new consumer counselling program will provide a new and useful services to local unions, city and state federations, and the national unions and AFL-CIO itself. Among them:

• Training in each community of union members capable of teaching others in the union how to launch consumer counselling.

• Study courses for union use in how to buy wisely, how to "shop" for loans, how to organize a credit union, how to file complaints with the proper public or private agency.

• Help in pushing for good consumer protection laws in the city and the state, such as laws to prevent garnishment of wages, laws to protect consumers against fraudulent claims, laws to set up state consumer counselling programs.

During the New Deal days the Department of Agriculture had a section called the Consumer Counsel, which worked with groups of all kinds interested in giving the consumer a break. The Consumer Counsel became a casualty of World War II, but the same war brought into being the Consumer Division of the Office of Price Administration where some effort was made to help the consumer make do under wartime shortages.

But businessmen, who began calling the tune in Washington during the war and still rule the roost, wanted no government help for the luckless family shopper, and no similar program has been in existence for many years.

Now, however, Sentator Estes Kefauver (D.-Tenn.) has introduced a bill to create a Consumer Department of cabinet rank to direct a broad program of consumer protection. It would embrace existing consumer services, and try to protect the consumer interest as it might be affected by legislation.

Part of CSC's plans to help workers become better-informed consumers, and more effective in defending their rights as shoppers, will lie in its cooperation with other departments of AFL-CIO:

Through the *Legislative Department* it will push for laws to protect the consumer's interest in such fields as utility and freight rates; in health legislation like the Forand Bill to provide medical care for the aging; in stronger laws governing work of the FTC and FDA.

Through the *Union Label Trades & Service Department* it will seek to link good consumer practices, union label, shop card and working button because good craftmanship is an important element in the quality of merchandise.

DEPARTMENT SET FOR CONSUMER COUNSELING

Official News, Union Label and Service Trades Dept., AFL-CIO, Winter 1958

The Union Label and Service Trades Department, together with the Community Services Dept., will give major attention during 1959 to the AFL-CIO Executive Council's mandate to provide union members and their families with "essential information" on "How to stretch the dollar," "How to get a dollar's worth," and "Why buy the Union Label way."

This joint campaign to safeguard unionists as consumers of goods and services will be carried out by the Department's Union Label and Service Trades Councils, representing approximately 4,000 local unions, and an estimated 3 million wives and daughters of union members who are active in ladies' auxiliaries. Community Services will bring to the joint venture its 163 full-time staff member in 76 major cities, plus nearly 120,000 trained counselors.

Although the Department will stress the importance of buying Union Label products and using Union Services, Secretary-Treasurer Joseph Lewis said, the main purpose of this program is to see that union workers get the greatest values for their hard-earned money.

WORKERS' FAMILIES CLIP HIGH PRICES BY USING UNION PURCHASING SERVICE

United Automobile Workers, December 1956

Thousands of Detroit and Michigan union members are packing Santa Claus' pack just as full as his jelly-like belly simply by stretching their dollars as they do their Christmas shopping this year.

No, they aren't printing their own five-spots on elastic — they simply have heeded an age-old union admonition—"Be Wise, Organize!" They are organized on the job — now they're organizing as consumers, too.

Members of 110 local unions, affiliated with different international unions, have found a way to establish a beachhead in the continuing struggle against inflation. They have seen the higher wages and better standard of living won through their unions at the collective bargaining table chipped away, sometimes in huge chunks, by unjustified price increases.

The dollar-stretcher for more than 20,000 Detroit area workers and their families—and more are signing up every day—is the Union Purchasing Service, a union membership-controlled organization which maintains a modest office, not far from downtown Detroit.

The Union Purchasing Service, sponsored by the union-organized Motor City Co-op, Inc., seeks out manufacturers, wholesalers and retailers of consumer goods who are willing to accept a lower markup in exchange for volume—in other words, take less profit on each item but sell so many items that their profit is higher than taking the high markup on fewer sales.

Here's how the plan works for the consumer:

Any AFL-CIO union member is eligible to register for identification purposes with the Union Purchasing Service. Non-union people can register, too, but they must pay a $1 fee.

Any registered member who is in the market for almost anything simply calls the service on the phone. He names the item he wants, giving the make and model number if possible.

The purchasing service quotes the lowest price available, issues a purchase order, and directs the member to one or more places where the item can be purchased at the price quoted.

How much can the buyer save? It depends. On photographic material, for example, the purchasing service can obtain prices at 20 to 30 per cent below retail prices. On major appliances — refrigerators, stoves, washers and dryers — the difference might be as much as 40 or 50 per cent below retail. On small items, it generally will be 20 per cent or more.

The Detroit program can provide almost everything in the home furnishing line as well as automobile accessories, toys, and such miscellaneous items as jewelry, watches, clocks, typewriters, cameras, portable tools, or luggage.

CREDIT UNIONS THRIVE IN ORGANIZED LABOR

Federation News (Chicago), December 5, 1959

It's 5 A. M. the day before payday when your brother's wife phones from 200 miles away: "Don's been in an accident; come right away!"

Where do you get the money to make the trip right now?

If you are a member of one of the more than 1,600 credit unions serving Illinois working people you'd have no problem. Many a credit union treasurer's been dug out of bed by a member in distress—and given him the help he needs.

This kind of "help each other" spirit is what makes Illinois credit union members so enthusiastic—and puts real life into their thrift program for the year.

Frank Seminara, treasurer of the Chicago Typographical Credit Union, said the first credit union was founded over a hundred years ago.

The basic principles of credit unions are still the same today:

1. Only people belonging to a credit union can borrow from it.
2. Loans are made only for provi-dent and productive purposes at low interest.

3. A man's character is the most important security for his loan.

The Illinois credit union law was passed in 1925 with the leading support of the Illinois State AFL-CIO President Reuben G. Soberstrom, a member of the General Assembly. Today, there are 1,680 credit unions in Illinois with 850,000 members and $375 million in assets.

About two-thirds of all credit unions serve occupational groups—employees of factories, stores, and offices. Thousands of these workers belong to organized labor. In addition, many credit unions are organized specifically for members of labor union locals.

Most members borrow from their credit union as a money-saving move, particularly when buying large items as stoves, refrigerators, and autos.

Credit unions stress regular savings, no matter how small the amounts. Average savings in Illinois are about $393. Savings in the credit unions are actually shares in the business, on which dividends are paid. Dividends paid by local credit unions last year were in the neighborhood of 4 per cent.

Most credit unions provide their members with insurance paid for out of the earnings of the credit union.

These credit unions carry loan protection insurance that pays an insured member's loan in full in case of death or permanent disability.

Many credit unions encourage members to save by providing them with a Life Savings insurance without charge. Insured members' savings are matched up to $2,000 in case of their death, in most cases.

ABOUT OUR LABEL

Electrical Workers' Journal, March 1958

It was back in 1905 that the IBEW first adopted its union label as we know it today, and it has been used in all the years between.

But we wonder if many of our members of today know *why* the union label came into being—if they are familiar with the story behind the story.

In the early days, there was only one way for labor unions and labor unionists to exist. How? By placing their union label on the products which they made and depending on their fellow union members in every trade to respect and demand it. And labor unionists followed through.

Many remember reading of the famous Danbury Hatters' case. It was only through demand by AFL unionists for the union label in the hats they wore, and rejection of those made by scab labor, that the Hatters union was able to survive. And that story was repeated many times over in the case of the Garment Workers and the Cigar Makers, and

in our own case in the electrical manufacturing field.

Did you know that in the early days some of our leaders went to jail because they refused to install wire and cable and fixtures on their union jobs unless the equipment bore the union label, and this action was regarded as restraint of trade.

Friends, the going wasn't easy in those early days, but staunch union men persevered and won for their respective unions recognition and security.

Today in "right-to-work" states, a union could be completely destroyed because the right to a union shop has been abolished. But, union labor has one very big and very strong trump card—the union label. A real demand for the union label on the goods we use and insistence on union services, can keep our unions strong in spite of any laws passed to destroy them.

The same union label exists today as it did 50 years ago. And the same insistent need exists for its use.

FIRST ILGWU LABEL SEWN ON DRESS

Justice, January 15, 1959

While cameras clicked and television viewers looked on, Mrs. Nelson A. Rockefeller hand-sewed the first industry-wide ILGWU Union Label into a street-wear dress. She

sewed steadily and with the professional skill of a finisher. When she was through, she showed the garment for inspection to the Governor of New York State and to the president of the ILGWU. Both approved. This marked the official start of the ILGWU Label campaign.

The ceremonies were held at the A. Goodman shop on the 17th floor of a Seventh Avenue skyscraper on the afternoon of January 9, 1959. While millions of labels have gone into the dress shops in readiness for the launching of the campaign, the drive officially started with Mrs. Rockefeller, in a Betsy Ross posture, sewing the first label in full view of a shop full of excited workers, officers of the ILGWU, her husband, Governor Nelson Rockefeller, former Senator Herbert H. Lehman, Mayor Robert F. Wagner, and Harry Uviller, industry impartial chairman.

Also this month, the ILGWU Union Label is being introduced on knitgoods, undergarments, childrens' wear and in centers and markets outside of New York.

First industry-wide agreement for use of the label was provided in the agreement that terminated the week-long general strike of the dressmakers last March. The ILGWU Union Label Department was established in June 1958 with Vice Pres. Julius Hochman as its director.

The scene at the Goodman shop, starting at noon, was one of increasing excitement. A small army of newsmen and photographers began to assemble as the time for the ceremony drew near.

Posters on the walls of the shop proclaimed: "Just a few more stitches for your security," "The best is union-made . . . Look for this label," "This label stands for humane, American working conditions."

A crowd of more than 300 persons waited at the entrance of the building to see the guests arrive. As they emerged from their cars to enter the building they were greeted by a committee comprised of Jennie Silverman and Frances Di Martino of the Dress Joint Board staff and Harry Shapiro, assistant manager of Local 10.

Pres. David Dubinsky introduced the speakers. The ceremony took place at the end of the plant of sewing machines. Mrs. Rockefeller charmed the gathering with the manner in which she remained unperturbed by the excitement around her and steadfastly plied her needle. Both the needle and the thimble she used were of gold, and were later presented to her by Pres. Dubinsky as a memento of the historic event.

Good-naturedly, the crowd inched forward, as Mrs. Rockefeller prepared to sew. It grew warmer, and someone made the obvious gag about sweatshops. No sooner had the Governor's wife made ready for the first stitch when Pres. Dubinsky stopped her. To make that stitch, she needed a union card—and he had one to present to her.

It is estimated that in the first year of the program, more than a billion labels will be sewn by ILGWU members into the garments they make.

WHAT'S IN A BRAND NAME?
PRACTICALLY NOTHING

Sidney Margolius in Textile Labor, January 1960

Remember the television comedian who wisecracked that his sponsors didn't care whether you bought their brand or Brand X, since they made both? Well, he may have been speaking the literal truth.

The fact is that a great many products sold under different brand names are made by the same manufacturers, often to the same specifications. Sometimes the lesser-known brand is the better buy. This is especially true of drugs, soaps and toiletries, car equipment, household appliances, mattresses, men's shirts and other clothing.

In drugs, the careful shopper has a useful guide in the USP mark on the label. Any drug, medicine or vitamin marked USP measures up to the same official government standard no matter what the name or price. So don't hesitate to buy the cheaper brand. It's just as good.

The government also grades poultry, meat, some frozen foods, some canned and fresh produce, eggs, butter and cheese. The shopper who bothers to read labels—a rare bird these days—can save a substantial amount of money. A survey by the University of Illinois' Bureau of Economic and Business Research found that supermarkets' private brands of canned foods cost an average of 11 per cent less than nationally-advertised brands of the same grade.

Or take soaps. Procter & Gamble make white floating soap for a number of retailers who sell it under different brand names. Even its leading detergent, Tide, is marketed by retailers under other brand names. Co-Op Breakwater, for example, is made by Procter & Gamble.

Nor is price any more reliable as a gauge of value than the brand name. The Hospital Bureau of Standards tested two dishwashing compounds. It found that the one costing 20 per cent more actually was inferior to the cheaper one. Incidentally, even professional buyers are confused by the many brands of detergents on the market nowadays. The Hospital Bureau reported that "one of the principal sources of this bewilderment is the utter lack of relationship between the price of the compound and its value in terms of performance."

In car batteries, not only are the private-brand batteries of large retailers generally made by the lead-ing brand-name manufacturers, but some of the big makers also sell more than one of the well-known brands.

Exide and Willard are made by the same company. Auto-Lite and Prest-o-Lite are both made by another corporation. Exide also manufactures some of the Mobil batteries. Gould-National produces a great many batteries sold under different brand names, including Co-Op, some of the Mobil batteries, Montgomery Ward, Gillette, Western Auto, Sunoco, Kelly-Springfield, Phillips 66, Pure Oil, Lee, Mopar, Amoco and others.

Similarly in tires, the dozens of different brands sold by large retailers and service stations under their own names are all manufactured by the seven or eight largest tire makers. U. S. Rubber makes the largest number of private-brand tires, including Co-Op, Atlas Montgomery Ward, Western Auto Stores, Co-Op and Cities Service. Sears' tires are made by Dunlop, in some cases by Goodrich and by several smaller companies.

Private-brand tires are made to retailers' own specifications. But in general, manufacturers themselves say, private brands of the large retailers are the same quality as the same grade under the manufacturers' own brand names.

In household appliances, too, the retailers' private brands are made by the large manufacturers. Many of Montgomery Ward's large appliances are made by Westinghouse. Sears' appliances are made by RCA-Whirlpool. In fact, Sears is one of the owners of Whirlpool. Eureka makes a number of the different brands of vacuum cleaners sold by retailers under their own names, including the Western Auto Stores. The AMC refrigerator sold by Associated Merchandising Corporation stores in various cities is made by Gibson.

BUSY SCIENTIST

Jane Goodsell in RWDSU Record, July 17, 1960

It just goes to show you never can tell about people. Take Charles Darwin, for instance. His father despaired of his ever doing anything worthwhile. Take Churchill. He got terrible grades in school, and seemed destined for obscurity.

Take me. My high school chemistry teacher only passed me on condition that I promise I would not sign up for his physics course the next year.

Yet here I am, one of this country's leading and busiest scientists. I don't mean to sound boastful, but it's such a thrill to know that I'm making a contribution to the great march of scientific advancement.

I have so many experiments going that some days I hardly know which to work on first. Of course, during the late summer months I concentrated on my peach-shaving. The peach season is short, you know, and I felt that it was vital to work on this important task while I had an abundance of scientific material. I often spent several hours a day, shaving the fuzz off peaches with my electric razor.

Even during the busy season, though, I didn't totally abandon my other projects. I managed to snatch a few minutes each day to test my paper napkins for wet-strength, and I kept up my research on writing in butter. And every evening before going to bed, I tore the paper off a Spring cigarette, and examined it over a strong light.

But now that the peach season is over, I can get back to my more time-consuming experiments. Today I washed half my hair in Woodbury and the other half in ordinary shampoo. That's no easy task, believe me. I also conducted a little experiment to determine whether Parkay margarine is actually move velvety and less shiny than other margarines, and a match for the high-priced spread.

I think I'll have to buy a card file to hold my charts and graphs. My reports on super-strength Alcoa wrap, alone, are voluminous. Every time we have a roast, I wrap one-third of the leftovers in Brand X foil, one-third in Brand Y and the remainder in Alcoa wrap. You'd be surprised how much time it takes to cross-check the leftovers for dryness and tastelessness, and the aluminum foil for ripping and tearing.

I spend hours summarizing the results of my research. My Shinola shoeshine charts are fairly simple. It's merely necessary to keep track of whether a Shinola shine actually lasts seven days. But working with percentages taxes my abilities to the limit. I was never very good at arithmetic.

Sometimes I feel like a split personality. I keep dividing myself in half. I already told you about my shampoo experiment, but that's only part of it. I treat my right hand with Jergens, and my left with a leading medicated lotion. I wash half the laundry in Tide, and the other half in an ordinary washday product to determine scientifically if Tide really produces the cleanest clean. For a truly controlled experiment, though, I should have two washing machines. Lack of money is a terrible hindrance to a scientist.

Tomorrow promises to be a busy day. I am going to conduct an experiment on the tires of our car. First I must ink them, and then lower the full weight of the car onto sheets of paper. The point of this project is to determine how the tire area compares to the area covered by my own two feet. This is vital for some reason which has momentarily slipped my mind.

WHAT? You want to know the results of my experiments? Ssh! For heaven's sake! You don't want the Russians to get hold of such vital information, do you?

"Tom-Foolery!"

CORK—
DRAWN FOR THE
AFL-CIO NEWS

HOW CORPORATE PROFITS INFLATE COST OF LIVING

Labor, October 10, 1959

Corporation spokesmen like to pretend that their profits are really very small and don't have much effect on the cost of living. But new figures show that the corporations' profit "take" out of the consumer's pocketbook is very substantial indeed—and rising sharply.

The government estimates that corporate net profits in 1959 will amount to $48.5 billion, up more than $1 billion over last year. In addition,

another $12 billion or more will go this year for the lush salaries of corporate officers, it's estimated.

Nearly all of this $60.5 billion in corporation profits and super-salaries is paid for by consuming families. It's paid for in the price of the goods they buy directly and also in the price they pay through taxes for the goods the government buys.

How much of a "cut" does this $60.5 billion represent out of the value added to the nation's economy by the goods and services corporations sell?

LABOR put that question to a leading government statistical expert. He replied: "We do have figures on what the corporations add to the national economy. Last year it was $194.4 billion." This year the figure is apt to rise to around $215 billion.

Out of that $215 billion, the "cut" for corporate profits will amount to over 22 per cent. The additional "cut" for the super-salaries of corporation officers will amount to nearly 6 per cent. In other words, out of each dollar the corporations collect for their productive activity this year, 28 cents will go just for profits and officers' salaries.

You can look at it also in another way. America now has about 51 million households. On the average this year each household, directly or indirectly, will have to pay over $1,000 of its living costs to supply the corporations with their profit and the corporate officers with huge salaries.

It should be noted that the $48.5 billion of corporate profits and the $12 billion of officers' salaries are counted before U.S. income taxes, and the government collects a substantial tax on both items.

But the consumer has to pay for the cost of the pre-tax profits and officers' salaries in the price of the corporation products he or she buys. The whole $60.5 billion is counted in the retail price. And that figure, remember, is up more than $11 billion from last year.

Clearly the soaring corporate profits, and the fantastic salaries paid to corporate officers, have a real effect on the cost of living and contribute to inflation.

BUSINESS SNUBS LAWS WITH DELAYING TACTICS

Labor, December 5, 1959

After 16 long years of proceedings in the Federal Trade Commission and the courts, the Supreme Court recently spoke what should be the final word on the FTC's case against advertising claims for Carter's Little Liver Pills. However, the lawyers for the makers of that old and widely-sold nostrum may still have some legal tricks up their sleeves.

The top court upheld a Federal Appeals Court ruling that Carter must take the "Liver" out of the name of its pills, stop asserting that they help the liver in any way, and "cease and desist" from making 14 other claims which the FTC had charged were false and misleading.

The commission launched this case way back in 1943, and since then it has been running the gauntlet of repeated hearings, trials in Federal District and Appeals courts, and finally the Supreme Court. This is only one of countless FTC cases which have been bogged down in what is called "the law's delays."

Another outstanding example is the commission's ancient case against the steel industry price fixers. After 29 years, this case still has produced no real results.

In 1920, the FTC began investigating the old "Pittsburgh Plus" system under which all purchasers of steel were charged the same identical price, no matter where they were located, who made the steel, or where it was made. In 1924, the commision ordered the steel companies to stop using that system, and they did.

However, they immediately adopted a "multiple basing point" system which was just as effective in fixing identical prices. The FTC got after them again; there were further long commission hearings, and endless proceedings in the courts and Congress.

Yet now, as a Senate investigating committee headed by Sen. Estes Kefauver (Dem., Tenn.) has revealed, and as practically everyone knows, steel prices still are "administered" in a way that prevents competition and usually results in identical prices.

The Justice Department has just launched a suit in Federal court at San Francisco, charging that some of the nation's biggest steel companies, *together* with a group of steel fabricators have been engaged in a conspiracy to fix identical prices on the sale of bars and rods used in steel construction in seven Western states. As part of the plot, competitors were frozen out and uniform, "collusive" bids were made on all construction projects, the department charged.

Undoubtedly, the corporations involved in that suit are little worried. If past practice is an indication, they'll drag it on in the courts for endless years—and if they lose, the same old game may be started over again in a new guise.

Why all this delay and futility? Probably some of the blame rests on the Justice Department and the FTC itself and some of their lawyers, who regard their cases as only a legal game to be played endlessly for its own sake.

Many observers also believe the fault lies chiefly in the courts. Many judges are not in sympathy with the anti-trust laws and other laws which the Justice Department and the FTC have the duty to enforce. These judges permit unnecessary delays and, even if they finally uphold the government, they mete out only light punishment in the form of small fines which scarcely make a dent in the profits piled up during delays.

The attitude of such judges was illustrated when one of them said "there is no moral obloquy in violating the anti-trust laws." That attitude helps explain why, under those laws, at this date, no Big Business man has ever been sent to jail.

HOW AMERICAN BUYING HABITS HAVE CHANGED

Stanley M. Seganish in Retail Clerks Advocate, September 1959

In 1888, the year the Retail Clerks was founded, the United States Department of Labor made its first survey to find out how people lived in the United States—what food they ate, what clothes they wore, what kinds of dwellings they lived in, what they spent on recreation and transportation. Over the years the Department of Labor has made periodic surveys of the ways in which succeeding generations of Americans managed their money.

The Labor Department has now published a resume of this 70-year period entitled "How American Buying Habits Change." The book charts a veritable transformation in a way of life.

The RCIA was honored when one of the first copies off the press was presented to Pres. James A. Suffridge by Secretary of Labor James Mitchell at the 23rd International Convention. In making the presentation, Mitchell said,

"I want to tell you a few things that are in that book, because I think it involves all of us. The book shows that the purchasing power of wages and salaries of the average city workers in dollars of constant buying power is three times as great today as it was in 1900. That figure does not include fringe benefits, sick leave, paid vacations, hospitalization, etc. The work week has decreased since 1900 by 15 to 20 hours. This means that the working people of this country rightly have been freed for recreation, education, travel, and and the broadening experiences that make him a better citizen.

"The book shows that for the average American worker there is no such thing as the 'good old days.' The 'good days' are here now and better days, it seems to me, lie ahead.

"This is especially true, as the book demonstrates, for the housewife. Some of you, I am sure, are old enough to remember that in the early 1900's the average home, a tenement, was heated with a coal cook stove, lighted by a kerosene lamp, and it might possibly have an icebox on the back porch. I can remember what we used to call 'railroad flats,' where there was no central heating, where in the winter time you clustered around the coal stove in the kitchen in order to keep warm. I can remember, too, the tough times there were to pay the $15 or $18 a month rent that was charged for a 5½ room railroad flat where the sunlight very seldom came in.

"Compare that today with your own lives: radio and television and hi-fi, vacuum cleaners, central heating, pop-up toasters—the things that we all take for granted here in America.

"You know, the average buying power of the family in America has increased 75 per cent since the turn of the century, and wages have *risen* even more sharply. Take, for instance, the contract I saw this morning, the latest contract negotiated, I am told, in the Los Angeles area. I understand that the average wage today of food clerks is $98 for a 40-hour week, plus all kinds of fringe benefits.

"And compare, this in the short space of a little more than 50 years, with $4 a week for 60 hours or more of work, with the only fringe benefit that you would get being the possibility that the last customer on the street might go home at 9 o'clock instead of 10 o'clock.

"This study points out two factors. It shows that all of this has been done in America because of the system under which we live, and it was done by increased productivity, enlarging the consumer base; and it has been done with the assistance and the help and the drive of organized labor."

These material changes mentioned by Secretary Mitchell were accompanied by other more profound metamorphoses. The country itself and all of society benefited directly from these improvements in living conditions of the mass of working people. Better participation in government, social reforms, the spread of education and many other advances can be traced directly to the reduction in hours of work and the opportunity of working people to participate directly in our democracy.

"The wage earner's way of life is well high indstinguishable from that of his salaried co-citizens," the book says. "Their homes, their cars, their baby sitters, the style of the clothes their wives and children wear, the food they eat, the bank or lending institute where they establish credit, their days off, the education of their children, their church—all of these are alike and are becoming more nearly identical.

"It is not only that the typical wage earner no longer lives in an identifiably 'working class' neighborhood or that his washing machine contains the same gauge sheet steel, the same electric motor as that of the wealthier man; or that they are both officers of the PTA, or are elected to public office or go to the same dentist. It is also that the American working man is conscious of the fact that he has attained a position in society not even approached by his counterpart in any other part of the world."

HOW ARE WE REALLY DOING?
The Machinist, February 12, 1959

How are we doing? Are we really any better off financially than we were 10 or 20 years ago? Have high prices eaten up all we've won in raises at the bargaining table?

These questions are being asked every day by thoughtful union members. Recently IAM Vice President Elmer E. Walker asked The Machinist to find and publish the facts so that union members will have the answers. Here are the facts:

In 1938 factory wages averaged 63 cents an hour.

In 1948 factory wages averaged $1.35 an hour.

In December 1958 factory wages averaged $2.12.

Over the same period, the Bureau of Labor Statistics reports, retail prices just about doubled.

Despite the higher prices of 1958, it takes less working time to earn the price of a loaf of bread, a pound of bacon, a shirt, a vacuum cleaner —almost everything is cheaper when you translate the price into minutes at the average hourly wage rate.

The Machinist tracked down the prices charged 20 years ago and 10 years ago on 28 items that are part of the cost of living of almost every family. For the most part, the prices came from old mail order catalogues that are available to anyone at the Library of Congress. Others came from the Government, trade associations and daily newspaper advertisements of the time.

Except for apples, cotton blouses and cotton dresses, the record shows that it doesn't take nearly as long to earn the necessities as it did 20 years ago. We lost ground on a couple of items since 1948, notably new cars and Blue Cross hospitalization.

Here is a comparison of the time it took to earn 28 different items in our daily cost of living in 1938, 1948 and 1958. Quality of the items compared is about the same in all three years. The results are worth studying.

Below are real prices in terms of minutes worked by average factory worker

	1938	1948	1958
LOAF OF WHITE BREAD	8.5 min.	5.75 min.	5.5 min.
QUART OF MILK	12 min.	8.5 min.	7.25 min.
10 POUNDS POTATOES	20 min.	23 min.	16 min.
1 POUND APPLES	4.5 min.	5.25 min.	4.75 min.
1 POUND BACON	35 min.	34 min.	21.5 min.
1 POUND CHUCKROAST	21.75 min.	28.5 min.	16 min.
MAN'S HAIRCUT	47.5 min.	55.5 min.	42.5 min.
MOVIE TICKET	57 min.	44 min.	35.5 min.
TWO PACKS CIGARETTES	24 min.	17.75 min.	12 min.
MONTHLY BLUE CROSS RATE FOR ONE PERSON	69 min.	49 min.	67.5 min.

— In Terms of Hours —

	1938	1948	1958
FORD V-8 TUDOR SEDAN	1015 hrs.	892.5 hrs.	945 hrs.
FOUR PLY TIRE—6.00 by 16	12.25 hrs.	9.75 hrs.	8.5 hrs.
100-MILE TRAIN TRIP, COACH	6 hrs.	3.5 hrs.	2.75 hrs.
AIRPLANE TRIP, N. Y.-CHICAGO, 1ST CL.	71.33 hrs.	32.66 hrs.	22.66 hrs.
FIVE-ROOM HOUSE	7,860.25 hrs.	6,486 hrs.	6,369.75 hrs.
PORTABLE ELECTRIC SEWING MACHINE	158.75 hrs.	92.5 hrs.	70.25 hrs.
UPRIGHT VACUUM CLEANER	55.5 hrs.	37 hrs.	30.5 hrs.
ELECTRIC IRON	5.5 hrs.	4 hrs.	2.75 hrs.
ELECTRIC REFRIGERATOR	147.25 hrs.	178.5 hrs.	71 hrs.
WASHING MACHINE, WRINGER TYPE	59 hrs.	80 hrs.	49.5 hrs.
ELECTRICITY (100 KWH.)	6.25 hrs.	2.5 hrs.	1.75 hrs.
MAN'S WOOL SUIT	28.5 hrs.	26 hrs.	23 hrs.
MEN'S WORK SHOES	4 hrs.	4.25 hrs.	3.5 hrs.
BOYS' SHOES	2 hrs.	2.5 hrs.	1.75 hrs.
MEN'S DENIM DUNGAREES	1.25 hrs.	1.5 hrs.	1 hrs.
LADIES' SHIRT, RAYON	1.5 hrs.	2.5 hrs.	1.75 hrs.
LADIES' COTTON DRESS	1.5 hrs.	2.25 hrs.	1.75 hrs.
LADIES' LEATHER HOUSE SLIPPERS	1.5 hrs.	1.75 hrs.	1.25 hrs.

10 | HEALTH AND MEDICINE

LABOR'S GOALS FOR MEDICAL CARE

Dr. William A. Sawyer in The Machinist, June 20, 1957

For labor, good health is a necessity. With an average income of $3,830 a year, workers have little "buffer," if illness sets in. The expenses of almost any illness can wipe out a family's small savings in short order.

Labor has taken a very broad view of the scope of medical care. It includes prevention and detection of disease, early diagnosis and treatment, prolonged care and rehabilitation where necessary, and, underlying each of these phases, a continuing program of education and counseling for constructive health maintenance.

This is what labor wants. And it wants coverage on this broad scope regardless of locale—doctor's office, home, or hospital. Labor's parallel desire, on an economic plane, is to finance this broad sort of health program on a prepaid basis, at a price it can afford, and through the medium of collective bargaining.

Actually, labor's interest in health is not a new concept at all. Many of today's unions had their start in mutual benefit associations, formed among workers years ago to mitigate the expense of illness and funerals.

Union health and welfare funds had their greatest impetus during World War II, when the National Labor Board allowed contributions by employers for union health and welfare programs as a fringe benefit, in lieu of wage increases. Since that time the financing of these programs has been made a matter of collective bargaining, and their cost is being met increasingly in this way.

The rapid growth in union health and welfare funds in recent years is startling. In the five-year period from 1948 to 1953, for example, the number of workers covered by these funds rose from about 2,000,000 to about 16,000,000, and the money expended from about $200,000,000 to about one-and-a-half billion dollars. This represents a considerable purchasing power.

By far the largest portion of these health funds goes into the purchase of commercial insurance. And yet insurance has little to do with a regular program of comprehensive medical care. All it can do is to help pay part of the cost of ill health when it develops.

I. A. M. President Al Hayes put it this way in his address before the 1955 convention of the American Hospital Association:

". . . We are told . . . that in the next 12 months one out of every three families will need hospitalization for one of its members . . . Granted the truth of the figures—which are appalling—shouldn't we ask ourselves this question: How many of those people who will need hospitalization could have been kept out of hospitals by preventive medicine or early diagnosis and treatment?

Medicine, in meeting the challenges of a changing world, will need to adapt its scientific and social attitude to the various collective forces in our society.

WE NEED TWO KINDS OF HEALTH INSURANCE...NOW!

Oregon Labor Press, February 6, 1959

A wise man said: "It is the proper function of government to do for the people what they cannot do for themselves."

We all accept this definition as it is applied across a wide spectrum of governmental functions, ranging from local fire protection to the conduct of foreign policy, from public schools to satellite research.

But it seems to us that one vital and proper function of government has been too long neglected, and that is medical and hospital care.

Consider these four facts:

1—A prolonged and serious illness can wipe out the life savings and financial security of any moderate-income family. Even well-to-do families can be pauperized by medical and hospital costs.

2—The only Americans who can afford a long and serious illness are the very poor (who must rely on charity), the very rich and those who are lucky enough to be covered by some group insurance plan.

3—Despite the recent growth of union health and welfare plans, and other forms of group medical insurance, only a small percentage of our population has such coverage—and it is often inadequate when serious illness strikes.

4—Those who have the greatest need for medical-hospital insurance are least likely to have it. This is particularly true of the elderly and the retired.

Many governments (far less wealthy than our own) have accepted this responsibility to their citizens—and have done so with outstanding success. Britain, Sweden, Norway and Denmark are four good examples.

But in the United States, every slightest move in the direction of government-sponsored health insurance has been blocked by the American Medical Association with its wolf-cry of "socialized medicine." We are glad to hear that there is now a possibility that the AMA may slightly soften its attitude.

We are not urging that this session of Congress consider an all-out National Health Insurance program. Such a proposal would only cause a hopeless knock-down-and-drag-out fight. But we *are* urging this Congress to enact two health insurance measures:

First, the Forand Bill. This would provide medical and hospital care, under the Social Security system, for those who are receiving Social Security benefits.

Second, government insurance to cover all citizens for long, serious and expensive illnesses. The idea is simple enough. It's like a deductible auto damage policy. Run-of-the-mill medical expenses would not be covered. But every family would be protected from the huge expense and financial ruin that prolonged and serious illness can bring.

CARMAN PRAYS FOR SON FACING OPERATION

Labor, January 2, 1960

EAST POINT, GA. — "It's wonderful what labor has done with this health insurance program," says James D. Parker. A car repairer for nearly 26 years and a member of the Brotherhood of Railway Carmen, Parker is thinking in very personal terms when

he offers that praise of the insurance program won by the "non-operating" rail unions from the nation's railroads.

Center of care and love at the Parker home here is 11-year-old Jimmy, Jr., the Parkers' only child.

Jimmy was a "blue baby" at birth, afflicted with a rare form of heart disease.

An operation at the age of three helped relieve the condition. But that operation also revealed holes in Jimmy's heart, which medical science at that time could not repair. Jimmy had to live quietly and with frequent pain. Nonetheless he grew up bright and cheerful, attending regular school and Sunday school.

Then, last Labor Day, the heart defect caused a blood clot in Jimmy's brain. He was rushed to the hospital for an emergency brain operation. The bill for that crisis came to about $4,000. Parker had to pay quite a bit of this himself but the health insurance paid a substantial part.

Recently, however, surgeons have developed an extremely delicate new operation for closing the holes in hearts like Jimmy's. Helped by the health insurance, the Parkers are planning such an operation for Jimmy. The medical journals so far, Parker says, have reported only six or seven full recoveries from this operation—but that hope does exist. "We expect that Jimmy will have this heart operation in the spring," Parker says.

The Parkers declare that God has been good to them and they ask only that He give them, and their boy, further strength to meet this new operation.

"I'm glad to have Jimmy's story known," Parker adds, "because it may encourage others with troubles like this never to give up hope."

(Incidentally, the railroad managements in their current rules notices served on the "non-operating" rail unions are demanding sharp cutbacks in the health insurance program which has helped the Parkers and many other railroad families. The unions vigorously oppose any such cutbacks.)

HOSPITAL COSTS HIT WORKERS' POCKETS

Lane Kirkland in AFL-CIO News, July 14, 1956

The rapidly rising cost of hospital services throughout the country presents a growing threat to the real value of health insurance plans to which millions of workers now look for protection.

In the case of service-type plans such as Blue Cross, this trend is reflected in higher premium rates. In the case of cash indemnity plans, it is reflected in the higher excess charges that members must pay out of their own pockets, over and above the benefits paid by their plans.

Unless a constructive solution is found, the purpose of these plans, to make good hospital care more widely available, will be defeated.

During the past ten years, hospital costs have risen at the rate of from 6 to 8 per cent per year. This exceeds the rate of increase in prices generally, and in consumer incomes.

Some of these cost increases cannot, and should not, be avoided. The wages and working conditions of hospital employees have long been notoriously bad. They still lag behind wage levels and benefits enjoyed by workers in other occupations, and should be further improved.

Perhaps the most crucial source of rising costs, however, is the excessive use of hospitals for the treatment of conditions that could be cared for outside the hospital, or could have been detected and corrected at an earlier stage.

Most health insurance plans, as well as the doctors who misuse hospital facilities, are themselves largely to blame for this. They tend to emphasize hospitalization and surgery in their benefit structure, and to neglect preventive care and treatment outside the hospital.

A Michigan study has shown that as much as one-fifth of the total cost of Blue Cross protection is spent on unnecessary hospital admissions and excessive stays. Faulty use of hospital care was found in as many as one-third of all admissions.

The solution does not lie in the curtailment of insurance benefits, but in the extension of those benefits so as to provide comprehensive protection and care, outside of as well as within the hospital. The emphasis in prepayment plans should be lifted to outpatient benefits, preventive care, and the early diagnosis and treat-

ment of conditions.

This can best be done through the medium of out-patient clinics and health centers providing the services of physicians and specialists on a "group practice" basis.

The experience of prepayment plans which do employ this approach has shown that the amount of hospitalization required can be substantially reduced while, at the same time, the quality and quantity of medical care provided the member are greatly improved.

N. Y. LAUNDRY WORKERS NO LONGER NEED WORRY ABOUT HEALTH COSTS

The Advance, February 1, 1960

Six years ago, the high cost of staying healthy—or of regaining health—was one of the bugaboos of practically every laundry worker in the Amalgamated, as it is of anyone who has to live on a wage earner's income.

Today, thanks to their Amalgamated Laundry Workers Health Center, no member of the New York Laundry Workers Joint Board need any longer stagger under this burden. Since its establishment on Oct. 18, 1954, no less than 311,103 patient-services have been dispensed by the Center—all without charge.

These and many other heartening facts were brought out at the recent biennial meeting of the Center's board of directors, held at New York's Hotel Astor.

Establishment of the Center over five years ago, with the cooperation of employers, was another step toward the Amalgamated's goal of "serving all its members from the cradle to the grave," said Louis Simon, Joint Board manager, at the meeting.

In an industry plagued with severe occupational hazards and consequent high illness and death rates among its workers, the existence of such a center is of crucial importance, Simon pointed out.

Through Dec. 31, 1959, the Center had served a total of 167,159 patients. Its pharmacy had filled 27,718 prescriptions. Nearly ten thousand separate individuals had made use of the Center's facilities. These include internal medicine, allergy, nose and throat, skin diseases, gynecology, neuro-psychiatry, ophthalmology, orthopedics, pathology, radiology, urology, and others. Dental services are also available.

Like the other three Amalgamated health centers—in New York, Philadelphia and Chicago—the Laundry Workers Health Center has a medical staff of leading physicians, including many prominent specialists. It is housed in a modern building erected and maintained jointly by the union and the industry, and it has the finest equipment obtainable.

Medical services are rendered free to all members, and few hesitate to avail themselves of them when the need arises. In September 1957, the Laundry Workers also decided to underwrite the cost of prescriptions to retired members.

The Center is now also serving members of Washable Suits & Novelty Clothing Workers Local 169, and arrangements have been made for coverage of the Neckwear Workers. From April 1 to Dec. 31, 1959 (the period covered by the latest report), there were 33,331 patient-visits to the Center. These included members and their spouses and children, and retired workers and their spouses. A total of 12,487 prescriptions were dispensed during that period.

In July 1958 the Center embarked on a program emphasizing preventive medicine and the value of periodic examinations. This patient health review includes a complete physical check-up, routine laboratory testing, electrocardiograms, cancer tests for women, urological examination for men, eye tests for glaucoma, as well as special tests where indicated. The Center has a deep interest in early cancer detection. The number of lives already saved through these free physical examinations is impossible to estimate, Simon said.

ILGWU 'HEALTHMOBILE' AIDS VICTIMS OF PUERTO RICO HURRICANE

Justice, September 1, 1956

The Garment Workers' Mobile Health Center for Puerto Rico has been initiated by being pressed into emergency service on the island less than 48 hours after its arrival.

The unit was dedicated in the heart of the New York City's garment center on July 25, 1956, and toured the city for public inspection during the following week.

A dedicatory ceremony in Puerto Rico had been planned with Vice Pres. Charles S. Zimmerman representing the ILGWU. But two days after arrival of the unit by ship on Aug. 10, Hurricane Betsy came roaring out of the Caribbean. The hurricane cut across the island and hit 20 Puerto Rican cities leaving a path of destruction and hundreds injured and homeless.

Zimmerman immediately reached Col. Miguel Munoz, head of civilian defense, and put the mobile unit at his disposal. On the day originally set for the ceremony, Col. Munoz ordered the unit to proceed to the little mountain town of Aibonito.

Manned by a crew consisting of Dr. Bajandas, a graduate of the University of Puerto Rico, Nurse Amy Haynes and medical technician Hector Colon, the mobile unit sped over the hairpin curves of the mountain roads on its mission of mercy.

In Aibonito the hospital was out of commission. Its roof had been blown off. The mobile unit moved in and took over many hospital functions. Meanwhile Puerto Rican defense officials, studying the situation, decided the unit was needed next to meet a greater emergency in Yabucoa, on the southeast coast of the island. In the early hours of dawn, the Health Mobile moved on to the next town.

Meanwhile, ILGWU headquarters in Puerto Rico continued to receive calls for emergency aid from union members in many parts of the island. Workers employed by Gordonshire in Cayey, by Hilmar in Arecibo, by Trio in Coamo found themselves homeless.

ILGWU Local 600 immediately set up emergency financial aid. Vice Pres. Zimmerman arranged for aid from Local 22 and other mainland sources.

The unit arrived in Yabucoa, and found the town in complete ruin, with no water, electricity or light, its hospital without power. The unit drew up in the hospital yard and began rendering its humanitarian services at once.

Wherever the unit moved about the island on its mission of aid, it was welcomed by the weary victims of the storm. Throughout the island, a good word is spreading about the union which sent the "clinica rodante" just in time to help in a moment of tragedy.

BREAK GROUND FOR $1 MILLION HEALTH CENTER

Federation News (Chicago), May 2, 1959

Ground-breaking ceremonies for the only union-management operated health center in Chicago's vast West Side medical district were held Wednesday at Polk Street and Marshfield Avenue.

The $1,000,000 out-patient clinic structure is financed by the Health and Welfare Fund of Chicago Office, Theater and Amusement Building Janitors Local 25.

City officials, health experts, labor leaders and employers participated in the ceremonies.

"You are helping to rebuild Chicago while providing for the health of your members," said Mayor Richard J. Daley, who helped turn over the first shovels full of dirt at the site. "The city's congratulations go to labor and management for their interest in the health of working people."

General President William L. Mc-Fetridge of the Building Service Em-

ployees International Union said that several locals now provide diagnostic service for members, but the Local 25 center is the only institution of its type providing complete medical care.

The center will be called the Olivia "Peg" Bautsch Health Center; it is named for the late secretary-treasurer of Local 25 who with Pres. Tom Burke pioneered the movement for union-management medical plans in Illinois. Miss Bautsch died in 1952.

Over 10,000 members of Janitors Local 25, General Service Employees Local 73 and Building Service Employees Local 199 are covered by the plan financed through employer contributions to health and welfare funds.

Comprehensive medical care is provided through the employer-paid plan, including diagnosis, x-ray, surgery and physical therapy. Part of employer contributions provide hospital care.

SIU CLINICS WINNING TB FIGHT

Seafarers Log, October 23, 1959

The long fight to wipe out tuberculosis among Seafarers is achieving its goal, and the diagnostic function of the SIU's clinics is playing an important role in achieving this objective. Reflecting the success of the campaign against tuberculosis, the number of Seafarers now hospitalized at the Manhattan Beach Public Health Service hospital is down to 19 from a high of 43 cases back in January 31, 1958.

While the 19 Seafarers do not constitute the entire roster of tuberculosis cases among Seafarers, the striking decline in the Manhattan Beach population is proving the worth of the yearly physical examinations given at the New York clinic and at SIU clinics in Mobile, Baltimore and New Orleans.

The two major requirements for controlling tuberculosis are early detection and effective treatment. The SIU clinics supply the first element and the Public Health Service the second, utilizing antibiotics and other improved methods of treatment.

With early detection it is often possible to treat tuberculosis without major surgery, greatly cutting the hospital stay and enabling the Seafarer to get a "fit-for duty," with his lungs intact.

Early detection is essential to check the spread of TB. Because of the confined nature of shipboard living, one undetected case of TB on a ship can result in infection of several other members of the crew.

The clinic has picked up many

early cases of TB before the Seafarers involved had the slightest inkling they were ill.

This routine has been successful in a number of other areas besides TB, notably in checking high blood pressure, arthritis, diabetes and other conditions of a chronic nature.

If the trend continues, and the Union is hopeful that it will, it will prove the contention on which the clinic program was based in the first place, that annual diagnostic examinations would improve the health of seamen and cut down on crippling and disabling diseases.

It was for reasons such as these that the Union originally negotiated the clinic program in contract talks with SIU operators.

UNION EYE CARE CENTER HAS $212,366 YEAR

The Cleveland Citizen, September 9, 1960

One year and 11,029 pairs of glasses later, the Union Eye Care Center of Cleveland is looking forward to doubling its volume of business in the next 12 months.

Totally owned and operated by organized labor, the Center did $212,-366 in business its first 12 months and offered glasses at as much as 60 per cent below prevailing retail prices in the Cleveland area.

How did Cleveland labor get in the optical business? William C. Lightner, president of the Center, explains it very simply: "We felt the consumer was not getting a fair break on optical prices, so we decided to do something about it. We had heard of successes in other areas and we felt we could do as well. We did some checking and felt we could set up in business if we had $25,000 worth of working capital. We just went out and got it the hard way, 25 cents at a crack."

Lightner, who is AFL-CIO staff consultant with the Cleveland Community Chest and an active member of the United Auto Workers, teamed up with Ed Moss, secretary-treasurer of District 54 of the International Association of Machinists. They sold affiliation fees to unions throughout Cleveland on the basis of 25 cents per member.

It was slow going at first, but finally the idea of low-priced eye care caught on. After nearly a year of almost daily appearances at union meetings throughout Cleveland, the Lightner-Moss team realized its goal of 100,000 affiliations, and $25,000 in cash was reached.

"From the very beginning we were lucky," Lightner said. "We hit upon an ideal, central location for the first Center. It was beautifully decorated and required little or no remodeling. Knotty equipment problems resolved themselves quickly. The problem of staffing the Center worked itself out almost overnight. We opened for business just a year ago and have been thriving ever since."

Officers of the Cleveland Center feel their optical prices compare favorably with the lowest in the country. Here are the averages for glasses and frames for the first year:

TYPE OF GLASSES	AVERAGE PRICE
4,244 Single Vision	$13.63
4,571 Bifocal	22.00
154 Trifocal	30.37
2,060 Safety	15.05

As the Center enters its second year, it has 162,000 union families from 232 locals affiliated. Plans are being completed for the opening next month of a second Center to be located on Cleveland's West Side. A committee is already busy selecting a location for a third site on the East Side.

What about the future? "It couldn't look brighter," says Lightner. "We only hope that other trade unions across the country will steal a page out of our book."

THE MINE WORKERS' MEMORIAL HOSPITALS

United Mine Workers Journal, September 15, 1959

One of the visitors to the Memorial Hospitals during this past year was the noted writer on medical care in the United States, Albert Deutsch. After making his tour through the Memorial Hospitals he wrote:

"You drive through the streets of Beckley, W. Va., a mining town of about 20,000. At a turn in the road, you come suddenly upon a modern, gleaming, steel-and-glass structure dominating a wild landscape of heavily-wooded hills. It seems strange, there, this mid-twentieth century architectural creation that stands out in dramatic contrast to its surroundings.

"It was my first glimpse of the Beckley Memorial Hospital, one link in a remarkable chain of ten hospitals strung along a 250-mile area in the southern Appalachian hills that serves coal miners and their families who are beneficiaries of the United Mine Workers of America Welfare and Retirement Fund. The feeling of awe evoked by this initial sight lingered as I was shown through the bright, cheerful interior, tastefully designed for maximum efficiency.

"The modern equipment was more than matched by the manifest skills of the doctors and nurses as they ministered to their patients in a therapeutic atmosphere not surpassed by the best metropolitan medical centers I had seen.

"Because the southern Appalachian region was most desperately short of good hospitals, the UMWA Welfare and Retirement Fund found it necessary to establish a network of ten facilities clustered close to the borders where Kentucky, West Virginia and Virginia meet. The Beckley Memorial Hospital with 193 beds, is one of the three larger hospitals in the chain.

"The patients—miners, pensioners, their wives, children and dependents —in all degrees of sickness and disability, were all treated not only with equal dignity and respect, but with efficiency by a group of doctors headed by specialists who could serve with distinction at the best medical centers. In fact, many were recruited from such centers, including the finest university hospitals.

"The Beckley Memorial Hospital is organized on a group practice basis—where the doctors work as a team, around a core of full-time salaried specialists. The doctors don't have to worry about the patient's ability to pay for expensive diagnostic or treatment procedures. They don't have to worry about bills. They can concentrate on giving the best medical service possible.

"Before the Williamson Memorial Medical Center—one of the three base hospitals in the chain, with 133 beds—was opened in 1956, there was only a handful of specialists in the area. Williamson had only one specialist—an internist. The next nearest qualified specialists — two surgeons, a urologist and a radiologist —were at Pikeville, Ky., 30 miles away. Another specialist, a pediatrician was at Logan, West Va., 41 miles distant in the opposite direction. The Williamson facility made available to the people of that mining region a hospital staffed by full-time specialists, all gathered in one place and prepared to render complete diagnostic and treatment services. Sick miners and their families no longer had to be moved hither and yon over many miles of hard road to get specialist care when needed.

"For decades, far-visioned medical leaders had beaten the drums for the 'regional hospital plan.' They envisioned chains of hospitals or health centers, especially in rural areas, with small facilities in more sparsely-populated areas 'feeding in' patients to medical centers located at strategic points in larger communities. The latter would have a wider representation of medical specialties together with special diagnostic and therapeutic equipment and facilities not available at smaller hospitals. Concentration of the more expensive equipment and special personnel in the central hospitals would be not only more economical financially, but more efficient, medically. The main benefits would accrue to the patient. Centralized purchasing of drugs and other medical supplies, together with personnel recruiting and business accounting, were also calculated to get better quality, more efficiently, at less cost.

"The concept of the regional hospital system was first put into wide-scale operation through the Miners Memorial Hospital Association chain. If it had made no other contribution, the UMWA Welfare and Retirement Fund would have earned a significant page in American medical history through this trail-blazing act alone."

During the past year, more than 20,000 hospitalized patients received the finest quality of medical, surgical and specialists' services through 279,321 days of hospitalization; more than 1,000 cases were treated daily in ambulatory patient departments.

The variety of acute medical problems found in both hospitalized and clinic cases disclosed conditions that many physicians have encountered only in the textbooks. A surgeon commented: "Respiratory problems far exceed those in any other area. The most interesting are our ever-present diseases due to coal dust and other chronic lung conditions.

"In the field of injuries, we treat almost as many cases as are found in the armed forces. These are multiple injuries of the chest, stomach, bones and muscles. The splintered and broken bones seen in this area exceed those found at any other time except during open warfare. Bad roads and high-speed vehicles increase the number of injuries and accidents seen here far beyond that

noted by surgeons in other areas . . . Scurvy and rickets top the general average for the country."

The number of specialists caring for beneficiaries has steadily increased. Pre-natal and well-baby clinics have increased in number and size; the number of diabetic patients meeting regularly for instruction and checkups has increased; family members come more frequently to the hospitals for special instruction on how to care for patients sent home for long periods of convalescence.

Education and research programs within the ten-hospital system focus on improving the quality of care. Educational programs have been established, with residency training at the three central Memorial Hospitals. Staff physicians are encouraged to attend postgraduate courses and professional meetings.

Active research programs have been developed, with clinical studies relating primarily to the problems of coal miners and their families.

"It'd be nice, Ed, if our Union Health and Welfare contract included dental care!"

Recognition of the high caliber of the Memorial Hospitals is implied in grants for construction of research buildings at Williamson and Beckley Hospitals. These grants were made by the National Institute of Health under the U. S. Public Health Service after review of staff qualifications and personal visits to the hospitals. Additional grants for research activity have been approved.

The program of training future staff, primarily local young men and women, has moved forward steadily. The Association now has four schools: Practical Nursing, Professional Nursing, Medical Technology, and Nurse Anesthetists.

HARPER WOODS WINS ITS BATTLE FOR A POLIO CLINIC

Michigan Solidarity, March 10, 1958

The City of Harper Woods held its polio clinic last week.

Sounds simple. The mayor wanted it, the women's volunteers health guild wanted it and the 13,000 unprotected adults and children wanted it.

The Wayne County Medical Society didn't want it. And for three months succeeded in preventing it.

The "battle of Harper Woods" has become one of the more publicized instances of the continuing fight between organized medical societies and volunteer civic groups over anti-polio clinics. Harper Woods has succeeded where most of the other groups gave up in discouragement.

The women of the Harper Woods Hospital Guild came up with the idea for a polio clinic late last year, but ran into a stone wall when they attempted to enlist doctors. They appealed to the city. Mayor Joseph Grossel got the same rebuff—and also got his dander up.

"To me it was a simple case of protecting our adults and children, and as rapidly as possible before the polio season begins," he pointed out.

The medical society, however, didn't share the mayor's feelings.

When the Detroit News in an editorial rapped the group for anti-clinic acts which suggested professional pressure on doctors, the society remain unmoved.

"We need a healthy, hearty return of the people to the family physi-

cian," was the flat-footed position of the society.

The impasse was finally broken when Mayor Grossel obtained the services of doctors outside of the society's influence.

Other groups haven't been as fortunate. Attempts by PTA and community groups to set up clinics have been frustrated. As far as can be determined, no doctors in Wayne County are now participating in volunteer polio clinics.

In Detroit, there is hope among PTA groups that they can mend the rift with the medical society through friendly talks, enabling them to proceed on clinics sought in many areas of the city.

Apparently there has been resentment among some doctors against the sense of ownership people have shown toward the Salk serum after contributing $30 million to its development. "We don't have people complaining about coming to a doctor's office and paying for smallpox or diphtheria immunization," was one lament.

More eloquent than any statement in the controversy are the figures on the polio picture at the moment:

• During 1957 there was one more case of polio in Wayne County than in 1956.

• The cost of maintaining a polio patient is $26 per day; the cost of serum is 96c.

• In the nation, 45 million persons under 40 haven't received even one polio shot.

HOW SOME UAW MEMBERS SAVE $ ON DRUG PURCHASES

UAW Solidarity, February 1960

Thousands of UAW members, both working and retired, have found a way to beat the high cost of vital prescription medicines.

It was done simply by getting together a large enough group of people interested in participating in a genuine discount plan, and then going out and finding a retail firm big enough to give substantial and genuine discounts to those presenting proper credentials.

Using this method, members of many Detroit area UAW locals as well as members of other unions have saved hundreds of thousands of dollars during the past two and a half years, when the first discount plan began.

Credit for starting the ball rolling must go to the union label committee of Dodge Local 3, which arranged the first such plan in June of 1957 with Regal, Inc., a retail drug chain.

Special cards were issued to every member of Local 3, entitling him to a flat 10 per cent discount on all purchases in the Regal stores including prescriptions. The item's regular discount price is clearly labelled in advance on every product, and the purchaser does not present his discount card until the cashier is ready to ring up the sale.

Today, 47 union groups in the greater Detroit metropolitan area, including 32 UAW locals and groups, participate in the Regal discount operation.

A few months ago, the Metropolitan Detroit Area UAW Senior Citizens Steering Committee negotiated a special discount plan for retirees with the Regal chain.

FIGHT PUSHED FOR FORAND HEALTH INSURANCE BILL

Labor, July 25, 1959

Organized labor, leading educators, consumer representatives and progressive lawmakers opened a new drive during the past week for enactment of a bill sponsored by Congressman Aime J. Forand (Dem., R. I.) that would provide badly-needed health and medical benefits for persons over 65.

First introduced by Forand in 1957, the measure would provide surgical, hospital and nursing home care for retired persons under Social Security. It would be financed by increasing the contributions of both employees and employers by ¼ of one per cent.

The bill is opposed by the American Medical Association, the powerful "Insurance Companies Lobby," Chamber of Commerce, National Association of Manufacturers, Farm Bureau and other rightwing groups, which continually raise the old cry of "socialism."

The Administration, which had previously refused to take a stand on the bill, this week aligned itself with the opposition.

AFL-CIO Director of Social Security Nelson Cruikshank told lawmakers the legislation was long overdue. He stressed, "The men and women in their declining years have earned a better deal than they are getting . . . The lack of protection against heavy medical costs is today's greatest gap in the security of older citizens."

The AFL-CIO spokesman said private plans, both non-profit and commercial, are "so costly that protection is too limited and aged persons are left under the ever-present risk of heavy medical bills which sap their modest resources."

"Medicine Man"

WHY CAN'T U. S. MATCH ENGLISH HEALTH SERVICE?

Federation News (Chicago), February 6, 1960

"You move too fast in your cities. You drink all your milk and swallow all your pills and go the same as us in the end."

This is how British unionist Jim Matthews looks at American life.

From the "cradle to the grave" is how Matthews describes the National Health Service of Great Britain. He said the richest man in Britain pays a premium of 11 shillings ($1.54) a week—the same as the poorest man.

The single contribution covers the comprehensive program which covers everything from maternity to funeral benefits.

Matthews said the British Medical Society opposed the program when it was first initiated. But now, he said, the American Medical Association can't find a single British doctor who will come to the U. S. and attack the National Health Service.

Matthews said we take care of our younger people adequately but neglect our older folk. "Look at the hue and cry against the Forand Bill."

"Why can't you match our health service?" Matthews asked.

11 | **RETIREMENT**

LABOR MUST CARRY THE BALL

The Carpenter, May 1956

Last month Ball State Teachers College, Muncie, Indiana, held its second annual conference on problems of the aging. Several hundred people from all walks of life were there to mull over the growing enigma of how the energies, skills and capacities of our aging citizens can best be utilized for the benefit of both the nation and the oldsters themselves.

The conference came up with no answers. However, that does not mean that it was not a success. The very fact that several hundred public-spirited citizens were interested enough in the problem to journey as much as several hundred miles to participate in the conference is an encouraging sign in itself. The conference may not have come up with any specific answers, but at least it put some of the questions into clearer focus — and knowing what the questions are is the first step toward arriving at the answers.

It will take time and study to develop a system whereby the contributions which senior citizens can make to our society are not lost through arbitrary and unrealistic taboos and regulations. This journal has repeatedly pointed out that ours is the only society in which gray hairs are a detriment rather than a blessing. Even in the tribes of darkest Africa, the oldsters are accorded recognition as senior statesmen. They are always on the councils and governing bodies where their experience, wisdom, and level-headedness can balance out the impetuosity of youth.

Here all the emphasis is on youth. Know-how scarcely counts. A worker who is perfectly fine as an employee on the day before his 65th birthday becomes a has-been and a detriment on the day after. It is neither logical nor an economically sound practice. But that is the way it will remain until such time as enough people make up their minds to do something about it.

Moreover, medical science is prolonging the life-span every year and as a result, the number of citizens "too old to work and too young to die" is growing year by year. Their plight can no longer be ignored.

That the universities and colleges are becoming aware of the problem is a good thing, but, in the final analysis, labor is going to have to come up with the answers. It is all right for colleges to determine that men in their sixties and seventies are just as productive and as efficient as lads in their twenties, but before very much happens, labor will have to take the bull by the horns.

Over the past hundred years, organized labor has spearheaded the drives that brought free schools, universal suffrage, Social Security and many other social advancements which make life in the United States and Canada meaningful and worthwhile. The labor movement is fully awake to the plight of our senior citizens in this dog-eat-dog society of ours. Perhaps it will take time, but sooner or later the labor movement will come up with answers that will eliminate the frightful waste of the talents and energies of our older people—a waste the nation can no longer afford.

20 LOCAL UNIONS STUDY PROBLEMS OF GROWING OLD, RETIREMENT

Federation News (Chicago), April 11, 1959

Delegates from 20 Chicago area local unions studied the Union's Role in Retirement at a conference at the University of Chicago.

Union, university and government experts gave their views on aging and retirement.

Clark Tibbetts, assistant director of the U. S. Department of Health, Education and Welfare's Special Staff on Aging, told the delegates the nation will be able to afford a $200 monthly income by 1965 for every retired worker, despite the increasing numbers of older persons. He said:

"This will be possible without jeopardizing the income position of the rest of our population."

Francis Henson, education director of the Machinists Great Lakes Territory, reported that a survey of unions in the AFL-CIO showed that nearly all feel that unions have a responsibility to help their members prepare for retirement both through pension plans and pre-retirement education programs.

Charles Odell, director, Department of Older and Retired Workers, United Auto Workers, said while unions like the Auto Workers can and do a great deal for older and retired workers, they should not try to go it alone. He said unions should seek the aid of other community groups such as social service organizations, fraternal societies and churches.

People get a lot more out of their jobs than just pay, according to Robert Havinghurst, chairman of the University of Chicago Committee on Human Development.

He explained that workers must find substitutes for the other satisfactions when they retire. Other benefits of working, he said, include prestige, self respect, friendship, avoidance of boredom and the opportunity to feel of service to others.

Dean Maurice F. X. Donohue of the University College claimed America can fulfill one of man's oldest dreams because American society is rich enough to free people from work.

But, he said, we must find ways to help the retired workers feel themselves a valued part of our national life.

TOWARD A BETTER LIFE FOR OUR OLDTIMERS

The NMU Pilot, January 31, 1957

When Herman Piontka drives to the village to pick up the morning newspaper he wears his old "high pressure" cap, a memento of more than 30 years at sea as cook and steward on the big trans-Atlantic passenger liners.

Herman is as happy a man as you'll find within 100 miles of Babylon, Long Island.

He's proud of his snug brick home, and of the fruit trees and flowers that grow in his carefully tended garden. He's proud of his career as a seaman and a good union man. He's a respected man in his community.

When a man nears his three-score years, then he can claim that he has earned his rest, and may with a quiet conscience settle himself down and enjoy himself. He has lived honestly and done his best — best for himself, his family and his country.

Unfortunately, however, only a pitiably small number of older people enjoy the fruits of their declining years. America is a land of plenty, truly, but not if you're over 65 years of age.

Nearly three-quarters of Americans beyond 65 either have no income of their own or earn less than $1,000 a year. And you know how well you can live on $20 a week. Not too comfortably, that's sure.

Older persons in our population (those over 65) are steadily increasing not only in number, but in proportion to our total population. Since 1900, the number of persons 65 and over has increased four times while the total population has only doubled. The over-65's now number over 14 million.

Among our rapidly increasing population over 65, 36 per cent have no income whatever, 38 per cent have less than $1,000 while 11 per cent have an income between $1,000 and $2,000.

In many cases, these incomes must do not only for the individual earning the money—but often support a spouse and other members of the family. Only 15 per cent of the oldsters over 65 earn or receive more than $2,000 a year.

Yes, Herman Piontka is a fortunate man, as he will cheerfully admit. When he retired on a National Maritime Union pension two years ago at the age of 69 his union allotment combined with his and his wife's Social Security payments, totaled well over $2,000 a year. This year Herman shared in a pension increase which added $10 a month to the pension check of each NMU old-timer.

The labor unions and other forward-looking groups in the community are continuing the fight to insure a better life for older people. The long range outlook is hopeful.

It has been said about seamen that they spend one-third of their money on women, one-third on whiskey, and the rest they spend foolishly. Of course, this was never wholly true, and is less true now that seamen have become first-class citizens.

Take Herman Piontka — since he worked as a $52-a-month ship's cook over 20 years ago, he's gathered a nest egg which, combined with his pension and Social Security benefits, allows him to live comfortably and even to share his good fortune with others. This Christmas, for instance, he donated a television set to the hospital in his community.

"Save your money, boys," advises Herman. A Twentieth Century Fund study puts it this way:

"To avoid the hazards of a dependent old age, an individual should set up his own program." They suggest these points:

1. Development of skills. Your muscles may not hold up after the age of 60, but special skills acquired in younger years will help to get and hold a job. Study some position or skill in your present employment or surroundings which represents a potential employment opportunity in your "after-60" period.

2. Set up an adequate savings program, regularly allotting a certain portion of your funds to United States bonds or savings.

3. Keep your installment buying down to a reasonable figure, as you mature. As you grow older, it is desirable not to burden your future earnings too heavily.

4. Learn your Social Security benefits. Go over them with a qualified adviser. You can only get the benefits you apply for. If you don't know about all of them you may miss benefits to which you are entitled.

OUR SOCIAL SECURITY SYSTEM

By Nelson Cruikshank in the Plasterer and Cement Mason, June 1959

Right now there are 12,800,000 people getting a monthly check from the Social Security system.

Now, 10,400,000 of these are older people. The average benefit that is being paid to each individual person is $71.62 a month. That isn't very high. But the average benefit of the person who is now retired, retiring this month, is considerably better. It is $84.50 in round numbers.

The average benefit that is being paid to a retired man and wife, under Social Security today, is $125 a month.

Again this is not high. But it is far better than the old way when all we had to rely on was perhaps charity or the help of one's family, friends and neighbors if we were destitute, or to rely entirely on savings. And what possibility does the ordinary working person, if he raises a family, have to lay enough aside that he can retire on his invested income?

You know the answer to that, and I don't need to give it.

Now, in 1956 we added a provision that pays benefits in case of disability. After age 50, if one is totally disabled, he can get retirement benefits, and benefits for most of his dependents.

There are today 255,000 working people in their wheel chairs, in their beds at home, in their hospitals, or just confined to their homes unable to work — 255,000 drawing their monthly disability check.

We only won that fight by a margin of one vote in the Senate, and believe you me it was an effort to get that one last vote.

But today $22 million every month goes out to these disabled workers.

In addition to the ten million old people who are drawing monthly checks, there are two million young widows with children who are drawing monthly benefits.

In the amendments of 1958, we succeeded in liberalizing these benefits, so that now a widow with two young children under 18 can draw up to $254 a month in the event of the death of the family breadwinner.

Now, again, some of you can remember when someone was killed on the job or when he died from disease or illness, and his widow and children were left without any protection.

Collections would be taken up on the job and in the shop. It would be announced that the Widow Jones was doing some baking on the side and taking in wash. And everybody pitched in to help. And then before long it would happen to another brother, and the Widow Jones would somehow or other be forgotten. That was a pretty poor system we had, even if we can call it a system.

Now, $254 a month isn't a great deal, but it is far and away better than the old system that we had.

Let's say, for example, these children are two and five years of age and there are two children in the family. The young worker is 35 years of age when he dies. The cash equivalent of that widow's protection under Social Security is $64,000.

In other words, he would have to carry $64,000 of life insurance to give him the same protection that he has under Social Security.

Now, this is not a bad protection when we consider the needs of working people. This, of course, is in addition to the fact that if he doesn't pass away in the working years of his life he has the retirement protection. And when he retires at age 65, if his wife is age 63, the cash equivalent of his retirement benefit is about $32,000.

In other words, he would have to purchase an annuity to give him the same protection as Social Security at a cost of $32,000.

This is all provided under our Social Security system.

Our system is good as far as it goes, but it doesn't go far enough. We need to increase the benefits, particularly for the higher wage earners, because today only the first $400 per month of our earnings counts on Social Security.

Another one of the major needs is to protect older people against the cost of medical and hospital care. Many of us have Blue Cross; we have negotiated plans for health and welfare. But for most people these cease when they first reach retirement age. Yet, when we reach retirement age is when we most need medical care.

We want to extend Social Security so that hospital costs and medical costs are taken care of out of the Social Security fund when people reach retirement age. This is one of the major risks, because we often see people with a pension plan, with Social Security, with some savings. They have bought their home and paid for it, and they are in pretty good shape until serious illness comes along and hits mom or pop, and then all their planning for security in old age is knocked into a cocked hat.

Now, we are a practical movement, the labor movement in America. We are not asking for much on social security when the retirement age comes.

We are just asking for a little decency and dignity, that when a man has acquired a skill, supported his union organization all his life and that union has by collective bargaining established a high wage level, that a substantial portion of that wage should be continued when the journey's end is near, and he has made his contribution to the economic welfare of his country.

THE 25-YEAR-CROWD

Local 1-S News, June 1960

*Will you love me in December
As you do in May . . . ?*
—*Popular song of 25 years ago.*

The Macy's "25-Year Crowd" held its annual party recently. It was pleasant, people say. The cocktails were many, the speeches were short. There were events and games, with prizes, and anecdotes to tug at the memory . . . of Macy's "firsts," the increase in Macy customers, and such-like.

The 25-year veterans of Macy's "had arrived," they were told by Board Chairman Jack Straus, who is known by the faithful as Mr. Jack.

"It is you who represent Macy's to the people," said Mr. Jack. "And Macy's wouldn't be the store it is without you."

How inevitably these words must have seemed just right. For when you have worked 25 years and more for an organization, you do feel you have contributed to it a substantial measure of your lives. You *have* represented the company to so many thousands of customers during this quarter century and more. It *is* true: the store would not be the same without people like yourself.

The 25-year veteran basks in this passing glow. The saleswoman feels the pleasure of this recognition; and it would be a poor thing to think of the wages and working conditions of 1935. The stockman forgets the tedium, and the pressure, and the quotas and injuries.

The flash bulbs of the cameras are popping, and there is much hand-shaking and reminiscence of the great and small who shopped in Macy's. And not for a moment will anyone speak of the ills and grievances—or of the years ahead which are uncertain, of the years ahead when oldtimers know they may slow down, and what will the supervisors say, and there will be no farewell parties, and who will speak all the words of praise then? And how will they live when they must retire? and what will Social Security be then, and what will the Macy's pension be then?

And will all these important executives, who are so pleasant and even democratic, will they love us in the December of our years, as they love us at this reception in the Statler Hotel?

The Union, too, has its reminiscences—rather different from those at the Statler. We have our recollections of negotiations to win decent pensions for these veteran Macy workers, negotiations which were difficult and long, and sometimes led to stoppages and strikes.

We remember our struggles for improved wages and job security, and the achievement of standards which meant respect and dignity for union members. And we think of these things, not always with nostalgia, but sometimes with bitterness.

Because deep within us, we know these parties of the "25-Year-Crowd"

represent the frosting on a "let 'em eat cake" philosophy of management. These parties do not provide the bread of sustenance which the older worker, and then the retired worker, must have to live.

In December of this year Local 1-S, the Union of these 25-year veterans, will have reached agreement on its demands for the next Union contract.

This Union will certainly demand a substantial increase in the Macy pension. We will demand that this increase be applied to members who have already retired.

We say that this substantial pension must be wholly independent of the present so-called "profit sharing" plan. The plan is based on percentages which discriminate against the lowest-paid employees, and most benefit the best-paid.

A genuine pension plan must be based on service and need; and the pension benefit must be *guaranteed*.

We shall—all of us—see if they love us in December as they do in May.

UNIONS TRIUMPH ON RAIL PENSION, JOBLESS BILL

Michael Marsh in Labor, May 9, 1959

Thursday, April 30, 1959, will go down as a red-letter day for America's active, retired and unemployed railroaders. On that day both House and Senate passed identical bills to improve rail retirement and unemployment benefits, climaxing a years-long struggle by railmen and their unions.

For the rail unionists it was a stirring victory. Carrier lobbyists had persuaded a majority of the House Interstate Commerce Committee to report out a drastically altered bill that was wholly unacceptable to the rail unions.

But when that bill reached the House floor it was ignominiously rejected. The railroaders' friends instead substituted a union-endorsed bill, and carried that substitute to

victory by 181 to 91. Congressman Harley Staggers (Dem., W. Va.) led the fight for the substitute, which bore his name.

Meanwhile the Senate had passed an identical union-backed bill without a single voice being raised against it. Sen. Wayne Morse (Dem., Ore.), with a strong assist from Majority Leader Lyndon Johnson (Dem., Tex.), guided that smooth victory.

President Eisenhower was not expected to veto the measure, in view of its overwhelming passage by both Houses of Congress. Earlier, Administration spokesmen had opposed the bill as too generous and House GOP Leader Charles Halleck (Rep., Ind.) fought against it on the House floor.

As passed by Congress, the railmen's bill has these major provisions:

1—Retirement and survivor benefits are increased 10 per cent.

2—Retirement taxes on both the carriers and the employees go up from 6¼ per cent of the first $350 earned in a month to 6¾ per cent of the first $400 earned.

3—Railroad unemployment benefits are generally raised by 20 per cent per day. In addition, a jobless rail employee who exhausted his unemployment benefits may draw up to 13 weeks of emergency extra benefits for specified periods.

4—Jobless railroaders with 10 but less than 15 years of service have a permanent right to up to 13 weeks of extra unemployment benefits. Those with 15 or more years of service have a permanent right to up to 26 weeks of extra benefits.

5—The ceiling on railroad unemployment taxes, paid solely by the carriers, is raised from 3 per cent of taxable payroll to 3¾ per cent.

None of the attempts by the House Interstate Commerce Committee to cut unemployment and sickness benefits and to abolish maternity benefits has survived in the bill as passed.

Likewise, the carriers bitterly opposed the idea of extending unemployment benefits for long-service railroaders, and the House committee bill provided no such benefits. The Staggers substitute passed by the House wrote them back in. Rail unions fought especially hard for these benefits.

In the Senate the railmen's bill sped through in the extraordinarily short time of 41 minutes. It was gotten to the floor by Majority Leader Johnson, who persuaded the Senate to lay aside its unfinished business to take up the Morse bill.

Not a single voice was raised in the Senate against the measure which passed by voice vote.

After the speedy Senate action, a debate on the identical Staggers substitute motion was nearing a climax. That news gave added impetus to the railmen's friends in the House.

Debate in the House centered on whether to accept the drastically slashed measure reported out by a Commerce Committee—or to pass the substitute offered by Congressman Staggers, as urged by the rail unions and by thousands of railroaders who wrote or telegraphed to their Congressmen.

On the showdown, the 181 to 91 victory in the House for the substitute was by a teller count of members. Thus there was no roll call and no way to identify which members voted against the substitute. However, it was admitted on the House floor that the Republican Policy Committee had circulated a "confidential report" to GOP members urging them to vote for the emasculated committee bill and against the more liberal substitute.

FORD PENSIONS MARK TENTH ANNIVERSARY

UAW Solidarity, April 1960

UAW retirees out of Ford plants across the country have collected over $66 million in pension benefits.

UAW Ford Department leaders and administrators of the UAW-Ford pension fund paused at March's end to look over 10 full years of pension payments to put together staggering figures that help tell part of the story considered "the most glorious chapter in UAW history."

Another 16,000 pension checks valued at $1.2 million had just been dropped into the mails—including

208 to 27 countries from Argentina to Yugoslavia—when fund administrators joined UAW officials and members in commemorating the 10th anniversary of negotiated pension payments.

Ford pensions, of course, are just part of the UAW's total pension story because another 90,000 UAW veterans from other plants are enjoying retirement in dignity, recipients of union-negotiated pensions. And the pensioner list is growing at the rate of 1,000 a month.

The Ford chapter is most significant. The agreement signed on Sept. 28, 1949, astonished millions of workers—including many Ford workers—who believed that company-paid pensions were a dream.

In late March 1950, into the mails went 643 letters containing the first pension checks to Ford workers.

UAW statisticians figure the average UAW member on retirement has 25 years of credited service and is drawing $60 monthly from the union-negotiated pension funds. He now also receives up to $119 a month in Social Security benefits and if his wife is living, the couple receives up to an additional $59 monthly for a total possible monthly income of almost $240.

Before the UAW's pension breakthrough, most of the nation's 10 million senior citizens could look to a monthly income on "retirement" of only $39—all from social security which had a benefit level unchanged since 1937.

UNION'S PROGRAM FOR AGED ON TV

AFL-CIO News, January 11, 1958

When the John Hopkins File 7 television program scheduled a telecast on gerontology — the science and study of aging — the producers looked around for a group which took the problems of its retired members to heart and did something about them.

It settled on District 65, Retail, Wholesale & Department Store Union, which has about 35,000 members and nearly 500 retired members in the New York metropolitan area.

The union's program was shown in action—art classes directed by a skilled artist who also is a retired member of the union; classes in typing, languages and home nursing; group discussions on current social legislation; weekly socials with singing, films, refreshments, etc.

And activities that are not wholly recreational — a toy repair shop, bandage making, various Red Cross projects, educational field trips and regular medical checkups to which each member is entitled as a part of his membership, which he retains after retirement.

All this is part of the union's overall security plan. This provides for retirement at any age from 55 to 65 with benefits, paid for life, based on the length of coverage and the age of the retiring worker.

"What is interesting to me about this union program," said guest expert Dr. James E. Birren, during the telecast, "is that it is difficult, according to the union, for one person to find time to be lonely.

"And the older person is still participating in the union—a significantly large part of the associations clustered about his job have remained with him. He isn't lonely and he isn't idle. The union has managed to make the activity of the older person meaningful."

DETROIT RETIREES WIN REDUCED BUS FARES

Auto Worker, May 1956

The UAW's long fight for reduced bus fares for retirees using Detroit's transit system has finally been won.

Last month, the city's DSR Commission, which controls Detroit's municipally-owned bus system, approved a special 10-cent fare for retired persons who are 65 or older and who are not gainfully employed on a regular basis. The regular Detroit bus fare is 20 cents, one way.

The plan will go into effect on May 15 for a trial period of at least four months.

If the four-month test period in Detroit proves a success, UAW local unions in other cities will seek similar plans for retirees in their areas.

7,000 RETIRED CLOTHING WORKERS TO HAVE OWN WELFARE CENTER

AFL-CIO News, January 19, 1957

New York — Some 7,000 retired members of the Amalgamated Clothing Workers in this area will soon have a health, recreation and education center of their own under a project to be set up by the ACW's New York Joint Board.

When it opens in the spring the New York center will occupy the top floor of the Sidney Hillman Health Center to make it convenient for retired members to visit the medical center for a physical check-up and then drop into the recreation headquarters.

Primary purpose of the New York center, like one in Philadelphia, will be to provide similar congenial surroundings where retired members can play chess, checkers, or other games, work on hobbies, watch television, attend educational affairs, or chat with old friends.

Dr. Morris Brand, director of the New York health center, said the location of the retired workers' center in the medical building would simplify the supervision of the health of the pensioned workers.

In announcing plans for the center in New York, Louis Hollander, manager of the N. Y. Joint Board of the ACW, said that "training for retirement is as necessary as training for work."

"Too many members eligible for pensions," he said "won't retire until they are on a stretcher, because they fear it means dying ahead of time. We want them to feel their lives still have meaning and usefulness."

TO RETIRE . . . OR NOT TO RETIRE?

Justice, February 15, 1958

"Retire? What for?"

Joseph Block, a straight-backed, smiling, 77-year-old member of New York Coat and Suit Pressers' Local 35, thinks the whole idea is foolish. "Why should I retire and spend my time puttering around with a lot of old people? I'd rather go into the shop and be with young people. It keeps me young," he says.

An ILGWU member since 1908, Block is one of many members of Local 35 — and older people everywhere — who think that retirement for a person well and vigorous enough to work is a great mistake.

They agree that the security provided by union retirement pensions and old-age pension laws is wonderful "if a person needs it." But they think it's definitely second best to the kind of security — and satisfaction — a person gets from being a functioning member of society.

"I've never considered retiring," said Sam Melowsky, age 72, during a recent discussion of the problem at the Local 35 office. "What would I do? Sit around the house?"

Waving a gnarled, broad-fingered presser's hand around the Local 35 office, Melowsky added, "This has always been an important part of my life. Why should I give it up?"

Harry Mindlein, another 72-year-old, wasn't even "in a mood to talk about retirement. I've been working since I was eight years old," he said. "The shop is my second home."

David Weissman, age 69, a member of the local executive board, thought that for a person like himself "it would be crazy to retire. I feel good. I can still do a day's work and lead an active life. Why should I retire and turn into an old man?"

Hyman Krenitzky, another union

veteran—all of the men had participated in the great cloakmakers' strike of 1910—said that he might retire next year, when he will be 70, "because my wife would like it."

"Yes," said Local 35 Manager Morris Kovler, "he said the same thing this year. He even made out an application. But then he withdrew it. He'll probably do the same thing next year."

Some Local 35 members enjoy retirement, Kovler said, but others can't stand it. "One of our members came back after three days of retirement and pleaded with us to take him into the local again."

"Retire? If you're ill and can't work, or if you have some good way to occupy yourself, sure. But it doesn't make sense otherwise. We have to ask ourselves what we are retiring to," the worker stated.

Nowadays, nearly all of the experts agree that this is the most important question a prospective retiree can ask.

THE COST OF RETIREMENT

Sidney Margolius in Seafarers Log, June 3, 1960

Conferences on retirement problems recently held in various states have brought out significant financial facts that even workers who have some years to go ought to know about.

This department has estimated a minimum budget for a retired couple based on data from the Community Council of Greater New York, the Bureau of Labor Statistics and other agencies.

Here is approximately what this budget would run in a typical U.S. city at today's prices:

	Monthly
Food	$ 62.00
Housing, utilities	77.00
Medical care	18.00
Clothing	13.00
Other goods, services	40.00
Total	$210.00

This budget is really the minimum. It allows only a dollar a day per person for food, and just a two or three-room rented apartment. It would provide a retirement of shabby respectability. You could pay your basic bills. But you couldn't own a car on it, nor have much recreation, nor any margin to cope with an expensive medical disaster.

Actually, most of the already-retired workers this reporter met at the conferences estimated that you really need about $250 a month for modestly-comfortable retirement. Florida state authorities, who have had a lot of experience with retirement expenses, also warn retirees they should have about $250 a month.

Looking at this estimate of modest living costs for a retired couple in a large city, your potential problems are:

1—Insufficient income to cover even a very modest budget. Even maximum Social Security currently payable to a retired couple, of $180 a month, falls noticeably short of the minimum budget.

2—Housing takes an unusual slice of the retired couple's budget—37 per cent compared to the more usual 33 per cent. Housing is the largest expense. The housing allotment in this budget includes furnishings, cleaning supplies and utilities.

3—Medical care also looms notoriously large in a retired worker's budget. It's given 9 per cent of the income compared to the 5½ per cent younger families typically spend.

4—Present Social Security rules are hard on widows especially. A widow gets only three-fourths the amount payable to her husband, or to put it another way, half what they got together. But her living costs are more than 50 per cent. Typical living costs of a single person are about 70 per cent of those of a couple. Thus, the most a widow can get from Social Security at this time is $90 a month. But the costs of this minimum budget for a single person would be close to $150 today.

You don't have to be an economics expert to look at these estimated living costs and see what's more urgently needed to assure retirees at least shabby respectability.

1—Most obvious need is to provide hospital and surgical insurance through the Social Security system.

2—Another critical need is moderate-cost housing. If a couple can arrange mortgage payments during their working years so their house is paid up on retirement, they will have taken a big step toward solving this costliest problem.

But many working families can't manage this. Other potential solutions are cooperative housing or Government-sponsored developments that will provide three-room apartments for $60-$75 a month including utilities.

Many already retired or about to, are reluctant to join housing co-ops when they have a chance. Often they say they "don't want to wait two or three years." This is a mistake. In two or three years many still will be living in the same costly flats.

A faster solution is now available. A new law permits renovation of existing small apartment buildings with FHA mortgage assistance.

3—Another urgent need is for financial, medical and nutritional counseling of older people. They are the targets of a number of health rackets, real-estate promoters, nutritional fads and insurance promotions. Widows especially seem to get snared.

'LIKE A SOLD ANIMAL' NO MORE

John Papa in United Automobile Worker, June 16, 1958

John Papa retired five years ago on his UAW-negotiated pension. He had been a benchworker at Ford for 29 years.

Now 68 years old and a widower, John Papa lives alone in his house on Detroit's east side.

But just because he's retired, John Papa hasn't given up his contact with his union. Recently he began attending a class for "new writers" at one of UAW's retired workers'

centers. The essay below was written for that class.

It was in 1922 when I first came to the U. S. of America. I came frightened, because I didn't have any knowledge of what things were like or of the American language.

I felt almost lost. But on Dec. 26 of the same year, I applied for a job at the Ford Motor Co., the Rouge plant, and I was hired.

I am not trying to tell anybody

that I was happy then, even though my first thought was to thank God, to thank America, and even to thank the Ford Motor Co. But working conditions at Ford were very hard, like slavery; we were treated not as human beings but almost like a sold animal.

In 1930 the depression came. Conditions turned to the worst. Almost everybody got laid off, except those who paid the foremen well, by giving them big presents, money. Really, it was pitiful.

If a laid-off employee wanted to get his job back, he had to buy it back, and the price was $75 to $100.

Personally, I don't believe that Henry Ford himself had anything to do with those terrible conditions. It was the management corruption, but as we all know, tyranny does not last forever.

Then 1937 came and the UAW-CIO came in. Thanks to one of the greatest Presidents America had (Franklin Delano Roosevelt), we, the Ford workers, were rescued from the slavery and regained our human rights, decency and consideration.

I have been a Ford worker for better than 30 years. Sure, I can tell the difference from before the union and after. And I can sincerely say the union has been a blessing and still is a blessing for the working people.

I am a retiree now, and who should I thank for all the good things I enjoy today? I wouldn't have them if it wasn't for the union.

I have a pension from the company, also social security which really is a blessing for us old-timers. That makes us independent from our children, especially with the new generation that does not want anything to do with the old people.

Also, it is good for the state when the pension and social security makes it not necessary to pay old age relief.

Not only that, but the retiree center where we lonesome people gather together, play cards, dance, get acquainted, and spend our time, I hope, will last.

Long live our union and God bless America.

12 | EDUCATION

LABOR'S STAKE IN THE PUBLIC SCHOOLS

Al J. Hayes, president of the International Association of Machinists in
The American Teacher, February 1957

When organized American workers led the campaign to establish our system of free public schools over a century ago, they were motivated by the realization that education is essential *1) to informed and intelligent participation in the affairs of government, and 2) to an individual's opportunities to advance.*

The American labor movement is concerned with the problems of our public schools today for the same reason. And it will continue to be interested in the affairs of our school systems just so long as free men wish to participate in the affairs of their government and seek a better life for themselves and their families.

There is no self-respecting American today who does not pay at least lip tribute to the ideal of equal educational opportunities for all.

But as the cost of education rises under the impact of mounting enrollment and broader concepts of the role of schools, there is a growing willingness by some groups and individuals to compromise the ideal for the false economy of trimmed school budgets. This is false economy because we pay eventually, not merely in too few and below standard classrooms and teachers, but in coming generations of citizens who are not fully qualified to comprehend and resolve the growingly complex problems of modern government, men and women whose capacities for useful and profitable lives are not fully developed.

The position of teachers is indicative of the plight of our educational system. I know of no group of employees who are more honored in the abstract and subject to more abuse in practice. Teaching is a noble and essential profession, whose practitioners are subjected to low wages, poor working conditions, the burden of worthy projects unrelated to teaching, stern public scrutiny, and, at times—less frequently now than in the past—the tyranny of autocratic administrators and political overseers.

Frankly, the plight of the teachers is in large part the fault of the teachers. Being members of a profession, they held themselves aloof from other workers and scorned their ways, seeking to equate themselves and acquaint themselves with other professional persons.

Teachers are professionals; there is no doubt about that. But they are wage-earning professionals, a fact which puts them in a far different position from the doctor, dentist and lawyer. The latter have a decisive voice in setting the levels of their own income. Teachers' salaries are set by a process which gives heed to the voices of many economic and political groups, but hardly those of the teachers.

To a large extent the school system itself suffers from the same miscontrued idea of professionalism. School administrators cultivate persons on the higher social, professional and financial level, seeking their support for the maintenance and development of the school system. In the past, boards of education and school committees were composed primarily of members of such groups. And let me add that we owe a great deal to the devoted service and unselfish efforts of such people.

However, devotion to ideals frequently comes face to face with practical economics, and it would be more than human for everyone to place ideals above financial considerations. So when extra classrooms are placed in the scale with increased taxes it is not surprising if the scale tilts more often than not in favor of tax considerations.

It is even less surprising if those who have a major part in decision-making have no children in the public schools, either because their children have passed school age, or because they are being accorded an education in the more exclusive private schools. Persons in such circumstances can approach problems of crowded schools and teacher shortages with a detached, if not an objective, attitude.

The problems faced by our public school systems and the nature of financial and tax decisions which must be made in solving them require that the schools have the broadest possible basis of support. I believe that the experience of the former National Citizens Commission for the Public Schools, the present National Citizens Council for Better Schools, and last year's White House Conference on Educa-

tion indicates that the interest exists and on a very broad scale. There is no reason at all why teachers and school administrators should not seek to cultivate it directly.

Throughout most of its history the organized labor movement has agitated and fought for a better educational system and better educational opportunities for all of our citizens. This is one of the primary objectives of organized labor today.

Such activities are undoubtedly helpful. But consideration, discussion and action on state, county and municipal levels are essential. Whether or not the Federal government increases its participation in financing our school systems—and I am confident that it will do so in the not too distant future—local interest, local action and local support will continue to be the fundamental foundation of our schools.

Those responsible for administering and operating our school systems would be well advised to seek the cooperation of city and state central labor groups in bringing about a greater degree of understanding of school problems and support of needed improvements.

The schools need the assistance of every American and every group of Americans in overcoming existing deficits in teachers, administrators and class-rooms and in meeting the growing demands which the future will impose upon them.

SCHOOL CRISIS BACK AT THE SAME OLD STAND

Robert B. Cooney in AFL-CIO News, September 5, 1959

School bells this September are announcing America's annual crisis: the classroom and teacher shortage.

The only change between this September and others is that the crisis is worse.

The U. S. Office of Education reported a few days ago that an estimated 42.7 million youngsters will enter classes from kindergarten

through the 12th grade this school year. This is an increase of 1.75 million over last year.

". . . the number of pupils whose education is being impaired in varying degrees by the classroom shortage is about 10 million," declares Health, Education and Welfare Sec. Arthur S. Flemming.

Flemming said recent reports on

public school enrollment show there were 1,843,000 pupils "in excess of normal school capacity last year."

These "excess" students were added to some 6 million in crowded urban elementary schools, and another 2 million in obsolete buildings to arrive at the total of 10 million.

And these statistics leave out urban high schools and rural schools.

The way in which overcrowding impairs education is reasoned this way: the desirable maximum class size is considered to be 30 pupils; if a class has 40 or 50 pupils, then everyone's education is hampered, not just that of the 10 or 20 "excess" pupils.

The effect of individual attention through smaller classes can be startling. Carl J. Megel, president of the American Federation of Teachers, was visiting a school in New York City earlier this year. A heavy snowstorm that particular day cut attendance from the usual 45 pupils to 16. A teacher reported:

"Mr. Megel, a very interesting thing happened today. A young lad, who has been a serious disciplinary problem, in this small class on this particular day, conducted himself in exemplary fashion and at the end of the day came to me and said: 'This is the first day that I have thoroughly enjoyed school.'"

If the problem of surplus students is handled simply by cramming more pupils into each classroom, the problem of the teacher shortage has multiple effects.

U. S. Commissioner of Education Lawrence G. Derthick had this to say a few days ago:

"The deficit of teachers will mean, in many communities, over-large classes or the employment of teachers without adequate training or both. In many instances, it will also mean curtailing the number of subjects offered."

Last year the nation's elementary and secondary schools were short 182,000 teachers. This year, Derthick said, the shortage will amount to 195,000.

Derthick said the teacher shortage is intensified by a teacher-turnover rate of 10.9 percent. Current studies show this rate to be more accurate than the 7.5 percent formerly used in calculating shortages.

Why are teachers increasingly leaving their profession?

"Low salaries, of course, still constitute the major reason for this exodus of teachers from their chosen profession," according to Megel.

"But, in addition to low salaries, the overcrowding occasioned by shortage of classrooms makes it impossible for the conscientious teacher to do a competent job in the classroom.

"Overcrowding increases disciplinary problems because teachers are unable to provide individual attention to so many boys and girls in such a few minutes of a class period."

Segregated schools, where they exist, add to the problem because they prevent the most efficient use of school facilities and teacher resources.

The nation's school-age population was 37.3 million in 1955. It rose 6 million to an estimated 43.3 million in 1959. This was a rise of over 16 per cent.

By 1963, the school-age population is expected to increase to a total of 48.8 million.

The classroom and teacher shortage has grown over the years even as the nation debated first whether it existed and then what to do about it.

One turning point was reached when a 1955 White House Conference on Education, stacked in its selection of delegates against federal aid to education, unexpectedly decided there was a need for federal aid.

Since then, school bills have come closer than ever to passage but have still foundered on such issues as civil rights, federal "control" or plain politics.

Probably the chief obstacle has been business opposition. Federal aid has been fought by the U. S. Chamber of Commerce, the National Association of Manufacturers and the American Farm Bureau Federation.

In Congress, a coalition of Republicans and Southern Democrats has sabotaged federal aid for schools, the latter in part because more schools would mean easier desegregation and a quicker tranformation of the South.

At present, such a coalition has bottled up in the southern-controlled House Rules Committee a four-year $4.4 billion Murray-Metcalf bill. It would raise teacher salaries as well as help build schools.

UNION HALL BECOMES SCHOOL ROOM

Justice, May 15, 1957

Any weekday, in South River, N. J., you can walk into the headquarters of the International Ladies' Garment Workers' Union at the corner of Main and Thomas and find the place filled not with garment workers, but with studious teenagers. These students are in union headquarters because there's no room for them in their crowded-to-bursting high school.

With a registration of 840, the South River High School has about 200 students more than it can accommodate. For the past school year, ILGWU headquarters has been integrated with the school; every ringing of the bell marking the end of a class period starts one line of students down two short blocks toward Main and Thomas while another marches informally back to the school building.

We visited South River the other day. We saw the young people come down the street, open the door marked ILGWU, climb the flight of stairs over which hangs an ILGWU banner, sit at the same table where later that night ILGWU members sit for a shop meeting.

We asked one youngster how it felt to study and work in a union hall. "It's clean and comfortable," he said, "and plenty of room." "I've been here before," said another, "before we began to hold classes. My mother's a member." One young lady replied, "What better place could you find for taking social studies and American history?"

South River is not an industrialized community. It lack big plants with heavy equipment such as may be found in other parts of New Jersey. Its largest single industry is the soft-goods, garment industry.

We talked with high school principal Fred Williams, backed into a cubby-hole office in his overcrowded school. What did he expect to do now that the school budget had just been turned down at a special township meeting?

"We included no request for capital outlay," he said. "The per-pupil cost of running this high school," he continued with the patient weariness of one doing a heroic job," is $323—the lowest in the county. We will need more teachers next year to meet the rise in our enrollment. My present teachers are bound to the school not by wages but by their fine sense of loyalty and community responsibility. But how will I be able to get additional teachers when any other community in the area will be offering newcomers more than I do?"

We asked Charles A. Eberwein, a member of the local Board of Education, how come. He explained that because the area had little heavy industry, the added tax burden of a higher budget would fall almost

entirely on the small property owners making up the community. "It's
not easy to ask people to raise their
own bills," he concluded.

Joseph G. Mark, president of
South River's leading bank told how
a flat rate of state aid fails to solve
problems of communities with low
income from local taxes. We drew
the parallel with federal education-

al aid to the states. Mr. Mark is
against it.

The ILGWU has lent a helping
hand by giving the high school the
use of its headquarters, rent free.
ILGWU Vice Pres. Israel Horowitz
says, "This isn't the first time workers have had to take measures to
insure proper educational opportunities for their children."

MORE AFL-CIO UNIONS OFFER SCHOLARSHIPS IN UNIVERSITIES

Willard Shelton in The American Teacher, March 1960

An increasing number of AFL-
CIO unions are developing college
and university scholarship programs
that reveal variety and imagination.

The AFL-CIO, in 1959, established
six scholarships, valued at $1500
each. Three go to members of families of union members, the other
three without regard to union affiliation. All are awarded regionally
on the basis of the familiar merit
examinations conducted by educators.

The Ladies' Garment Workers in
1958 set up 10 scholarships of $500
each, awarded and renewable each
year, for the children of ILGWU
members. The Communication Workers annually awards two $2,000
graduate fellowships for research on
labor-management relations in private and government-owned telephone systems.

The Retail Clerks in 1958 established a fund to finance scholarships
for RCIA members or their children.

The Seafarers offers each year, to
young members or the children of
members, four 4-year Andrew Furu-
seth Memorial Scholarships worth
$1,500 each.

The Joint Council of Dining Car
Employes, affiliated with the Hotel
and Restaurant Employees, gave a
$1,000 scholarship in 1958 to the
daughter of a union member, Elizabeth Eckford, who was one of the
Negro children completing her high

school work at Little Rock's Central
High School.

The Air Line Pilots Association
offers a 2-year civil aviation medical
fellowship, open to physicians graduated from a Class A medical school
and with one year of interneship.

Pace-setter for all is the Amalgamated Clothing Workers, which has
channeled from the Sidney Hillman
Foundation a whole group of scholarships—$2,000 at Chicago Medical
School, $4,000 for Roosevelt College
in Chicago, $2,000 at   New York
State's School of Industrial and Labor relations, $1,000 at Albert Ein-
stein Medical School, Yeshiva University, Maryville College and the
Education Foundation for the Apparel Industry.

William Green Memorial Fund
Scholarships, created by the AFL-
CIO, support two undergraduate
scholarships of $800 and two grad-
uate fellowships of $1,800 each at
Ohio State University. The International Labor Press Association offers a one-year scholarship, valued
at $1,250, at the Columbia Graduate
School of Journalism.

Among the state labor groups,
scholarships in the latter part of
1958 were awarded by seventeen.
The Alaska State AFL-CIO offers
$500; the Arizona State AFL-CIO
offers three $500 scholarships. The
California Federation increased its
$500 awards from three to six. The

three new awards are provided by the Building Trades Council, the Regional Railroad Trainmen and the L. A. Painters. The California Building Service Employees offers a $750 scholarship.

Idaho awards $500; Illinois two for $500 each; the Iowa Federation one of $500. Kansas uses its funds primarily to assist future teachers: it grants $150 scholarships to students at several schools.

The Massachusetts State Federation gives two $500 awards and others are given by these local central bodies: Brockton, Lowell, Lynn, New Bedford, Northampton, Quincy, Springfield, Westfield and Worcester.

Minnesota offers four scholarships ranging from $250 to $500; the Electrical Workers State Council offers four of $150 each; the Minnesota Machinists Council grants $100.

The New York State Machinists offers $350; the Oregon AFL-CIO grants three $500 awards, and three of $100 each; the Tennessee State AFL-CIO three of $500 each. The Virginia State AFL-CIO offers $500.

The Texas State AFL-CIO has $500 and $250 awards, plus five varying from $50 to $250 from union groups and 21 others of comparable value from labor sources in Austin, Dallas, Fort Worth, Houston, Odessa, San Antonio and Wichita Falls.

As of the middle of 1958, a substantial number of scholarships were offered by 18 city central groups and by nearly 100 local unions or councils of local unions.

NOSE CUTTING

Texas State AFL-CIO News, Aug.-Sept. 1958

We never cease to be amazed at the insistence of some Texas newspapers and Texas governmental leaders in following the age-old practice of cutting off their noses to spite their faces.

That's just about what the present public debate over Texas acceptance of certain types of federal aid amounts to. The Hale-Aikin Committee, which is supposed to represent the best of public opinion in developing a projected public school program, advocates discontinuing the programs in which the federal government helps to provide hot lunches for Texas school children.

It also proposes discontinuing federal aid for vocational education. Some Texas governmental leaders advocate refusing to take part in the National Defense Education Program.

With regard to the school lunch program, one commentator carries the objection to the extreme by claiming that the program means that you'll have the federal govern-

ment keeping kids in line at the lunch counters.

How silly can you get?

The school lunch and vocational programs have been going on for years, and there has been no indication that the federal government is attempting to influence the philosophy of public education. The National Defense Education Program is designed to help provide scientists, and other badly-needed technical experts this country must have if it is to survive.

Would these haters of the Federal government deny school children enough to eat, deny Texas youths training for jobs and deprive America of trained scientists just to prove that Texas is independent?

Success for their hate-the-federal-government attitude would not result in any tax-saving for them (and that is their objective) but would only mean that Texas tax money would be spent in places other than Texas. We not only wouldn't have our cake; we also wouldn't get to eat it.

BRICKLAYER-TEACHER IS NAMED PRINCIPAL

Dick Lewis in The Bricklayer, Mason and Plasterer, August 1959
(From the Schenectady Gazette)

One Schenectady educator can say he knows the schools "inside out."

For 42-year-old William K. Flynn, soon to take over as principal of Riverside elementary school after six years in the city school system, has during more than 17 years as a bricklayer taken part in the construction of the "outsides" of several area schools.

And, as soon as the administration affairs at Riverside are brought to a close, Flynn will again shed his pedagogue's garb for coveralls, and pick up his tools for a summer's session with mortar and trowel.

The bricklayer-teacher started out to be a teacher. He was graduated from Union College in 1941 with a B. A. degree and teaching certificate. However, before World War II, Flynn's highest offer from the teaching profession was $1,300 a year.

And so, the young Union graduate put aside his diploma and, with the aid of his journeyman-bricklayer father, worked as an apprentice bricklayer for three years until attaining the higher-paid rank of journeyman.

In 1950, still employed as a bricklayer, Flynn began taking evening courses at Siena College for his master's degree in education, which he was awarded in 1956. Midway through his master's requirements, in 1953, he became a school teacher.

Since becoming a teacher, and now an administrator, Flynn has retained membership in the Bricklayers' Union and worked each summer on some contracting job. Included were three high schools.

Flynn at one time was president of the Bricklayers' local in Schenectady and taught apprentice bricklayers.

CHICAGO PLUMBER SORRY HE LEFT TOOLS BACK IN 'STATES'

AFL-CIO News, March 3, 1956

OXFORD, ENGLAND (PAI) — Early last year Tom O'Brien, a member of Plumbers Local 130 of Chicago, dropped his tools and went to Oxford to study at Oxford University in England.

He wishes he had brought his tools with him.

Following is an Oxford newspaper account of O'Brien as carried in the the Chicago Federationist:

"Tom O'Brien is probably the only American plumber studying at Oxford.

"When Tom, now aged 28, left high school in Chicago, he was apprenticed as a plumber. Instead of dating girls or going to cinemas he

spent his time over books, and took his B.A. degree.

"Then he won a scholarship from the Institute of International Education and was awarded a year's tuition at Oxford, including board and lodging and $392 in spending money.

"So he packed his tools away and sailed on the Queen Elizabeth.

"First thing he did when he took over his digs at Oxford was improve the heating system.

"'I can't get used to the lack of central heating here,' Tom said.

"'I caught a cold when I arrived and I've had it ever since.'

"The Little 'In-the-Red' School House!"

"He views the ancient university city, not with awe as a seat of learning, but with the critical eye of the plumber.

"He wishes now he hadn't left his tools at home—because he expects lots of people will be asking him to fix their burst pipes when they learn he's a plumber as well as a scholar.

"'Back home, we don't have much trouble with burst pipes,' he says, 'because our pipes are built-in and protected. But here your pipes are exposed all over the place.'

"When he returns home he will go back into overalls and start plumbing again. He is studying economics and labor relations."

RUTGERS SCORES 'FIRST' WITH UNIONISM 'CERTIFICATE PLAN'

The New Jersey Labor Herald, December 1959

A "Certificate Program" in Labor Unionism, the only one of its kind in the United States, is attracting wide attention in labor education circles, as the Rutgers Institute of Management and Labor Relations gives it top priority.

Objective is to train union men to develop long-range, disciplined self-study programs, according to Dr. Herbert A. Levine, Labor Program Director. Four AFL-CIO business agents and eight local union officers are registered for the course.

Required course work is scheduled so there will be no time loss from regular employment. The student must complete a curriculum equivalent to 30 hours taken over a minimum period of two years.

One-third is "core courses"—English and Communication Arts, general economics, principles of U. S. government or history, psychology or sociology—offered at four Rutgers Extension Centers.

Two-thirds of the curriculum is offered by Rutgers Institute's Labor Program in cooperation with education departments of labor groups. A one-year field project provides an opportunity to apply theories learned in the Certificate Program.

"The course is adjusted in recognition of the necessity for educational programs to meet the needs of the membership," Dr. Levine said. In this special course, the unionism studies are concerned with: 1) on-the-job internal union needs and problems which arise out of employment contracts; 2) broad economic, political, and social problems which face labor and other organized segments of the community."

TEACHING COLLECTIVE BARGAINING

Shirley Ward in The American Teacher, December 1959

Recently I decided to make collective bargaining a meaningful term to my students studying U. S. history.

I have, in the last 10 years, become weary of history books that define capitalism only in management's terms. The public schools are turning out too many citizens ignorant of the fact that free enterprise and our amazing standard of living are not only the result of shrewd investment and management, but of the process of collective bargaining.

What I did was simple. There were rough edges when I had finished. But I was gratified enough to feel that this exercise would be a permanent part of my lesson planning. I had three classes in U. S. history last semester; very average

groups. They had completed a study of corporations after the Civil War.

But the unit to follow on labor was inadequate in the text, sympathetic as it was with the great strikes of the same period. Thus, to give the students a better understanding of labor's problems during the last 100 years, I allowed each class to become a union for the three weeks' study of the era.

After two to three days of defining terms and general discussion, each class elected a chairman, steward, and secretary. I conducted the elections. Then for two class sessions I remained out of the room while the chairman conducted the following business in a democratic procedure. They were to decide:

Name of the organization; membership (union shop); termination of the agreement; assignments for the three weeks; grading; absence and tardy policy; late paper and homework penalties; policy on non-participants in discussion, and seating arrangement.

When this had been done, I returned to the room, the representative of management, ready to write a bargaining agreement on the above items. I stressed that their chairman and I were on equal terms.

I found, to my astonishment, that all classes had come through with fair arrangements. In anticipation of a deadlock, we had decided that arbitration would follow, but arbitration was not necessary.

We set forth immediately upon our agreements with seriousness. The chairman was to open the class each day, the secretary take minutes and the steward report the grievances. I went about my teaching under the policies contracted by the students.

There were two demands I made arbitrarily. I had to decide the time of termination. Secondly, the students had to realize that a strike could not be tolerated in a learning situation. We would have to come to agreement or accept arbitration. They responded with restraint.

Assignments were reasonable. Grading was turned back to me in all classes. Penalties were varied but fair, and all seemed to have a greater interest in assignments, activity, discussion, and evaluation. The students desired that I keep command of the classroom, yet they appreciated having a voice in making assignments.

I noted with amusement that all insisted on the union shop agreement and seemed annoyed with the less than one per cent who favored the open shop.

At the conclusion we set a day in each class for final evaluation. All three classes were in close agreement. Positive conclusions were: collective bargaining definitely improves interest and morale of the worker and that the democratic process in the labor union offers the only real opportunity for choice and self-responsibility within the corporate structure.

On the other hand, the students noted dangers: the need for education of the membership; the necessity for the members to be alert, participating, and willing to compromise for the betterment of all; and that leadership had to be responsible, able, and democratically selected. They had learned that democracy means effort and concern for the betterment of all.

There is no end to the searching and learning that can take place by trying such a project for a limited amount of time within the classroom.

TEACHER-BACKED BOARD LIFTS BAN ON U.N.

Edward A. Irwin in The American Teacher, November 1959

A touch of sanity found its way back into the rules of the Los Angeles board of education when that body voted to stop labeling the United Nations a "controversial subject."

The old policy, put into effect in 1953, not only halted such activities as essay contests on the UN, but cast a shadow of fear over teachers, who indicated in more than one survey that they felt they could not even discuss "controversial" subjects.

Leading the fight for change of the policy was Mrs. Georgiana Hardy, a board member elected two years ago with wide community support, including that of teachers and labor.

She pointed out that the old governing policy for the study of current public problems had singled out the UN, but "no other issue or organizations."

While Mrs. Hardy led the fight, the change in rules was possible only because of the election of two new board members this spring by a coalition of liberal forces.

At a public meeting, nine speakers appeared against the measure and 11 for the change, including Hank Zivetz, executive secretary of the Los Angeles Teachers Union, the only teachers' organization to appear.

Zivetz declared, "Facts on the United Nations, on the Soviet Union, on sex education, or on any other 'controversial' subject, do not constitute the danger. Rather, the denial of free discussion, the refuge we take in narrow conformity, the magnified fear of controversial facts of life are the real subversives in our democratic midst."

THE GOLD MINE ON THE CORNER

Catering Industry Employee, April 1959

For union members, every public library is like a range of hills where there is gold to be found for the digging. Suppose you're a union officer, or a shop steward, or plain rank-and-filer? What could you find for the looking?

Jacob S. Epstein of Cincinnati puts it simply:

"There's gold in those shelves!"

And Mr. Epstein ought to know. In 1952 he started Cincinnati's department dealing in books and services for organized labor.

So you drop in on this cheerful gent, and his round face breaks into a happy smile when he finds out you want to ask what good a library is to a union and its members.

"Well," says Mr. E.—his friends call him just plain Jake—"you take the story of how unions got where they are today. It's one of the most exciting chapters in the life story of the land. Talk about excitement! Why no western thriller's any better than the true stories of the Molly McGuires in the Pennsylvania coal fields!

"Or take the tragedy of the Triangle Shirtwaist fire that spurred the International Ladies' Garment Workers' Union to launch its big organizing campaigns of 50 years ago!

"Or take the downright chilling facts of the period in the Thirties when mobsters were trying to move in and take over unions. Matthew Josephson's history of your own union tells that story well, and how your members won the day. Union House, Union Bar is one of the best, and you'll find it in a surprising number of libraries.

"Lots of union members, I'll bet," says Jake, "aren't aware of the fact that the history of organized labor in this country goes all the way back to 1619, when some glassmakers in Virginia struck to get the right to vote.

"And the whole story's right here. Books on the Wobblies, the Knights of Labor and lots more. Of course the classic is John R. Commons' History of Labor in the United States. Another, more recent, is Labor in America by Mark Starr and Harold Faulkner."

Sometimes, he acknowledged, people find history heavy going. They'd rather read biographies, or fiction, to get the feel of a subject. So he takes you to a shelf loaded with books about men who have led labor: Gompers, Lewis, Hillman, Reuther and others. Or novels about working people and their struggles to find a way to the dignity of the bargaining table.

A more practical side of a Public Library's range of service for a union and its members is in the bread-

and-butter facts needed to help the union do a better job.

Take laws. Everybody knows there's a tangle of statutes governing workers and their unions, federal and state and, often, city or county laws.

"You'll find your public library has the texts, not only of the Taft-Hartley Act itself, but of dozens of NLRB rulings."

But how can an ordinary union guy find his way through all that tangle of statutes and stuff?

Jake smiles. "That's why we have trained staff people. To help you find exactly what you want. You tell us what you're interested in, and we know how to find exactly the right page in exactly the right book. That's our business, you see."

Mr. Epstein feels strongly that so few union negotiators use the library in getting ready to meet the boss at the bargaining table.

"Here we are, just around the corner, loaded with ammunition to pass along, and only a corporal's guard of your folks make use of it.

"Like up-to-date cost-of-living figures for any area in the U. S. Or like copies of contracts that have been won recently by other unions.

Or material on fringe benefits. Or suggestions on better health-and-welfare planning. It's all here, free for the asking."

But, knowing a lot about unions, Jake knows it isn't all bargaining. There are other concerns, too. Training leadership, for instance. Or planning better union meetings. Or getting facts on some candidate's record. Or arming the membership with chapter and verse to back up a local drive for housing, civil rights, health. Or a national drive to get Social Security benefits on tips.

"You name the subject," he says. "We can help you dig out what you want."

Back in his office, Jake has a message for the union officer and the union member, too. It's just this:

"Any public library will buy and develop special collections for any group that's interested. We only need to know what the public wants. If unions will use the library, the library will stock the things the union needs. They'll train staff to serve union people in the ways the service can be most useful.

"But we've got to know your needs."

13 | HOUSING

THE UNION'S STAKE IN URBAN RENEWAL

Electrical Workers' Journal, February 1960

In a time of growing national prosperity, millions of American families are still forced to live in dilapidated, overcrowded slum tenements because they can't obtain decent homes within their means. The continuing deterioration of many of our slum areas and the desperate need for more and better housing are problems that are important to every union member, from the standpoint of economic growth as well as human need.

By 1980 the United States population is expected to be 260 to 275 million. It is estimated that at least 90 per cent of this increase will go to metropolitan areas, which means that 20 years from now these areas will have twice as many people as they do now.

Suburban areas will bear almost the full impact of this rise in population; downtown areas will absorb only a small part of it. But unless action is taken, city slum areas will continue to deteriorate as they become more crowded and as more and more homes become substandard. There is a great need for modernization of downtown areas.

The Federal Government's Urban Renewal Commissioner, David H. Walker, said recently, "Urban renewal is one of the greatest markets the building world could ever know." He said the building industry would find opportunities not only for profit but for contributing to the most exciting, moving challenge in America, if it would try its hand at conservation and restoration of in-town homes.

Just replacing homes that are now substandard or will become substandard in the next 15 years is a major challenge. An indication of the need is seen in these estimates the AFL-CIO has made for the years 1960 to 1975:

Homes substandard now	15,000,000
Becoming substandard	7,500,000
Total	22,500,000
Suitable for rehabilitation	5,000,000
Total to be replaced	17,500,000

This is an average of about 1,200,000 substandard homes that should be replaced each year for the next 15 years. In addition, many thousands of homes must be built to meet the needs of our increasing population. Altogether, we need to build more than two million new housing units a year—about twice the number now being built.

Urban renewal projects are not confined to renovation of substandard homes. They involve new office buildings, urban industrial centers, modernization of downtown stores, parks and malls, adequate parking facilities and new transportation approaches to relieve in-town congestion.

The tragedy of slum areas is not only that they lead to human suffering, but also that they are costly. These slum areas are costing every taxpayer money and they will cost even more unless something is done before the inner-cities are hopelessly decayed. The money a city collects in taxes from these blighted areas is only a fraction of the cost of servicing them.

In Boston the City Planning Board estimated several years ago that police protection, fire department, health and social services cost the city $48.24 per family in slum areas, compared to $10.81 per family in other residential sections.

A similar survey in Buffalo indicated police and fire protection and health and social services cost the city $139.86 per family for the city as a whole but climbed to $340.12 per family in slum areas.

How can slums be eliminated? Primarily through action by local groups. Some of the essential elements for a sound rehabilitation program are:

1. An adequate local housing and health code that can be enforced.

2. A master plan for community development.

3. An inventory of neighborhood areas and a plan to promote neighborhood understanding.

4. An effective organization to run the program, representative of all interested parties.

5. Sources of capital at moderate interest rates to carry out rehabilitation projects.

6. Rehousing of displaced families in decent homes they can afford.

What part can unions play in meeting these needs? They can interest themselves in the problems of distressed metropolitan areas. They can voice the need for constructive planning and take part in action programs in their community. They can check their city codes and, as some IBEW locals have done, press for adoption of adequate, effective electrical codes as a step toward sound housing codes. They can urge state redevelopment acts in those states which have not acted. They can support Federal legislation designed to spur and assist urban renewal projects.

It is estimated that the construction of every new home provides enough work for two men (one off-site and one on-site) for an entire year. Larger building and industrial projects provide even more work for our members. More construction means more electrical equipment and appliances, more of the things made, installed and serviced by IBEW members.

Everyone has a stake in slum clearance and urban renewal. The opportunity to obtain a good home in wholesome surroundings is a right which no American family should be denied.

$5,000-A-YEAR FAMILY PRICED OUT OF HOUSING

AFL-CIO News, May 3, 1958

What the country needs even more than a good, 5-cent cigar is good, middle income housing, according to Byron M. Radcliffe, a director of the four-year building curriculum at Michigan State University.

Americans have an average income of around $5,000 a year, he explained, thus limiting to $12,500 the price of a home they can buy. Most lending institutions, including the FHA, are not inclined to lend on a mortgage of more than 2.5 times the borrower's annual income.

But up to mid-1957, he went on, only 27 per cent of the houses built were in this category, and 44 per cent sold for more than $15,000, which would require an income of $6,000 or more. About one-third of all American families are in this classification.

Radcliffe claimed construction costs can be cut not by chiselling on labor or material, but by careful planning, attention to construction methods and techniques, and close supervision of the job.

ILGWU BY-PRODUCT: HOUSING

Justice, May 15, 1957

"Nowhere in the world are so many people crowded together on a square mile as here," Jacob A. Riis wrote about New York's East Side in the final years of the last century. The sweatshop flourished in the tenements and Riis, a great reporter, pictured the plight of masses of workers trapped by poverty.

At the start of the new century, the ILGWU was born on the East Side. It launched its great crusade against the sweatshop, for a shorter workday, for higher pay, for getting the children out of the shop and the shop out of the home.

Today, the hopes of past generations of garment workers are reflected not only in improved standards of work and pay but also in the magnificent apartment buildings which comprise the ILGWU Cooperative Village in New York City.

It is one of the major miracles of a free society that the struggle of organized garment workers to win security on the job and safeguards against ill-health and old-age has produced the important social by-product of housing development. There will soon be Air Force families near Reno and Little Rock, and Puerto Rican families on the outskirts of San Juan, who, like the families in the ILGWU Cooperative Village, will be enjoying the heritage of those who marched on the picket lines in past decades.

This must be a source of mounting pride for all ILGWU members. Each has a right to feel that he or she has made a direct contribution to providing these needed homes.

The housing problem will not be solved by the trade unions. With all of the great reserves accumulating in health, welfare and retirement funds, only small portions of these so far find their way into government-insured housing developments. Furthermore, the needs are so great that they will be met only when a meaningful housing program is enacted by government.

Meanwhile, our ILGWU is pointing the way in which unions can add still another socially desirable aim.

Pres. Dubinsky has declared that about 30 per cent of union funds are going into housing investments. This will strengthen the funds by giving them a larger return on investment. At the same time, in places far distant from the dark canyons in which our pioneers lived out their work-burdened lives, it will bring about the erection of fine new homes.

HOW OUR MONEY IS INVESTED

IBEW Pres. Gordon M. Freeman in Electrical Workers' Journal, May 1957

With all the publicity attending the recent Senate investigations and the alleged misuse of union funds by a few AFL-CIO unions, Secretary Keenan and I thought it appropriate to bring our members a brief analysis of how IBEW funds are being used.

As you know our books and financial records are completely audited every three months by certified public accountants, so that our members may be sure our accounts are being kept properly and our financial records sound.

It has always been the policy of our Brotherhood to invest its funds so as to earn as much money as possible on them, safely. Our readers may like to know that, in rough figures, 20 per cent of our funds are invested in United States Government Bonds, 20 percent in safe "blue chip" corporate stocks and bonds, and 60 per cent in mortgage loans.

It is about these mortgage loans that we especially want to inform you today.

Our readers are aware of the current "tight-money" situation. Because of it, some of our union contractors were unable to carry on their business, resulting in some of our own people being thrown out of work. We could think of no better way of investing the funds of our Brotherhood than in mortgage loans which would accomplish three goals:

(1) Help keep union contractors in business;

(2) Give employment to our members and other union workmen;

(3) Help provide low and medium-cost housing that working men can afford.

Here is how our plan works. In a number of major cities, we contacted old, reliable firms of mortgage bankers. These bankers contacted union builders in the area. *Only 100 per cent union contractors are loaned any IBEW money.* The mortgage bankers with whom we deal inform the union builders that money is available for investment in low-priced housing, at prices which our own people and other working people can afford. In recent months many IBEW members have purchased homes financed by IBEW funds.

The loans which we make are all insured by the FHA or the Veterans Administration.

The cities in which IBEW has invested money in mortgage loans are: Baton Rouge, Chicago, Cleveland, Detroit, Miami, Minneapolis-St. Paul, New York, St. Louis and San Francisco. We hope to be able to make funds available in other cities in the near future.

Now some of our readers may ask, "Are these good investments?" Every loan of IBEW funds made has the approval of your International Secretary and International President. We feel we can say with confidence that they are splendid investments. Because of the "tight-money" situation, we are getting "cream of the crop" loans. They are all confirmed by the United States Government which appraises all projects and backs up our judgment with its national guarantee.

And we might say, and we feel our people will agree with the theory, there can be no safer investment for the funds of working people, many of them engaged in the building trade, than in homes for those people.

WITH AMALGAMATED SPONSORSHIP
SLUMS . . . BECOME HOUSING . . .

The Advance, January 15, 1960

For the fourth time in three decades the Amalgamated has agreed to help New York City solve its housing and slum clearance problem.

The ACWA has undertaken sponsorship of a new housing project. This time it will be in Brooklyn. When it is completed it will provide apartments for about 2,300 families at an average monthly rental of about $23 a room.

It will be known as Amalgamated Town.

The site of the Amalgamated's fourth venture into low-rent, co-operative housing is the Warbasse project facing the Atlantic Ocean on the south side of Brooklyn.

When the co-operative, which is a project of the United Housing Foundation was first announced in 1957, many members of the Amalgamated were among the first to make applications for apartments.

In announcing the Amalgamated's sponsorship of the project, general president Jacob S. Potofsky said "this development gives us the opportunity to round out our housing program begun more than 30 years ago."

That program began in 1927 when the Amalgamated sponsored the development facing Van Cortlandt Park in the Bronx, a group that has expanded over the years until it now includes 1,435 apartments.

When the Amalgamated undertook responsibility for the Van Cortlandt Park project, it was sponsoring the first co-operative to be built under the limited dividend companies' law.

Three years later, in 1930, the Amalgamated sponsored a group of 236 apartments on the lower east side of Manhattan that became known as Amalgamated Dwellings.

Then, after World War II when the city again faced a housing shortage, the Amalgamated sponsored another group of 807 apartments, also on the east side of Manhattan, near the East River, which are called Hillman Houses.

Thus, before assuming responsibility for the new project in Brooklyn, the Amalgamated has been instrumental in providing 18 apartment buildings housing 2,500 families.

These up-to-date structures represent an investment of over $22 million.

In each instance, the Amalgamated-sponsored structures were built in areas blighted by wretched slums. Besides the completely modern apartments, the Amalgamated projects were landscaped and laid out with recreational areas to replace the ugly tenements that had blighted the neighborhood.

Potofsky pointed out that "the Amalgamated and the United Housing Foundation have decisively demonstrated that low-cost co-operative developments, sponsored by the labor movement, built soundly and managed wisely, have done and can do more to fill the demand for low-income and middle-income housing than any other agency or institution in the city."

Potofsky contended that "New York City needs more low and middle-income housing and needs ft desperately. We are pleased to be in a position to fill this need."

UNION TO HELP SAVE DOWNTOWN AREA, JOBS

Federation News (Chicago), September 7, 1960

A bold, ambitious plan to insure the future of downtown sections of the nation's major cities and maintain jobs for thousands of wage earners was announced this week by the Building Service Employees International Union.

Chicago, national headquarters of the BSEIU, has been chosen as the first city in the union's project.

Building Service plans to build a $25 million skyscraper apartment and commercial project on the north bank of the Chicago River. The project will be called "Marina City."

William L. McFetridge, BSEIU president, said the Chicago development will be a pilot project in a national program of using union reserve funds to insure the future of downtown areas in major cities.

The union's 250,000 members depend on these areas as their main source of jobs.

McFetridge said he is interested in starting similar programs in New York City, Philadelphia, Pittsburgh, St. Louis, Cleveland, Denver, Los Angeles and San Francisco.

The union announced the plan after buying a choice location nearly a block in size for almost $3 million.

The project is expected to be completed in 1962.

The plans calls for 1,200 apartments in two 40-story buildings. These "towers" will rise above a four-story building covering most of the site. Office and commercial space will be included in a 10-story building along with the four-story unit.

The main building, the four-story plaza, will provide storage space for 400 cars, more than 1,000 motor boats, a 1,000 seat auditorium, shops, restaurants and offices.

All of the apartments will be air-conditioned. The housing portion of the project will be financed by the Federal Housing Authority.

THE CRISIS IN HOUSING

Abraham E. Kazan in Justice, May 1, 1960

In a period of relative prosperity, or at least superficial prosperity, we are in the midst of a seriously declining housing market. Private homes and apartment buildings are just not being built fast enough to meet the needs of the nation. At a time when we should be building 1,700,000 units a year, we are now building only one million units—and perhaps less than that this year.

What is the reason for this situation? For the past several years the interest rates in mortgage money have been steadily increasing. This is the major factor in the decline of the number of houses and apartments being built. The last session of Congress increased the interest rates on GI-insured mortgages to 5¼ per cent and on FHA insured mortgages to 5¾ per cent.

The intent of increasing the interest rates on these mortgages, which are guaranteed by the government, was to induce financial institutions to make more mortgage loans to home owners. The factor which was not considered is that veterans and others cannot afford the monthly carrying charges to pay for housing at such high interest rates.

The rates on conventional mortgages, those not insured by the government, have continued to rise and now are at about 6 per cent for interest and 2 per cent for amortization. Families with average incomes cannot afford housing at these rates.

The Governor of New York put forward a program to finance middle income housing. He proposed to mix $100,000,000 of public funds with $200,000,000 of private funds from banks and insurance companies. This was a program we long advocated. However, the interest rates demanded for the private money was so high that even when mixed with cheaper public funds the program will not provide housing to benefit the average working family very much.

On Oct. 1, 1959, most of the savings banks increased the amount they would pay for the use of depositors' money from 3¼ to 3½ per cent. A few days later the federal government offered the public 5 per cent for the use of their money. Nearly half a billion dollars was invested by the people in these government notes in two days. This is part of the paradoxical situation: the people are rich in money but poor in housing. Large numbers of people are living in substandard conditions while drawing interest and dividends on their savings bank accounts, government bonds and common stocks.

This money is being used to rebuild not the slum areas, but to rebuild Park and Fifth Avenues with ultra-modern office buildings, and to finance plant expansion of factories they will never see. The savings of the people are being loaned to build luxury apartments in which most people will never live. Only office buildings and luxury apartments can afford to pay today's high interest rates.

If we tried to analyze who is responsible for such conditions we find that the fault lies not with the government, not with the bankers or insurance companies, but with the people themselves. For it is the people who have given their savings to others to manage for them. The people seem to be much more interested in dividends than in housing.

It is very probable that the housing situation is going to get much worse before it improves any. It is unlikely that the situation will improve until a great many people learn some responsibility in controlling their own financial affairs.

MEAT CUTTERS LAUNCH HOUSING PROJECT IN BRONX

Labor Chronicle (New York City), June 1960

The Meat Cutters and the State of New York have signed an agreement for construction of a $96,000,000 middle-income housing project by using the air space above the Mott Haven Railroad yard in the Bronx.

Union officials have applied for, and state authorities have signed, a commitment for a $25,000,000 mortgage loan to build the first section of Concourse Village, to consist of seven twenty-story buildings containing 1,686 apartments.

Tenants will pay $6,000,000, or an average down payment of $700 per room, plus carrying charges of about $28.00 per room per month.

Construction of the first section will start late this year. Another 2,400 apartments will be started six months later, and the remaining 1,120 before the end of 1961. They will house an estimated 22,000 persons in 5,206 apartments.

Bronx borough officials have approved the new development, which marks the first use of air space in New York City for a middle-income housing project. Such space has been used for office buildings and stores.

Jerome Belson, the union's housing director, said the space above the railroad yards provides an excellent site in a central location without destroying other buildings.

"The Meat Cutters are proud," Belson said, "to help provide desperately needed housing for the middle-income wage earner. There is low-cost public housing for those on low salaries, and luxury housing for the wealthy. But few cities have housing for the family with $7,500 yearly earnings."

UPHOLSTERERS OPEN VILLAGE IN FLORIDA FOR RETIREMENT OF COVERED MEMBERS

The Dubuque Leader, January 25, 1957

Palm Beach County, Florida — It would be difficult to find a more appropriate memorial to the dream of one man than Salhaven. Named after President Sal B. Hoffman of the Upholsterers International union, it is the retirement and convalescent village for members of that union.

Other unions have provided homes for their aged and disabled members, but so far as is known the UIU is the first to do so on a family basis. It is the second to choose the balmy sunshine of Florida.

The product of 12 years of planning since establishment of a UIU health and welfare fund in 1944, Salhaven was dedicated last December. It is laid out in U-shaped courts, each court consisting of 10 to 12 cottages, each court complete with swimming pool and bathhouse.

Eventually it will include 240 family cottages and 10 bachelor lodges, the latter with eight apartments apiece, on its 614 acre site. Located some 15 miles from Palm Beach, Salhaven has its own waterworks and sewage disposal system, police and fire departments, and hospital.

The UIU has spent $2 million of a $5 million planned total for the village. The completed community will include a 500-seat auditorium, a public restaurant, a commissary, rental cottages for UIU families on vacation, a hobby shop, and a work shop.

Cost of the accommodations for individual homes has been set at $50 per month for retired families. Vacationing members will be charged reasonable fees for use of facilities which have not been taken by pensioners.

THERE'S A SHORTAGE OF SHELTER
FOR 15 MILLION U.S. FAMILIES

Federation News (Chicago), March 12, 1960

Fifteen million American families —about one-fourth of the total number—are still ill-housed.

Thirty-five million new housing units must be built in the next 15 years—at least two and one-quarter million a year—to provide a decent home for every American family by 1975. This means expanding the current housing construction rate by about 900,000 units a year.

Increased housing activity would improve the living conditions of millions of families. It would also make an important contribution to the nation's overall economic prosperity.

If we build 900,000 more houses each year, this would create 1.8 million more jobs for workers, about half in actual construction and an equal number in factories producing materials and equipment needed for housing. This 1.8 million equals about half of the current unemployment.

Moreover, experience has demonstrated that residential construction trends help determine overall economic activity. Thus, in both of the most recent economic recessions, 1953-54 and 1957-58 a decline in housing activity preceded and helped to generate a general economic cutback.

Housing bills have been enacted in each session of Congress in recent years but they have failed to deal effectively with the most urgent housing needs.

As a result, virtually no new housing has been made available within the means of millions of low-income and minority families victimized by poor housing. The need of moderate-income families for suitable homes within their means has also been largely ignored.

The AFL-CIO urges the Congress to enact housing legislation aimed at assuring construction of at least 2¼ million homes a year. The major features of such legislation should include:

• A large-scale low-rent public housing program to provide decent homes for low-income families. A minimum of 200,000 low-rent public housing units should be authorized.

• Low-interest, long-term loans should be made available to provide homes at reasonable charges and rents to hundreds of thousands of moderate-income families priced out of today's housing market.

• An effective program to meet the special needs of elderly couples and individuals.

• A federal policy to assure every family an equal opportunity to obtain decent housing without regard to race, color, creed or national origin. All housing built with the aid of federal funds or credit or any other form of financial assistance should be made available to minority families on an equal basis with all other families.

• Authorization of at least $1 billion a year in federal funds for the next 10 years to assure an expanded slum clearance and urban redevelopment program.

• Effective encouragement for metropolitan planning to assure that artificial and outmoded boundaries do not block housing and redevelopment, and dynamic urban growth.

• Additional measures, including encouragement for cooperative and moderate-priced rental housing; farm housing, especially for migrant farm workers and their families; required payment of the prevailing wage in any housing construction involving federal financial assistance; and protection of home-owners against foreclosure in the event of temporary unemployment, illness or other emergency.

III

Labor
And the Nation

EDITORS' NOTE

Wage earners join unions so they can influence economic conditions, so that they can have some say, not only on their own wages and conditions of work, but also about the nation in which they live.

Union members have acquired some understanding of the economic forces in their lives. They know that many of these forces—depressions, competition, technological change, living costs, the quality of our public schools, repressive legislation—cannot be controlled through contract negotiations on a shop-by-shop or even on an industry-wide basis.

For that reason, union members have become more and more conscious of the importance of electing to public office liberal, fair-minded men and women, men committed to working for the greatest good for the greatest number.

This concern has resulted in the labor press giving more and more attention to providing union members with information on legislation, on voting records, on economic issues, civil rights, and labor's own internal problems. It has also resulted in the development of educational material to help union members to register and to make a well-informed decision on election day. This section of *Labor's Story* reflects labor's growing concern for good government.

14 | LAWS, CANDIDATES, ELECTIONS

LABOR'S PLACE IN POLITICS

*Ed S. Miller, President, Hotel and Restaurant Employees, in
Catering Industry Employee, September 1958*

There is almost no aspect of a worker's life, in or out of his union, which isn't affected in some way by the politics of our time. His rights as citizen, his health, his kids' education, his housing; the prices he pays as well as the taxes; his minimum wage standards and his union security—all are in some way politically determined in city, state and nation.

We're going to need to apply a great deal more, and a great deal better, political education and action than ever before in all unions, everywhere.

No. This is no time to get out of politics as has been argued. But it may be worth while to search out the reasons why union members seem to be afflicted with a bad case of Stay-At-Home-itis.

Why are so few union members registered to vote?

Why do so few of those who get registered follow through by getting to the polls on Election Day?

Why is it like pulling teeth for AFL-CIO's Committee on Political Education (COPE) to raise those vital voluntary dollars needed to help elect candidates ready to fight for labor's program?

One answer to such question is the contention that most rank-and-filers feel left out when it comes to deciding what labor's program ought to be. It's his view that union members, feeling ignored by labor's leadership in determining labor's policies, register their dissent by staying away — from meetings, from picket lines, from registry offices, from polls and from COPE collectors.

Now there is no doubt that in any social institution—a union, a town meeting, a church, a corporation, a lodge or anything else—the rank-and-file have less to say on policy as the institution gets bigger and bigger.

What happens is that more and more of the decision-making takes place in boards and committees and conventions. It's hard to see how we could have it any other way. Part of the price of modern organization is this cleavage between members and leadership. And it's certainly true that people who want a healthy democratic society need to work at the job of findings ways to overcome this weakness.

It is more serious when this cleavage develops in a union. Because a union, by definition, must be democratic. It must operate in a goldfish bowl. It belongs to its members, not its leaders, and unless its members have a real share in decision-making the union will find itself in trouble. Some have in recent times, as everybody knows.

It is interesting, and possibly instructive, to think about our movement as having three levels of life:

There is the top national leadership, including not only those at AFL-CIO's Washington center, but those in charge of all the affiliated and independent unions, too. At most I suppose this group will include 1,000 individuals.

These are the "men who lead labor," and to the general public—including lots of union members—the headlines often give the impression that they are the labor movement. It is these whose names get in the papers with comments on everything from Russia to recession, from bombs to bargaining.

Nearly all are earnest, honest, hard-working men. All have been elected to office, and all try to reflect what they feel are the true desires of the mass of the movement.

But the very nature of their work, the nature of modern organizational life, may mean that in some ways they are isolated from the rank-and-file. In large measure they must depend upon the second level of leadership to keep them posted on what the members want.

This second level may include, say, 1,000,000 men and women. These are the line officers and the noncoms of labor's Gideonite host—the regional administrators, field representatives, officials of state federations and city bodies, and the array of local union officers, business agents, executive board members, shop stewards and committeemen.

By and large these, too, are honest, hard working and devoted men and women. Most are elected, many are unpaid. It is they who spend their days and nights at meetings, at bargaining tables, knocking on doors to organize the unorganized, buttonholing city councilmen, settling grievances, planning and directing strikes and picket lines, badgering people about registration, hauling them to the polls, serving on Community Chest boards and appearing as spokesmen for the union along Main Street.

Like the national leadership, these hometown leaders are "in politics" in various ways. They're likely to be registered, and to remember to vote. They get to hearings at city hall and keep an eye on the courthouse. Often they will run for city council or school board, sometimes for state legislature, once in a while for Congress.

But it's the base of labor's pyramid that counts. This is where the latent political power lies. Here are 17 million, more or less, of all crafts, kinds and conditions. Here are Republican, Democrat and independent; white, black and brown; Catholic, Protestant, Jew and folks with no religious preference at all.

The question is—can we get that latent political power into motion?

It may require a new look, and some new methods. But there's one thing which needs to be understood before we can answer that question.

One thing every shop steward and business agent learns early is that out of every 100 union members there are many who are willing to go along with the union, but not willing to invest their spare time and energy in the union's work. Some prefer to give their time to their church, others are red-hot bowlers, others have to hold down another job to feed the kids. And so it goes. But among every 100 union members will be some who are willing to help do the union's work because they like it.

The number of these in any local union is likely to depend on a lot of factors, including the willingness of the local's officers to accept their ideas and their help. But it's upon those who are willing that organized labor must depend if it hopes to mobilize a substantial political activity among the others.

And, as everybody knows, it is foolish to talk about "delivering" a "labor vote." Nobody can do it. The best any union political program can do is to get most members to the polls to vote as they please. In the nature of things, most of those who mark their ballots will vote to serve their best interests.

For some time now I have been urging all who will listen to take steps to quicken the sense of partnership union members feel in their union's work in order to win more and more to the point of wanting to help.

As in most matters, those steps can't be taken in Washington or Cincinnati. They can't be legislated by Congress or even an International convention.

They've got to be taken where the people are. And generally, they need the cooperation and interest of alert, responsive local union leadership.

It is a whole lot easier to organize effective political action around an issue in your home town than it is to organize that action around an issue raised in Washington. Here, it seems to me, lies the key to solving our problem: politics begin at home.

When union members come to grips with an issue right where they work, they discover that politics isn't something remote. And they discover that they aren't left out—that they're needed to win the home-town battles.

There is an astonishing variety of signs of life in labor's democracy at the level that counts—the rank-and-file:

• The angry protest from waiters and waitresses in Los Angeles and New York on the tip tax issue. In this case, action from below generated an orderly attack on a problem of great importance to hundreds of thousands of our members.

• The recent case when hotel workers decided to come to grips with job discrimination is a good illustration of political education at its best.

• From Ohio, California, Washington and other places are coming stories of grassroots action by rank-and-file members to deal with imminent threats to their unions from the "right-to-work" forces. In scores of towns union members are volunteering to serve without pay in the mammoth undertaking of checking union rosters against voter registration lists.

The point of these illustrations is simply this:

When the issues are close to home, many union members will become active partners in making union policy through action.

I'm not suggesting that such things are occurring in all local unions. All of us know of places where spontaneous actions of this sort are discouraged by local officials of limited, selfish vision.

But even this barrier to rank-and-file partnership can be, and is, overcome when union members are willing to take the time and trouble to tackle the job.

The best political education is action. The kind of discussions workers have in generating action is policymaking at its best and most fruitful.

GOP-DIXIECRAT COALITION STRONGEST 'PARTY' IN CONGRESS

Henry Santiestevan in UAW Solidarity, April 1958

WASHINGTON — It was the afternoon of March 22, as the House was debating a civil rights bill, that a querulous voice raised a fabricated question.

Michigan's testy, reactionary Rep. Clair Hoffman (R) asked Virginia's dixicrat Rep. Howard Smith (D):

". . . What became of that coalition that we had back in the time when we put through the Taft-Hartley bill when we overrode Mr. Truman's veto? Do you remember? There was a coalition of Southern-

ers with somebody on this side—I do not know what to call them, but I was one of them and that coalition worked pretty good."

Smith replied, "I will say to the gentleman that the coalition which you are speaking of is all in the past . . ."

The question and answer—really intended as barbs aimed at the civil rights measure—were meaningless because the GOP-Dixiecrat coalition was still very much alive, and both Smith and Hoffman knew it.

The coalition of Republicans and Southern Democrats can be traced back to 1937, the first session of the 75th Congress. During that session, when the Roosevelt Administration was fighting to get the nation out of a massive depression, almost 10 per cent of all roll calls in the House showed Republicans and a majority of Southern Democrats voting against a majority of Democrats from the rest of the country.

Right after the war, the GOP-Dixiecrat coalition used its power to pass the Case anti-strike control bill, to exclude farm labor from NLRB jurisdiction, to turn over the U. S. Employment Service to the states, and to take the first steps toward gutting the price control program. This soon resulted in a wave of speculation, profiteering and inflation which cost the American public billions in purchasing power.

After the election of the GOP-dominated Congress in 1946, the coalition reached its greatest strength. It pushed through the Taft-Hartley Act and overrode Truman's veto; it reduced coverage under the social security act, further weakened price and rent controls, and overrode Truman's veto of the "rich man's" tax reduction bill.

During the Eisenhower administration, the GOP-Dixiecrat coalition has played an ever more dominant role. It has fought against a decent public housing program, federal aid to education, effective civil rights legislation, an increase in the minimum wage and various other liberal measures.

"Down Boy!"

On paper it appears that the Democratic majority in the House is the largest since the New Deal—280 Democrats, 152 Republicans. But the real "party" alignments are the GOP-Dixiecrat coalition on one side and the liberals on the other.

A study of three rollcall votes in the 86th Congress' first session showed the approximate alignment of the two groups:

Coalition — Southern Democrats, 80; Border Democrats, 9; Northern and Western Democrats, 6; Republicans, 130. Total: 225.

Liberals—Southern Democrats, 20; Border Democrats, 15; Northern and Western Democrats, 143; Republicans, 18. Total: 196.

What's really happened to the GOP-Dixiecrat coalition? Nothing. It's still the strongest "party" in Congress.

THE HIGH COST OF POLITICAL ACTIVITY

The Hat Worker, February 15, 1960

Political argument, political persuasion has always been a costly business. It has become infinitely more expensive in modern times. Any extensive distribution of a printed item can run into thousands of dollars. The mere mailing of a sample ballot will be a big expense.

TV time is practically prohibitive in cost. The press, so heavily loaded with propaganda against you, demands premium rates for space if you want to advertise your point of view there.

And yet, unless you get your point of view across, unless you can make yourself heard, the opposition will walk all over you.

The one advantage we do have over our enemies is that we are so many. The little we can contribute, the little we can expend amounts to a lot when it's totalled up. What's more, we can build our political defenses just as we build our economic defenses—by volunteer effort. Unions came into being not because of hired organizers alone. It was the devotion of the idealists, the devotion of the volunteer workers in the unions that have built our labor movement.

Under these circumstances do you think it is too much to call on you to chip in a little money? To contribute a little work?

We hope not. We hope you will not resent it if your shopmate or union officer comes to you with a subscription list for COPE. On the contrary, we hope you yourself will volunteer as a committee man, you yourself will be the first to go on the subscription list with the dollar or more for political needs. How else can you expect to get rid of the oppressive laws against you, how else can you hope to get laws passed in your favor, except as you pitch in with money and work for your own side?

THE BOSS WANTS TO 'EDUCATE' YOUR VOTE

UAW Solidarity, May 1960

Management these days has been sending many of its bright, eager young men back to "school."

The boss' goal is to educate them to "educate" you.

"As one executive puts it," Business Week magazine said recently, " 'Lobbying is passé. It's the voters who have to be influenced.' "

Management's "education" programs, therefore, are aimed at influencing you, and thus getting your vote.

Its bombsights are meetings, discussions, speeches, advertising, house organs, door-to-door chats, and the $2 billion a year reading rack industry, among others.

Each of these seeks to build up acceptance among wage-earners and their families of the economic, political and social policies that the leaders of management and of business pressure groups think best for you and the rest of the country.

In addition, they want to cut down —some want to wipe out—the pressure that workers put on companies through their unions. They want to cut down your demands and to make you and your co-workers less critical of reactionary, selfish company policies.

These management "education" programs, therefore, serve to emphasize why year-round education activities such as UAW's are needed, urgent and meaningful.

Many of the management programs were in effect to some extent long before factory workers organized their unions. Since that time, they've been considerably stepped up.

Today, estimates of the reading rack industry's take alone stand at about $2 billion a year.

Fortune Magazine, the businessmen's $1.25-a-copy journal, has reported that more than 200 individual companies are putting out "educational" material for the boss to pass along to you.

Take a look at the reading rack technique. Each rack contains a lot of interesting and useful "how to do it" material. But there are other pamphlets there, too, and management is itching for you to read them.

The Wall Street Journal, for example, quoted a General Motors official as saying:

"Any overdoing of the economics material would be a quick way to kill off interest. We try to mix in pamphlets that have no relation to business or economics, but are personally interesting and useful to employees and their families."

The idea of "mixing" those in is to get you to take the "business or economics" stuff when you pick up the others.

These, however, are the old tried-and-true methods. What is more recent and lately expanding is management's open concentration on "educating" its boys politically to turn them loose on you, your neighbors, your friends.

Political "education" is nothing new to management. Companies were in politics up to their necks long before there were unions. That's a big reason labor always has had such a rough time. Unions usually have to operate under laws pushed through by Big Business.

Company political "education," therefore, is as old—and stems from the same roots—as Big Business lobbying.

"Sure, we have boys who hobnob in politics," the Wall Street Journal quoted one auto company official as admitting. "We call them the anonymous department."

The behind-the-scenes activity which has popped into the open, however, is the stepped-up, widespread intensity with which company after company now is carrying on management's political "education."

The National Association of Manufacturers has a full-course kit of political medicine to spoon-feed the boss' boys in "education classes"— and it sells it for $300 a kit.

The Chamber of Commerce says it is shipping out manuals for its own courses at the rate of 1,000 a week. Iron Age, the steel industry magazine, reported last June that "top management is sincerely throwing its weight behind it, authorizing the tools and necessary programs."

The magazine quoted J. J. Wuerthner, Jr., of General Electric as saying that business has "tens of thou-sands" of management people going "through company or area programs of political indocrination."

Companies such as American Can, Gulf Oil, Sears - Roebuck, Aerojet, Republic Steel, Standard Oil, F. W. Woolworth — all are blossoming out in the political "education" field.

Ford, moreover, has laid out a month-by-month program of political education and action over two years.

Michael D. Reagan, a political science lecturer at Williams College, commented on this trend in the March-April issue of the renowned Harvard Business Review.

Reagan pointed out that unions are associations of people while corporation are associations of capital, as illustrated by the fact that in elections of corporate boards of directors, voting is on the basis of one share of stock, one vote, and not one man, one vote.

"If the resources of a billion-dollar corporation can be thrown into the political balance by officers who are in effect accountable only to themselves, what happens to the principle of political equality?" Reagan asks.

This is what UAW's education program is concerned with, too.

"Target Practice"

BIEMILLER TELLS LABOR'S LOBBY ROLE

AFL-CIO News, April 6, 1957

Most people think of labor lobbyists as pushing wage and hour legislation. But Andrew J. Biemiller, director of AFL-CIO Dept. of Legislation, told an entirely different story in a televised interview with Drew Pearson.

Pearson's interview with Biemiller included the following exchange:

PEARSON: What type of bills has the AFL-CIO been interested in passing in recent years?

BIEMILLER: Well, we've worked very hard for a lot of different kinds of legislation. We've worked hard for social security bills, minimum wage bills, bills affecting labor relations, bills improving our public health service, taxation legislation, bills to strengthen the Pure Food and Drug Act. Those are just a few illustrations.

PEARSON: Let's take a few of those. Why is your group interested in the Pure Food and Drug Act?

BIEMILLER: This is obviously the best protection the housewife has against adulterated food, the best protection that all citizens have against bad patent medicines, quackery that goes on in the medical field from time to time. And we have been trying very hard to get an adequate appropriation so that the inspectors in that poor, little, neglected Pure Food and Drug Administration can really take the laws that are on the books and enforce them.

PEARSON: What has labor done up on the Hill regarding public health?

BIEMILLER: People who don't understand the function of the public health hospitals seek to have them cut down in size or obliterated. We have on several occasions helped save those public health hospitals and the great work they have done against cancer and others of the dread diseases of mankind. Likewise, we've also assisted many good, honest citizens in the drives they have put on to get increased appropriations for the Institute of Public Health. We think that the results that are coming from those funds, in research on all of the dread diseases, are well repaying the taxpayer the dollars that go into those funds.

PEARSON: How much do you think you've increased the appropriations for public health?

BIEMILLER: Well, the appropriations for the Institute of Public Health have nearly trebled in the last decade.

PEARSON: How many other things that have nothing to do with wages and hours have you, as a labor lobbyist, been working on?

BIEMILLER: Actually most of our work is on matters that do not primarily deal with wages and hours. Take the whole social security program, the allied public welfare program. This is a program which from the very beginning in 1935 has had enthusiastic labor support.

PEARSON: Incidentally, the bill of last year which was passed on social security, what did you have to do with that?

BIEMILLER: That bill we regard as our greatest triumph in the past few years. This bill did essentially two things: it cut the retirement age for women to 62, and it established disability pensions for everyone on the social security rolls at the age of 50. That is, pensions for those totally and permanently disabled who are 50 or over. This bill was primarily labor's bill. We conferred with members of the House Ways and Means Committee, and then after we got over to the Senate, the Senate Finance Committee. We found that we had bitter opposition on this bill. We ran smack into the National Association of Manufacturers, the Chamber of Commerce, the American Medical Association, and the Administration. After a bitter fight, it was passed by a vote of 47 to 45.

HOW TO BE A LOBBYIST

The CWA News (Communication Workers), February 1960

CWA members have a vital interest in helping to achieve labor's legislative goals. John L. Crull, vice president in charge of legislation work for CWA, calls attention to the need for action at the membership level. He says:

"We shouldn't wait for suggestions from international headquarters before contacting our Representatives or Senators on these matters. Spontaneous, self-initiated action often is more effective than action stimulated by a common source.

"The following how-to-do-it suggestions should help in attaining the desired objective."

● Action begins where you are. This means work in community or neighborhood groups and organizations, activity in civic agencies or political parties. Your conclusions should reach and affect local and state politicians and influential citizens.

● Express your convictions. Occasionally visit your Congressman or see him at public gatherings. Decide for yourself what kind of lawmaker he is. On urgent issues, write, wire or telephone him in Washington.

● Initiate and continue a regular correspondence. Write a useful, friendly, positive letter, keeping it to one page. Avoid form letters. Begin by establishing a common interest or point of contact, perhaps recalling the last time you heard him

speak or conversed with him. Commend him if possible.

● Deal with only one issue in each letter. State the purpose in the beginning of the letter, set forth your reason for writing. If possible relate the matter by title and number to a specific legislative bill.

● Develop your viewpoint with valid reasons. It is useful if you can give personal information or experience that bears on the matter and which your Congressman otherwise might not receive.

● Conclude by asking questions that will obligate him to give a reasoned reply to your position. On some issues ask where he stands.

● Don't forget other public leaders in your writing program. At times this may include the President, cabinet members, department and agency heads.

● Act promptly. Unless urging Presidential veto of undesirable legislation, letters should be sent before Congress acts. Early interest in legislation is usually more effective. Over 90 per cent of all bills pass Congress in the exact form they are approved by committee.

● Whatever your opinion is, express it.

In urging action on this program, Crull says:

"If we want these legislative goals, we'll have to go to work—and keep hammering away."

'COPERAMA' IN TEXAS

Jerry Holleman, Union President, in Texas State AFL-CIO News, May 1958

Have you ever tried letting other people put words in your mouth? That's exactly what happened to your hired hands at the COPERAMA dinner here in Austin, and the result was pretty hilarious. At least it was hilarious for the audience, although the "actors" may have

thought some of the lines weren't so funny.

We had decided the $25-a-plate guests would rather have a gridiron-style program than a speaker. So John McCully was assigned to write scripts for the rest of us — Fred Schmidt, Hank Brown, Sherman

Miles, Doris Cates, Don Ellinger and myself—and Don took on the job of writing a script for McCully and Houston Clinton. None of us was allowed to see the scripts until they were handed to us as we went to the stage.

Our two script writers did themselves up proud and turned out scripts which did just what they were supposed to do: Make us point out—and I must say, exaggerate—some of our own shortcomings, a sure-fire method of getting laughs.

Everybody had so much fun doing the skits, and the audience got so much fun out of listening to them, that it is likely the same scheme will be used in the future. I wouldn't say the entertainment was worth the $25 per plate, but at least it made the separation of money from diner a little less painful.

The COPERAMA dinner was a great success, although we naturally would have liked to have doubled the number attending. Tentative plans call for similar affairs annual-

ly, and in time it could come to be a much better fund-raising affair than this one. Make a mental note to try to make the next one. Maybe we'll needle somebody besides ourselves next time.

* * *

Every local union in Texas can learn a lesson from the tremendous job that Oil, Chemical and Atomic Workers Local 4-367 in Pasadena has done in selling COPE memberships. We often hear the complaint that it's easy for a small local to get 100 per cent membership but that it's just flat impossible for a large local to achieve. Yet here is a 5,000-member local which is knocking at the door of 100 per cent contributions and fully expects to reach that level before very long. It already has collected $3,170 or around 75 per cent participation.

We won't attempt to pass out credits for the great job that has been done except to say that it has taken a lot of hard work by a lot of people in the local to do this job.

HERE IT IS, GOP: DEMOCRACY IS OUR SECRET WEAPON

George Ryder in UAW Solidarity, November 10, 1958

The "political labor boss" the Republican party screamed so loud about in the campaign that just ended isn't quite as they pictured him.

If you're wondering what he's really like, look in your mirror.

He might look just like you—if you're the kind of a union member who takes enough interest in his country's future to get out and work at the drudgery of a political campaign.

For it is truly those who spend their free time ringing doorbells, handing out literature and talking about the issues with the voters who really determine the outcome of an election.

Why? Because they're the ones who get the voters to come to the

polls and cast their ballots. And it is those ballots that are rung up on a machine or folded and put in the box that decide which candidates will win and which viewpoint will prevail in city, county, state and national government.

True, the doorbell-ringer has to be a part of an organization. So any political campaign is organized, and the way labor unions organize to get out the vote may seem complicated. But it isn't.

In a general election, each Congressional district is organized as a separate unit.

Within each district, an effort is made to find two precinct workers —those are your doorbell ringers. Usually one of them is elected by the party. If the elected delegate isn't particularly interested in labor's viewpoint, then the union's political action department offers a member who'll work independently —but in cooperation with—the party's elected representative.

From seven to 10 precincts are grouped into zones. Each zone has a chairman elected by the precinct workers themselves.

These 30 or so zone chairmen constitute the steering committee of the Congressional district organization. They're sort of its executive committee.

Meetings of this committee—or of all the precinct workers—are presided over by a district chairman, who, along with the district secretary, is elected at a meeting of the precinct workers.

As election time draws near, special steering committee meetings are called. At these meetings, steering committee members break up into their various state districts and interview the candidates who have written asking for labor's endorsement.

These meetings may call for the committee members to spend a couple of evenings—very often for four or five hours at a stretch—to conduct the interviews and then gather together to assess the answers the candidates have given.

A few days later, there will be a meeting of the entire district's precinct workers to hear the steering committee's recommendations about which candidates to endorse.

If there is a division of opinion among steering committee members, the candidates themselves may be asked to appear before all the precinct workers to present their arguments for endorsement.

When the precinct workers have decided upon which candidates they want to endorse, these recommendations are sent to the county council's policy committee. Then to the council's executive board. Then to the eventual authority, the council's delegate body.

Altogether, it's a helluva obstacle

course for any candidate who wants labor's endorsement.

But even before he goes through this coffee grinder, a candidate for the legislature in a state where UAW is politically active has to fill out a questionnaire.

When he gets it, his first reaction almost automatically is "Whew!" It's rigorous.

Besides a fairly complete personal biography, the candidate's political history is run down in minute detail—other offices he's held or just any political experience that he's been exposed to.

Sample questions: "What experience have you had in connection with legislation? Have you ever acted as a lobbyist or as an interested person in behalf of any particular legislation? Specifically, what did you do in behalf of this? Was this legislation enacted? Anything else happen as a result of your actions? Why are you running for the state legislature? What legislation are you interested in?"

Then the questionnaire asks pointed questions about taxes, social welfare and civil rights, labor laws, industrial - agricultural - rural - urban economic development, public education, election laws and legislative apportionment, public conduct of the legislature, recent legislative controversies in the state and the candidate's idea of how a legislator ought to conduct himself.

His personal habits are not above inquiry—perhaps indolence (if he's an incumbent) during crucial debate or lax attendance at committee meetings during the legislature's sessions.

If the candidate survives this gauntlet and gets labor's endorsement, what then are the precinct workers supposed to do?

First of all, they must canvass their precincts. They must set up books listing the voting habits and party preferences of every voter in the precinct.

They must find out what issues are of particular concern to each citizen.

They even are expected to ferret out particular neighborhood gripes, and then apply a little community service—nagging the city for another street light on a dim corner near an elderly woman's home, or agitating for playground improvements in a neighborhood with a heavy population of children. They must show an interest in obtaining for the voter services in which the city may be negligent or deficient.

And, finally, they must show enthusiasm, interest and energy — or expect the PAC committee in their local to replace them.

Hub of activity is the district headquarters. Usually, it's an empty store, rented for the few weeks before an election. Its windows are plastered with signs and its door is almost always open.

Here the precinct worker comes to get his literature, exchange information with his brother door-bell ringers, discuss the day's news and its effect upon issues and voter interests, make his reports, meet a candidate who may have sauntered in to find out how he's doing in the district — and, if there's any time left, get a cup of coffee.

Here neighborhood rallies are planned, set in motion and reported upon. Here trends in voter sympathy are discussed, dissected, analyzed and figured out. Techniques to arouse voter interest are traded. Here the precinct worker can find out what there is about a certain candidate

that is causing uncertainty in the voter's mind.

Here, too, if he comes and talks to precinct workers, the candidate can get a first-hand report on his campaign. He can find out what he ought to talk about in his next rally speech. He can find out on which issues he must press harder.

If a political campaign generates fever, the district headquarters surely is the thermometer.

Finally, comes the day for which the precinct worker has given up his leisure, scuffed his shoes trudging the streets, calloused his finger ringing door bells, inked his hands passing out literature — the day for which he has talked, cajoled and pleaded.

Election day is here.

Activity is at a fever pitch. Arrangements are made to haul to the polls those who can't go or would neglect to go.

Finally the precinct worker himself does what he has so often urged the indifferent, uninformed or lazy citizen to do—he goes to vote himself.

He steps into the booth, yanks the lever that closes the curtain and turns down the pegs for the candidates he knows will try to remedy the never-ending problems, social grievances and inadequate protections that nag and gnaw at an everchanging society such as this country is.

He is truly on this day the "labor political boss."

NEW YORK WORKERS REGISTER SOME PROGRESS IN ALBANY

TWU Express, April 1959

Workers may benefit indirectly by action taken last month in the closing hours of the New York State Legislature. However, in a number of other areas definite dangers were created.

The railroad commuter aid program will aid an ailing industry. The

exclusion of bus and taxi firms from paying the higher taxes on gasoline and oil probably will keep many transit firms from going out of business. The welfare of workers in both industries is related to both matters.

But negatively speaking, the investigation in the state's "full crew" law bodes no good for working men in that such a probe will be aimed not so much at a study of actual conditions as it will be to find ways for the railroads to inflict even sharper economies upon their workers.

There are also many misgivings on the measure called for by the Governor, and passed by the legislature, requiring union financial reports and setting various curbs on the activities of unions and their leaders. This is a much watered-down version of the vicious bill that Gov. Harriman vetoed last year on labor's instance.

State AFL-CIO, however, opposed even this bill—arguing that this field was properly the area of regulation by Congress.

Another definitely dangerous measure passed by the legislature was the legalizing of injunctions in disputes that involve the transportation of perishable farm or dairy products.

On the credit side of the legislature's activity were these:

● Extension of unemployment insurance to all employees, effective Jan. 1, 1960 instead of just those working for employers with two or more persons.

● Extension of workmen's compensation and sickness disability to employees of employers with three or more workers instead of four or more as previous.

● Extension of temporary 13-weeks extra jobless benefits to July 5, 1959.

● Extension of residential rent control for two years, with provisions bringing rooming houses under control in certain cases.

● Increased funds for vocational rehabilitation program.

● Killing of bill providing injunctions against organization picketing.

● Increasing of number of dwelling units under state bond money from 7,000 to 21,000 by combining one-third bond funds with two-thirds private funds.

● Killing of proposal that one-year residency in state be required of all relief recipients.

● Added to New York City Charter the city's new code of ethics for public employees.

LABOR TURNED OUT THE VOTE FOR 'KEEF'

Gene Kelly in AFL-CIO News, Aug. 20, 1960

NASHVILLE, TENN.—The men and women of Tennessse labor deserve a big slice of the credit for the smashing primary election victory of Sen. Estes Kefauver (D). "The Keef" said so himself.

"From labor, farmers and business people I have had wonderful support," Kefauver said after getting 65 per cent of all the votes cast in a record-breaking Democratic primary. "I want to express my appreciation for the effective efforts of labor, working through their fine organization, the AFL-CIO Committee on Political Education, and its state director, Charles Houk."

During Kefauver's 12 years in the Senate and 10 in the House he made a record his supporters said is based on liberalism in the economic field, and of moderation and tolerance in the civil rights field.

The Tennessee election was considered a test of whether a nationally recognized senator of Kefauver's caliber, with his voting record, could be driven from office in a southern border state.

The senator won nomination for a third term by overwhelming Circuit Judge Andrew T. ("Tip") Taylor. Two years ago Taylor made a strong race for governor, and was considered a good bet to win his next statewide bid for office. But Kefauver changed all that.

Labor precincts in Chattanooga and Memphis voted for Taylor in 1958, against him in 1960. What happened?

COPE made 60,000 telephone calls, mailed 300,000 copies of Kefauver campaign material, distributed 160,-000 leaflets and handbills, set up central files with the names of 65,000 union members, got many of them registered, and helped many turn out to vote.

"For the first time," says Dan Powell, area COPE director, "we were able to get through to labor people. The campaign became a labor issue."

And Stanton Smith, coordinator of state and local central bodies for the AFL-CIO, adds this comment: "We broke through the racial barrier, for the first time in the South."

Kefauver ran a vigorous campaign, emphasizing his hearings on price "gouging" by the drug industry and explaining his voting record. The race issue, raised by supporters of his opponent, fell flat on its face.

"This is by far the best job labor ever has done in Tennessee," said Smith. The job was started in May of 1959, when the executive committee of the state AFL-CIO endorsed a broad education and registration program. It was agreed that full-time COPE people would be assigned to four major cities, and central card files set up in each.

Smith says the card file was the key. Without it, there would have been no checking of union registrations, no extensive mailings, no telephone campaign. It kept 200 members of the COPE Women's Activities Division, and some men, busy for weeks.

The WAD and the COPE coordinators got new membership lists from union locals, checked names against voter registration lists, notified locals and individuals of the names of those not registered. The result was the highest concentration of registered voters in the South, perhaps in the nation—80 per cent of the union members, 70 per cent of the spouses in Knoxville, raised from 50 per cent by intensive plugging.

Copies of three Tennessee labor newspapers were mailed into homes of union members, along with a Kefauver picture story in The Machinist, national weekly of the IAM.

In Nashville, members of the WAD typed 15,000 names on cards, checked them in the city directory, telephone books and voter lists. A COPE precinct organization was set up, lists of non-registered voters sent to precinct captains, and a registration drive conducted.

In Chattanooga, the WAD produced a card file of 10,000 names. Fifty women volunteers addressed 40,000 mailings, made 15,000 phone calls on election day, loaned their services also to Volunteers for Kefauver. Carl D. Mills, of Boilermakers' Local 656, was COPE coordinator here.

The Knoxville card file was brought up to date before election, and 50,000 items of information addressed and mailed. On primary day, 96 women volunteers worked on the telephones, and other men and women acted as car-drivers, baby sitters, and general handymen. Members of three women's auxiliaries and 17 local unions made 16,000 phone calls from the Plumbers' Hall. The Knoxville COPE coordinator was J. D. Porter, head of the Knoxville AFL-CIO and COPE chairman.

In Memphis, secretaries of local unions manned the telephones after a registration and informational campaign by COPE.

A COPE reporter summed up the campaign this way:

"Sen. Kefauver won renomination against bitter, heavily financed opposition marked by the irresponsible use of scurrilous literature designed to inflame voters on the segregation issue.

"The Tennessee campaign was a clear example of what COPE can achieve against the organized forces of big business when the basic, back-breaking work of getting our members registered and voting is pitted against a flood of corporation money."

15 | CIVIL LIBERTIES

'WE WILL CARRY ON THE FIGHT AGAINST BIGOTRY IN ALL ITS FORMS'

AFL-CIO Pres. George Meany in the AFL-CIO News, April 7, 1960

I know it sometimes seems to our friends that we move very slowly indeed on matters that are of deep, primary concern to them. Are we doing enough on the minimum wage law? Some of our own affiliated unions would say we ought to be doing more. Are we doing enough on the Forand bill? Not enough to satisfy everyone who is interested in medical care for the aged. What we are doing is the very best we can.

We find the same situations when we come to an even more fundamental issue—the issue of civil rights, of equal opportunity. It has been said by some, as you well know, that while the AFL-CIO supports civil rights legislation in Congress, we have not been vigorous enough in ridding our own movement of practices based on bigotry and discrimination.

I do not propose to argue, a century after the Civil War, that discrimination will disappear if we just leave it alone. We haven't left it alone; we're not leaving it alone today; and we will never leave it alone until we wipe it out.

Second, while I do not pretend to enjoy criticism, I do not resent it when it is honest and factual, although sometimes I wish our friendly critics would keep in mind the ground we have covered, as well as the distance we have yet to go.

I think the record proves we have come a long way. Many of our older unions were born and grew up in an earlier and less enlightened period. They reflected the attitudes of their communities—prejudice based on ignorance.

It is a measure of our progress that where discrimination still survives in the labor movement, it is a bootleg product, sneaked in by subterfuge. Even those who practice discrimination know that its days are numbered. And we are going to make sure of it.

I do not mention our progress with any feeling that we deserve praise for it. We do not deserve plaudits for doing what is obviously the right thing. On the contrary, I agree with those who are not satisfied, who believe the status quo is not good enough. I am not satisfied either.

There are still some units within the AFL-CIO that engage in discriminatory practices. And there are others in our ranks, whose own records are clean, who think it is unwise for us to take a vigorous, public stand on civil rights.

They argue that we have enough problems and enough enemies without inviting more. They say that the civil rights issue is used to prevent union organization in the South, and to weaken the unions that exist in that part of the country. They say that some southern Congressmen, who might otherwise be receptive to some parts of our legislative program are alienated.

I have heard all these arguments at first hand. They have not changed my convictions in the slightest.

I say that if we have to practice discrimination to organize workers, then organizing will have to wait until we educate the unorganized.

I say that if we have to lose a vote in Congress on minimum wages, or the Forand bill, or unemployment compensation because we take a stand on civil rights, that is a price we are prepared to pay.

The labor movement is a brotherhood — a brotherhood of workers. Surely it cannot set its face against the brotherhood of man.

I assure you that we will carry on the fight against bigotry in all its forms, wherever it is found. To me, this is not merely a fight to enforce the laws of man; it is a fight to fulfill the word of God. I will be satisfied with nothing but total victory.

JUSTICE WHEN IT COUNTS MOST

Charles Zimmerman, AFL-CIO Civil Rights Committee Chairman, in IUD Digest, Summer 1958

The foremost concern of our labor movement has been to achieve for every worker a measure of job security, and a set of standards to govern his hire, tenure, and conditions of employment.

Unions, through collective bargaining with management, have succeeded in writing into a contract a set of rules—rules of fairness and justice—to be followed by the employer in hire, promotion, transfer or dismissal of his workers.

In recent years, many of our unions have also insisted on including in the collective bargaining contract a non-discrimination clause. Such a clause simply establishes the rule that in hire, layoffs, promotion and in all other terms and conditions of employment, there is to be no discrimination because of race, creed or color of workers covered by the union contract.

This rule is now law in a major portion of American industry—not law laid down by the government or the courts, but voluntarily established on union initiative and accepted by management.

Thus, through the instrumentality of collective bargaining, union labor is evening out the unequal burden of privation and distress of unemployment, to make sure that this burden is shared equally, without regard to race, creed, color or national origin.

In order to make sure that employment opportunities for union workers are fair employment opportunities, union labor carries its fight for equality for all beyond the assurance of non-discrimination in hiring and layoffs. It also fights discrimination on the job: discrimination in promotion, advancement, and in the rates of pay for work performed. The AFL-CIO insists that dual seniority lists discriminating against workers because of race be eliminated throughout industry.

Denial of equal opportunity in one area starts a vicious circle running through every aspect of life.

The non-white worker not only bears the brunt of unemployment in a recession, he is also placed at a disadvantage economically by being forced down the income scale.

By being pushed down toward poverty, the non-white becomes more subject to diseases caused by malnutrition and dietary deficiency. He becomes more easily the victim of foreclosure, of repossess and of all the handicaps that come with the inability to make ends meet.

Perhaps the most crucial form of discrimination that puts the Negro citizen and his family at a disadvantage is in housing.

When Negro families are barred from access to homes only because their skin is the wrong color, they are forced into all-Negro ghettoes. And as segregated neighborhoods develop, it becomes difficult to resolve the problem of segregated schools and to rub out the color line in other phases of community life.

In the heart of the industrial North, trouble broke out when the William Myers family moved in as the first Negro residents of a huge 15,000 home development. The representatives of the AFL-CIO, along with those of its affiliates, joined hands with other civic-minded organizations in forming the Citizens' Committee for Levittown to set up a program of studies, meetings and conferences to build good-will and neighborliness in the community.

Labor has also fought for the enactment of the first law in the nation banning private housing, signed by Mayor Robert Wagner of New York City on December 30, 1957. The measure was a major breakthrough in segregated patterns dominating private housing in many communities.

Labor is pressing its fight against discrimination in employment, in schools, in places of public accommodation, in public transportation, in medical care and in housing. It is doing this in pursuance of its firm resolve to secure equal rights for all Americans in every field of life.

Justice is indivisible. When the going is tough, when adversity aggravates and multiplies the denial of justice, we must redouble our efforts to make it prevail. For that is when justice counts most.

SPUTNIK AND THE BILL OF RIGHTS

Catering Industry Employee, October 1957

Two recent news items, one from Moscow, the other from Madison, Wisconsin, seem to be worth considering.

One revealed that a "sputnik," or earth satellite, was successfully pitched aloft and is whirling through outer space at fantastic speed.

The other disclosed the findings of a poll among students at the University of Wisconsin: fewer than one per cent approve the principles of our Bill of Rights.

Many greeted news of the "sputnik" with cries of fear and hysterical alarm. They conjure for us visions of cities laid waste, and millions in the agony of irradiated death.

Ours is a calmer view. We see the man-made "moon" less as evidence of Soviet superiority than as proof of the soaring, searching spirit that is the mind of Man. It is a great victory over the Unknown, and it began long ago when thoughtful people started to ask themselves about the stars. Generations yet unborn will share its fruit, whatever their nation, their politics, their color or their creed.

We believe, too, that this first invasion of outer space advances by many years the moment when statesmen, after whatever painful adjustments of view, shall have arrived at a useful recipe for peace.

No, it strikes us that the news from Madison is more alarming than the news from Moscow. For if the students at one of America's most liberal, fruitful colleges have lost confidence in the Bill of Rights, then they have lost confidence in themselves, and in their neighbors. What shall we do for tomorrow? What shall we have to defend?

There can be no doubt that this cancer of distrust has spread to our children from ourselves. Their parents have been dishonoring the Bill of Rights for 20 years by failing to speak up for the freedoms there spelled out. Instead, we have enshrined the champions of conformity to give our children an ugly trinity indeed: the informer, the Congressional inquisitor, and the Man In The Grey Flannel Suit.

Here is a deep sickness in our so-ciety. Unless we can find the cure, and find it soon, it is much more likely than pushbutton missiles to destroy the land we love.

STATES' RIGHTS AND LABOR'S RIGHTS

Black Worker, March 15, 1958

Probably the greatest single menace to labor's rights and civil rights is the so-called doctrine of states' rights. Like an ugly hydro-headed monster, it bobs up to plague the forces of racial, liberal, civil, political and social progress. It gets solace and sympathy in certain circles because it claims to be the philosophy of the local community or the "town hall" where the people speak their piece in behalf of local government. Under the cloak of representing the basic democratic roots of American life, the idea of states' rights has won nation-wide consideration and support.

Its primary aim is to have complete control over the life of Negroes in the South, with complete freedom to deny them the status of human beings which civil rights legislation seeks to guarantee. Rejecting federal intervention of any kind, including the 13th, 14th and 15th amendments to the Constitution, it is always ready to wheedle and wangle federal funds from the government to help bolster the weak economies of southern states.

As a matter of fact, southern politicians are the most active, skillful and scheming in getting the federal government to establish army, navy and air bases in southern communities which, in many instances, constitute the main economic foundation of these communities.

While it is contended that the launching of Sputniks I and II by the Soviet Union into outer space placed the communist world far ahead of the free world, it may be correctly pointed out that the backward and archaic policies of racial-ism in the South have placed this country far back of the communist world in the struggle to win the allegiance of the uncommitted peoples of Asia and Africa.

Perhaps the greatest damage which has been done to the name of the United States among the peoples of Europe, Asia and Africa results from the policy of discrimination and segregation based upon race and color under the cloak of states' rights.

And while states' rights is used hypocritically by the South to keep their citizens of color in bondage, responsible leaders of the North who claim they favor civil rights and labor's rights continue a policy of appeasement of the South.

Little Rock has posed a question which this country will not be able to answer to the satisfaction of the free world until Negroes in America have complete political, economic and social equality.

What is true of civil rights is also true of labor's rights in relation to states' rights. Labor has begun to understand the "right-to-work" laws that would strangle the free trade union movement have come up under the cover of states' rights. Under Section 14b of the Taft-Hartley Act, special provision is made for the enactment of "right-to-work" laws if they are more restrictive of the rights of labor than federal legislation of that type. This was a legislative invention of the late Senator Robert A. Taft and Congressman Hartley. While Senator Taft was not particularly concerned about catering to southern states' rights doctrine, he used it to help throttle organized labor.

Now the forces of reaction led by the National Association of Manufacturers and the United States Chamber of Commerce, in addition to employing the doctrine of states' rights to strangle organized labor, are also utilizing the doctrine of individual liberty.

Every man has a right, they cry, not to join a union and still keep his job. So frantic have the advocates of "right-to-work" laws become that the union shop constitutes a controversy of great magnitude.

Of course, labor can and will succeed in its fight eventually in putting down this wave of "right-to-work" reaction. But labor can not be complacent or too optimistic about expecting favorable results against the "right-to-work" movement which would destroy the union shop and organized labor.

This is one battle labor cannot afford to lose.

DISCRIMINATION COSTLY TO ALL
AFL-CIO News, December 1, 1956

Employment discrimination in the U. S. reduces national income more than $25 billion a year, Harry Fleischman, director of National Labor Service, declared on a radio program, "Is Labor Color Blind?"

Interviewed on As We See It, presented by the AFL-CIO on ABC network, Fleischman said that the average non-white family has $1,929 less a year to save and spend than white families.

"The added purchasing power (that would have come from an end to discrimination) would have gone a long way toward eliminating those pockets of unemployment we had last year," he said.

"Make no mistake, the cost of discrimination must be borne and shared not only by Negroes and other minority groups, but by the whole community—investors, producers, distributors and workers—in terms of curtailed production, sales and returns on investment, and in decreased employment opportunities."

Fleischman pointed out that "discrimination costs white southern workers money as well as Negro workers. They don't like to see their wages remain substantially lower than that of northern workers—primarily because workers in the South are kept divided and unions weak."

JANUARY SHEET STAMPEDE
United Paper, January 1958

This is the month of the "white sale" at the local department store.

January 1958 also turned out to be free sheet month for a batch of American Indians living down North Carolina way.

Seems the Ku Klux Klan objected to one of the Indian women dating a white man. Discarding a tradition that went back to Capt. John Smith and a gal by name of Pocahontas, the Kluxers decided to burn a cross and generally put the fear of bedsheets into the Indian population.

But the Indians apparently looked up their history on a Gen. Custer and decided to surround the opposition. This they did without a scalp lifted . . . .but in sufficiently convincing fashion to send a good portion of the Klansmen packing fast enough to forget their muslin and percale trappings.

We were intrigued with the comment on this by Illinois' Sen. Paul Douglas, to wit, "Seems the earliest Americans decided to do something about un-American activities."

"Page 1"

SEAMAN

KENTUCKY LETS MA BELL CURB EMPLOYEES RIGHTS

AFL-CIO News, March 3, 1956

FRANKFORT, KY. — The Kentucky Legislature has allowed the Southern Bell Telephone Co. to abridge the right of its employees to seek elective or appointive office.

Seven members of the Communications Workers were threatened with discharge by the southern arm of the Bell System unless they withdrew as candidates from local and state election contests.

The company gave a variety of reasons for its directive to employees. No workers, the firm said, could give his full time and attention to the public service while seeking office. And, they added, there was the danger that an officeholder might favor one group of subscribers over another.

So, said the advisory letter, "we cannot permit the campaigning for or holding of" political office.

CWA replied with introduction of a bill in the legislature providing that no company policy could deprive an otherwise qualified citizen from seeking election.

The union pointed out to the legislators that companies often scream piously about abridgement of workers' rights by unions but here was a concrete example of a firm thwarting a right every citizen considers inherent.

The House agreed and passed the

bill 82 to 3. It failed of passage in the Senate, however, mustering only a 13 to 11 vote with 16 votes needed to carry.

A similar move by the same company in Louisiana last year back-fired. Two CWA members running for legislature were given the choice of quitting the contests or their jobs. Outraged, they took the issue to court and the company backed down in the face of an injunction.

FOOD FOR THOUGHT

Trainman News, June 27, 1960

It is still too early to determine the effectiveness of the Salk anti-polio vaccine, and that is the word from the U. S. Public Health Service. But one of the arguments being advanced by some who are highly critical of Dr. Salk and his vaccine presents not only a ridiculous but a despicable situation.

There are those in the nation who frown upon Dr. Salk and will have nothing to do with the vaccine he has discovered because he happens to be a Jew.

One eminent physician who conducts a medical column in a number of newspapers said recently that some of the greatest scientists the world has ever known have been Jews, and the world is all the richer because of their great contributions.

How right he is.

We're heading into the peak of the polio season with the advent of mid-August, and every precaution must be taken against that dread disease.

In Chicago where a record out-break of polio in one sector of the city is causing great concern, the number afflicted so far this year has risen to 609, at this writing. Three hundred and fifty-five of the cases have been paralytic.

But, according to Dr. Herman Bundesen, president of the Chicago Board of Health, only 59 of the paralysis victims have had the full series of three Salk shots; 12 have had two shots and 46 one shot.

This all adds up, said Dr. Bundesen, to "definite proof" that the Salk vaccine can sidetrack the threat of an epidemic in the peak of the polio season.

It gives us food for thought.

Dr. Salk has made a valuable contribution to mankind in the fight against a terrifying, crippling disease.

Can any of us afford to blind ourselves to the potentialities of his vaccine in winning the battle against polio because Dr. Salk is a Jew?

Think it over.

REPORT TO OUR READER-OWNERS

East Bay Labor Journal (Oakland) July 3, 1959

San Francisco is slightly out of our bailiwick, but the present writer has a personal interest in the dispute over banning discussion of politics and religion in Union Square. For, like many workingmen very short on formal education, he has always felt that the Public Library was his university and the Public Park was his campus.

When snow was on the mountains in Oregon, and timber was coming down the Hood River, there was idle time in Portland, and many discussions on religion and politics in the Public Park. In Seattle, too, San Francisco, and San Jose, one got so many ideas—many of them cuckoo, of course—by listening to the gassers in the Public Park.

This was in the now vanished era of steam beer, when one had to like it, in order to have a right to the big free lunch. Steam beer is going out fairly quietly, but it would be a shame if free speech went out quietly from Union Square.

Ernest Besig very aptly quotes a decision of the U. S. Supreme Court of twenty years ago to the effect that parks are traditionally used for "communicating thoughts . . . and discussing public questions."

That's it, and there is a terrible smell of conformistic respectability about some of the announcements of the commission in San Francisco charged with managing the park system.

The contacts in a park are very much at random, and should remain so. For instance, the present writer remembers so well the seedy little salesman whose shoes barely hung together who, in a random conversation in San Jose's St. James Park, gave him the idea of going and asking for a job in a newspaper office, and thus getting him started on work he's followed ever since.

Surely there are still wandering young workingmen who might make new starts in life through meeting seedy folks in the parks not acceptable to conformistic respectability.

If they shut down on free speech in Union Square, why not shut down on free books in the public library also, and go whole hog? According to many articles in the Chronicle, it's one of the worst public libraries in the U. S., anyhow.

WHAT IS YOUR UNION DOING TO FIGHT DISCRIMINATION?

Federation News (Chicago), January 30, 1960

Local unions which received awards at the 4th and 5th Labor Conferences on Civil Rights for their work in bettering human relations took action on specific problems as well as general work in this area.

What is your local union doing to fight discrimination? Are you doing enough to promote and protect your members' rights to win a civil right award?

The following Civil Rights Guide prepared for staff representatives of international unions by the Jewish Labor Committee will help you find the answer.

1. Does your international have a civil rights policy and program? What are the responsibilties of the Chicago area local unions to this program?

2. Does your international have a civil rights committee? Does it urge local unions to set up committees also?

3. Does your policy seek to have included non-discrimination clauses in the contracts? What success have you had in the Chicago area as to the inclusion of such clauses?

4. Have your locals received grievances or complaints about discrimination? How are they handled?

5. Do the application forms of the employers you deal with include references to color, religion, or national origin?

6. Do your employers have federal government contracts? If so, do they post the mandatory non-discrimination provisions?

7. Do your locals participate in apprenticeship plans? If so, how are the apprentices selected?

8. Do your contracts include medical welfare provisions such as Blue Cross and Blue Shield? If so, do all the members have equal and adequate access to medical institutions and services covered by these welfare provisions?

9. What specific action have your local unions taken to promote local, state and federal civil rights legislation?

10. Do your local unions have showings of civil rights films, speakers, and/or distribute literature on the subject of civil rights?

11. Would your local unions be interested in a union program and state legislation to obtain middle-income housing?

12. Do your Chicago area locals introduce or actively support civil rights resolutions in their respective State bodies, the Illinois State AFL-CIO, and international union conventions?

TRUSTEESHIP TO END SEGREGATION UPHELD

AFL-CIO News, July 2, 1960

The U.S. Labor Dept. has upheld the action of the Auto Workers in placing under trusteeship a Memphis local which refused to desegregate washrooms and drinking fountains in the union meeting hall.

The government rejected a complaint from a group of members of the local charging the trusteeship was not established for purposes authorized by the Landrum-Griffin Act. The group also charged the international had no right "to force integration."

The Labor Dept. pointed out that an objective of the UAW's constitution is "to unite in one organization, regardless of religion, race, creed, color, political affiliation or nationality, all employees under the jurisdiction of the international union."

In ruling in favor of the international, the Labor Dept. said an inquiry by its Bureau of Labor-Management Reports showed the UAW had followed the union's procedural requirements and set up the trusteeship to carry out legitimate objectives.

About 500 of the 1,800 members of Memphis Local 988 are Negro. These members, the Labor Dept. reported, sought action to end racial discrimination and segregation, "alleging systematic exclusion of Negroes from all union committees and segregation of rest rooms and water coolers in the union hall."

The UAW executive board, after conducting a hearing last January, adopted a resolution authorizing a trusteeship over the local.

The UAW, in a report to the Labor Dept., said it instituted the trusteeship action because "the local union was continuing a course of discriminatory and unequal treatment of members on the grounds of race . . ."

TEXTILE UNION BARS FUNDS FOR SEGREGATED SCHOOLS

United Mine Workers (PAI), June 15, 1960

The Textile Workers Union has officially barred the use of union funds to support segregated schools.

The union's recent convention supported its international officers in declaring that Local 371 at Front Royal, Va., had violated the union's constitution in offering to invest $8,000 in debentures to help an all-white school escape integration.

The funds have been sequestered and Local 371 has been placed under an administrator. The convention action, which left the door open for outside arbitration of the dispute, was the result of an appeal by Local 371. This was based on a decision of the union's Appeals and Grievance Committee which held that the proposed financial support violated the civil liberties clause of the TWUA constitution.

"We, as a union, must hold our heads high and not go pussyfooting on such an issue," said Pres. William Pollock. "Let's tell the world we reject segregation."

PA. ILG'ers SPURN SEGREGATED FOOD

Justice, August 1, 1960

"I wouldn't want it to happen to me," said ILG'er Mary Oberholzer. So when Negro co-worker Gladys Saunders was refused service at the Hot Shoppe in Alexandria, Va., 30 garment workers got up and walked out of the restaurant.

The incident occurred on a bus tour to Washington, D.C., sponsored by the Northeast Department. Mary Oberholzer was captain in one of 18 buses, and spokesman for the workers at Asba Manufacturing Co. in Greencastle, where she is shop chairlady.

The story reached ILGWU Pres. Dubinsky who congratulated "all the workers who participated in this splendid demonstration of belief in racial equality and human brotherhood, and is in line with the traditions of our union."

(As Justice went to press, word came that Hot Shoppes decided to abandon the color line in the restaurants in Alexandria.)

PROMOTERS OF RACE HATRED ALSO ENEMIES OF LABOR, COUNCIL DECLARES

AFL-CIO News, September 19, 1959

"The fight for fair practices—in employment, in training, in schools, in churches, in housing and in all public facilities and services—is labor's fight," declared the AFL-CIO Executive Council in its report to the 1959 convention.

The report recorded "important advances" during the past two years toward labor's goal of "equality for all."

"To be sure," the council noted, "there are in labor's ranks those who do not believe in equal opportunity.

"Our task has been to strengthen these weak links that endanger the strength of the whole trade union movement and to reinforce the bonds of brotherhood that make the union strong."

The council stressed that "the promoters of race hate and of acts of violence" that shattered homes, schools and churches "are also labor haters."

The council pointed out that unions in many southern localities have led the community and taken the brunt of "vicious" employer attacks utilizing race hate to defeat unions.

This is what labor is doing, the report said:

• Complaints of discrimination are checked by the Civil Rights Dept. and labor's field staff. In nine out of 10 cases, "prompt and helpful responses" have come from unions involved in complaints.

Where further steps are needed, the hearing process can take a case through the Civil Rights Committee to the council.

Civil rights committees have been set up by AFL-CIO state central bodies in Arizona, California, Colorado, Connecticut, Delaware, Indiana, Maryland, Massachusetts, Michigan, Minnesota and Rhode Island. All local unions in turn are being encouraged to set up civil rights committees.

AFL-CIO Pres. George Meany has appointed a Southern Advisory Committee on Civil Rights in May 1959. The group, headed by Pres. Stanton E. Smith of the Tennessee State Labor Council, held its first meeting in Louisville, Ky., in June.

• In employment, the report said, labor has been working to eliminate discrimination in hiring, advancement, tenure and job conditions.

"We likewise are driving for non-discriminatory operation of all training and apprenticeship programs," the council declared.

One key tool used by unions to ensure job equality is the non-discrimination clause in contracts, a provision which now covers a major portion of industry, the council said.

• In voting, housing, community services and schools, organized labor has fought hard to end discrimination, the report said.

"In its own ranks, labor is still short of its declared civil rights goal," the Council concluded. But labor is making progress with "firmer determination" and "greater speed" than any other segment of the community, it added.

NAACP BACKS UNIONS, ASKS END TO ALL BARS

AFL-CIO News, July 2, 1960

The National Association for the Advancement of Colored People reiterated its support for organized labor at its 51st national convention here but charged a "disparity" between labor's civil rights policy and the practices in some unions.

A comprehensive resolution on labor and employment opposed "right-to-work" laws and urged NAACP branches to prevent the use of Negroes for strikebreaking purposes during labor disputes.

"Colored workers especially," the resolution said, "need the protection of a vigorous union movement to prevent economic exploitation."

The resolution contained also a section declaring that the NAACP "as a last resort' will call on the National Labor Relations Board to enforce provisions of the Taft-Hartley Act against any unions which bar Negro members.

The statement noted the contributions by unions in the struggle for Negro rights and the support by organized labor for FEPC laws in many states but added that some unions operating in the South, "in seeking to avoid conflict over racial issues, are permitting racist elements to gain control of local union operations."

At the NAACP's annual labor dinner, Ralph Helstein, president of the Packinghouse Workers, pleaded for Negro and labor unity, declaring that "this is not a fight any one group can win; it can only be won together."

THINGS TO REMEMBER IN THE RACIAL ISSUE

Oil, Chemical and Atomic Union News, March 19, 1956

Speaking to the District 9 Council meeting on March 3 in Atlanta, Ga., OCAW Pres. O. A. Knight, said:

"I would be derelict in my responsibilities to you as members of this union if I failed today to make some mention of a serious problem which threatens our union, particularly in the South. I refer to the racial tension which has been building up in recent weeks.

"I want to suggest to you that when you, as members of this union,

are confronted with the problems and the discussions surrounding this racial tension, you bear in mind three things:

"First, remember the teachings of your religion. Don't let anyone convince you that there is one God for one race and a different God for another race.

"Second, remember you are citizens of the best country in the world, offering the greatest democracy and opportunity. Don't go

272

LABOR'S STORY

against the laws of that country.

"Third, remember that you are members of this labor organization and that you have taken an obligation 'never to knowingly harm a fellow member.' That obligation applies to all, regardless of color.

"Don't listen to extremists on either side."

Knight then charged that among those who are agitating and stirring up racial hatred in the South are some of the most notorious anti-union people in the South. In support of this charge, he read off a list of leaders in the White Citizens Councils who have long and conspicuous records of fighting labor unions.

"Above all," Knight repeated, "don't let them tear your union apart. Nothing in the world has done so much for human beings as has organized labor in the past few years. It has brought people from abject poverty to comfortable well-being, and it has just got started. We still face a big job or organizing and of improving the wages and living standards of people who work for wages."

COLORADO UNION TELLS COMMUNITY HOW IT FIGHTS AGAINST DISCRIMINATION

AFL-CIO Education News and Views, May-June, 1960

Laborers Local 578 of Colorado Springs, Colo., has lifted the color bar simply by practicing the Christian rule of brotherhood.

What's more, the union is spreading the good word through the community.

Members of the union have appeared before a Colorado College sociology class, an interracial harmony group known as Unity Council, and on television to describe in their own words the way a change of heart brought true equality into the 1,000-man organization.

"I believe there is only one kind of man on earth. I've been taught that, ever since I started in Sunday school almost 35 years ago," said Theodore C. Erickson, business agent of the local.

Thomas Maestas, the union's Spanish-speaking financial secretary, agreed. So did Jim Brown, a Negro from Arizona, and Felix Scott, a Negro from Louisiana, who came to Colorado Springs to find a better life.

Spanish-Americans make up more than half of Local 578's membership; Negroes, about 15 per cent; and whites, about 30 per cent. Yet for many years the union was dominated by the white minority.

"If your skin wasn't the right color or if your command of English wasn't so good, you weren't sent out on the more desirable jobs," Maestas said. "If you complained in a meeting you were called 'out of order.' "

Today Negroes and Spanish-Americans enjoy the same job referral rights and a full democratic voice in Local 578's affairs.

"The first step, two years ago, was the election of Ted and me on a platform of fair play for all," Maestas explained. "The next step was getting the various racial groups better acquainted.

"We formed a job stewards' club. The club meets frequently and doesn't hesitate to discuss questions of color."

When tensions do arise "we just iron out our problems before they get out of hand," Scott said. For example, a white leader in the local talks it over with a white who may have become a source of difficulties, and the same method is followed among the Spanish-speaking and Negro groups.

Opposition to Local 578's harmony effort was mainly passive: "Nothing can be done." Erickson maintains that the fact it was done is proof that the best approach to civil rights is "grass roots action like ours—not the passing of laws from above."

Brown said discrimination by contractors is "not nearly as bad as it used to be. It's dying out, here."

If a contractor shows strong bias, representatives of Local 578 call on him. Only after persuasion failed would the local refuse to supply him with men, but that step has never been necessary.

In current contract negotiations, Local 578 seeks hiring hall procedures that would exempt job referrals from prejudice on account of race or religion. The union also wants to create a joint union-employer board of appeals on a man's job qualifications. "Not qualified" has too often been used as a pretext for discrimination, Erickson says.

Erickson advocates political action, "but first we must get our people to the polls. When you realize that in your own local union only one person in nine is exercising the right to vote, you can see what a lot of educating has to be done."

Sam Gadd, Colorado Springs Labor Council secretary, reports that the Laborers' equality program has been "wonderfully heartening, in the very best spirit of our democratic tradition."

TELL YOUR CONGRESSMAN: ACT NOW ON CIVIL RIGHTS

UAW Solidarity, February 1960

UAW members have been urged to write or wire their Congressmen to support a petition in the House of Representatives to get a civil rights bill out of the Rules Committee to the floor for action.

Two UAW departments, citizenship and fair practices, joined in the appeal to the membership to take action on behalf of the discharge petition.

As Solidarity went to press, a reliable source in the nation's capital released the names of Congressmen who had signed the petition. Newspaper reporters are not allowed to inspect the petition, kept at the Speaker's desk, because of House rules.

On Jan. 21, when the list was released, the petition had been signed by 145 Democrats and 30 Republicans. To break civil rights legislation out of the Rules Committee, a total of 219 signatures are required.

UAW President Walter P. Reuther charged at the AFL-CIO Legislative Conference held in Washington, Jan. 11-13, that a "cynical political deal" was made by Dixiecrats and the GOP in which Republicans agreed to kill civil rights legislation in the last session of Congress in exchange for the Landrum-Griffin bill.

Some 80% of the Republican members of the House had not signed the discharge petition at the time the list was released.

UAW members were urged to ask their Congressmen to vote for a "meaningful" civil rights bill which would include:

1. Clearly stated Congressional support for school desegregation decision;

2. Restoration of a revised Part III (stricken from the 1957 civil rights bills) which authorizes the Attorney General to seek injunctive relief for citizens denied their civil rights;

3. The right to appoint federal registrars in districts where citizens are barred from registering and voting in federal elections because of discrimination;

4. Technical and financial assistance for schools in communities that desire to desegregate, and where states withheld funds;

5. Legislation aimed at preventing hate bombings and other violence, and at apprehending those guilty of such actions.

16 | PROBLEMS AND PERSPECTIVES

16-a   A Balanced View on Strikes

HOW TO INTERPRET 'STRIKE NEWS'

AFL-CIO Secretary-Treasurer William F. Schnitzler
in AFL-CIO News, May 9, 1956

Our system of free collective bargaining has given this country basically cooperative and productive labor-management relations. Let us not be misled by the publicity focused on the cases of labor-management dispute and turmoil. Viewed in perspective, and balanced against alternative systems, it is an incontrovertible fact that we have developed a remarkably fine record of harmonious labor-management relationships.

Unions and management may disagree, mind you, and may drive a hard bargain and irritably fuss and fume with each other, but they are normally prepared to work out practical compromises and reach solutions that both can live with.

Unfortunately, a large part of the public has been led to believe that labor-management relations and union activities are characterized by strikes. The press coverage of labor relations has built and reinforced this misconception. Apart from questions of editorial bias, the press has focused on the conflict rather than the peaceful-agreement situations.

Let us examine this in detail for a moment. With millions of Americans depending on the press for their information, I am disturbed that the daily papers' reporting has been a barrier rather than an avenue to public understanding.

Look at an average daily newspaper. It may report one day that a large strike has flared up in, say, Los Angeles. The next day it may have a story on a threatened strike in New York. Maybe two days later it will headline a labor dispute in Cincinnati. And so some strike story appears almost every day, creating an atmosphere of frequent and continuing strikes, although in fact each strike may be a rare occurrence in its own community, and most communities proceed for years without any work stoppages at all.

Strike situations, incidentally, are normally described as "labor trouble," although we well know that strikes normally are attributable to management practices and indeed are sometimes purposely provoked by management.

Consider a hypothetical but typical example. Assume a bargaining situation in which a union and a company, which get along well with each other, are reaching the expiration date of their agreement and are negotiating for a new one. Perhaps a week before the contract is scheduled to expire, the union may, in

"Same Old 'Bull'!"

keeping with the requirements of its constitution to poll its membership, conduct a vote to authorize a strike if no new agreement is reached.

The local newspaper and probably others in the state would run a simple item headed "Union at XYZ Company To Take Strike Vote." The next day it may report "XYZ Company Employees Votes Strike." Then, maybe a week later there is a headline saying "Strike Deadline Nears at XYZ Company." And then another, "Strike Due Tomorrow at XYZ."

By that time, the company, which

does not want to push the union into a strike, makes some concessions. And the union, which does not want to undergo the serious sacrifices involved in a strike, says "Well, we can't press any more, and the company's offer is now up to a reasonable point." So they work out a last-minute settlement.

(It is possible, instead, that the company or union may misjudge the extent to which the other would compromise. Or perhaps the company may want to see if the union really would back up some proposal. And so a strike may actually take place, with more headlines. But such a strike is normally settled very quickly.)

The agreed settlement is probably reported in the paper. But by then the average reader, who doesn't care if the XYZ workers get an 8-cent rather than a 12-cent increase, has already formed the impression from the cumulative newspaper reporting that crises, bitterness and strikes are typical of labor relations at the XYZ Company.

This problem accounts for so much of the public underrating of the effectiveness of our system of labor relations. In fact, considering the number of situations in which strikes could arise, there are sur-prisingly few of them. In all, some 75,000 to 100,000 agreements are signed each year without any work stoppage.

Look at it another way: The U.S. Department of Labor adds up all the time lost because of strikes in a year. The total lost time comes to less than ¼ of 1 percent of all working time. And much of this is accounted for by the one or two large disputes which do crop up each year. This lost time, by the way, is less than in many years during the 1920's and '30's.

Of course, the number of strikes is not always the best indicator of the health of labor relations. In Russia there are no strikes at all. Where unions are too weak, or where the employment situation is so depressed that workers are too afraid to strike even though their demands are just, the absence of strikes may well signify a disgruntled, underproductive workforce.

Our present record of relatively few strikes is a tribute, in my estimation, to the increasing maturity of labor-management relations in most parts of the economy and is heartening evidence of the willingness and ability of labor and management to arrive at equitable settlements.

AMERICAN NEWSPAPERS CHALLENGED TO GIVE LABOR A 'FAIR SHAKE' IN NEWS COLUMNS

The Railway Clerk, December 15, 1957

Grand President George M. Harrison hurled a challenge to the American press to give labor a "fair shake" in handling labor news stories. He declared at a recent New Orleans meeting of the Associated Press Managing Editors Association: "For years I've been reading in the newspapers how labor unions should be run . . . I'm going to express my views about how I think newspapers should be run, particularly when it comes to presenting labor news."

Brother Harrison made it clear that labor doesn't want slanted stories on either labor or business, but that labor isn't getting the "fair shake" it deserves. He cited these examples:

"The newspapers of America have been covering the trials and tribulations of the labor movement with a great deal of glee. That's all right with us—just save a little space for the other fellows.

"Tell about these men who charge too much for their product; about the bankers who charge too much for their money. They will be the real culprits if we have another depression, not the man who takes home a small paycheck each week which just about covers the cost of his food and his rent and his clothing."

Brother Harrison said that the McClellan Committee hearing on the misdeeds of some in labor was big news until wrongdoing on the business side came up and the hearing "suddenly stopped being front page news in many newspapers." He observed that the first business witness was from Sears, Roebuck, "a pretty big advertiser."

"I say that the newspapers have failed to point out that the dishonesty and racketeering revealed before the McClellan Committee have involved just as many businessmen as labor leaders—for every labor man who took a 'bribe or a kickback' there was a businessman who gave it," he added.

Quoting the statement of Senator McClellan castigating management for some of the shady practices revealed by his committee, Brother Harrison dared the newspaper editors to say where they had been published. He answered the question this way:

". . . The only place I've seen those quotes myself has been in our organization's official journal, The Railway Clerk. And that's not because I don't read newspapers. I'm sort of a labor union Sputnik constantly orbiting between Cincinnati, Chicago, Washington and other points around the country. I spend a lot of time on trains . . . and I read a lot of newspapers. I'm probably one of the best customers you have.

"Now, let's go on to those 'juicy' stories which labor has, but which management does not have. Here are just a few which were either missed, or underplayed.

"First, one of our railroad companies spent a lot of money to build a hunting and fishing lodge for use by its officials and charged the expense to maintenance. It's called a 'demonstration project,' possibly it was intended as a 'demonstration' of how to chisel their stockholders, their customers and their Government. It is reported that guards with police dogs patrol the high wire fence so that interlopers won't get too curious. There are fishing ponds, worm beds, stables, kennels, and all of the rest. Now, any journalist with the imagination that's been used on some labor stories, could do a real job there.

"When the Interstate Commerce Commission brought this company into court on 20 separate counts for falsifying their accounts the company pleaded nolo contendere, paid a $1,000 fine on each count—a total of $20,000 more of their stockholders money, and went back to do a little more 'demonstrating' on their project.

"Then there was the nice 'juicy' story about the General Electric salesmen in New York who were providing 'call girls' for big buyers of appliances. That could have been developed into a real story, but somehow it slipped by most papers, and the ones which did run it put a 'boys will be boys' sort of label on it.

"I contrast this with the treatment given the Teamsters on the Portland and Seattle stories.

"If labor writers would treat unions like financial writers treat business," Brother Harrison said, it would make quite a difference, adding:

"Here's what I mean: If a labor writer goes to a convention which lasts a week and at which scores, even hundreds of delegates get up and speak, he's as likely as not to refer to the convention as being 'dominated' by some 'labor boss' or group which 'steamrollers' things through.

"How much nicer are the words used on the financial page.

"Here's how one financial writer reported the annual meeting of Procter and Gamble, a firm which did more than $1 billion in business last year. First, the writer reported that this meeting was 'smooth-meshing' and then he went on to say:

" 'While some companies put on a razzle-dazzle show, P&G does it more sedately. The meeting started promptly at noon. Thirty-three minutes later, Chairman Deupree closed the fast-paced meeting attended by approximately 100 stockholders.' "

"Can't you imagine some newspaper reporting: While some unions put on a razzle-dazzle show, the Brotherhood of Railway Clerks goes at it more sedately. The convention started promptly at noon. Thirty-three minutes later, Chairman Harrison closed the fast-paced convention attended by approximately 100 delegates."

16-b Who—and What—Causes Inflation?

WHO BOOMS PRICES?
BIG BUSINESS RIGS THEM, BLAMES YOU

UAW Solidarity, October 27, 1958

There's no need to write a story about what has happened to prices. Every wage-earner — and every housewife—knows the sad tale.

The real question is not what, but why.

Have you been told that your hard-won wage increases—and those of other workers—are responsible?

You probably have.

But before you accept this "guilt," stop and think. Who told you this myth?

Your daily newspaper? Sure—but whose side is that same paper on when elections roll around? Whose side does it take in collective bargaining? The Republican big business side, just like the advertisers.

Maybe it was your boss who told you wages were pushing up prices. Well, ask him about his own pricing policies—especially if he's a BIG boss, like General Motors, or U.S. Steel, or Standard Oil, or DuPont, or National Dairy Products, or any one of the handful of leading companies in our basic industries.

Regardless of what newspapers keep saying, the truth is that big business pricing policies are responsible for your having to stretch your budget like a rubber band.

It has happened not once but many times in one of our basic industries, steel, dominated by the gigantic United States Steel Co.

Take the spring of 1957. As a whole the steel industry was winding up the most profitable six months in its history. U.S. Steel alone showed profits for the first quarter of the year that were the highest—both before and after taxes—in its corporate history. Its dividends were at record levels.

This in addition to the industry having set new records for profits and dividends only the year before, in 1956.

Then in July 1957, the United Steelworkers bargained themselves a wage increase. They were able to do it, in part, by showing how between 1947 and 1957, the steel industry had raised its prices 96.3 per cent while its unit labor costs had gone up only 34.7 percent.

But U.S. Steel blandly announced it was upping the price of steel $6 a ton.

The result was that in every other

industry that depended upon steel—and this obviously includes the auto industry—the U.S. Steel "price steal" had to be swallowed and passed on some way to the consumer—that's you.

UAW's research department made a study of the 30 firms that dominate 10 key industries — steel, auto, oil, rubber, aluminum, electrical products, chemicals, food processing, paper and glass.

From 1947 to 1957, these 30 companies (all with brand names any consumer knows) increased their share of corporate profits after taxes in all manufacturing—not just their own industries—from 17.5% to 31.1%.

Their sales zoomed 167.6 percent. Their assets expanded 175.2 percent. They grew far more rapidly than the rest of American industry.

In fact, their profits were so large that in spite of record dividends, they were able to invest billions of undistributed profits in new plants and equipment.

Yet the big corporations are those yelling loudest that "labor costs" are pushing up prices. They yell and yell, without ever telling the truth about their swelling profits.

For the simple truth is that they cannot explain or justify price increases on the basis of unit labor costs.

THE CONSUMER IS BEING TAKEN FOR A RIDE

The Railway Clerk, December 15, 1957

The "press has given considerable space to the popular misconception that wage increases alone are responsible for price increases," Grand President George M. Harrison told a recent meeting of Associated Press editors. Voicing strong opposition to that viewpoint, he quoted a recent editorial in the Catholic magazine *Sign,* which proved that U.S. Steel has made far more profit than could be charged to wage increases. Hitting hard at the newspaper practice of blaming labor for high prices, Brother Harrison continued:

"There have been nine wage boosts in the steel industry, but 21 price boosts. Why shouldn't there have been only nine price boosts if wages alone are to blame?

"In other industries the same trend holds true. Wage increases have added $3.50 to the cost of producing 1000 board feet of lumber during the past five years—yet, production has increased so that the actual production cost has been lowered 63 cents. Overall, labor costs have gone up two per cent in the same period, but

wholesale industrial prices have gone up 11 per cent. Why?

"The Labor Department reports that since the end of the war, price increases have exceeded wage increases in nine out of ten cases. No, workers aren't getting the money, and wages are not the real culprit in skyrocketing prices. The real culprit is Big Business. The giants of industry who have discovered that they no longer have to seek 'risk' capital, that they no longer have to go into the market place and sell stock when they want to expand or build a new plant. They just simply raise their prices, buy their new equipment and build their new plants with the unreasonable profits they take from the consumer.

"The consumer, rather than the investor, puts up a large share of the money to expand industry and when it is all over they split the stock and make a distribution to the stockholders.

"Industry no longer uses 'risk' capital as it did in the old days when America was building and growing great. In the 10 years between 1946 and 1956, U.S. corporations spent $226 billion on new plants and equipment, but floated only $23 billion in stock—the other $203 billion came out of exorbitant profits. Healthy profits are fine, but not exorbitant profits that cause inflation.

"This ability to fix prices is something new on the industrial front. It is above the old law of 'supply and demand.' This year, for example, industrial output is down, yet prices are still rising. Auto sales have been slipping slightly over the past several years, nevertheless prices this year are higher than ever. U. S. Steel shipped 4½ per cent less steel during the first six months of this year, yet it made 10½ per cent more profit.

"Where's the law of supply and demand in that?

"These giants have the ability to control prices because they control our basic commodities. Four companies control 100 per cent of all aluminum made in this country; three control 97 per cent of all autos produced; four do 66 per cent of the rubber business; and another four do 60 per cent of the steel business.

"Yes, something has happened to that law of 'supply and demand' we were taught as youngsters — and, something has also been happening to the laws governing inflation. Normally, inflation comes when there is too much money around and a shortage of goods. Who has too much money today? Certainly not that factory worker with his three kids and $75 a week.

"I'll tell you who has the money. The industrial giants of America, such as the Ford Motor Company. Ford, and it is like the others, has boosted its profits 250 per cent during the past ten years, while its labor costs were going up 70 per cent. Ford, by the way, recently announced that it was 'planning no financing to take care of future plant expansion.' It doesn't have to. Every time you see a Ford go by you see a man who should be a stockholder riding in it. But he's not. He's not getting stock for that additional puffed-up price he's paying for his Ford—he's just being taken for a ride."

THE FIGHT AGAINST JOBS FOR ALL

AFL-CIO Federationist, December 1959

The attack on unions and collective bargaining under the guise of "fighting inflation" is basically a fight "against economic expansion and full employment," AFL - CIO Pres. George Meany has declared. He levels the charge in an article in The Annals, the publication of the American Academy of Political and Social Science. His article is part of an issue devoted to the subject of inflation.

The nationwide campaign on inflation, Meany writes, "has distorted reality" and "has submerged the crucial problems facing the nation" —national defense, public service needs of a growing population, economic aid for the uncommitted nations and adjustment to automation and technological change.

The phony inflation campaign is thoroughly exposed, Meany says, in the nature of the attack on unions and bargaining.

"Americans have been told incessantly," the AFL-CIO president writes, "that wage increases are an inflationary evil, since they are supposed to have resulted in both excessive consumer demand for goods and great increases in costs per unit of production."

The facts are, he points out, that "there was no excessive consumer demand" from mid-1955 to mid-1958 when prices were creeping up.

"There was no general shortage of goods. Instead there was weakness in consumer markets during most of that time and there was a growing gap between the economy's ability to produce and its ability to consume."

As for unit costs, Meany observes, "since 1947 output per man-hour of work has risen at a faster rate than in previous periods, despite the slow pace of economic progress in the past few years." He adds:

"It is the attack on trade unions and collective bargaining that exposes the underlying drive of the structive force for achieving higher living standards and making possible greater economic progress.

"We reject arguments that collective bargaining has had any inflationary effect or that it has in any campaign for restrictive economic policies. The entire campaign is basically a fight against economic expansion and full employment.

"The attack against trade unions, as well as the propaganda for 'tight money' and budget surpluses at low levels of output and income, is an attempt to achieve a slow pace of economic progress and high levels of unemployment.

"What the restrictionists have not yet fully developed is a formula by which they can attain sufficiently high levels of unemployment to satisfy them and win elections at the same time."

The need for national survival and continued progress can be met by economic expansion of at least 5 per cent a year. Continuing wage and salary increases, Meany writes, should be encouraged if growing consumer markets are to be attained.

There must be an end, he adds, to the incessant propaganda campaign about "runaway inflation." Rapid economic expansion to sustain full employment and meet the nation's needs will do more than anything else to stabilize the price situation, he emphasizes.

Later Meany, in a letter to Sen. Paul H. Douglas, chairman of the Joint Economic Committee of Congress, asserted that policies of tight money, high interest rates and attempts to balance the federal budget at relatively low levels of output and incomes should be halted.

His letter to Senator Douglas declared that a substantial revision of the government's tax policies is required to provide a more equitable basis for raising federal revenue and for achieving a better balance in the flow of economic returns to consumers and business.

Mr. Meany said that collective bargaining has been a positive, contribution to the economy and in no way impeded advances in technology." And he emphasized, "Examination of wage-price movements makes clear that the cause of rising prices in the postwar period is not collective bargaining wage settlements."

16-c T-H and L-G: Repressive Laws

EVILS OF T-H STILL EXIST AFTER 10 YEARS

Eugene A. Kelley in AFL-CIO News, June 22, 1957

America's anti-labor law, the Taft-Hartley Act, marks its 10th birthday June 23.

On that day in 1947 Congress voted to override former Pres. Truman's veto and put T-H on the nation's lawbooks.

The roll-call that day in the House

found 225 Republicans and 106 Democrats joining to override the President.

In the Senate, 48 Republicans and 20 Democrats, mostly from the South, voted for passage, three Republicans and 22 Democrats voted against.

Fortunately, during the last decade, America has not experienced a depression which would incite employers to use all the weapons in the legal armory which Taft-Hartley makes available.

Nevertheless, Taft-Hartley's anti-union restrictions have placed serious crimps on union effectiveness —and, as a Senate committee later found, they served as a prime buttress to the determination of southern textile operators to keep the union away from their plants.

Unions have learned what Hartley meant when he told the House with unusual candor "you are going to find there is more in this bill than may meet the eye. . . ."

But labor acted swiftly and effectively to meet the new challenge. The rebuff it suffered stung unions into greater political actvity than ever before.

Much of the credit for Pres. Truman's re-election in 1948 goes to the labor movement, as well as credit for removing from the capital scene many who voted for Taft-Hartley. Hartley himself refused to take his chances at the polls that year and was not a candidate. The interest in politics which intensified then has never slackened.

The act never became the "slave law" that some of its framers hoped it might be but it has had tremendous impact upon the growth and activities of unions.

The handcuffs imposed by the law have hampered organizing efforts despite the countless thousands of man-hours and dollars expended. In the dozen years when the Wagner Act was the national law, membership in unions skyrocketed from 3.72 million in 1935 to 14.9 million in 1946. In non-agricultural industries membership rose from 13.4 precent to 34.9 percent.

When Taft-Hartley was passed there were about 15.4 million union members in the United States. In the 10 years since membership has risen about 2.5 million but the labor force has gained eight million workers.

Taft-Hartley's infamous Sec. 14(b) invites and encourages states to pass even more restrictive legislation than the parent act itself. The result has been that 18 states today have "right-to-work" statutes on their books and similar legislation is under consideration in other states.

The use of injunctions in labor disputes has been increased in the Taft-Hartley decade, the closed shop has been banned, economic strikers have been barred from voting in NLRB elections if they have been replaced by scabs, secondary boycotts have been outlawed and the full weight of government is thrown on the side of the employer in "national emergency" strikes.

The late Sen. Robert A. Taft suggested and supported some modifications of the law of which he was a co-author, but the changes never disturbed the worst features of the legislation.

Candidate Eisenhower in 1952 and 1956 took the stump to advocate changes in the law but Pres. Eisenhower never followed through.

His appointments to the NLRB, however, have made changes that go far beyond the intent of Congress.

The board members and some of its officials have seemed determined to shape the national labor policy in accord with the will of business and management. In so doing they have exceeded anything the framers of the law would have attempted to achieve through legislation.

M. G. Ratner, onetime assistant general counsel for the NLRB, commented in 1955:

"It is apparent that the Eisenhower-appointed members of the board are using the power of their office to substitute for the labor relations policy which Congress enacted in 1947 a new and vicious anti-labor policy of their own.

"The sweeping and crucial character of the policy changes which the board has made . . . taken together amount to amendment of the statute in a manner far more drastic than anything this Administration has proposed to Congress."

These policy changes have resulted in removing even the scant protection afforded by the Taft-Hartley Act to millions of workers as the NLRB slashed the types of cases over which it would assume jurisdiction.

No longer is it an unfair labor practice for an employer to deliver hate-filled anti-union speeches on the eve of an NLRB election. Nor is it any longer forbidden for an employer to interrogate individual workers about their union membership or activity on behalf on a union.

Not until the legislation is substantially amended or repealed will labor consider the tragedy enacted 10 years ago a "Black Monday" to have been erased.

ON LIVING WITH THE LANDRUM-GRIFFIN LAW

Ed. S. Miller, general president, Hotel and Restaurant Employees,
in Catering Industry Employee, November 1959

We had hoped to bring our readers a useful and reliable analysis of the new labor law. But the law was drafted in such haste that it carries dozens of doubts. Until the lawyers have had a chance to examine it line by line, and until the Secretary of Labor has had time to write the administrative ground rules, that analysis must wait.

In many ways this is a remarkable statute. Here are some of those ways:

● It is the first in U.S. history to require affected organizations to inform their members of its contents. Corporations have never been required to inform their stockholders concerning laws affecting business; nor farm organizations to explain farm laws to farmers.

● It is the first in U. S. history to invade the internal affairs of private, voluntary associations with detailed rules of conduct affecting meetings, elections, membership rights, and many other matters. No savings and loan association, Community Chest, veteran's group, lodge, bank, corporation, mutual insurance company—all of which handle "other people's money" and are, in various ways, private bodies "clothed in the public interest," has ever been so closely regulated.

● It is the first to name a "czar" of any kind, let alone a government official—in this case, the Secretary of Labor—with sweeping powers over the duly-elected officers of a private organization. What a howl we'd have heard from the Chamber of Commerce had Congress made the Secretary of Commerce such a czar for business!

● It creates at least 17 new federal crimes! Time was when these were largely robbing mail trains or making moonshine, but things have changed. At least 16 of the 17 are aimed at union officials if they fail to toe the line, including filing various reports.

● It imposes upon unions bonding requirements "for faithful discharge of duties" by their officers far more costly in money, and far stricter, than Federal law requires of bankers and company executives.

• It creates for working people a kind of "split-level citizenship." The full protection of the U. S. Constitution is made available to all workers covered by the NLRB's rules as of August 1, 1959; but those not then reached by those rules are left at the mercy of a crazy-quilt of 50 different kinds of state law.

• There is a kind of sick humor in the fact that this law, billed by its backers as a padlock on union treasuries, is itself a massive raid on those funds. Not only is its Section 502 a bonanza for the bonding business, but labor's bills from printers, accountants and lawyers will skyrocket as a result of its adoption. It may be stated without hesitation that the labor control law will cost unions far more money than the total sum alleged by the McClellan Committee to have been misused by union officers. And its built-in barriers to organization will cost the unorganized, in pay raises they won't get at the bargaining table, many times as much. Nor is this all: the Secretary of Labor has already announced he'll need $12 million of our taxes, over and above his regular budget, to administer the law in its first 21 months!

• It forces conscientious union members, on pain of severe punishment should they refuse, to violate deep-rooted trade union principles by crossing picket lines and handling scab goods.

It is a harsh measure. It is a bill of attainder directed against a single sector of society. Its backers openly declared they sought a bill to damage your union severely. It was adopted in a period of unprecedented Congressional hysteria under the boldest, baldest thumbscrew tactics in political history.

Its effect is to punish the U. S. worker—organized and unorganized alike—by hobbling the unions which are his chief defense against a corrupt and predatory business system.

But our labor movement will learn to live with Landrum-Griffin. We will survive this bold move to weaken us, just as we have survived every other attack during organized labor's 150 years on this continent.

Let it be clearly understood that your union, like most unions, has for many years practiced nearly all the rules spelled out in the Landrum-Griffin law. Since 1899 we have published detailed monthly financial reports showing every penny of income and outgo. Annually we have published an audit made by a rank-and-file committee. This document, in our journal, has been available to the public in scores of public, university and government libraries. Our International Constitution, and local bylaws, are in most respects very close in their meaning to the "bill of rights" in Title I.

The very language of the law, meant to hogtie unions, will force new approaches, new methods. It should revive the ancient spirit of trade union solidarity. Its challenge will bring forward at many levels bold, imaginative new leadership.

It will be months, perhaps years, before this piece of punitive patchwork with its confusing, often contradictory, language can be untangled. Many of its sections, one may hope, will be found to be unconstitutional once they may be drawn to the attention of the U. S. Supreme Court.

Despite the severe hazards imposed upon such service unions as ours by the control law's Title VII — the Taft-Hartley amendments — we will continue to organize the unorganized. We will find the way.

This union of ours was on the job for 68 years before the business lobbies saddled us with Landrum-Griffin. We will be here long after Landrum-Griffin has been stricken from the statute books by a disillusioned people.

LANDRUM-GRIFFIN 'CONFUSION, IRRITATION' HIT BY AMERICAN BAR ASSOCIATION REPORT

Harry Conn (PAI) in Michigan AFL-CIO News, September 22, 1960

The first year of the Labor Control Act of 1959 (Landrum-Griffin) has been one of "confusion and irritation," according to a report adopted by the American Bar Association's Section on Labor Relations Law.

The serious problems raised by the report offer much support for the charges of union leaders and labor attorneys in their attacks on the law.

Professor Clyde W. Summers of Yale University, who presented the report to the ABA's Committee on the Development of the Law of Union Administration and Procedures, said the Department of Labor, in its interpretations, had tried to make "some sense out of nonsense."

The committee is made up of attorneys in the labor and management field. In addition to Summers, other co-chairmen are labor attorney David Previant of Milwaukee and Washington attorney Helen Humphreys.

The committee reviewed the operation of the act for the first year, including interpretations by the secretary of labor. Following is the ABA's analysis of sections of the act:

The study is concerned with six kinds of reports required by the act, saying: "The reporting requirements present the most burdensome task, both for those subject to the act and those charged with administering it."

It notes that "the problems created by the reporting provisions are numerous and complex, inevitably producing a multitude of small problems and annoyances."

On the question of union officer and employee reports, the ABA points out that "the section bristles with uncertainties as to who must report and what transaction must be reported."

A "most serious question" raised by the bar association is whether this section "violates the privilege against self-incrimination." It observes that "commentators are divided on this issue, although all recognize the presence of a serious problem." The report concludes that the section "could be unconstitutional."

"No single provision of the act," the ABA report declares, "caused more initial confusion and dismay than Section 502 requiring union officers and employees, who handle union funds to be bonded. This provision, which received relatively little attention in the legislative debates, was shortly seen to contain a bramble of ambiguities which threaten to make it unworkable if not unbearable."

Interpretations by the Secretary of Labor may have eased the problem, the report said, but certainly did not solve it.

"In spite of the Department of Labor's efforts," the report declared, "through extended consultation with representatives of unions and surety companies, to make the section understandable and workable, much confusion and uncertainty remains.

"Surety companies, cultured in caution, have tended to fix rates which will be certain to cover all eventualities until experience guides are developed. As a result, the costs to the unions have been extremely heavy, in some cases six times that prior to the statute."

At the end of the first nine months, the number of cases for investigation had reached 1,287.

However, the report notes that the Office of Compliance and Enforcement, which handles investigations, does not need any formal complaint to start probing. "A letter suggesting a violation is enough," the ABA declared, "and it may be addressed to almost any official or agency such as a Congressman, the NLRB or the Department of Justice."

What the filing of groundless complaints means is explained as follows:

"The filing of an unfounded complaint brings investigators, who, by their questioning of union members, may create unjustified suspicions and fears. The investigator often explores all possible leads before interviewing the union officers against whom the charges are filed.

"By the time the officers have an opportunity to demonstrate that the charges are groundless the damage has been done. In some instances unsupported complaints have been filed by an opposition group within the union for the purpose of distorting the democratic process.

"The very fact of an extensive investigation inevitably creates a cloud which is not easily dissipated, but this is aggravated when the department refuses to disclose the results of the investigation."

The ABA was critical of the fact that the emphasis seems to be heavy on catching violators and not in correcting violations. The air of secrecy symbolized by insisting that all investigation reports are confidential inevitably irritates those who seek to comply but are constantly fearful of making a mistake.

The Department of Justice was also criticized because in enforcement it mixed criminal and civil liability.

"When the act was passed," the report said, "union spokesmen expressed fears that unions would be harassed by a flood of litigation initiated by dissidents and crackpots. This fear has not materialized. Less than 25 published court decisions have been found and questionnaires to all members of the section have turned up 11 other cases, most of them still pending."

This small number of cases produced little "substantative law," according to the report. It has been established that the law has no effect on events prior to signing of the act, Sept. 14, 1959.

It was noted that many other complex problems, particularly in the area of remedies, "have received no illumination."

16-d Job Security—and Its Opposite

RIGHT-TO-WORK ECONOMICS

Milwaukee Labor Press, March 6 and June 26, 1958

The Milwaukee Labor Press, along with other labor publications throughout the country, has been devoting considerable space to the so-called "right-to-work" legislation being pushed in many states.

We have pointed out repeatedly that this misnamed legislation is nothing more than a super-duper union-busting drive which is being backed by the National Association of Manufacturers and the Chamber of Commerce. Its total effect would be to cripple, if not destroy, the entire American trade union movement by outlawing all forms of union security.

And what would it do to the economic side of the workers' paycheck? A startling example was revealed last week in Phoenix, Arizona where the law has cost the five basic building trades union members an average of 25 cents an hour according to Mason M. Warren, president of the Phoenix and Maricopa County Federation of Labor.

Warren says this is the result of

the "work" law despite two important facts.

Relations between the building trades and the Associated General Contractors are good. For this reason and because the state has experienced booming conditions, employers have been using the kid gloves approach rather than the mailed fist which is embodied in the RTW law and the anti-picketing, implementing legislation.

In an interview with Joe Barr for the California Labor News Service, Warren said that organized labor had been hit hard by the "work" law.

"Under the restrictive laws," he declared, "we can't organize the unorganized unless the employer is willing to cooperate. When you deal with an employer who is not cooperative, you find that he can lay off the union men as quickly as you organize them. We've been trying to organize one concrete pipe plant for two years. The contractor, who sells most of his product to agricultural users, fires union men as soon as we organize them. Under our RTW and anti-picketing laws we can't picket him until 51 per cent of employees are union members.

"Even when we've had all the people in the union, the employer refused to sign a contract. And when we take the people out he hires a new crew. Since the RTW work clause specifically robs men of union security, we find ourselves right back where we started: the plant remains non-union."

These misnamed right-to-work laws can wreak havoc not only on labor unions but deal the entire economy a crippling blow by depressing wages with resulting lack of purchasing power.

'Right to Work?'

Some four million workers are unemployed. Soon there may be as many as five million jobless.

A heavy proportion of these jobless workers live in the 18 states that have adopted so-called "right-to-work" laws.

But the unemployed don't seem able to enjoy the right to work.

Maybe they can call on their local Chambers of Commerce to provide them jobs. Maybe the Chambers of Commerce, which have endorsed and fought for the passage of the "right-to-work" laws, will be able to explain to the unemployed why the "right-to-work" laws don't provide work.

Maybe, in fact, some of the more honest Chamber of Commerce officials will admit that the "right-to-work" title of those laws is as phony as a lead nickel. Maybe they will concede that the "right-to-work" laws are laws to end the union shop and weaken democratic unionism.

But no matter how they try to explain it, they don't be able to explain why "right-to-work laws" won't provide the right to work.

353.

"Our most important problem today is—How can we white-wash our lousy voting records?"

SING A SONG OF SLAVERY

*Thomas J. Lloyd, president, and Patrick E. Gorman, secretary-treasurer,
AMCBW, in The Butcher Workman, November 1958*

Some years ago, when large corporations needed help they would advertise: "Hands Wanted." There was not much thought given to the dignity of the worker. His hands were needed—nothing else.

It is the same now, though corporations are not so frank. They never wanted the worker to think they needed anything more than the use of his hands. Those hands prepared him for the right to work . . . those hands did not give him the right to work.

His right to work then, as now, depended upon the employer's need for help. Every individual has a right to work, except when the boss does not have a job for him. At present, there are 5,000,000 healthy workers with hands capable of doing honest work, and yet they look for jobs which they cannot find. Their right to work is a myth.

The most hypocritical phrase yet conceived to fool the voters of our nation in matters of proposed legislation is the phony label, "right-to-work." It is a brazen lie. The whole purpose of such laws is to destroy organized labor.

These pious destroyers of workers' unions argue that a man ought not to be compelled to join a labor union. At the same time, the companies impose rules upon workers in which the workers have no right to even express an opinion whether these company rules are good or bad for them.

Without strong unions in every industry, workers have no choice and no rights. The boss is master over their lives. The worker can be moved about, or kicked about from pillar to post at the whim not only of straw bosses, but a host of other bosses ranging up to the plant superintendent. For those who do not belong to trade unions, there is no freedom except the freedom to obey or else!

The advocates of phony "right-to-work" laws shout that a fellow has the right to join any particular church, and that this should apply to labor unions, especially unions which have union shop clauses in their contracts. In this, these phony advocates are speaking out of both sides of their mouths.

A doctor would not think of practicing without belonging to the Medical Association, and the Medical Association would usually find ways to discourage his practice without such membership. And the lawyer—just try to find one who does not belong to the Bar Association! Chambers of Commerce and manufacturers associations are strong for the closed shop as far as their own welfare is concerned.

These advocates, however, would deny these rights where workers insist that, after a majority has decided, all workers should belong to the union. These advocates shout loud and long for the majority rule on practically every proposition, except where it applies to workers' rights, or to the unions to which they belong.

Organized labor will always be opposed to "free riders" in industry. These are the parasites who do not belong to the union, but take all of the benefits the union secures for them. A worker should be ashamed to take an increase in pay if he did not cooperate with the union which secured it for him. It is an act of cold ingratitude for such non-union workers not to join with their fellow men to make things in life a little better for all.

It seems only yesterday that in this nation there were staggering breadlines, apple peddlers on every corner, and soup houses in every city. Did these unfortunate jobless have the right to work? Today, even a big shot in a corporation does not have the right to work if the corporation decides to fire him. Those who vote in favor of phony "right-to-work" legislation are voting the workers into semi-slavery whether they know it or not.

There is no right to work guaranteed to any individual. However, there certainly is a guarantee to every individual of the right to vote. In exercising this right, every worker can demonstrate to the enemies of organized labor that at the ballot box they can use their heads, as well as their hands. By voting a positive "No" to the intended tyranny behind such "right-to-work" laws, we can prove that we will never agree to sing a song of slavery.

NEW REPUBLICANISM & $$$ BEHIND INDIANA 'WRECK' LAW

Peter E. Terzick in The Machinist, March 14, 1957

New Republicanism and a $860,000 slush fund added up to a "right-to-wreck" law for the workers of Indiana. The Indiana Senate, by a vote of 27 to 23, has placed its stamp of approval on a measure to prohibit all forms of union security. The measure had already cleared the House by a 12-vote margin.

Governor Handley, a prime example of the New Republicanism which talks like Eugene Debs but votes like Calvin Coolidge, refused to veto the bill.

Indiana thus achieved the dubious distinction of becoming the first highly industrialized state in the nation to include such a law on its statute books.

Last November, Indiana voted overwhelmingly for New Republicanism, and New Republicanism repaid the State by passing the "right-to-work" measure.

Two New Republicans, George Diener, Speaker of the House, and Crawford Parker, Lieutenant Governor and Chairman of the Senate, personally engineered the measure.

New Republicans in the Senate voted better than 4-to-1 for the measure while Democrats voted better than 7-to-1 against it. In the House, New Republicans backed the bill by about 2-to-1 while Democrats lined up better than 7-to-1 against it.

However, the measure did not spring up spontaneously in the legislature. Rather it was pushed by an Indiana "right-to-work" committee which has been active in the state ever since the 1954 elections.

Long before the Legislature met, the committee was beating the drums for "right-to-work" legislation. For all the valiant opposition that Indiana labor could muster, the law was railroaded through the General Assembly.

Now that "right-to-work" forces have succeeded in Indiana, there is little doubt that many other highly industrialized states will become targets in the near future. A few lessons from the Indiana battle are herewith presented:

• "Right-to-wreck" laws are promoted or discouraged at the ballot box. If too many of the wrong people are elected, no amount of lobbying during legislative sessions can change things very much.

• "Right-to-wreck" propaganda is subtle and deceptive. Every bit of propaganda put out by the "right-to-wreck" backers exuded love for organized labor. The only aim of their bill, they claimed, was to strengthen unions. Such ballyhoo is very effective with the general public.

• Indiana newspapers were virtually 100 per cent in the "right-to-wreck" camp. In one week, four editorials praising "right-to-wreck" appeared in Indianapolis newspapers. In addition there were four vicious cartoons, 21 stories besmirching all labor for the sins of a few evil-doers in scattered parts of the country, plus numerous references to labor czars, bosses, etc.

● Educating rank-and-file members to the dangers of "right-to-wreck" is a tremendous job. For all the fine work done by labor leaders in Indiana, too many rank-and-file members still failed to realize all the implications contained in the wreck law. States which hope to keep out wreck laws must educate their members before bills reach the life-or-death stage in the Legislature.

● The impact of New Republicanism on wreck laws transcends state boundaries. U. S. Representative

Madden of Indiana recently charged Secretary of Agriculture Benson had been using his Indiana employees to promote the "right-to-wreck" legislation in the State. Someone thoroughly organized the farm organizations of Indiana solidly for "right-to-wreck." Only the Farmers Union was not behind the bill.

● Employers, too, were somehow or other intimidated. Many who privately expressed themselves as opposed to the wreck measure quickly backed away from any suggestion they go on record.

If there is any moral implicit in the Indiana situation, it is a two-pronged one: first, the best place to really beat the "right-to-wreck" legislation is at the ballot box; second, the time for all unions to start educating both their own members and the general public is right now.

ONLY 60 OF 10,000 NEW JOBS IN INDIANA DUE TO 'RIGHT-TO-WORK' LAW

AFL-CIO News, October 15, 1960

Indiana's so-called "right-to-work" law has had virtually no effect in attracting new industries and new jobs to that state, according to a survey by a management research organization.

Forbes Marketing Research Inc. reported that only 60 of the 10,503 jobs created by industries which moved into Indiana since enactment of the "work" law in 1957 can be credited to the ban on the union shop.

The survey, made at the request of the Indiana Council for Industrial Peace, demolishes the principal argument of "right-to-work" supporters, that the compulsory open shop boosts the state's economy by attracting new industries.

To make the survey, the research firm interviewed officials of 55 new industries and 45 firms which conducted major expansions of facilities during the past three years.

The companies surveyed were certified by the Indiana Dept. of Commerce as "representative of the more important new industry locations and expansion of Indiana facilities."

Ninety-three of the companies, including all of the largest new industries, indicated that the "right-to-work" law was not a factor in the decision to locate in Indiana. Market locations, labor supply and access to raw materials were the principal factors listed by management.

Favorable aspects of Indiana's labor climate, including union and employee-employer relations, productivity and employee attitudes were cited by management as far more important factors in the decision to locate in the state. Six of the seven new or expanded firms which mentioned the "right-to-work" law did not consider it as the primary reason for locating in the state.

SAN FRANCISCO UNIONIST SEES OPEN SHOP AT WORK

San Francisco Labor, March 21, 1958

One San Francisco union member, at least, has learned the hard way what the compulsory open shop means to a working girl.

She is Leona Wolf, a member of Department Store Employees Union, Local 1100, who recently went to work in a San Francisco specialty shop at the rate of $1.60 an hour, plus 1 per cent commission. She works a 5-day, 40-hour week, with appropriate overtime pay, paid vacation, paid holidays, health and welfare plan and job security.

Miss Wolf returned to San Francisco after working in Phoenix, Arizona. Arizona, of course, has a compulsory open shop, known there as a "right-to-work" law. During her stay there, she worked in three Phoenix shops. Here's what a job looks like under the compulsory open shop:

In her first job, Miss Wolf was paid $40 a week, worked 45 hours.

She was made assistant manager and raised to $50 a week, but her hours were raised to a 6-day, 48-hour week. Her lunch period was 20 minutes; she had no relief, no coffee break.

Job number 2 was in a high-priced women's shop, where the lowest priced garment was $22.50. Conditions here were better: she had a half hour for lunch. When she asked about a coffee break, she was told:

"You are in Phoenix now and we make our own rules. If you take a coffee break, don't bother to come back."

Miss Wolf was an assistant manager or buyer on job number 3. But she worked ten hours a day, 6 days a week, with a half-hour lunch and no breaks. She also sold in other departments, closed sales for other salesgirls when they had difficult customers, did janitorial work and also buying for several other departments in the store.

16-e The Strength of American Labor

'LABOR MONOPOLY' TAG EXPOSED AS COVER-UP FOR UNION-BUSTING

Arthur J. Goldberg, general counsel of AFL-CIO Industrial Union Dept., in IUD Digest, Winter 1958

The ultimate objective of those who cry out against "labor monopoly" is to put our unions under the federal anti-trust laws.

Should this objective ever be accomplished, organized labor will be weakened to a point of almost complete ineffectiveness. National and international unions will be prohibited from bargaining for their members at the plant level and all traces of company-wide negotiating will be

eliminated. All this will be done under the guise of monopoly busting.

Employees working for any of the multi-plant employers who dominate the American economy will be restrained from using their collective strength in bettering their wages and working conditions.

Instead, workers will be forced to bargain directly with the plant where they are employed as if that plant was a separate entity, completely devoid of the employer's other interests.

For the great majority of organized workers, the enactment of such legislation will mean a return to the 19th Century when employers with vast holdings held tremendous economic power.

Those who would return to the so-called "good old days" have resurrected the charge of "labor monopoly" as a front for their real goal. If they can convince the American public that labor is a monopoly, then "protecting the public interest" will necessitate placing this "monopoly" under restrictions of anti-trust legislation.

Like the phrase "right to work," "labor monopoly" is now being drummed into the public mind as the first part of this anti-union campaign. Both phrases are equally misleading.

As "right to work" has nothing to do with a worker's right to a job, "labor monopoly" has no connection with our nation's concept of monopolistic practices.

The American public considers "monopoly" a bad word. We say that monopolies are bad—whether created by business organizations or by business organizations in conspiracy with labor organizations.

Essentially, our argument with monopoly stems from the fact that competition is economically desirable and should be the major regulating force in a free-enterprise economy.

There are, however, areas where we recognize the fact that competition among suppliers is undesirable. For example, we do not object to one supplier of electric power, a single telephone service or a one-ownership urban transportation system. Similarly, our patent laws give inventors protection against their competitors for a limited period of time.

In such areas, we do not ordinarily apply the epithet "monopoly," although in a technical sense monopoly does exist. We do not use the term because in these areas, the lack of competition is considered socially desirable.

What type of competition does a labor union destroy? Competition among whom? These are questions that must be answered if the charge of "labor monopoly" is to be considered seriously.

Technically speaking, of course, any labor union is a monopoly in the limited sense that it eliminates competition between employees for the available jobs in a particular plant or industry. By concerted economic action, these workers attempt to increase the wage at which the employer will be able to purchase their labor.

If the monopoly concept is to be applied to unions—under this false notion—all labor organizations should be forbidden and replaced by auctions at which jobs can be parceled out to those willing to supply their labor at the lowest wage.

If this is not the type of competition envisioned by those who speak the loudest of "labor monopolies," there would seem to be only two other types of competition they seek to encourage. These are: competition between unions to see which will supply labor at the lowest rate; and competition between employers in the sale of their products, based strictly on a difference in labor costs.

Neither of these alternatives will stand the test of careful scrutiny. No one really proposes to establish an economic system under which unions would compete with each other to supply labor at the lowest possible cost.

Those who make the "labor monopoly" charge are not really concerned with competition or its negative counterpart, monopoly. Their real goal is the weakening of unions and especially those unions they believe are too strong. The "labor monopoly" charge against American unions is false from every viewpoint.

POWER OF CORPORATIONS VERSUS THAT OF UNIONS

Labor, September 19, 1959

Claims that organized labor has "too much power" were sharply and appropriately refuted the other day on the floor of the House by Congressman Roman Pucinski (Dem., Ill.), a veteran Chicago newspaperman.

"We cannot properly assay the role of labor unions in America without an understanding of the nature and concentration of modern corporate power," he said.

"Approximately 50 per cent of American manufacturing today is held by about 150 corporations, reckoned on the basis of asset values.

"Taking a larger group, it is probable that about two-thirds of the economically productive assets of the United States, excluding agriculture, are owned by a group of not more than 500 corporations. . . . And within that 500, a still smaller group has the ultimate decision-making power.

"This is the highest concentration of economic power in history."

In terms of individuals, this trend is even more striking, Pucinski said. He cited findings of the National Bureau of Economic Research showing that in the last year for which detailed figures are available, in 1953, "the wealthiest one per cent of the population owned about 30 per cent of all wealth, at least 90 per cent of all common stocks, and virtually all state and local government and corporate bonds."

Moreover, "each corporation is a highly centralized authoritarian institution in which the officers and boards of directors control policy with almost no check or veto from the stockholders." By contrast, nearly all unions are subject to democratic control by the members, and the power they allegedly exert is miniscule compared to the vast control and authority exercised by the captains of industry, he said.

IS LABOR *TOO* STRONG?

Robert W. Tighe in Building Service Employee, August 1956

The view that unions were conspiracies to raise wages, and to raise and fix prices, was popular during the last century.

As the "loaded" word "monopoly" became more popular, it tended to replace the word "conspiracy," and unions were charged with this evil.

The most notorious court decision upholding this view was delivered in 1907. In this case the members of the Danbury hatters' union were found guilty of violating the Sherman Anti-Trust Act. They were fined $234,000 — because they had asked fellow unionists not to patronize a struck plant! Most of them lost their homes and life savings as a result.

Despite the effectiveness of the

"monopoly" slander, however, unions had been growing stronger and more national leaders came to see that unions and business monopolies (or trusts) could not be compared.

William Jennings Bryan, the nation's best known orator, analyzed the comparison in this way: "The 'trust' and the 'labor organization' cannot be described in the same language. The trust magnates have used their power to amass swollen fortunes, while no one will say that the labor organization has as yet secured for its members more than their share of the profits arising from their work . . . In a trust, a few men attempt to control the products of others; in a labor organization the members unite for the protection of that which is their own, namely, their own labor, which, being necessary to their existence, is a part of them."

A better popular understanding of unionism led to the passage of the famous Clayton Act in 1914. This law said specifically that unions were not conspiracies in restraint of trade.

It was hailed as the "Magna Charta" for labor, but proved not to be that important. However, it did deal a body blow to the forces behind the "labor monopoly" theory.

Sixteen years later the passage of the Norris-La Guardia Act gave the theory a knockout punch by practically assuring unions of freedom from prosecution under anti-trust laws. By 1935, with the passage of the Wagner Act, the false "labor monopoly" theory seemed to have been buried permanently.

But old slanders never die, and in 1948 and 1949—just after the passage of the Taft-Hartley Act — a movement was started to make the "monopoly" label stick to unionism. This campaign had as its objective making unions subject to the Sherman Anti-Trust Act.

It was financed by those anti-labor employers and associations which felt that the Taft-Hartley Act was not digging the pit under unionism fast enough. Today it is being revived.

Most people can understand the use of the word monopoly in terms of some specific product, like sugar, for example. The businessmen who control a sugar monopoly can sell or refuse to sell, can advance or lower the price, can destroy all or part of their stock in order to increase prices. The people who "control" a labor union—that is, the members—can occasionally, usually once a year when the contract expires, refuse to sell their labor.

The "price" of labor is actually set through negotiations with management—not through arbitrary action on the part of labor unions.

Organized labor is not monopolistic basically because labor is not a commodity. But there is another important factor which differentiates the business monopoly from the labor union—it lies in the location of the power to control.

In a monopoly, control comes from the top. In a union, the control of the members and their labor rests in the members themselves. This is why unions are strong, and are becoming increasingly stronger, and why they are an important development in the progress of democracy.

But, people say, are not unions too strong? Doesn't the AFL-CIO merger put labor in a position of being able to dictate not only to businessmen but also to the U. S. government?

Of course, labor is stronger as a result of the merger. In fact, it was to gain strength that the mergers were consummated. But anyone who understands the nature of the merged federation knows that their strength does not lie in an ability to dictate.

The AFL-CIO is a relatively loose federation of autonomous international unions. It does not control the leadership, finances, or other resources of the affiliated internationals. The AFL-CIO can not call a strike or initiate a boycott.

The federation is a voluntary association which was created in order to work toward greater unity of objective and effort within the labor movement, and in order to give the voice of organized labor a better chance to be heard in the councils of this nation.

The basic ideals of labor remain unchanged. Organized labor in the United States has always fought for the preservation and extension of the democratic processes.

Moreover, while unions have grown, business enterprise has also grown. The economic horizon today is studded with successful corporations—some giant-sized, others relatively small, while business profits have reached all-time highs.

In the words of Theodore Roosevelt, written long ago, unions "are growing constantly in wisdom as well as in power . . . (and are) . . . one of the most efficient agencies toward . . . the achievement of industrial democracy, and the attainment of a larger measure of social and industrial justice."

Far from being monopolistic and a threat to our system of government, unions are opponents of monopoly and promoters of democracy.

'MONOPOLY POWER' CRY: WHAT IT REALLY MEANS

Labor, October 17, 1959

Reactionary politicians, industrialists and editorial writers love to denounce labor's alleged "monopoly power." But just what does this phrase mean?

Suppose you turn the phrase around. The opposite of monopoly is free competition. What would "free competition" mean in the field of labor?

It would mean each man for himself. Each worker would have to bargain individually with the company where he sought a job. On the job, he would have to bargain individually for every raise. Everything about his job rights, seniority, work load, overtime, would be an individual matter between him and the boss.

Under this "free competition" for labor, there would be no strikes. The only choice would be to accept the company's terms or quit.

Does this picture sound highly theoretical? It isn't. That's the way things were in the 19th century, before unions developed their supposed "monopoly power."

Those were the "good old days" when a dollar was called "darn good pay" for 12 hours of heavy work. Those were the days when you held your job at the foreman's whim. The days of the sweatshop, of the poorhouse, of kids aged 12 trudging off in the dark winter mornings to work in the mine or mill.

This type of "free competition" for labor still has not vanished in America. Millions of workers still toil for barely enough to keep body and soul together — in occupations where unions have not been able to gain a foothold.

By and large, though, most American workers have very different conditions from these. Why? Because they, and their fathers before them, banded together in unions. Because they refused to work without a collective agreement. Because they dared even to strike—collectively— to achieve their goals. And millions of non-union free riders have benefitted also from others' collective action.

This collective action is what labor's critics are really attacking when they denounce the unions' "monopoly power." Labor, they say, has become too big." They want it to become small again. Chipping away, now here, now there, they seek to break the unions down.

One step toward this goal is to tie unions up in the courts. Another step is to put unions under the anti-trust laws. Another is to forbid industry-wide bargaining or industry-wide strikes.

The reactionaries will deny it, but their ultimate aim is clear: to restore the sort of "free competition" in labor that ruled in the 19th century. Then labor would have no "monopoly power," and workers once again would be defenseless.

16-f   Ethics and Ideals

FRATERNALLY SPEAKING

William L. McFetridge, general president, BSEIU,
in Building Service Employee, January 1959

Once upon a time, a long time ago, many trade unions had elaborate induction ceremonies, with applicants taking pledges and being given lectures on their fraternal responsibilities.

The elaborate early charters of local unions, hanging on the walls of many a labor temple, reveal how early trade unionists considered their organizations a fraternal fellowship as much as a bargaining agency.

All of this was a long time ago, and no one is going to try to turn back the clock. But there was a recognition of a basic fact in that early fraternal emphasis that we dare not overlook.

A trade union must be a fellowship, a brotherhood of those who share the same goals, same ideals and same interests.

We read a lot, and have written some, about democracy in labor organizations. But the structure of democracy is not enough. Without the cement of shared beliefs and ideals, no voluntary organization will prosper, no matter how democratic its constitution or procedures.

Unless people believe together, work together, and like to be together, the bricks do not make a building.

"I am tired of men with talent," the late Supreme Court Justice Louis D. Brandeis once said, "Give me men who care." In an organization like ours, it is the men who care, who believe in their union and work hard for it, who spell the difference between success and failure.

The foes of organized labor seek constantly to open a breach between the officials and members of trade unions. When we forget that a union is a fraternal fellowship, we fall into their trap of thinking of a union as a government, rulers on one side and the ruled on the other.

Actually, the strength of the labor movement, at the polls or at the bargaining table, is the fact of fellowship—members of a larger family bound together by ties of shared beliefs and ideals. It is the fact of worker fellowship that has built and will maintain the American labor movement.

OUT OF THE BASEMENT

William L. McFetridge, general president, BSEIU,
in Building Service Employee, June 1959

A current best-seller among nonfiction books is one called The Status Seekers, written by Vance Packard. It's "an exploration of class behavior in America," and, in the chapter on job prestige, author Packard writes:

"In Chicago, a labor union has succeeded in raising the income of janitors to the point where they make more money than many of the white-collar tenants of their apartment buildings. This has produced a delicate situation with not a little resentment on the part of the tenants of the expensive status symbols the janitors flaunt. Furthermore, the union has been endearing itself with members by a crusade to move the janitor and his family out of the basement into a first-floor apartment, bespeaking the new dignity the janitor so much desires. Many school janitors are now called 'custodians.' "

To tell the truth, we couldn't exactly figure out if author Packard approves or disapproves of this upgrading of the job status of building service employees. But he's given us a good slogan—"out of the basement."

For that is a major and continuing objective of our Building Service Employee unions. We want—and intend—to get service workers out of the basements of substandard wages, poor working conditions and low-man-on-the-totem-pole job prestige. In many areas, we've largely won that battle. In others, we have a way to go. But we're at work and that's our goal.

For trade unionism is not just a matter of improving wages, important as that usually is. Trade unionism is a matter of asserting the dignity of the worker—and his right to be treated as a person, not as a doormat. No one wants to be a mudsill, and building service workers are not going to be known for letting others walk all over them.

MEANY RIPS CORRUPT 'LABOR LEADERS'

United Automobile Worker, May 1957

Lashing out at those who "betray union law" through their actions, AFL-CIO Pres. George Meany told the 1957 UAW Convention in Atlantic City that the merged labor movement will meet the problem of corruption in labor "head - on, without evasion and with no attempt to sweep it under the rug."

Pointing out that it was the job of labor unions to keep their movement clean and devoted to humanitarian purposes, Meany declared:

"Whether the District Attorney or the grand jury moves or not, this is still our job. Whether management is involved in some of these crimes — and perhaps committees or public officials are not as zealous in going after management as they are after labor—that doesn't make any difference. It provides us with no excuse not to do our job."

In an obvious blast at Teamsters' head Dave Beck, Meany told the delegates:

"Borrowing money without the knowledge of the membership and without them being informed that you borrow it, and without paying interest may not be against the law of the land. I don't know, but it is against the trade union law.

"Buying property as an individual and the making of a decision as the head of the union that the union will buy that property at an exorbitant profit to the individual may not be against the law. It may not be illegal, but it is against the trade union law.

"Taking the Fifth Amendment which is part of our basic law and is designed to protect the innocent and protect the average citizen from being compelled to testify against himself—that, of course, is not illegal. It is part of the basic law, and all citizens have a right to take the Fifth Amendment.

"But taking the Fifth Amendment on the question of personal corruption in connection with the handling of trade union funds, the refusing to give an account of the stewardship of those funds, while that may not be against the law, it is against the trade union law, and no one has the right to hold a trade union office who takes that position."

Pres. Meany made the following points:

1. The exposure and elimination of corrupt practices — whether accomplished by the union movement or by the government—"is good for the trade union movement, and we will profit by it."

2. The AFL-CIO has "no intention of waiting for the public authorities to act in order that they may act on our own law of trade union ethics. That is our job, and we are going to do it."

3. "The main reason" that we are against racketeering in labor is "not just because it is bad for the labor movement, but primarily because it is wrong."

4. Anyone who is conducting the business of a union in a corrupt manner is playing into the hands of American labor's enemies."

5. The Ethical Practices Committee "is going to handle all the cases that come before it" . . . and it is going to "interpret the Constitution of the AFL-CIO in the same manner for a big union as it does for a small union. No big union is going to be immune. . . ."

6. "American labor has come of age . . . we have 15 million people organized in the AFL-CIO; and, if that is Big Labor, then we must assume big responsibility . . . the American people have every right to expect that we discharge that responsibility in keeping with the highest ethical and moral standards possible."

Facing Meany as he addressed the 3,000 UAW delegates—who had already endorsed the ethical practices program of the AFL-CIO — was a huge banner at the back of the auditorium with the slogan "No Tolerance For Corruption . . . In Business, Government, Labor."

ETHICAL PRACTICES: LABOR'S VIEWPOINT

Al J. Hayes, chairman, AFL-CIO Ethical Practices Committee, in The Machinist, March 6, 1958

I believe that the most significant contribution of the Ethical Practices Committee has been to provide the labor movement with a code of ethics of its own—a code separate and distinct from that of the business world.

The simple truth is—that until recently there were no such rules— and trade union officials had only the ethics of a business society to guide them. Unfortunately the ethics of a businessman are not good enough for a trade union officer. What might be admired as no more than "sharp practice" or clever dealing when it is engaged in by an employer, becomes corruption and unethical practice when indulged in by a trade unionist.

Let me give you one example to

show you what I mean. A few years ago a syndicate of business speculators took over the control of the transportation system of an eastern city. They looted the treasury and raped the reserves in a grand manner—and after they had squeezed every possible penny from the wreckage, they pulled out and left the city with a shattered transportation system.

What they did to the people of an entire metropolitan area was, in my view, criminal. But within the framework of our business system it was not only smart, it was practically admirable. So far as I know there has never been any concerted outcry in the papers against this kind of business practice.

It seems to be accepted that this

is nothing more than smart business; just as it is considered smart for a businessman to pad his expense account, print misleading and untrue advertising, cheat a little at income tax time, and play with the truth in order to make a big sale.

The business ethic—or the lack of it—naturally spills over into other institutions. We know that lawyers are not above shady practices, that doctors are not above hidden fee-splitting and commercial operations, and that some of our greatest educational institutions are not above buying the services of football players.

I do not intend to belabor the point—nor do I make it is an excuse for those in organized labor who have enriched themselves by following the ethics of business. Rather, I am trying to demonstrate that in patterning its ethics on those of a business society, organized labor has laid itself open to special condemnation — a condemnation that has not been extended to the businessmen who have fashioned this ethic —nor to the outriders of the business system—the professionals, the educational administrators, and the legislators — who have extended it into other fields.

I venture to say that organized labor has gone further than any other private institution in our nation to establish and to police standards of ethical behavior on the part of its members. I also venture to say that if the ethics of organized labor were compared objectively with those found in business, professional, academic or political life we would find that they are certainly no worse—and are, in fact, probably better than those of other institutions.

Some may think that is exaggeration on my part. If so, it is probably because they have been conditioned by five years of clever propaganda to believe that union officers are the "bad guys," and employers are the

"good guys," in the field of industrial relations.

For in this year of 1958—believe it or not—five years is just how long organized labor has been under the gun of continued Congressional investigation. In rapid succession, the labor movement has been investigated by the Hoffman Committee, the Ives Committee, the Douglas Committee, and the McClellan Committee. One after the other these committees have intensively examined every aspect of union activity. They have been over the books and the records of most every major union in the nation. At this moment the McClellan Committee has 86 full-time investigators combing the country—talking to all manner of cranks, malcontents, strikebreakers, and anti-union employers.

And because of the sensationalism with which their hearings have been reported by the daily press, many people have come to believe that corruption and racketeering are the rule in the labor movement.

Now—what are the facts regarding the extent of corruption and un-ethical practices in the 140 unions affiliated with the AFL-CIO? What has been the foundation of all the headlines, news stories, editorials and radio commentaries that have succeeded so well in convincing so many Americans that the labor movement is indeed a honeycomb of corruption and a hiding place for racketeers?

It may surprise you to know that all of these committees together— over a span of five years—have uncovered facts of dishonesty—proven or probable—on the part of less than 40 trade union officers. (And I would like to add that this includes eight men whose unethical activities were first spotlighted by the Ethical Practices Committee, rather than by Congress.)

Now there are undoubtedly many more, but even if that number were doubled or tripled, this would still be a very small proportion of the more than 16,000 full-time paid national and international officers and the 420,000 local union officers, in the 140 unions affiliated with the AFL-CIO.

I very much doubt if industry, business, the professions or the politicians could have come out with any better record after five years of intensive investigation, especially when one considers that according to Fortune and Life, $5 billion changes hands in the business world each year in kickbacks, payoffs, and bribes, and that according to FBI estimates, more money is stolen by white collar embezzlers than by all the nation's pickpockets, burglars, armed robbers, and auto thieves combined.

So—we come now to a crucial question—Why? Why has organized labor been singled out for such special attention from Congressional committees and for such sensationalized coverage by the nation's press and radio?

I think the answer lies in the fact that the labor movement has made great progress over the past twenty-five years — too much progress to satisfy that small, but vocal group of economic recalcitrants who yearn for the old days when the boss was the boss—unhampered by the united voice and strength of his employees.

These prophets of the past know better than to attempt a frontal attack on the principle of collective bargaining. That is too well accepted and established in the public mind. Instead they are making a flanking attack against the only instrument which can effectuate that principle. They are attempting to destroy the faith of the general public —and of the rank and file union members—in the leadership of the American labor movement.

By creating an atmosphere of distrust for unions— yes, even within unions—they can also create at atmosphere for repressive legislation. Unfortunately, that is exactly what

is happening. We in the labor movement are being attacked on many fronts. We are losing legislative debates now that we would have won five and ten years ago. Only last year, for example, Indiana became the first industrial state to enact a law prohibiting the union shop—a type of law which, in spite of its high-sounding name, is fashioned solely and deliberately to weaken the structure of trade unions and to lessen their ability to bargain collectively.

This, and many other types of restrictive legislation are being proposed in other states, and on the Federal level. Just let me note, however, that the labor movement does not have a closed mind on the subject. We do not, for example, object to legislation which is designed to safeguard pensions and health and welfare funds. We do, in fact, actively support such legislation—and we want it to apply to all funds.

It is a curious fact, however, that the National Association of Manufacturers and the U. S. Chamber of Commerce oppose the application of such legislation to funds administered by employers—even though 90 per cent of all workers covered by health and welfare funds come under plans that are exclusively employer-administered.

But we do not support — we are unalterably opposed to — legislation which would put the government into the business of controlling and regulating the internal affairs of unions. We sincerely believe that a free trade union movement — even one that makes mistakes—is necessary to a free democratic society. We also believe that government regulation of unions would be the first step toward government regulation of the subject matter of collective bargaining.

In other words, wages, hours, and working conditions instead of being settled by mutual agreement at the bargaining table would—as they are in many other parts of the world—

be settled by government decree!

In summing up, let me emphasize that the free American labor movement has historically been a force for good in the nation. Not only have workers—through their unions—been able to share in the long-term technical progress of American industry by getting higher wages, shorter hours, and better working conditions—but organized labor has customarily carried the ball for progressive social legislation of benefit to all the American people.

MR. BUSINESS UNIONIST: WHAT MAKE HIM TICK?

Oregon Labor Press, August 3, 1957

The decline and fall of Dave Beck has focused public attention on a disease known as "business unionism."

We have seen frequent mention of this malady since Beck began to have his troubles with the McClellan committee, with the AFL-CIO and with his own union. It might be instructive to take a closer look at it. What is business unionism, and how does it differ from genuine trade unionism?

In simplest terms, a business unionist is a labor union official who looks upon himself as a businessman and sees his union as a commercial business venture.

Sounds very neat and efficient, doesn't it? No one will deny that it IS efficient—but it isn't democratic and it isn't unionism. Look at the many basic differences between the business unionist and his old-fashioned, idealistic counterpart.

The business unionist believes unions should be run from the top down, like a corporation. The democratic unionist believes unions should be run from the bottom up, by their members, even if the machinery runs a little less smoothly this way.

The business unionist thinks of himself as an executive dealing in a special commodity — labor — just as other businessmen deal in steel or lumber or machinery. He tries, of course, to get the highest possible price for his commodity, but he's also interested in the greatest possible profit and power for himself. (And what's to stop him from a sweetheart contract now and then?)

The democratic unionist rejects the idea that labor is nothing but a commodity. To him, labor is people and union members are much more than payers of dues. To him, unionism is a tool of idealism and social progress—a way of creating a better world.

Mr. Business Unionist believes he should be paid as much as the executives of industry with whom he deals. He calls this "equality at the bargaining table."

Politically, Mr. B. U. is likely to share the conservative views of the industrialists and businessmen with whom he compares himself. He's opposed to strong political action by unions (unless, perhaps, he can see something in it for himself).

He sees nothing wrong in a union constitution that perpetuates him in office; along with his loyal lieutenants, and vests great power in union officials who are appointed, not elected.

He's a businessman, yet strangely enough his decisions are not always easy to understand from a business point of view. Many democratic unions invest their surplus funds in GI mortgages and slum-clearance housing projects, where their money serves a worthy social purpose and earns a good rate of interest as well. But Mr. Business Unionist is more likely to invest his union's millions in a palatial headquarters, where the chief yield from the investment is a personal sense of luxury and power.

Mr. B. U. is proud to tell the world that he's a "bread-and-butter union man." He's for high wages and some fringe benefits, but he has nothing but bored contempt for such things as ethical practices codes . . . better public education . . . fair employment practices . . . civil rights . . . foreign policy . . . broader Social Security coverage . . . and democratic unionism.

He is often impatient when he must work with other unions—especially the ones that follow the slower and sometimes inefficient prac-

tices of democracy. To him, the "labor movement" is neither a reality nor an idealistic goal. It is merely a handy speechmaking phrase.

This, then, is a thumbnail sketch of Mr. Business Unionist. Sometimes he is financially honest and sometimes he's a plain crook. He does not exist in large numbers in American labor, thank God. But, wherever he is found, his existence is threat to the integrity and vitality of labor unions.

UNIONISM: A CRUSADE—NOT A BUSINESS

Justice, April 1, 1957

Dave Beck, the Teamsters chief, was careful not to incriminate himself during his appearance before the special Senate committee last week. But he didn't mind incriminating the labor movement with conduct which Pres. Dubinsky characterized as a tragic spectacle.

The vast majority of those who serve the labor movement look upon their calling as a crusade. They understand the great responsibility which rests on them as officers entrusted with safeguarding the security and welfare of millions of individual union members. They realize that the funds they administer have been accumulated not to generate profits, but rather to provide protection for working men and women on the job, in sickness, in old age.

But if Beck is guilty of the terrible charges made against him, it is only because he has brought with him into the labor movement the concept that trade unions are not a cause, but just another business, to be considered the personal property of union officials. But unions must not, cannot be so considered. They are not the property of any official, no matter what his title. They belong only to their members. And legislation alone, punitive or not, cannot provide the complete remedy for the cash-value approach to unionism.

The AFL-CIO Executive Council, at its Miami Beach meeting in January 1957, established a new cardinal principle for organized labor. No union officer, the council declared, should continue in the labor movement if he finds it necessary to hide behind the Fifth Amendment in refusing to report to a proper government body on his handling of union funds.

It is to the credit of the organized labor movement that this policy, as proposed by AFL-CIO Pres. George Meany, was adopted by the council in a sweeping vote of 24 to 1—with the sole dissenting vote being Beck's.

This new policy reflects the progressive and aggressive leadership of President Meany, as well as the spirit of the united labor movement. It threatens only such stragglers from the field of big business who, like Beck and Brewster, invoke union autonomy and the Fifth Amendment in order to cover up their freewheeling administration of union funds and who refuse to recognize that the time of irresponsibility and of autonomy alibis is a thing of the past.

In its decision at Miami Beach, the labor movement proclaimed that the sense of responsibility is an indispensable requirement for trade union leadership. Those who lack it don't belong in the labor movement.

GOLDBERG LISTS SIX BASIC RIGHTS — PLUS RESPONSIBILITIES OF UNIONISTS

AFL-CIO News, November 26, 1957

Trade union members possess at least six basic rights and five major responsibilities as a result of their membership in the American labor movement, the Conference on Freedom and Responsibility in the Industrial Community was told. AFL-CIO Special Counsel Arthur J. Goldberg, speaking at Northwestern University Law School, declared that each union member is entitled to the following rights "vis-a-vis his union:"

1—The right to a democratic union.

2—The right to due process of law in union disciplinary proceedings.

3—The right to a clean, honest union.

4—The right to an effective union.

5—The right to a union free from discrimination because of race, creed or color.

6—The right to a responsible union, responsible not only to its members and employers, but to the community and to the nation as well.

Noting that "the vast majority" of union officials endeavor honestly to safeguard the rights and forward the interests of their members, he added that "union members who fail to exercise and practice their responsibilities as union citizens bear a high degree of accountability for abridgement of their rights."

"These rights," he continued, cannot be achieved by a union membership that does not exercise its responsibilities, a union membership that sits back, bored or smug, and challenges its officialdom to pull economic and ethical rabbits out of the union hat.

"When union members regard their unions as slot machines which may pay back a quarter for each nickel invested, or as an insurance policy that can be obtained at little cost, then, that union member is devaluating his union," he declared.

LABOR AND PUBLIC RESPONSIBILITY: A SYMPOSIUM

Clair M. Cook in The Guild Reporter, December 11, 1959

Close to a hundred professional labor educators gathered at the University of Wisconsin recently from the AFL-CIO, international unions, universities and related organizations. They explored under the sponsorship of the National Institute of Labor Education a vital and timely question, "Labor's Public Responsibility." Here are excerpts from some of the papers given on that subject:

Jack Barbash, Professor of Labor Education, University of Wisconsin— "Nobody knows for sure what the public responsibility of unions is in respect to their internal affairs because there are a variety of publics. . . . My conception is that the union

owes the public—and more importantly in many ways, it owes itself —effective democracy in the management of its internal affairs. . . . Union leadership is generally committed to the idea of democracy in running the union, but the idea needs refinement, concreteness and implementing skill to make the idea effective. . . ."

Emory Bacon, Director of Education, United Steelworkers—"Since the problems of men in our industrial society are so pressing, and the needs of labor members and staff so acute, either a bold step must be taken to expand and extend labor education in the immediate future or the cause for which we stand may again be set back for years. . . ."

Gus Tyler, Director, Training Institute of the International Ladies Garment Workers Union—"Our earliest unions came into being precisely because working people—true believers in the Declaration of Independence—felt themselves set poles apart from their 'betters.' The central function of American unions has been to immunize this polarity—to redistribute wealth, to equalize rights, to democratize both economy and government.

"As unions win these rights, they can participate even more fully in the problems of the community, sensitive to the sufferings of their fellow men and eager to extend mutual aid, whether the source of the suffering be a germ, a dictator, a flood, a foreign dialect, or an epidermal pigmentation. . . ."

George W. Taylor, Professor, Wharton School, University of Pennsylvania—"There is then a considerable feeling the unions have a public responsibility to take broad national economic interests into account in labor negotiations. . . . At the very same time there is perhaps an equally strong belief that unions should become more responsible than they have been to the aims and aspirations of their own constituency.

"These will inevitably tend to be short-run aims and aspirations. It is expecting far too much of mere mortals . . . to accept with alacrity the loss of their own jobs or to relinquish prized conditions because that will likely tend to contribute to long-term economic growth or even because that is necessary to insure better and more secure jobs in the long run for their fellows. . . ."

Russell Allen, Director of Education, AFL-CIO Industrial Union Department—"Quotations from a constitution notwithstanding, the primary job of a union is to represent its members vis-a-vis their employers. Such representation can sometimes carry with it such tasks as clinging to work rules that affect labor costs.

"But to characterize such advocacy as 'irresponsible' is to lose sight of the union's primary representative function. It represents its members not because they are always right, or always liberal according to someone's definition, but because it is the workers' representative or no one is. A union that is not responsible to its members' wishes is irresponsible in the only sense that is meaningful to those members."

Ben Segal, Director of Education, International Union of Electrical, Radio and Machine Workers—"I believe there is a growing awareness and realization by a number of union leaders of the broad—in some instances, continually widening—gap between the pronouncements and resolutions of the unions and the deep-rooted beliefs and opinions of the local union leadership and rank-and-filers, especially on political issues, civil rights, civil liberties and international affairs."

Mitchell Sviridoff, President, Connecticut State AFL-CIO—"This brings us back to the fundamental role of the labor movement and its goals. If its function is exclusively economic and materialistic, then a standard of comparison with banking, business and even many of our honored professions is entirely appropriate.

"But if we conceive our functions to be broader, our goals to be loftier, indeed, our purpose to be more a mission, then not only must we expect higher standards of behavior to be imposed upon us, perhaps they ought to be self-imposed as many unions have already done."

David B. Truman, Professor of Government, Columbia University—"From its own point of view, the chief public problems of the labor movement are those that reflect its own maturity. . . . A price of its new status and of its continued influence is not merely that it act as a claimant for its members but also that it take its place as an equal among the trustees of the society and the political system."

IV

Labor
In a World
Of Crisis

EDITORS' NOTE

From factory, to community and nation, to the world at large —the interests of unions have expanded as they matured during past decades.

In 1919, AFL president Sam Gompers helped found the International Labor Organization, which is now a UN agency. However, it was not until the 30's that American labor fully recognized the dangers of the emerging dictatorships, Fascist and Communist. Working people, as citizens, soldiers and unionists, then came to understand the meaning of these 20th Century tyrannies, and their destruction of all liberties, including free trade unionism.

After World War II, labor unionists took an active part in world labor bodies. They served as labor attaches, and as friends and visitors to trade unionists overseas. Labor had its own little Marshall Plan, and it has helped union men—whether in ravaged Europe or emergent Africa—to organize democratic unions.

The American unionist is no stranger to poverty or workers' struggles for dignity and a decent living. He speaks the common vocabulary of all working people, whatever their language, culture, garments, climate or habitat.

Today, the union card is a unique passport in this age of revolution and social change. The articles and news stories which follow illustrate how valuably the union card—and the experience it represents—symbolizes constructive alternatives to Communist imperialism and its programs of infiltration and conquest.

17 | THE QUEST FOR PEACE AND FREEDOM

STAND FIRM ON PRINCIPLES, MEANY URGES FREE WORLD NEGOTIATORS

Saul Miller in AFL-CIO News, April 23, 1960

The danger of aggression and war can be reduced if "our leaders at the conference table . . . convince the Communist leaders that we have the determination, the resources and the power to deter any aggressor . . . in order to preserve world peace and human freedom," AFL-CIO Pres. George Meany has declared.

In a speech keynoting the AFL-CIO Conference on World Affairs, Meany warned that if the "free nations begin to retreat at the summit conferences on the future of Berlin" or any other major issue, "it will be interpreted as a sign of weakness."

Appeasement of Khrushchev at the summit, he declared, "would prove just as disastrous for the cause of peace and freedom as was the appeasement of Hitler at Munich in 1938."

America and the free world, he added, "cannot afford to underestimate Soviet strength—military and economic — nor should we become overawed by it." America has what it takes to win the struggle for freedom, he asserted. "The greater danger is default rather than defeat."

The American labor movement, Meany said, favors taking "every necessary, practical and every safe step to prevent war," and firmly believes that "our government should negotiate with Soviet Russia at the summit and at every other level. But let us negotiate as realists."

He warned that official communiques from the summit "paying lip service to pious platitudes" would serve no good cause, that "smiling photographs and public handshakes can perpetuate a monstrous fraud if they do not symbolize anything deeper than surface politeness."

Meany pointed out that there "is no magic formula in sight for the immediate solution of the major problems that beset our world. The best we can hope for is a gradual subsiding of international tensions through a step-by-step program of acts of good faith by both sides. The road to peace is an uphill climb all the way."

Examining the background against which the summit conferences are taking place, Meany sketched the potential awaiting mankind in eliminating hunger and disease, providing decent homes and adequate clothing for all the world. Illiteracy and ignorance can be wiped out in a generation or two and we are now witnesssing the beginning of the end of color "as a divisive force in society. At last the world will recognize only one race—the human race."

These goals are attainable in our times, the AFL-CIO president said, if the "great negative potential in world affairs today," atomic war or cold war, military war or economic war, is removed. The "continuing threat to human survival and progress stems from one source and one source only—Soviet Russia."

308

In the final analysis, Meany said, the outlook for world peace and freedom "depends primarily on our own efforts. We cannot bank on any Soviet concessions given in false coin."

Comparing the U. S. and Soviet intentions, Meany noted that "America has no aggressive designs now or in the future against Soviet Russia. No other free nation entertains such foolhardy notions. If there can be any one certainty in international affairs, it is this — that the free world is willing to live and let live."

In contrast the Soviet record is one of repudiating every agreement with her former allies, Meany said, and suppressing "with brutal and overpowering force" revolutions in Hungary, Poland and East Germany.

Moscow, he added, "invented and initiated the cold war" and while there have been changes of faces in the Kremlin" there is "not one scrap of evidence of any change in the fundamental Communist determination to dominate the entire world by every available method, even war."

NEW POLICY NEEDED IN BATTLE WITH TYRANNY, REUTHER TELLS WORLD AFFAIRS PARLEY

AFL-CIO News, April 23, 1960

Free world labor is the "most effective anti-Communist force in the world" and wherever labor is strong the forces of tyranny are "weak and without influence," AFL-CIO Vice Pres. Walter P. Reuther told the AFL-CIO World Affairs meeting in New York.

Reuther declared that the new power struggle is not for supremacy but for survival, and that in this struggle military power is a "negative aspect of foreign policy that buys time" so that an offensive can be mounted on the political, economic and social fronts to win over tyranny.

"We will prevail," he said, "by demonstrating that our society can provide solutions. . . . Peace or freedom cannot be made secure in a vacuum."

The free world is losing ground in the struggle for the uncommitted nations, he added, because "we're not really trying." Our policies "are shaped in the image of our fears not of our hopes," and in too many areas we are identified with the forces defending the status quo, "a status quo that is unacceptable."

Everywhere humanity is on the march, he said, and this country must move with it.

We must identify ourselves still more sympathetically with the rise of nations in Asia and Africa and wherever peoples are striving for social justice and freedom, he continued.

As part of a total effort to win the peace Reuther urged a national list of priorities topped by an intensive effort to improve and extend education to meet the Soviet challenge and a complete identification of the U. S. with the global struggle to eliminate racism, to stamp out the master race theory and to "give us more credentials in the world."

In the foreign area there is a need for a greater emphasis on wiping out hunger by making full use of our food surpluses and creating regional world granaries to provide food capital for those countries that need it, Reuther said.

He urged greater channeling of efforts through the United Nations and creation of scholarships for Americans and other peoples to create a "UN Peace Corps" to serve in economic, technical and social assistance roles around the globe.

Reuther called also for exertion of every effort to set up a ban on nuclear testing with a universal in-

spection and control system. He
urged that the Chinese Communist
problem be considered realistically
because no arms agreements can be
made effective if they are outside
such a pact.

"Our potential to fight and win
wars must be used to battle and
win the peace," Reuther declared.

He added that labor must lead the
way in bringing about full employment and full production for peace
as it has in the past for war.

The major task, he concluded, is
to shake the country out of its com-
placency and mobilize it completely
for the battle for peace and freedom.

DIPLOMACY IN OVERALLS

The Carpenter, July 1956

In the day-to-day operations of
this sorry old world of ours, the men
in the striped pants make all the
news. The pushing and pulling and
jockeying for position of the diplo-
mats, ambassadors and ministers
rate all the headlines. More often
than not, the headlines contribute
little to undisturbed sleep.

Using the good old batting average as a yardstick, the silk hat boys
strike out pretty often. For all their
conferences and compacts, tensions
and mistrusts diminish little, if any.
The governments that trust each
other and cooperate with each other
completely can be counted on the
fingers of one hand.

Fortunately, however, there is another facet to international relations
—the intercourse among people in
overalls and sweatshirts. In this
field, the box score is much better.
The little people everywhere are
drawing closer together as understanding and mutual respect increase.

What is bringing about this increased understanding and mutual
respect?

Many things, probably—and one is
that thousands upon thousands of
ordinary Americans are working in
foreign lands helping to build better
lives for the impoverished and ignorant.

Recently there came to the General Office a report from Brother
Emile Bilodeau, a member of Local
Union No. 1822, Fort Worth, Texas,
who is working with the U. S. Operations Mission to Iran, a part of
the Point Four program. The report
makes you proud to be an American.

It is not that the program is cur-
ing all the Iranians' ills overnight.
Far from it. There are still ignorance and poverty and prejudice.
But American technicians are showing Iranians how they can overcome
these things by their own efforts.

Iran is 80 per cent illiterate. Only
one-fourth of her villages have a
school. But 28,000 teachers have
been trained by the Point Four program. Villages all over the land are
organizing their own schools without waiting for the Ministry of Education to act. It may take years to
achieve, but illiteracy is doomed in
Iran.

In health, too, there has been a
great improvement. Over 3,000,000
men, women and children have been
innoculated against smallpox, ty-
phoid and diptheria. Numerous clinics have been organized and put into
operation. Hundreds of courses in
child care, nutrition, etc., have been
organized. The value of sanitation
has been stressed.

But after he has learned to stay
alive and read, a man has to have
some way of earning a living. In the
field of economic development the
Iran mission has been particularly
effective. Thousands of Iranians
have been taught how to farm better
so that they could go out into the
highways and byways to pass on to

farmers the benefit of their knowledge. Through crossbreeding, an Iranian cow that produced 1,500 pounds of milk has a daughter that produces 5,000. A field which barely produced enough to keep the farmer's family alive is producing a surplus for sale at the market place. The wooden plow, an exact duplicate of the plow used 2,300 years ago at Persepolis, is giving way to cooperatively-owned farm machinery.

In the cities, modern production methods are being introduced in factories; nothing to rival Detroit, but a tremendous improvement over age-old hand methods. Transportation, housing, etc., are improved as fast as natives can be taught the rudiments of American methods. Not even unionism is being neglected, for American unionists are there to help.

So, while the men in silk hats are yak-yaking and debating, the little people are working together to build richer and fuller lives for all.

The final chapter in the world struggle between democracy and communism may not be written for generations. But win, lose, or draw, Americans can be proud of the contributions they have made to human progress. Never in history has a people given more generously both of its money and talents to elevate the status of others.

When man's inhumanity to man finally comes to an end, the boys in overalls will be much more responsible than the boys in the silk hats.

NYET!

Justice, July 1, 1959

Life without labor strife is on display in New York. The show is called "The Soviet Exhibition." It was organized under the direction of the USSR Chamber of Commerce. Its purpose is "to tell Americans about the Soviet Union, its economy and culture, as well as the progress and aims of its people."

This is a most noble purpose and, at a time when all peoples in the world long for peace, such an exchange of information takes on added signficance. This newspaper therefore dispatched a reporter to the press review of the exhibition. His instructions were simple: In the interest of getting to know the Russians better, do a piece on how trade unions in the Soviet Union operate. Based on materials at the exhibition, draw the parallels or the differences with American trade union practices.

Our reporter made the circuit of the glossy exhibits. He goggled at the three-story-high pylon posters, admired the miniatures of parks and airports the Soviets plan to create, was awed by the scale model of continuous metal casting mills, and atomic-powered ice-breakers, studied the animated statistics and stood in wonder before the nose of Sputnik.

He then inquired of a press officer where the section of the exhibit showing the work of the Soviet trade unions might be found.

He was relayed down the line by five officials. He then asked three young guides on the main exhibition floor. One of these took him to his leader, who replied that there was no separate section on the trade unions. Pressed further, he added there wasn't even a joint section. In fact, there was in this vast array of Soviet imagination, culture and wish, nothing on the Soviet trade unions.

A tarnished millenium is on exhibition in New York. Sections depict heroic Soviet history (without the shadow of the shadow of Stalin showing). A display of Soviet literature tells of a tremendous edition of Tolstoy's books (but doesn't even hint at Nobel Prize winner Pasternak).

Luscious food and colorful garments are displayed, (but without price tags). A tractor of enormous dimensions roars out (but there is no full or scale model of the kind of tanks that subdued the Hungarian revolutionists).

If these shortcomings constitute the price a people and a nation must pay for other advantages, this surmise is not documented by the exhibit.

We strongly recommend this exhibition to all industrialists who dream of doing away with strikes—for the Russians have no strikes. We recommend it to all tycoons who hope for a return to a time when they no longer have to bargain with unions over wage rates or work schedules — for the Russians don't bargain either.

We think that this exhibit can mark the beginning of a period of true friendship among kindred spirits—for example, the U. S. Chamber of Commerce and the USSR Chamber of Commerce which, judging by the displays it selected, seems to know just what would please the American businessmen with whom it hopes to do increased business.

Hooray for the tractors, tovarischi! Bravo for Sputnik! And three cheers for the American Confederacy, which with its slaves could share the pride of the slogan emblazoned on your high poster, and boast with you that it, too, had wiped out unemployment. But please, comrade, could you tell us where is the section of the exhibit on the Soviet trade unions?

LABOR CHECKING RED INFLUENCE

Edward P. Morgan, radio commentator sponsored by the AFL-CIO, in the AFL-CIO News, August 18, 1956

Events can almost never be reduced to a simple equation of cause and effect. A number of circumstances are always behind international happenings but in the stark blackness of the first headlines many important developments behind the news are often blotted out.

Take for example the constant effort to check the influence of communism in western Europe. This is not just a matter of contact on high but remote levels among friendly governments. This is a job that has to be done at the level of ordinary people, for the primary targets of Communist propaganda and proselytizers are, of course, the workers, the girl in the shop, the man in the factory.

This may come as something of a surprise if not a shock to Sen. Goldwater and others who are so eager to equate trade unionism with the bubonic plague, but the fact is that the most responsible elements of organized labor in the United States have had a very influential hand in the international struggle against the Communists. Their effectiveness comes in large measure from the fact that they approach the individual wage-earner on his own level and talk to him directly, or through people he knows, in terms he can understand.

Without fanfare, a group called the Intl. Metal Workers Federation, which is a part of the ICFTU, the Intl. Confederation of Free Trade Unions, has been making measurable progress against Communist-dominated unions in Italy, France and Trieste. On a somewhat different accent the group has recently begun a campaign against communism in Japan, one of the approaches being a defense of the rights of workers and small landholders caught up in the projected expansion of U. S. military installations on the island of Okinawa.

American unions supporting the metal workers are the Machinists, the Auto Workers, Steelworkers and the Intl. Union of Electrical Workers. The federation has spent between $80,000 and $100,000 a year in France over the last several years and similar sums in Italy on special campaigns, which have helped to bring these dividends:

Spectacular losses of strength by Communist unions at Fiat, sometimes called the General Motors of Italy, in the Fiat plant at Turin and other factories; also a victory of free trade unions in negotiating a new contract with the Renault automobile works in France last spring.

How are the workers weaned away from the Communist-dominated unions which so long have had a "monopoly" on the French and Italian labor forces? The answer is chiefly by education and organization, such as training of shop stewards in the give and take of democratic union processes, something about which they knew or understood virtually nothing.

'BERLIN BLEIBT FREI' — BERLIN REMAINS FREE

John Herling in UAW Solidarity, May 1959

WEST BERLIN—The people of West Berlin turned their 1959 May Day demonstration into a triumph for the free world. Representing American labor, UAW President Walter P. Reuther, added a new dimension to the dramatic occasion by his speech and his presence.

Berlin's hard-fighting, hard pressed, free trade unions organized this greatest outpouring of people in this city since 1949—the year of the Soviet blockade. They represented not only labor, but every group in the community; both Socialists and Christian Democrats teamed in a firm anti-Communist alliance.

More than 600,000 Berliners marched in groups or walked with their families. Then they stood, eyes glinting in the welcome sun, to affirm their faith that "Berlin Bleibt Frei." This means not only "Berlin Remains Free" but that it's going to stay that way, come what may, despite Nikita Khrushchev and Soviet threats.

Now in 1959, crisis has returned to Berlin. The Soviets have issued an ultimatum and stepped up their war of nerves against the free world—and Berlin.

So, on this May Day, 1959, the men and women of this city kept streaming into the Square of the Republic. From the lofty platform six-foot letters proclaimed, "Berlin Bleibt Frei."

You see the Brandenburg Gate, way off on the left, the border between West Berlin and the Soviet-controlled East Sector—the cut-off point between freedom and democracy. You see the charred Reichstag building, the slowly healing relic of Hitler's arson in 1933.

The people yelled, "Hullo Willy, Hullo Walter," in high spirits, roaring their laughter and gesturing good will. Bands and an orchestra made the occasion festive and satisfied all musical tastes. Banners spelled out a variety of slogans revealing a wide range of opinions, but "Berlin Remains Free" was the recurring theme.

Tough and tested Ernst Scharnowski, head of the Berlin Federation of Labor, was master of ceremonies. Years before, Scharnowski had rescued the Berlin trade unions from the control of the Communists. They hate him with deadly intensity.

But he scorns them, works hard and crackles with a crusty humor. He told the world: "They're again trying to break our nerves. They never stop. They will never break our nerve or our spirit. We Berliners are like eggs. The more they boil us, the harder we get."

Through the loudspeaker came Scharnowski's voice, introducing "our friend, Walter Reuther, who brings the greetings of 16 million American workers to us in Berlin."

The roar of welcome thrilled Berliners and visitors alike. Here was "people-to-people diplomacy" on the grand scale. The solidarity of the world's free peoples had on this occasion an outward, visible symbol; and the U. S. labor movement was represented in person.

Reuther spoke in German, a fact which delighted the crowd. This was one of Reuther's shorter speeches— about 15 minutes. He told them that American labor and the American people as a whole joined in their determination to keep Berlin free. The world's free labor movement, he said, understood how important a role history had cast for Berlin and its people.

The climax of the meeting came with the speech of Willy Brandt, Berlin's mayor.

The jubilant freedom bells began to peal, pouring over Berlin's people. Slowly and, it seemed, almost reluctantly, the great May Day meeting came to an end.

HUNGARIAN STRIKE CRIPPLES PUPPET REGIME

Gervase N. Love in AFL-CIO News, December 15, 1956

The workers have become the core of Hungary's grim battle for freedom as a general strike that crippled production, transportation and communications turned into wide-scale disorder and fighting.

In Budapest, the Soviet-dominated Kadar government "outlawed" the Central Workers Council, the nucleus of resistance, before the strike was to become effective.

But though Russian soldiers, backed by tanks and heavy arms, seized leaders and threw them in jail or hustled them out of the country, the council continued to function and renewed its demands on the government.

Direct negotiations between council leaders and Premier Janos Kadar had broken down when the puppet leader rejected a series of worker demands for greater freedom.

Additional hundreds of Hungarian workers, backed by students and liberals, fell before the all-powerful Russian arms, but the grim resistance continued and grew, with rank-and-file workers at times forging ahead of their leaders.

Widespread walkouts had cut production to a minimum even before the general strike call. Factories and mines were damaged. Workers willing to return to their jobs could do little but clean up the debris.

Meanwhile, relief agencies, assisted by the financial support of free labor throughout the world, continued despite the fighting to try to feed the Hungarians and to take care of the additional thousands of refugees moving steadily into Austria via a new underground railway.

At last count, approximately 130,000 men, women and children— most of them with nothing but the clothes on their backs—had successfully found succor in Austria.

The United States, after red tape had slowed immigration to a trickle, got a huge air and sea lift plan under way through which it was planned to move 21,500 to this country by the end of the year. About 3,000 have already arrived, most of them at Camp Kilmer, N. J.

With the world opening its heart to the Hungarian fugitives, American workers were doing more than their share. The AFL-CIO is collecting funds from its affiliates to help them through the AFL-CIO Intl.

"The Rebirth"

SEAMAN

Free Labor Fund. It is closely co-operating with the Red Cross drive for a $5 million emergency fund and the CARE campaign for funds for food packages.

Many unions have offered to help bring refugees here and assist them to get settled in jobs and homes. The Glass Bottle Blowers made a firm offer to take care of 50. Pres. David J. McDonald announced he would ask the Steelworkers' Executive Board to authorize guarantees for 1,000. Other unions were planning to follow suit.

Meantime, the Intl. Confederation of Free Trade Unions, through which the bulk of free labor's aid has been channeled, announced receipt of $505,000 in aid funds, with more arriving daily.

Most of this money is being spent through the Austrian Federation of Trade Unions, which has thrown all its resources into the effort to care for the refugees.

In all free countries, including the U. S., trade unions have organized public meetings and mass demonstrations of support for the Hungarians, and have deluged the United Nations with pleas for assistance. In many democratic countries, workers have refused to handle ship cargoes coming from or destined to go to Russia.

SOVIET BOYCOTT ASKED IN HUNGARIAN CRISIS

AFL-CIO News, November 10, 1956

Soviet heavy weapons were still pouring their deadly fire into workers' apartments and Red Cross hospitals when AFL-CIO Pres. George Meany wired Pres. Eisenhower a demand for a virtual boycott of Russia by the rest of the world.

Specifically, Meany called on the government to:

"1—Urge every country outside the Iron Curtain to sever all cultural, scientific, technical and economic relations with the Soviet dictatorship and, forthwith, discontinue the exchange of any delegations with the USSR.

"2—Energetically block every effort of Moscow to seat in the United Nations the venal puppet regime it has imposed by brute force on the Hungarian people.

"3—Seek to have the UN specifically condemn the Soviet representative for having deliberately deceived its General Assembly on Nov. 3, 1956, in regard to his government's plans and preparations to overwhelm Hungary, another member of the UN, by military force in violation of the UN Charter."

FREE HUNGARIAN LEADER ASKS UN PROBE OF REDS

Gervase N. Love in AFL-CIO News, November 17, 1956

A white-haired lady with the blue eyes of a fighter and a black dress in mourning for her dead sat at the big conference table in the AFL-CIO Executive Council meeting-room and told the heart-chilling story of what has been happening in tragic Hungary.

She was Anna Kethly, a leader of the Hungarian Social Democratic party, a member of former Premier Nagy's ill-fated cabinet, former president of the Teacher's Union in her native country, a veteran of resistance to tyranny with a spirit undimmed by more than seven years in totalitarian jails— three years under the Nazis, the rest under the Communists.

Her appeal for understanding and help for the country she loves passionately was made at a press conference at which AFL-CIO Sec.-Treas. William F. Schnitzler presided.

To newspaper, radio and television men and women she told the now-familiar story of the spontaneous revolt touched off when secret police fired into the ranks of demonstrating students. She told about the Nagy coalition government, and of how its self-appointed first task of calling free elections was shunted aside by the necessity of getting the Soviet army out of Hungary.

And she told how the Russians, in as cynical a double-cross as history knows, ended negotiations on the removal of their army by jailing the Hungarian bargainers, turning loose an overwhelming force of tanks and heavy arms, and setting up their own puppet government.

Miss Kethly was in Vienna, representing the Nagy government, when the Soviet guns blazed and tanks rumbled. She continued on to New York to lay her case before the United Nations.

She appealed for moral and diplomatic support with pressure—especially by the uncommitted countries —on Russia through the UN.

She made it clear she was not appealing for armed intervention.

"Above all, we want a UN commission to make a survey and report its findings," she said. "We are convinced that such a course would have a great effect on the Russians themselves.

Miss Kethly endorsed the suggestion of Pres. George Meany that the free world, in effect, boycott the Soviet Union, calling it an "important proposal."

As she talked, all but the last trace of fighting against the Russians had ended in Hungary, but the workers had called on another powerful weapon—the general strike.

Practically every worker in the nation had followed the lead of the bakers, who stopped work when the Russians seized the bread they made to use it as bribes to end the revolt and get people back on the job.

FREEDOM FIGHTERS PLEDGED ASSISTANCE

Arnold Beichman in AFL-CIO News, December 22, 1956

CAMP KILMER, N. J.—American labor will welcome Hungarian workers who have fled to freedom in the United States "on the basis of equality," Pres. George Meany told several hundred Hungarian refugees.

In a bare, dimly-lit hall, he spoke to Hungarian men, women and children, the majority of whom had arrived in this country via the Air Force airlift a few hours earlier.

"We shall continue our efforts," he pledged, "to secure the most generous contributions from our membership to help the Hungarian freedom fighters who have found a haven in this or other free lands.

"Now that you are here, you can live in peace, freedom and dignity. We of American labor welcome your garment workers and steel workers, your auto workers and construction trade workers, your craftsmen of all trades and skills."

When the speech was over, a most touching scene occurred. Meany left the platform and started down through the auditorium. The entire audience arose as one and stood silently. From the rear, a few voices began singing the Hungarian national anthem, Isten Alld Meg A Magyart — God Save the Hungarians. It was picked up by the entire assembly, this slow, sad song. The men stared ahead as they sang while many of the women wept or covered their eyes with neckerchiefs and shawls to hide their tears.

Then many of the refugees crowded around Meany to shake his hand. Some took out little books and showed them to Meany. They were their union books, and they wanted to show him that they had been workers and union members and they wanted to join, as a young ironworker said, a "real American union."

SPAIN SCORED FOR ARRESTS OF UNIONISTS

AFL-CIO News, December 20, 1958

Recent wholesale arrests of union members and professional persons suspected of democratic leanings by the Franco dictatorship in Spain have been strongly protested by the Intl. Confederation of Free Trade Unions and the Workers Defense League.

Underground information from reliable sources inside Spain is that around the middle of November at least 100 arrests were made of men known not to be Communists. The dictatorship usually pins the "Communist" tag on those who incur its displeasure.

They include Amat Echeverria of Madrid, active in the exiled Spanish labor movement, and Jaime Carner, minister of finance in the Republican government in 1931. The use of "third degree" methods is feared.

The ICFTU's protest was sent directly to Generalissimo Francisco Franco by Gen. Sec. J. H. Oldenbroek, and was the latest in a long series that shows free world labor support for democracy in Spain.

BRITISH, U.S. UNION COOPERATION URGED TO HELP NEEDY NATIONS

Robert Cooney in AFL-CIO News, Sept. 6, 1958

Bournemouth, Eng.—American and British unions must work together to do more to aid the less fortunate peoples of the world, AFL-CIO Vice Presidents George M. Harrison and Jacob Potofsky told the 90th annual conference of the British Trades Union Congress here.

Harrison, president of the Railway Clerks, and Potofsky, head of the Amalgamated Clothing Workers, attended as AFL-CIO fraternal delegates.

Delegates, shocked by racial violence in England, applauded Potofsky when he said American labor is "appalled" at the actions of Gov. Orval E. Faubus of Arkansas, and is moving to eliminate all vestiges of racial discrimination in U.S. unions.

A strong majority rejected a resolution proposing talks between the Intl. of Confederation of Free Trade Unions and the Communist-dominated World Federation of Trade Unions.

WFTU unions are "slaves of their own governments," TUC Gen. Sec. Vincent Tewson charged in opposing the resolution.

The TUC urged renewed efforts by heads of governments aimed at ending the manufacture and testing of nuclear weapons, and to bring about disarmament and study the effects of radioactivity.

Speaking frankly to British unionists as chairman of the AFL-CIO Intl. Affairs Committee, Harrison said the abandonment of nuclear arms or nuclear tests will not assure peace and security.

"Those who butchered Budapest and murdered Nagy, those who took away independence from 10 European countries, those who deny even their own people every democratic right," he said, "will not hesitate to use non-atomic weapons of mass destruction.

"Our peace will constantly be in danger until the problem of the underprivileged and the half-starved is solved," the railway leader added.

There has been much publicity on the doings of former Pres. Dave Beck and Pres. James R. Hoffa, of the Teamsters, in Great Britain, where honesty in union leaders is prized. Potofsky was applauded when he said the AFL-CIO "never will compromise with corruption."

JOURNEY TO INDIA

Joseph D. Keenan, IBEW International Secretary,
in The Electrical Workers' Journal, May 1959

When I was a boy on the west side of Chicago, I thought I saw the real face of poverty and want. I also thought I saw it when I was working in the deep South and, of course, very vividly during the height of the American Depression. But I never saw it so sharply as during my recent journey to Asia, where I journeyed to India, to Japan, to Hong Kong, Singapore, and the Philippines.

In India, thousands upon thousands of families are expected to carry out their entire cycle of life and death in the streets. In fact, in Calcutta, there is a Catholic religious order whose major duty is to retrieve the bodies of people who have starved to death and to provide them with a decent burial, or to make comfortable the last remaining moments of the dying. A visit to Calcutta's railroad station—

not far from the fashionable Chowringhee district—was an unforgettably appalling sight. Here, thousands of refugees live in filth and grinding poverty. A face of a mother peering out of the dark recesses of a dirty, burlap tent is haggard and unsmiling, although—in the miracle that is childhood — her little boy stands grinning broadly in the mud outside.

Meanwhile, the population of India—which is nearly 400,000,000 now — grows at the rate of 6,000,000 souls a year — outstripping rapidly the present rates of productivity.

For their part, the Communists—like the buzzards we saw on the road to Agra—are waiting to pick up the pieces. They have become an aggressive force throughout India. They already have political control of Kerala, an important Indian state. They are also moving in to take control of the Indian trade union movement. They are interested in plant or plantation, blue, white, or "no-collar" workers. What is worse, they are having alarming success in the very heart of India's industrial "Ruhr," which covers the great states of Bihar, West Bengal, and Orissa. At Jamshedpur, where the Tata Iron and Steel Works are located, the Communists participated in a violent and bloody strike last year.

Although the free trade union at the plant was able to withstand them, they still have a very strong foothold in that area. At Bhillai, where the Soviet Union is building and will operate a gigantic steel producing installation, the Communist union will have an even easier success. There is also a German and British "turn-key" operation.

In fact, a great deal is being said about the way in which Russians have been bending over backwards to be kind ot the Indian technicians and workers at the plant which they are constructing. They have developed an outstanding sense of good community relations which helps their cause.

(For example, when an Indian worker was injured, two of the Soviet technicians have been known to pick up the victim and carry him long distances rather than to wait for an ambulance.)

It is not only want, however, which helps the Communists advance their power and prestige among the workers. They appear to have unlimited supplies of funds. In West Bengal, we were told that three organizers, a jeep and 11 bicycles have appeared "as if by magic" for the use of Communist organizers. Coinciding with the much heralded arrival of India's Communist Party leader, S. A. Dange, visiting an industrial area, there also appeared a brand new jeep. In his speech to workers there, Comrade Dange—who is also Vice President of the Communist World Federation of Trade Unions—said that this jeep was a result of donations "from the workers themselves." Of course, the workers knew better.

Communist efforts are exerted not only among the unions but also among the intellectuals, the small businessmen, the women, and the millions who are members of the so-called "scheduled" castes or "untouchables." In particular their work among the high school and college graduates has been bearing fruit, for in this group there are legions of perpetually unemployed. Many young, eager students find that there is no way to use their training and talents. It is not at all surprising that they listen—in desperation—to the blandishments of Communist orators. The government worker is also a special target. Living on a fixed salary—in many cases fundamentally unchanged in a decade— he has many desires that outstrip his pocketbook.

Another fundamental fact that has to be reckoned with when one talks about India is its proximity not only to the Soviet Union but to Communist China. The recent explosion in Tibet brought this graphically to the attention of the world. But even apart from the Tibetan clash, there has been a continuous fear and awe in India as to what the Chinese are accomplishing in the realm of productivity and production. There is a real rivalry for leadership between India and China in this part of the world.

When I returned from India, I had a number of discussions with our own State Department officials concerning the urgency of India's need in the area of economic development. The Indians anxiously hope that the United States will finance a major steel plant in their own "Ruhr." In fact, AFL-CIO Pres. George Meany has written to Under Secretary of State of Economic Affairs C. Douglas Dillion, supporting this request which, if realized, would go part of the way in meeting a very real and dangerous economic challenge.

Strictly speaking, there are two dominant free trade unions which are trying desperately to change the prevailing picture. The Indian National Trade Union Congress, which is the largest free trade union group, has been accused of being too closely tied to the dominant Congress Party, and therefore the Government. The other and smaller free trade union organization, known as the Hind Mazdoor Sabha, has been accused of engaging in popular fronts with the Communists in certain areas. Both of them are faced with a growing Communist union, known as the All India Trade Union Congress.

A basic problem, I believe, is the slowness of the free trade union leadership to develop young "cadres" to take their places. While the Constitution has abolished the caste system—a fact vigorously applauded by the free trade union leadership—it is still often reflected in practice. Most of the Indian trade union leadership is drawn from the upper classes or castes. When we mentioned to an Indian trade union leader that it was essential to develop rank and file leadership, he said, "But they are illiterate."

I then related to him the story of the early days of organizing in the South when many new members of unions signed their name with an "X." They may have been illiterate, but they certainly knew where their best interests lay. In fact, provided with an opportunity, a number of the "X-signers" became local leaders.

Whatever is the case, I know there is a tremendous desire on the part of the rank and file to move forward, to have a voice in their future, and to walk with pride. There is also an eagerness to learn more about America and how our unions operate. There was a surprisingly large reserve of good will for us in India, and in fact, all of Asia.

I kept wondering whether it wouldn't be possible for some of our unions to find a few good solid, young organizers who would be willing to go to India, live and work among the people as "labor missionaries," and help budding Indian unionists to find their way.

This could be done under the banner of the ICFTU and through the International Trade Secretariats. That isn't to say that we have the only "prescription," or that our way of doing things is best for different countries with different backgrounds and culture. I am convinced, though, that there is much in common between India's struggling workers of today and the developing labor movement of America's recent past. We too had a tough, hard fight with the employers, as well as the Communists. And we won it on the basis of solid work and "fight." We won, above all, on the principle that we have a right to walk with the same dignity as our fellow man, and the opportunity to feed, clothe and educate our children. In any case, perhaps something very valuable will come out of the experience, both for India and for ourselves.

MALAYAN PLANTATION WORKERS UNION
A MILESTONE OF DEMOCRACY

Arnold Beichman in Electrical Union World
(Local 3, IBEW in New York), February 1, 1960

KUALA LUMPUR, MALAYA—On the second floor of the handsome, three story headquarters of the National Union of Plantation Workers (NUPW), there is a bronze plaque which reads:

"The AFL-CIO salutes the National Union of Plantation Workers for its successful and constructive efforts to improve social and economic conditions through democratic trade unionism."

The plaque was presented to the NUPW at the building's formal dedication one day before Malaya became an independent country. But years before that, this skillfully-led plantation union had demonstrated a vigor and independence which have made its name a byword in Asian trade unionism.

Within the Malayan Trades Union Council, the plantation union, led by Gen. Sec. P. P. Narayanan, a 37-year-old immigrant from South India, is outstanding because of its democratic base, its financial strength, its sound organizational methods and its successful opposition to totalitarian infiltration.

What makes the NUPW with its 180,000 members unique in this part of the world has been its insistence on combatting the evil of racial and cultural separatism which plagues labor movements in other parts of Asia and Africa.

This land of 6.6 million people is divided into three major racial groups: 49 per cent indigenous Malays, 36 per cent Chinese and 12 per cent Indians. Most of the workforce is employed on rubber plantations.

Each group not only has its own language but the Chinese have different dialects. The result is that most union officials must know at least two or three languages, including English which necessarily is the most common instrument of communication.

Union meetings are conducted in one of four languages with interpreters standing by to do consecutive translations. The union bi-weekly magazine is printed on its union-owned presses in Malay, Chinese, Tamil and English.

Because of this racial problem, the parent MTUC and the NUPW eschew partisan political activity. When the first parliamentary elections took place, trade union officials quite conspicuously stayed as far away from speech-making as possible. They endorsed no candidates or parties although most of them belong to the Malayan Labor Party, a socialist organization.

Union officials are barred from running for office or from openly supporting a political party. Of course, no powerful institution like the NUPW can, realistically, stay out of politics so that there is much behind-the-scenes activity. But with pro-Chinese parties, pro-Moslem parties and pro-Hindu parties and interracial parties, it would be suicide for unions with multi-racial memberships to become mere political adjuncts.

National union officials are elected by a mail referendum. Members who want to run for local, or estate, union offices must have been employed on the same estate for two consecutive years. A reason for this provision is that in two years, it is possible to uncover whether a candidate believes in democratic unionism or is a crypto-Communist.

Finances are controlled centrally and dues collections which come from all parts of the country's plantations are deposited within a week

of receipt. The NUPW also has an
education department, and a research division and is now thinking
of building schools, hospitals and
old-age homes and establishing university scholarships for children of
members. In the back of Narayanan's
mind is an idea for buying and operating a union-owned rubber estate
as a "model" for the industry.

Malaya still has a Communist
problem — the existence of several
hundred jungle terrorists who make
travel in some parts dangerous. But
that problem is under control.

The NUPW's real crisis is still to
be solved—whether racial, religious
and cultural differences can be kept
out of union politics, whether the
union's democratic structure can be
perverted by racialist demagogues.
The MTUC and the NUPW both
have had excellent beginnings
thanks to ICFTU aid and two able
British trade unionists, John Brazier
and Tom Bavin.

With such a foundation, Malayan
labor leaders have reasonable justi-
fication for optimism about the future.

INDONESIAN RAILMEN FIGHT REDS WITH AID OF CO-OP

Labor, January 2, 1960

A 37-year-old rail labor leader
from Indonesia, visiting in Washington this past week, told newsmen
how his railway union has established a unique cooperative project
to raise the living standards of railroad workers in Indonesia, and
thereby help head off Communism.

He is Buntuangin K. J. Tambunan,
secretary general of the Indonesian
Free Railway Workers Union, representing 29,000 employees of all
crafts on the government-owned Indonesian National Railway.

In the United States on a Rockefeller Foundation scholarship, he is
studying for a degree in labor-management relations at Cornell University.

Tambunan came to the nation's
capital as a guest of the Railway
Labor Executives Association. While
here he met with U. S. rail labor
leaders, toured the new Railway
Labor Building and visited at LA-
BOR's editorial, business and mechanical departments.

The story of the co-op came out
at a press conference: Five years
ago, Tambunan's union—the Indonesian Railway Workers Union —
known as PBKA—established a Social Welfare Cooperative Service to

provide goods and services for all of
the railroad's workers.

The co-op is no ordinary enterprise. Licensed by the Indonesian
government, it purchases and dis-
tributes food to workers and their
families, has a savings and loan
department, operates factories that
produce low-cost clothing and shoes,
has a clinic, and is planning a housing project.

Furthermore, the co-op has become a useful weapon in PBKA's
struggles against a rival Commu-
nist-led union, SBKA. This is of
vital importance in a nation that is
the scene of a day-by-day struggle
between the forces of freedom and
Communism.

Although the SBKA is still somewhat larger than PBKA, the latter
has been closing the gap rapidly,
having virtually doubled its membership since 1950.

Since the co-op is licensed by the
Indonesian government, it has received funds from our International
Cooperation Administration. Tambunan described this aid as "invalu-
able." ICA has also sent technicians
to Indonesia to help train co-op
leaders.

"This is the form of aid that is

needed not only in Indonesia but in other countries threatened by Communism, which thrives on poor living standards. It is helping us to help ourselves," Tambunan declared.

Tambunan described his union, a member of the International Transportworkers Federation, as an organization "completely free from any party domination."

OPERATING FREE TRADE UNIONS POSES PROBLEMS FOR JAPANESE

Ray Davidson in Oil, Chemical and Atomic Union News, January 12, 1959

From the American standpoint, Japanese unions are weak, disunited and quite confused about what course to pursue. There are more than 30,000 separate unions, most of them small, independent unions. Many are paper organizations, with little membership participation and support.

Most Japanese unionists appear to be aware of their weakness and appear very eager to create more strength and unity. For that reason, they ask endless questions about how we operate American unions.

As the Japanese unionists are the first to admit, their unions were handed to them by the American occupation and were not won by struggle, as were our unions. When the American occupation said "it is proper to have unions" and secured passage of laws guaranteeing the right to organize, Japanese workers hastily set up unions.

Management at that time was in no position to resist. So unions came into being. Most of them sprang up on a company basis, rather than on the industry-wide basis we know.

There is confusion in Japan between the economic and the political objectives of labor. We spent a great deal of time explaining that in America, political action and collective bargaining are two separate things, that in our view the first and basic job of the union is to negotiate with the boss for better wages and working conditions.

The larger Japanese union federation—Sohyo—has a strong political orientation and seems to put economic action in a secondary role. Its political complexion ranges from mildly socialist to Communist. The other major federation — Zenro — is more mindful of economic action and apparently wants to shape up more along American trade union lines. Most, if not all, of its leadership supports the Socialist party.

It should be explained that in Japan there are only two substantial parties — the so-called Liberal-Democrat which is conservative, and the Socialist which might be compared to the British Labor Party.

One thing which hinders Japanese efforts at progress is the paternalistic, almost feudalistic employment custom. Once a man has secured employment he never thinks of changing jobs.

On the other hand, a company seldom lays off a permanent employee because it would be a loss of face for the boss to admit he could not use his people.

This hesitation to lay off workers prevents intolerable unemployment in over-populated Japan.

The methods by which pay rates are established seem to have no relation to the work done. When a man goes to work, his salary is set on the basis of the amount of education he has, with apparently no regard for the job.

Each year he gets an increase, and in most cases there is also an increase if he gets married or has a child. Apparently job classifications are rare; a man simply does the work to which he is assigned. So a man working at one machine may make twice as much pay—if he is an old-timer — as a younger man working at an identical machine.

Aside from wages, there are other benefits. In many cases, company-owned housing is available at rentals far below the normal rate. There are free medical services. Many companies pay lump retirement benefits at age 55.

A major item of income for the Japanese worker is his semi-annual bonus, which the unions make a major negotiating point. Such bonuses sometime amount to the equivalent of three months pay each half year. But pay rates are so low that few luxuries or major consumer items can be bought from regular pay; appliances, luxuries, new clothes and vacations are usually financed from bonus money.

A well paid industrial worker receives the equivalent of $80 to $90 a month in salary and bonus—but prices vary and he lives distinctly better than one could live in America on that much money.

PHILIPPINE LABOR LAUDS USW MILITANCY

Steel Labor, December 1959

Luis R. Mauricio, Philippine labor leader who served as a guerrilla fighter during World War II, says that members of the United Steelworkers of America can be proud of their militancy.

"It has served to help labor groups in foreign lands in their own battles for decent wages and better living standards," said Mr. Mauricio who recently visited the USW International headquarters at Pittsburgh as guest of the State Department.

He has been impressed in his visit to America—his first—by the labor consciousness of a great majority of the people.

"We have laws patterned after the United States and have the counterpart of the Taft-Hartley and the National Labor Relations Board (NLRB)," Mr. Mauricio declared. "But we have no laws against secondary boycotts or picketing.

"We can be enjoined by the courts if a dispute concerns national interest — meaning the security of the state.

"We in the Philippines have had many strikes—mostly due to management's active resistance, aided and abetted by the courts. The only violence has occurred when police and the constabulary are sent in to break up peaceful strikes and picketing," the Philippine labor leader explained.

REPORT ON ISRAEL

Leon Stein in Justice, July 15, 1960

The group of U. S. labor paper editors who toured Israel last month as guests of Histadrut found that the organized labor movement of that nation plays a leading role in every phase of national life. This is in sharp contrast to the condition in our own homeland, where the world's largest labor federation must campaign continuously to influence reluctant legislators.

Uniquely, Histadrut — founded in 1920 — antedates by more than a quarter of a century the country in which it functions. This means that long before the state of Israel was established, Histadrut was building industry, stimulating agriculture, providing funds for these enterprises, setting up schools to train workers and their children, organizing transportation. It was, in fact, performing many of the functions of the state in anticipation of its creation.

This accounts for the laboristic spirit of Israel. Many of the same men and women now directing its government agencies are of the generation which, through Histadrut, helped pave the way for the establishment of Israel. Until now there has, for this reason, been very little of that kind of class conflict or union-government difficulties found in other countries.

It is startling to visit Histadrut's bank, to study, as we did, the vast construction programs undertaken by Solel Boneh, one of its divisions, to watch Histadrut members load Histadrut products on to Histadrut-operated ships.

But most surprising is the fact that, in many instances, Histadrut is both management and union in the same enterprise. For us, with the memory fresh in our minds of U. S. labor's code of ethics, this commingling of managerial and trade union functions was most challenging. In our own country, in recent years, organized labor has sought to make a clear separation of these functions.

But a higher ethical goal has been achieved in Israel through Histadrut. The labor movement in Israel makes no distinction between building the fledgling state and improving the welfare of its workers. The enterprises it creates and manages are under the control of the same workers who control its unions. The surplus or "profits" earned by these enterprises are not distributed to private businessmen. Instead, most of it is used to build new enterprises that the country needs.

We saw much in Israel that, on the other hand, reminded us of our own country. There is a drive to domesticate the desert which is so much like our own efforts to conquer our West that when we came coasting into Eilat, the southernmost city of Israel on the far side of its desert, it suddenly seemed like high noon in a western U. S. town, as if any minute the cowboys would come riding down from the hills.

Leaving Tel Aviv, at about the point where the two-lane highway begins, we suddenly found the street lined with automobile repair shops and spare parts stores. Grimy mechanics worked on the hybrid cars much as one sees them working in American repair stations, except that here they were often putting together parts from as many as a score of vintage makes. This is Israel —shreds and patches and ingenuity and irrepressible drive.

Among Israel's newcomers there are vast differences of culture, class and color, of language, custom and status. Some have come from lands where they lived in medieval squalor, others from centers of middle-European, twentieth century culture.

We remembered how in our own land, prejudice and segregation are still facts of national life. Then we saw in the Lachish region, running across the middle of Israel, a profound experiment in human rehabilitation. Here, a number of years ago, villages were created in advance to receive the newcomers and to make their transition to new patterns of life easier and, above all, to develop a national awareness that would override all the differences they brought with them.

In cities it was found that this process could be speeded by putting together newcomers in the factory and in apartment houses.

Following this pattern, they were also commingled on the Lachish cooperative agricultural settlements. But it didn't work. The relationships of newcomers under industrial discipline did not serve as a model for the relationship, traditionally tribal, of newcomers on the land.

The pattern on the land was changed and each of the Lachish centers was made ethnically homogeneous. This worked; departures from the farm dropped and production rose. And the challenge of integration, now proceeding rapidly, was met by Histadrut which helped create central villages, Kiryat Gat and Nehora—a kind of joint board —for the circle of cooperatives.

It is in these centers—with their Histadrut factories, Histadrut stores, Histadrut training centers, Histadrut health clinics—that an integration process far more complex than our own is taking place.

ICFTU MOBILIZES RESOURCES TO HELP BUILD FREE, STRONG UNIONS IN AFRICA

Arnold Beichman in AFL-CIO News, July 9, 1960

Brussels, Belgium — The world's free labor movement, the Intl. Confederation of Free Trade Unions, is streamlining itself for achieving as swiftly as possible its major goals within the next few years.

Primarily, the ICFTU will direct its resources to help organize strong unions in the newly-independent countries of Africa. Where such unions already exist in Africa, as well as Asia and Latin America, the ICFTU will utilize these resources to reinvigorate them so that they will be able not only to stand up against employers and unfriendly governments but also against the dangers of Communist subversion.

For the real and immediate job ahead in Africa is to beat the Communists to the punch. Both the Soviet Union and Communist China are already moving into Africa, pinpointing their ubiquitous target — unorganized, underpaid, hungry workers.

Under the leadership of Omer Becu of Belgium, the newly-elected secretary general of the ICFTU, a team of four assistant general secratries will be designated to carry out crucial assignments.

To finance this crusade, the stronger labor organizations in the ICFTU have pledged to try to raise $10 million between 1961 and 1963 for the Intl. Solidarity Fund for the specific purpose of building union strength in less developed countries.

Becu is expected to confer early in September with the AFL-CIO Committee on Intl. Affairs in regard to the future policies of the ICFTU. AFL-CIO Pres. George Meany and Vice Pres. Walter P. Reuther participated in the recent sessions of the ICFTU executive board in Brussels.

Among major decisions at the ICTFU sessions were:

• A warning against admitting Franco Spain to the North Atlantic Treaty Organization (NATO).

• Denunciation of the Cuban government for its rapid drift in the direction of communist totalitarianism. The ICFTU charged that the Communist Party today controls the Cuban Confederation of Workers and that anti-Communist labor leaders have been removed.

• To consider a call to the United Nations "to consider adopting economic sanctions against the Union of South Africa."

• A sharp attack against the Soviet Union for "torpedoing the Geneva conference on disarmament at precisely the moment when new proposals were to be presented." The statement appealed to the democratic powers "to continue to show their readiness to resume negotiations, either direct or sponsored by the United Nations" for disarmament.

• Asked member governments of the Organization of American States to break off diplomatic relations with the Dominican Republic and to consider "imposing effective economic sanctions" against the Trujillo regime.

• To send trade union missions to Indonesia, Japan, Turkey and the French-speaking part of Africa. The Turkish Trade Union Federation, Turk-Is, with about 800,000 members, has been affiliated to the ICFTU pending completion of formalities.

• Other new organizations admitted include those from Liberia, St. Vincent, Bahamas and Mauritius. The ICFTU now has 135 affiliates from 102 countries comprising a total membership of 56.5 million workers.

COMMON BOND

Emil Rieve, chairman of Textile Workers Executive Council, in Textile Labor, March 1957

In some ways a union card is almost as valuable to a traveler as a passport. I found this out during my recent AFL-CIO mission to Africa which began in the Gold Coast city of Accra. My trade union credentials opened the door to many memorable experiences and won for me a warm and friendly reception.

What brought me to Accra was the all-African trade union conference of the International Confederation of Free Trade Unions. I was there together with Secretary-Treasurer William F. Schnitzler to bring the greetings of the AFL-CIO to some 150 delegates assembled there from 17 African nations and to strengthen the bonds between them and us.

As you might expect, it was a colorful event; a few of the delegates even wore ceremonial native dress. But this was no gathering of men lately from the desert or the jungle. The African labor movement, embracing 1,200,000 workers, is led by intellectuals, with a liberal sprinkling of Oxford graduates, if you please. Although it is roughly where American labor was in the early Thirties, its delegates were at least one step ahead of us: They met in Accra's best hotel; we couldn't afford hotels in our early days.

The African delegates, of course, were not concerned with problems like Taft-Hartley although those from places like Kenya and Tanganika know full well what anti-union repression is. Their main concern, and properly so, appeared to be with freeing their members from colonialism and spurring economic development under democratic methods.

Accra itself was bubbling with the spirit of freedom while we were there; in fact, by the time you read this, the Gold Coast will be an autonomous part of the British commonwealth and will be known as Ghana.

We managed to see enough of the country to be assured that textile exports will be no threat to TWUA members for perhaps 50 years to come. Accra has only a few shops employing about 500 workers engaged in the weaving of coarse cloth used in native robes.

Its basic economy rests on cocoa and when the world price falls, so do this country's fortunes. In this respect, the Gold Coast is like an American community which depends solely on textiles.

We had several meetings with American-educated Prime Minister Kwame Nkrumah and found him to be a very staunch friend of labor. That's no surprise: During World War II he belonged to the National Maritime Union while serving in the U. S. Merchant Marine.

He has an enormous job cut out for him. While his country is on the move and is fired up by its new spirit of independence, there is great poverty, at least by American standards. Industrial development is limited by power shortages. Shipping facilities are primitive. Cargo is still brought in by small boats from ships anchored 304 miles off shore; all this in the shadow of a fort where slaves once were held for shipment abroad.

Democratic procedure, however, is not new to the Gold Coast. Many tribal customs are rooted in this tradition. Tribal chiefs, for instance, have always had to stand for election and can be removed by their followers.

We had an opportunity, too, to spend some time in Morocco, also a newly independent nation. Here we found a vigorous labor movement of more than 600,000 members with central headquarters in an eight-story building in Casablanca.

Of course, I made sure to visit the textile union and received a warm welcome. Their members are engaged mostly in the manufacture of silk and rugs. Moroccan unions resemble ours more closely than any others in Africa; in fact, they're organized on an industrial basis and function very much like ours.

Our hosts took us on an inland trip which included a traditional meal on a farm. Here we squatted, shoes off, on cushions and ate a variety of meats roasted on spits. We ate with our fingers, as is the custom, and the food was exceptionally good.

I mention this incident to underline the fact that a common bond exists between all unionists, no matter how great the difference between them in culture, history and tradition. Nowhere was this more evident than in that farmhouse near Casablanca.

BOURGUIBA LAUDS LABOR'S ROLE IN FIGHT FOR INDEPENDENCE

AFL-CIO News, December 1, 1956

American labor's vital role in helping Tunisia to achieve independence was given high praise by Prime Minister Habib Bourguiba, speaking at an AFL-CIO dinner in his honor.

Bourguiba expressed "the deepest appreciation" of the Tunisian people for the friendship and support manifested by American labor when Tunisia was striving to win its independence and since this victory was achieved. He recalled that the AFL-CIO rejected the charges of "communism" leveled against freedom-seeking Tunisians by those who wanted Tunisia to remain a colony.

The Tunisian leader praised the AFL-CIO for its democratic philosophy and its great practical achievements.

"The work of American labor gives us an image of what free labor can accomplish in a free country," he said.

Pres. George Meany, who had returned from South America only a few hours before, declared that the AFL-CIO will keep fighting for "the freedom of all states" and for free trade unionism in every country.

CHILEANS LEARN ABOUT THANKSGIVING

The Chronicle (Cincinnati), December 4, 1959

Eight Chilean trade unionists were introduced to fine old Yankee ways of feasting and celebrating last Thursday. They became acquainted with Thanksgiving Day, and they did it in Cincinnati—at the home of Mr. and Mrs. James P. Healy.

The South Americans are union printers. They arrived in the United States Sept. 27, under auspices of the Department of Labor and the International Cooperation Administration, to study industrial relations and development, and administration of trade unions.

Before arriving here they studied printing and publishing installations in Atlantic City, New York, Chicago and Kingsport and Knoxville, Tenn.

But Thursday they devoted their attention to turkey, trimmings—and even cranberries—at the home of Mr. Healy, team manager of the exchange visit.

A former officer of the Cincinnati Stereotypers, Healy speaks little Spanish, the language of Chile. So just about all the conversation was through interpreters.

Friday the party visited and interviewed officers of Local No. 3, International Typographical Union, in the Brotherhood of Railway Clerks Building. They discussed with Frank Gorsler, president, union matters including area wage rates, contract negotiations, grievance procedures, fringe benefits.

They inquired particularly about Federal labor laws and the effect on union operations. They were impressed with the civic role played by labor here in community affairs such as support of United Appeal, Sunday observance, drive against smut, aid to juveniles, and the recent construction by building trades of a recreational hall for homeless boys.

TRAINING PROGRAM FOR LATIN AMERICAN UNIONISTS WINDS UP

The CWA News, December 1959

The Communications Workers of America and four other U. S. communications unions three months ago embarked on a unique trade union experiment, a people-to-people training institute where 16 young Central and South American trade union leaders have been trained to do a better job for the workers they represent in their respective countries.

The program — carried out at CWA's Front Royal, Va. institute— was designed to 1) strengthen the ideological position of communications workers in Latin America, and of the Latin-American labor movement as a whole; and 2) provide labor unions in this area with qualified individuals, fully trained in all

aspects of trade unionism, prepared to plan, direct, and carry out trade union education.

They graduated as full-fledged union instructors, equipped with projectors, screens, charts and visual materials of many kinds (with battery-operated machines for areas where electricity is not available).

The 90-day study and observation period in the United States is to be followed by nine months of work in their own countries. Leaves of absence have been arranged and the 16 instructors will be on the road for nine months following their U. S. stay.

In this way, secondary union leadership throughout the communications field in Latin America can have the opportunity to learn and contribute to a stable, aggressive democratic trade union movement that can contribute to the general public welfare while serving the best interest of the workers.

Defining the purpose of the course, CWA Pres. Beirne said:

"It is to help you help yourself and the people you are privileged to represent through your trade unions.

"We would not be so foolish as to tell you that we have all the answers to all problems. Rather, what we are going to try to do through this program is acquaint you with some of the trade union skills and techniques that we have found effective in our union education programs.

"We will show you how we have trained our staff personnel, local officers and stewards in the art of building a union. Each of you has different problems in each of your countries. However, we all share some problems in common."

ROMUALDI REPORTS ON LATIN AMERICAN RIOTS

The Machinist, May 22, 1958

Serafino Romualdi, Latin American representative of the AFL-CIO, accompanied Vice Pres. Richard M. Nixon on the first part of his recent tour of Latin America.

Back at AFL-CIO headquarters last week, Romualdi was interviewed by THE MACHINIST.

The big question: What was behind the outrages perpetrated on Vice President Nixon in Peru and Venezuela, and attempted in Colombia?

Romualdi was positive about part of the answer.

In none of the demonstrations against the United States did any Latin American unions take part, nor did any union officers take part so far as anyone knows.

In Uruguay the Vice President met with a delegation of union officers without incident.

In Paraguay, Mr. Nixon met with officials of the labor organization affiliated with the International Confederation of Free Trade Unions. The discussion was friendly.

In Bolivia, the Trotskyite element among the union leaders boycotted the meeting with Mr. Nixon. All other union elements were represented and reported a cordial and fruitful discussion.

In Ecuador a scheduled meeting was canceled but not because of any hostile labor sentiment.

In Colombia, Mr. Nixon presented the labor movement with a library of 300 books about trade union and collective bargaining subjects.

In Venezuela, on the night of the disorders at Caracas, Dr. Romulo Betancourt, leader of the Democratic Action Party to which the overwhelming majority of union officers belong, took to the radio to express his regret publicly.

"In understanding the situation in Venezuela," Romualdi points out, "it is necessary to understand that the Communists have the strongest influence among the student bodies in the universities. Part of the reason is that these young intellectuals are plagued with unemployment, economic insecurity and low salaries."

During the Jiminez regime, hundreds of students were arrested and tortured by the secret police.

"While this was taking place, the United States Government showed uncalled-for friendship for the dictator and President Eisenhower even gave him a medal for his contribution to democracy," Romualdi declared.

"The demonstrations against Vice President Nixon are a harvest of the bad fruit of years of neglect in Latin America."

INTERNATIONAL LABOR ORGANIZATION FIGHTS POVERTY AND INJUSTICE THROUGHOUT WORLD

C. Edmund Fischer in The Advance, March, 1957

"We must change the fate of these men. We must rescue them from degradation; we must combat and conquer their wretchedness . . . We cannot fail."

Thus read a report by the International Labor Organization about 7 million Indians who barely exist in the cold, wind-swept Andes mountains of South America. It was a report that very well could have been written about hundreds of millions of other impoverished people throughout the world, for most of the globe's two billion inhabitants are ill-fed, poorly-clad, and miserably-housed.

For 38 years, ever since its founding in 1919, ILO has wrestled with social injustice on the premise that world peace depends on the elimination of poverty; that so long as there are down-trodden peoples there will be unrest. In brief, ILO has sought to raise the living, the health and educational standards through international agreements and technical assistance.

Seventy-seven nations comprise ILO at this time. Although we did not join until 1934, prominent Americans like labor leader Sam Gompers and Prof. James T. Shotwell played leading roles in its formation and affiliation with the League of Nations. When the League was dissolved, ILO continued as an independent organization. It is now a specialized agency of the United Nations.

A unique feature of this UN agency is its annual policy-making conference which is made up of four delegates from each country: two from the government and one each from labor and industry. In the U. S., the AFL-CIO nominates the labor delegate and the U. S. Chamber of Commerce and National Association of Manufacturers jointly nominate the industry delegate.

ILO, with principal headquarters in Geneva, has a permanent staff of approximately 700, whose tasks include collecting and disseminating information, research, and publishing reports and studies of concern to the ILO.

In addition, the ILO office has several technical divisions whose experts provide advice and assistance to member nations on such items as labor relations, work standards, industrial safety, manpower, social security, etc.

(Incidentally, when the Federal Government and Congress were working up the Social Security Law in the 1930's, the ILO provided technical assistance based on studies of similar laws in other nations.)

Just how successful has the international labor body been in its quest to eliminate hardship and deprivation?

Needless to say, there is still much poverty in the world. And there will be for some time to come. Yet, there has been progress, principally through technical assistance, a phase of its activities on which the ILO is placing increasing emphasis.

The 7 million Indians, mentioned at the outset, are beneficiaries. Through the labor organization and several other UN specialized agencies, these people are being resettled, are being taught new skills and improved farming methods. They are learning to read and write, and they are being shown good health practices. Their standards are being raised.

Or take the case of orange picking in Israel. A small matter? True, but because experts assisted the Israel Productivity Institute double the amount of oranges are being picked, and an industry has been helped.

There is the example of an ILO productivity team creating increases of from 100 to 200 per cent in bus manufacture and reconditioning in India, and raising output in a Pakistani textile mill by 34 per cent.

These illustrations do not even scratch the surface of the hundreds of assistance programs that have taken place, or are now underway. These projects have a special meaning for every American worker. As the result of an improving economy in their own lands, the workers abroad will, in the end, have more money to spend. They will be able to go into the market and buy things they never before could afford. Some of these items will be made in the United States.

Moreover, the factory and shop owners, seeing their own industries growing, will need more machinery, more tools, more raw materials. American industry will benefit; so will employment.

While technical assistance is on the upswing, ILO works in other fields aimed at eradicating child labor, unemployment and sickness and injury resulting from hazardous jobs, and at providing a universal maximum work week, equal pay for equal work for women, more harmonious labor-management relations and a host of other items to improve the welfare of workers and their families.

ABOUT ATOMS FOR PEACE

*Gordon M. Freeman, IBEW president, in The Electrical Workers' Journal,
September 1958*

Good will is not just a gift bestowed on man with no effort on his part, nor is peace. They must be achieved by taking thought against the morrow, by looking deep into himself and his neighbor with the spirit that has been at the heart of all the world's major religions.

The best hope to counter the threat of war is the will of the old Adam to control himself and to meet his fellow man with good will in the "parliament of man," organized for living instead of for killing.

It is just 13 years since the first atomic bomb burst on Hiroshima. Last month in Geneva, 5,000 scientists from 67 nations gathered to discuss what progress the world has made toward harnessing the atom for peaceful uses. It was not an optimistic conference. The collective judgment of the group was that putting atomic energy to practical, economic use throughout the world is far from imminent. There are still many difficult technological and engineering problems to be overcome before atomic energy, particularly to generate electricity, will be wide-

ly practical and profitable.

We would never dare to differ with the 5,000 learned scientists in their evaluation of the progress of atomic energy to date. We would, and do dare to differ with them, and the news reporters, that the atomic energy outlook is "sobering" and "pessimistic."

It is only three years ago that the first Atoms-for-Peace Conference was held, following which the secrets of atomic energy were first made public and widely shared. It's only three short years since we first began to "beat our atomic swords into nuclear plowshares." We have come a very long way in those three years. This year, 1958, the United States put its full-scale reactor into operation at Shippingport. It has seven more reactors with less capacity in other sections of the country. The universal problem facing all nations in the matter of atomic energy is to reduce the cost of nuclear power so that it will be competitive with electricity generated by the conventional fossil fuels.

By common estimate of the scientists, it will take at least another decade before nuclear energy becomes economical in the large countries, and perhaps 20 years in some of the small, underdeveloped nations of the world which need help so desperately.

The world had to wait thousands of years for man to open the secret door to atomic energy. That door was opened in a burst of destruction. Now only 13 short years later, we have atomic power plants in opperation. We have atomic-powered submarines running under the North Pole. We have the world's first nuclear-powered merchant ship, the "Savannah," under construction. Radio-isotopes are coming into common use in industry, agriculture and medical research throughout the world.

Of course, for the peace of the world and the good of all, the more quickly atomic power can come to the power-poor nations of the earth, the better.

But after waiting thousands of years to use atomic energy at all, it seems to us we have come a long way in 13. It does not seem a hardship either, that another decade or so must pass before nuclear generation of electricity becomes practical.

Our Government and our science can play a vital role in stepping up our atomic programs, and many of our citizens can help.

THE NEW ATOM AND THE OLD ADAM

The Dubuque Leader, December 21, 1956

Peace on earth and good will toward men seem a bit shaky this year.

This is hardly surprising. There have been wars and rumors of wars since before the dawn of recorded history. But it may be that our awareness of the danger is a good sign. A false sense of security in the past has too often been the calm which preceded the sudden and terrible destruction of war.

There is an ominous character to the most deadly weapons ever known to man, the newly split atoms releasing energy for history's most deadly bombs—uranium, hydrogen, and what have you. Yet it is conceded that the very deadliness of these new weapons may shock humanity into realizing that civilization and war cannot both forever exist on an ever shrinking planet.

The moral awareness that war must be prevented whenever and wherever possible sprang into official being the same year—1945— that the atom bomb was thrust upon mankind with all its awful powers of destruction. Man had learned to utilize the new atom at the same time that he awoke to the need for control of the old Adam who has been at the bottom of all wars— himself.

Nation upon nation has depended in the past upon armaments and alliances, only to bring more war upon the world. Many a country which thought itself the best prepared or supposed itself aided by the best allies has come to ruin.

The climate of war has always been one in which the "good guys" triumphed over the "bad guys." Those on one side were all good, those on the other all bad. At last this childish notion may be supplanted by one in which wrong actions are bad, regardless of who does them, and in which the community acts—not the "enemy."

A world which long relied upon organizing for war has now found hope for the future in organizing for peace through the United Nations.

V
Looking Ahead

EDITORS' NOTE

Labor newsmen are familiar with the realities of the market-place, the legislative chamber and the collective bargaining table. They have seen greatness and meanness in every phase of our national life.

Few union editors would claim that the labor movement is the repository of all virtue. Yet probably all would say that, taken as a whole, American trade unions are this country's most stead-fast, major force for progress.

From time to time, the labor press articulates the great social thrust of working people and their institutions. Labor editors know that the core meaning of our national life lies in that senti-ment of Walt Whitman: America is a continuing experiment in how much democracy a society can bear.

As the following articles reveal, trade unions will continue to contribute measurably to this "experiment," to our national purposes, our current history and our future.

18 'FOR THE GOOD OF ALL AMERICA'

POWER — FOR WHAT?

AFL-CIO Pres. George Meany in Kentucky Labor News, September 26, 1959

There's a great deal of talk these days about the "power" of labor. Newspaper editorials and speeches by industrial tycoons emphasize the growing membership of unions, the increase in their financial resources and their developing political potential. The public is led to believe that the trade union movement has become "too powerful."

Too powerful for whom? Too powerful for what?

Are they talking in terms of exploiting the many for the benefit and enrichment of a few? Certainly not! The truth is just the other way around.

Those who have enjoyed monopolistic power over the nation's industrial life naturally fear and resent having to deal with labor on a basis of equality. And, by the same token, the politicians who serve business interests look with alarm at the political education programs conducted by the trade union movement. They are not happy about the political enlightenment of the voters. They know their control is jeopardized when the citizens of our country go to the polls in record-breaking numbers on Election Day.

I see no harm in power, if it is power dedicated to human values, if it is power for good—and that is what the trade union movement seeks.

Obviously, concentration of power in the hands of a few can be dangerous to the general welfare. But when unions become more powerful, it means that the people of this country become more powerful. It is merely a practical application of the basic principle of democracy.

Our forefathers meant it to be that way. They believed that the enjoyment of freedom depended upon rule by the great masses of citizens. They were against monopoly of power by the wealthy. They were against monopoly of power by the military. They were against monopoly of power by the aristocracy. They were convinced that the free way of life could be safeguarded only when power over the economic, social and political life of our country was shared by the many. That is exactly what the trade union movement has tried over the years to bring about.

Let us look back a bit to the time when the trade union movement had very little power but consistently used what power it possessed to advance causes of benefit to all the American people.

When Samuel Gompers and his associates lobbied in the state legislatures and the national Congress for an 8-hour day, was their purpose to degrade the worker? When they campaigned for universal free education, was their objective to exploit the worker? When they battled for workmen's compensation laws were they trying to injure the interests of the American people? When they fought for union recognition and free collective bargaining, were they trying to create new millionaires at the expense of those who worked for wages?

Or was it to make life better for the worker, to obtain for him a larger share of the wealth he helped to produce, to give him greater purchasing power so that American industry and American agriculture could find a ready market for their rapidly growing productive capacity?

The record shows—beyond contradiction—that from its very inception the trade union movement has consistently used whatever power it had to raise the American standard of living, to promote the interests of all the American people and to enhance the power and prestige of the nation as a whole.

Yes, the record is clear. It proves that the trade union movement has always been in the forefront of all action—whether in the shop, in the community or at national and international levels—to obtain a better break for the average citizen. It has been an agency not only for democracy, but for democratization. Because of union efforts the immigrants who came to our shores learned that America was really a haven for the oppressed of the world. They learned through their unions to speak the language and to appreciate the blessings of freedom. They discovered that here in America men and women could stand together and fight for justice and progress with reasonable hope of success.

America's emancipation from isolationism was won the hard way—and the trade unions made a significant contribution toward the development of a more mature international policy.

We did not shrug our shoulders, as some did, and say it was none of our business if dictators engaged in wholesale murder and the degradation of humanity in other parts of the world. We insisted it was our business. We saw the inherent danger to our free way of life, whenever freedom was destroyed in other lands.

There was a time when many Americans applauded Mussolini for getting the trains to run on time in Italy. But it took an American trade unionist of Italian descent like Luigi Antonini, to awaken our people to the outrages committed by the Fascists. In like manner, labor led the opposition in America to the atrocities of Hitler and the Japanese war lords. We recognized them as enemies of all freedom. No group in America, from the very beginning, has been more adamant in its opposition to Communism and more active in resisting Soviet infiltration than the American labor movement.

Labor's influence in foreign affairs has not been merely negative. We have fought for justice and fair play for oppressed peoples everywhere. After the war, we helped the workers of Germany re-establish their free trade unions as a bulwark of democracy, social justice and peace. We have played a vital role in rallying support for the Hungarian and Algerian peoples in their struggle for national freedom. We are proud of the fact that we have been able to extend a helping hand, through Histadrut, to the people of Israel.

Colonialism is now a dangerous anachronism. We of labor believe that target dates should be set for ending it in Africa, Asia and wherever else it still exists. The perpetuation of colonialism by any segment of the free world merely plays into the hands of Communist imperialism.

Along with freedom, labor relies implicitly on the preservation of peace as the only sure road to human progress.

Thus far, the cold war has proved a heavy burden to all of us. But the price of our national defense program cannot be considered too high as long as a hot war can be avoided. Nor can we hesitate to provide the military and financial aid required to sustain our allies and to prevent underdeveloped nations from going down to oblivion behind the Iron Curtain. America has always extended a helping hand to those who wish to be free and are willing to defend their freedom and American labor whole-heartedly supports this policy.

It is rather strange, in view of

labor's constructive record, that in this day and age there are still people who cling to the notion that America would be better off without trade unions.

Those who keep insisting that unions are "too powerful" actually want to render unions powerless—powerless to impede big business monopolies, or to seek further improvement in the American way of life.

In this effort to destroy the trade movement, our opponents have enlisted—at a fee, of course—a small army of professional promoters. They have organized a widespread campaign to enact state "Right-to-Work" laws which guarantee no rights to anyone but seek to wreck union security.

These "pitch men" have now come up with another gimmick to exploit. They say businessmen must get more active in politics, learn more about it and do more about it. As if this were something new!

When I was a young boy, workers trying to earn a living encountered "pink slip" days which came around each year just before election time. The workers were told, by way of a pink slip inserted in their pay envelopes, that if a certain party or a particular candidate did not win, the factory would shut down the day after election. This form of intimidation, along with heavy campaign contributions, comprised the main expressions of business political activity. In fact, some businessmen made contributions to both parties, just to make certain they would be in good shape no matter who won.

Yet certain spokesmen now say business must enter the field of politics to meet the "threat" of big labor. Well, all I can say is: "Welcome. Come on in. The water is fine."

The more they get in with their financial resources, the greater interest will be stirred up among workers. Perhaps it will help us eventually to succeed in our efforts to encourage all workers to perform

their duty as citizens by exercising their right to vote.

And when we get down to such a contest between workers and big business we will do all right, because there happens to be a few more of us than there are of them.

The big propaganda stick our opponents are using against us, of course, is the exposure of corruption in some segments of the labor and management field. They feel this is too good an opportunity to let pass. They are hungry for the kill. They propose to use the exposure of the sins of a very small minority as a means to bring about the punishment of all labor. They are going all out for the enactment of legislation, not to meet the corruption problem, but to hamstring the labor movement as a whole and render it powerless.

The trade union movement met this problem head-on at the meeting of the AFL-CIO General Board in April 1958. We pointed out we had taken effective and rigorous steps to clean house. We said we would go further and cooperate with Congress in the drafting of legislation to make it more difficult for anyone to misuse union funds.

Yes, we volunteered to cooperate in writing such legislation. But, we also said in April 1958 that we will not accept punitive legislation designed to hurt the trade union movement under the guise of a law against corruption.

This was a truly significant action. Here was a group of private citizens saying to government: "We will assist you in writing legislation to regulate and govern certain of our actions." Where else in American life is there a parallel? What business organization has ever done such a thing? And the record shows that business is not immune to sin nor free of racketeering elements.

What other group in American life, business or professional, would, in the interests of morality, ethics and self-respect, cut off 10 per cent of its membership and income as a self-enforcing action against those responsible for corruption?

The AFL-CIO did that very thing by expelling organizations whose leadership was found to be tainted.

Where is the business or banking association which has shown equal courage under similar circumstances? Show me any business organization which has set up a moral code for its membership which matches the Ethical Practices Codes adopted by the AFL-CIO.

Labor still stands on the position it took in April 1958. We are still willing to cooperate—and we have cooperated—in drafting anti-corruption legislation, but we still make the reservation, and we will not withdraw it, that we will not accept punitive or anti-labor legislation as part of this package.

Now, as in the past, labor must continue to fight for its very existence as a free association of free men and women. We still have to fight for the right to conduct our own business in our own way, for the right to make our maximum contribution as free citizens to our free society.

In America, we have a system of government which, while not perfect, has proved itself to be of greater benefit to its citizens than anything else yet devised by the mind of man. At a time when that system faces its greatest challenge, when its very existence is threatened by totalitarian aggression, you would think that the mutual interests of free labor and free management would draw them together. Yet we find American business mounting a furious attack upon the trade union movement which has proved a bulwark of defense to the free enterprise system.

This is typical of the short-sighted, bull-headed policy of big business through the years. Perhaps there are some aspects of life in the Soviet Union that appeal to them. Under the Red Flag there are no strikes, no slow-downs, no absenteeism, no labor problems at all. But our employer friends should realize that the Russians don't have any profit problems either.

Our road is clear. Our ideals are untarnished. Our record means something to us. We know where we are going, what our objective is. Ours is the very simple objective, in a democratic society, of securing for the workers a better and ever better share of the wealth of the nation which they help to create.

And we are going to pursue that objective with all the strength we possess.

When our opponents talk about the power of labor, their exaggerations carry little conviction. Our power is not the power of money. It is the right of free men and women in a free society to withhold their labor in the interests of justice.

Yes, the right to strike is labor's ultimate power—a power which we cannot be deprived of without fracturing the entire democratic structure of our nation. In these modern days we don't like to use the strike weapon unless we are forced to do so. That doesn't mean we have forgotten how to use it. If employers refuse to bargain in good faith and think the time has come to get tough with labor, they will learn this truth to their sorrow.

We also have a basic political power—the power of numbers. The 17 million organized workers of America, together with their families and friends, constitute a significant number of votes in any election.

It is only since 1947 that labor has entered the political area in an organized way. We learned then, from a very simple demonstration by Congress in enacting the Taft-Hartley Act, that the gains and achievements we had won over the years could be taken away from us overnight by legislation. So the decision by labor to go seriously into the political action field was really made not by the leaders of labor but by the architects of anti-labor legislation.

We are determined to pursue our

activity in this field with all earnestness. I will concede quite frankly that an effective political organization cannot be built in a day or a year. But we decided in 1947 that we had to get into this political business and stay in it until we succeeded in organizing a permanent, progressive and successful program and we are making steady progress toward that goal. In view of the increasing opposition from big business, I would predict even more rapid progress by labor's political arm in the years to come.

Using our economic strength, our political strength and any other weapon that we have the right to use, we are going to continue labor's efforts to make America a better place for all its citizens—not merely union members. Yes, even to provide a better and more stable climate for constant prosperity for employees and management.

Labor wants America to become more than an idealistic symbol for all the people of the world who believe in human freedom. We want to prove to them and to ourselves that we can make democracy work.

It is our intention to continue the fight against racial and religious discrimination until this ugly blot on our good name is eliminated.

We are going to carry on our drive to wipe out poverty and human misery not only in America but everywhere in our world.

We will use all the power and influence we have to see to it that the great scientific discoveries and inventions of our time are used not for the purpose of destruction, but for the enrichment of human life.

Let no one mistake or distort our purpose. Labor has no desire to take over America or make over America. We are not out to push any one else down or around. What we seek is a balance of power in the economic and political life of the nation. Only thus can the proper atmosphere be created for the gradual but steady improvement in the standards of the American people.

In pursuit of our objectives, we may employ new methods from time to time but we will never depart from the democratic principles laid down for us by the founders of the trade union movement 75 years ago.

Yes, labor has gained in power in America. We arc proud of the way it has been used. We hope in the years to come that we will achieve greater power to work for the good of all America.

TRENDS IN COLLECTIVE BARGAINING PROPOSALS

Peter Henle in AFL-CIO News, July 27, 1957

Some of us in the trade union movement hear, from time to time, the question, "Are unions running out of collective bargaining proposals?"

To those familiar with collective bargaining, this question seems on a par with such other questions as "Are the Yankees running out of pennant-winning ball players?" or "Is Milwaukee running out of beer?"

The answer to this question is "No." Unions *will* try to win continued improvements.

This is assured by the nature of

our economy and by the outlook of the American people. Americans don't believe in resting on yesterday's laurels or yesterday's living standards. They think in terms of a continually improving standard of living.

However, when this question about bargaining proposals is raised, the questioner usually is wondering not whether unions are running out of *demands* but whether they are running out of *new ideas*.

At a recent Conference of the AFL-CIO Industrial Union Department, Pres. George Meany was asked to talk on "A Labor Philosophy for Today." He explained simply that "the philosophy of the trade union movement of 75 years ago is good enough for today." He also pointed out: "Of course, we have to adjust our methods; we have to adjust our actions and our approach to our problems."

Most new union goals normally will not be totally new but old demands in new forms and with new refinements—simply because our rapidly changing society creates new problems, new needs, new concepts.

Almost all union bargaining proposals have certain common objectives: higher wages—increased purchasing power—to provide a rising standard of living; increased leisure time; seniority and protection against arbitrary treatment and against emergencies and financial strains; and good working conditions in terms of health, safety, cleanliness and convenience.

Most future proposals will be on old-fashioned lines, focusing on wage increases and liberalizations of existing benefits.

Actually, the combination of old-fashioned gains — 2 more paid holidays here, a 10-cent hourly increase in wages there, another week's vacation, a broadened medical-coverage plan—add up in several years to a dramatic cumulative change. Such gains have truly been reshaping American living patterns of leisure, buying power, medical care and income stability.

It is easy to lose overall perspective. A disproportionate share of publicity may be given to the more novel demands, those with some new twist, without recognizing the cumulative significance of familiar bargaining gains.

Each union has to decide for itself what it will seek and when, in terms of its own practical situation. A proposal adopted by one union may well be rejected by another.

With this in mind, let us examine some union proposals likely to receive major attention at the bargaining table over the next 5-10 years.

1. Continuation of emphasis on winning sizable wage increases commensurate with the increase in the economy's productivity.

Indeed, wage increases must require almost the full attention of many unions; since they operate in low-wage industries the worker's first concern must be to boost his living standards.

How high can we expect wages to go? There is no reason to put any upper limit on the economy's efficiency, or on the nation's living standards which such efficiency makes possible. If we assume an annual increase in productivity of three per cent, this should permit real wages to increase by over one-third in ten years and to double at the end of 25 years. There is no reason why over this period this nation cannot utilize its growing productivity to abolish the remaining areas of poverty in this country.

2. There will be union proposals to make up for gaps and inadequacies in benefit programs to meet the hazards of sickness, old-age and unemployment.

In the last decade some type of program has been negotiated in these areas by almost all unions. In total effect, these benefit programs have wrought a peaceful revolution in American theory and practice in the welfare field. They have been a notable demonstration of the American pragmatic approach to human problems.

Faced with federal and state legislatures reluctant to pass, or hostile to welfare legislation, unions have attempted through bargaining to win for their members what they were unable to convince the government to provide for all citizens.

In so doing, trade unions have helped to prod the legislatures into making improvements in welfare programs for all.

Initially, union bargaining efforts in the welfare field put first things first: They sought, primarily, protection for their members against sickness, old age and unemployment. Follow-up demands in later negotiations usually have bolstered the skimpy starting plan, but still have not attained desirable, comprehensive standards.

Today additional experience with existing health and welfare plans points up shortcomings, and unions are shifting their emphasis to fill out existing plans and extend them to meet needs not previously reached.

Unions are becoming increasingly interested not simply in benefit payments but rather in *medical service,* including preventive care, under which a worker can meet all his family health needs.

In the field of retirement and old-age needs, experience with pension plans negotiated in recent years is leading to a number of new emphases. Here are at least four areas worth noting:

Unions are putting on the bargaining table demands for vesting provisions to permit workers to take with them accumulated pension credits if they leave a company before retirement age. Then, at retirement age, they would be entitled to whatever pension their credits had earned, regardless of subsequent employment.

2. Pensions for disability as well as for old-age have been a trend in recent years.

3. Medical protection after retirement is another need moving to the fore. Workers who have been protected by a negotiated health and welfare plan suddenly find this safeguard against economic disaster is gone when they retire. At retirement age, health insurance is extremely costly, if available at all. Unions are moving to meet this problem both in the legislative and the collective bargaining areas.

4. Protection for widows is also attracting attention. Union-won pensions have generally ended with the death of the retired worker, cutting abruptly the income of the surviving widow to the reduced level provided by the social security law. Continuation of existing private pensions to widows for an extended period is often a serious need.

In the field of protection against employment instability, a major forward step has been taken with the negotiation in the auto, rubber, steel and other industries of supplemental unemployment benefit plans. These plans protect workers against sudden drastic slashes in their income as a result of unemployment. They provide payments to laid-off workers to supplement their state unemployment compensation.

These plans, which do not yet provide a desirable degree of protection, vary widely in details. In fact, far more variety in union efforts to deal with the hazards of unemployment can be expected than in dealing with the hazards of old-age or illness.

Along with supplementary unemployment benefits have come negotiated savings plans. Some unions will give savings plans increased attention in collective bargaining, although these plans could only be feasible in relatively high wage industries where workers might persuade management to contribute to savings funds available for any emergency.

In any event, this central theme of a cushion for workers against layoff and other emergencies will receive continuing attention in bargaining.

3. There will be bargaining proposals centering around a demand for increased leisure.

Increasing productivity is enabling large parts of the economy to produce or handle more in less time. With less time—or fewer workers—needed, it will be possible to reduce hours of work without any reduction in pay.

In one sense, proposals for shorter hours are hardly new. "Shorter hours" was a rallying cry for unions well over a century ago. But with industrial and social progress, the demands of old for a 9- and then an 8-hour day and for a 5-day week now become, in a different setting, the demands for a 6-hour day or a 4-day week today or tomorrow.

Some unions may seek a cut in the number of hours per day, looking toward the 6-hour day. This has already been done in the ladies garment industry, where well over 400,-000 union members have had their workday reduced from 8 to 7 hours without reduction in total pay, and in the printing industry, where the unions have negotiated reductions to 7½, 7¼ or 7 hours a day.

Other unions, however, may put top priority on reducing the number of workdays per week from 5 to 4. Each possibility involves many detailed scheduling and other problems which would have to be tailored to the requirements of the individual company or industry.

In the move toward more leisure time, other unions may put more stress, not on reduction of the standard daily or weekly hours, but on reducing the hours through substantially longer vacations, or an increased number of holidays.

One possible development is to add holidays, not to celebrate historic occasions, but because they would fit the desires of workers for longer breaks from work and would suit the production schedules of the employer. There is a noticeable trend toward making the Friday following Thanksgiving, Memorial Day and the Fourth of July a holiday.

At any rate, we should not expect or hope for uniformity in the ways in which bargaining will provide increased leisure. There may well be many workers who will prefer more pay to more leisure.

4. There will be new bargaining proposals arising because of changes in the economy, proposals to meet problems posed by shifts in the character and structure of industry.

Many unions will develop new bargaining programs because of (A) the rapid pace of technological innovation, particularly automation; (B) shifts in geographical location of industry, as a result of plant migration and business mergers; and (C) changes in the workforce, particularly the relative increase in white collar and technical workers.

Changing technology and automation pose real issues for collective bargaining. New questions of transfer policy, retraining, and seniority are bound to come to the fore. Changes in job classification and wage structures are inevitable. To a large extent, collective bargaining has always been handling these issues but the new technology is bound to raise new applications of old formulas. Indeed, it may require entirely new bargaining proposals.

Increasing relocation of industry presents special problems for a number of unions. When a company shuts down a plant in one community to produce in another area, the blow is a hard one for the workers in the abandoned community. More unions are turning their attention to the protection of workers against the possibility of such shutdowns.

In addition, the increasing proportion of workers required in skilled or technical work may lead to new emphasis in bargaining. A new emphasis on skill wage differentials may become apparent in some negotiations.

Because all the foregoing may indicate a rather full schedule for future collective bargaining, I would call attention to the fact that some controversial questions do fade as issues between labor and management. For example, union security has been a very hotly disputed question. Today, however, over 80 per cent of all collective bargaining agreements recognize the principle of union security, and many major corporations which previously opposed granting the union shop have recently accepted it.

SETTING NEW SIGHTS FOR ORGANIZING
THE UNORGANIZED

AFL-CIO Sec.-Treas. William F. Schnitzler
in AFL-CIO News, August 27, 1960

The trade union movement is setting its sights on new advances in organization during the coming year.

We believe that conditions will be auspicious for further gains in union membership:

1. From all indications, the political climate will be improved. While the 1960 campaign is just getting under way, candidates endorsed by the AFL-CIO appear to have the edge. All the public opinion polls point to the conclusion that America wants more liberal, more progressive and more active government.

2. At the same time, anti-labor forces are in retreat. The trend toward legislation restricting union activities has lost its momentum. Now the emphasis is on removing legislative curbs on legitimate union activities. The AFL-CIO has not only survived the scandals resulting from the exposure of corruption within a few organizations, but it has gained in stature, prestige and public respect.

3. Equally important, we can look for a revival of industrial activity with a new Administration in Washington. It can safely be predicted that there will be increased expenditures for national defense, housing, education and road building. It can also be assumed that the tight-money policy will be lifted. Once this inhibiting policy is removed, the national economy will be able to move forward vigorously again with higher employment and greater opportunity for sustained industrial expansion.

It must be pointed out that the AFL-CIO has not been sitting back and waiting for a better break before launching a strong organizational drive. On the contrary, during the past few years we have taken advantage of every opportunity to organize workers and we have succeeded beyond what could be expected, considering the handicaps we faced.

The figures show that our affiliated unions have enrolled more than a million new members since the merger. However, the total membership does not reflect this gain, because an equal number has been lost as a result of high unemployment in the mass production industries.

This condition, we trust, will be of short duration. A higher rate of economic growth is essential to keep America strong and it undoubtedly will be attained. When that occurs, our past membership gains will become fully apparent, as will our future organizational opportunities.

The trade union movement must be ready to take advantage of these opportunities. Our organizations cannot be conducted as exclusive clubs. Their first duty, as enunciated by the founder of our movement, Sam Gompers, is to "organize, organize, organize!" Just as America can maintain its strength only if it keeps growing, so the American trade union movement can remain strong only if it continues to organize and enlarges its representation.

The AFL-CIO believes there will soon be unparalleled opportunities for more intensive organization in virtually every industry and every area of the nation.

However, there are two broad fields where thus far we have scarcely scratched the surface and where we must make up for lost time.

First of these are white collar workers. The AFL-CIO is now making a careful survey to determine what new approaches and new organizing methods may be necessary to bring the benefits of union organization to millions of workers in this broad category.

Second are the workers employed by Federal, State and local governments. Some branches in this group are highly and effectively organized. Others are virtually without any union representation. This is another huge reservoir of potential membership which we can and must tap.

In a Federation like ours, the prime responsibility for organizing the unorganized rests upon affiliated national and international unions. The AFL-CIO itself can plan, it can point the way and it can assist. We are doing this and we will continue to do so. We will also do everything in our power to erase jurisdictional difficulties which impede organization.

Let this Labor Day be the signal for a real forward push in organizing the unorganized. The trade union movement is on the mark, it is all set and it is ready to go.

LABOR PUBLICATIONS REPRESENTED IN THIS VOLUME

(Arranged Alphabetically by Name, Publisher and Editor)

THE ADVANCE—Amalgamated Clothing Workers of America, Max Awner.

AFL-CIO COLLECTIVE BARGAINING REPORTS—AFL-CIO, Stanley Ruttenberg.

AFL-CIO EDUCATION DEPARTMENT NEWS AND VIEWS—AFL-CIO, Lawrence Rogin.

AFL-CIO NEWS—AFL-CIO, Saul Miller.

AMERICAN FEDERATIONIST—AFL-CIO, George Meany.

AMPLIFIER—Local 1048, Electrical Workers, Joseph Nichols.

THE AMERICAN PRESSMAN—International Printing Pressmen & Assistants' Union of North America, Anthony J. DeAndrade.

THE AMERICAN TEACHER—American Federation of Teachers, Marie L. Caylor.

THE BLACK WORKER—Brotherhood of Sleeping Car Porters, A. Philip Randolph.

BRICKLAYER, MASON & PLASTERER—Bricklayers, Masons & Plasterers Union, Joseph Murphy.

BROTHERHOOD OF MAINTENANCE OF WAY EMPLOYEES JOURNAL—Brotherhood of Maintenance of Way Employees, E. C. Crotty.

32B—Local 32B, Building Service Employees, Richard Strunsky.

BUILDING SERVICE EMPLOYEE—See Service Employee.

BUILDING SERVICE LOCAL OFFICERS QUARTERLY—See Service Employee.

THE BUTCHER WORKMAN—Amalgamated Meat Cutters & Butcher Workmen, Patrick E. Gorman.

THE CADILLAC STEWARD—Cadillac Local 22, Automobile Workers, Fred Quick.

THE CARPENTER—United Brotherhood of Carpenters & Joiners, Peter E. Terzick.

CATERING INDUSTRY EMPLOYEE—Hotel & Restaurant Employees & Bartenders International Union, Frederick B. Sweet.

THE CHRONICLE—Cincinnati Central Labor Council, J. W. Dolan.

THE GARMENT WORKER—Central & Western Pennsylvania District Garment Workers, ILGWU, Marvin Rogoff.

CLEVELAND CITIZEN—Cleveland AFL-CIO Federation of Labor, John F. Cummins.

CWA NEWS—Communications Workers of America, A. B. Herrington.

THE DUBUQUE LEADER—Dubuque Federation of Labor, Roland A. White.

EAST BAY LABOR JOURNAL—Alameda County Central Labor Council & Building Trades Council, R. L. Burgess.

ELECTRICAL UNION WORLD—Local 3, Electrical Workers, Arnold Beichman.

ELECTRICAL WORKERS' JOURNAL—International Brotherhood of Electrical Workers, Gordon M. Freeman.

ENGINEER'S OUTLOOK—American Federation of Technical Engineers, Russell M. Stephens.

THE FEDERATION NEWS—Chicago Federation of Labor, Irwin E. Klass.

FIREMAN AND OILERS JOURNAL—International Brotherhood of Firemen & Oilers, Anthony Matz.

GLASS HORIZONS—Glass Bottle Blowers Association, Lee W. Minton.

THE GUILD REPORTER—American Newspaper Guild, Charles E. Crissey.

THE HAT WORKER—United Hatters, Cap & Millinery Workers International Union, J. C. Rich.

HENDERSON FREEDOM FIGHTER—Locals 578 and 584, Textile Workers of America, David George.

HOTEL—New York Hotel Trades Council, Sol Abramson.

INTERNATIONAL OPERATING ENGINEER—International Union of Operating Engineers, Hunter P. Harton.

IUD BULLETIN—Industrial Union Department, AFL-CIO, Oscar Jager.

IUD DIGEST—Industrial Union Department, AFL-CIO, Oscar Jager.

IUE AFL-CIO NEWS—International Union of Electrical, Radio & Machine Workers, Al Hartnett.

JUSTICE—International Ladies' Garment Workers' Union, Leon Stein.

THE KENTUCKY LABOR NEWS—Kentucky State AFL-CIO, Ann S. Coates.

KEY AND SOUNDER—Commercial Telegraphers Union (Western Union Division), F. C. Poli.

LABOR'S ECONOMIC REVIEW—AFL-CIO, Stanley Ruttenberg.

LABOR—17 Standard Railway Labor Organizations, Ruben Levin.

THE LABORER—International Hod Carriers, Building & Common Laborers Union, Joseph V. Moreschi.

THE LAMPMAKER—Local 663, Automobile Workers, Bernard J. Schuck.

LOCAL 1-S NEWS—Local 1-S, RWDSU, Norman L. Sobol.

THE MACHINIST—International Association of Machinists, Gordon H. Cole.

MICHIGAN AFL-CIO NEWS—Michigan AFL-CIO, Ted Ogar.

MICHIGAN SOLIDARITY—See UAW Solidarity.

MILWAUKEE LABOR PRESS—Milwaukee Federated Trades Council, Ray W. Taylor.

OFFICIAL NEWS—LABEL TRADES DEPARTMENT—AFL-CIO Union Label and Service Trades Department, Joseph Lewis.

NEW JERSEY LABOR HERALD—New Jersey State Federation of Labor, Lewis M. Herrmann.

NEW YORK LABOR CHRONICLE—New York City Central Labor Council, James Quinn.

NMU PILOT—National Maritime Union of America, Bernard Raskin.

OIL, CHEMICAL & ATOMIC UNION NEWS—Oil, Chemical & Atomic Workers Union, Ray Davidson.

OREGON LABOR PRESS—Oregon AFL-CIO and Multnomah County Labor Council, James W. Goodsell.

PAI PRESS SERVICE—Press Associates, Inc., Harry Conn and Alex Uhl.

THE PAPER WORKER—International Brotherhood of Pulp, Sulphite and Paper Mill Workers, George W. Brooks.

THE PLASTERER AND CEMENT MASON—Operative Plasterers' and Cement Masons' International Assn., Edward J. Leonard.

PLUMBERS' JOURNAL—See United Association Journal.

POSTAL RECORD—National Association of Letter Carriers, Jerome J. Keating.

THE PUBLIC EMPLOYEE—American Federation of State, County & Municipal Employees, Arnold S. Zander.

RAILWAY CARMEN'S JOURNAL—Brotherhood of Railway Carmen of America, Robert H. Jamison.

RAILWAY CLERK—Brotherhood of Railway & Steamship Clerks, Freight Handlers, Express and Station Employees, George M. Gibbons.

RETAIL CLERKS ADVOCATE—Retail Clerks International Association, James A. Suffridge.

RWDSU RECORD—Retail, Wholesale & Department Store Union, Max Steinbock.

SAN FRANCISCO LABOR—San Francisco Labor Council, David F. Selvin.

SEAFARERS LOG—Seafarers International Union, Atlantic & Gulf District, Herbert Brand.

THE SENTINEL—Local 1397, Steelworkers, John E. McManigal.

SERVICE EMPLOYEE—Building Service Employees International Union, George E. Fairchild.

SOUTHWEST LABOR—Local 425, Amalgamated Meatcutters & Butcher Workmen of America, Virgil Talbot.

STEEL LABOR—United Steelworkers of America, Vincent D. Sweeney.

TEXAS STATE AFL-CIO NEWS—Texas State AFL-CIO, Jerry R. Holleman.

TEXTILE LABOR—Textile Workers Union of America, Irving Kahan.

TOLEDO UNION JOURNAL—Local 12, UAW, Walter Murphy.

TRAINMAN NEWS—Brotherhood of Railroad Trainmen, George H. Hennemuth.

TWU EXPRESS—Transport Workers Union of America, Joseph J. Kutch.

THE TYPOGRAPHICAL JOURNAL—International Typographical Union, James Bettle.

UAW SOLIDARITY—United Auto, Aircraft & Agricultural Implement Workers, Frank Winn.

UNION LABEL NEWS—New York Union Label and Services Trades Department, Harry Avrutin.

THE UNION POSTAL CLERK—National Federation of Post Office Clerks, P. Cline House.

UNITED ASSOCIATION JOURNAL—United Association of Journeymen & Apprentices of the Plumbing & Pipefitting Industry of United States & Canada, William C. O'Neill.

UNITED AUTOMOBILE WORKER—See UAW Solidarity.

UNITED MINE WORKERS JOURNAL—United Mine Workers of America, Justin McCarthy.

UNITED PAPER—United Papermakers & Paperworkers, Richard A. Estep.

UNITED RUBBER WORKER—United Rubber, Cork, Linoleum & Plastics Workers, George Scriven.

VALLEY UNION—Central Labor Councils of Merced, Stanislaus and San Joaquin Counties, Sheldon F. Sacks.

VOICE OF THE CEMENT, LIME, GYPSUM & ALLIED WORKERS—United Cement, Lime & Gypsum Workers International Union, Felix C. Jones.

VOICE OF 770—(Retail Clerks Local 770), Joseph T. DeSilva.

ACKNOWLEDGMENTS

The editors wish to express their appreciation to the many trade union editors whose cooperation and interest made this volume possible. Particular thanks go to Saul Miller, AFL-CIO Director of Publications, and Bernard R. Mullady, secretary-treasurer of the International Labor Press Association, for their aid, counsel and encouragement.

We are also pleased to acknowledge the many courtesies of Dorothy Oko, of the Labor Education Service of the New York Public Library, and of Merkle Press, Inc., which provided 14 of the photographs on the dust jacket.

For permission to use copyrighted material, thanks are due to Sidney Margolius, Jane Goodsell, Edward P. Morgan, Arthur J. Goldberg, John Herling and PAI Press Service.

Not least, we wish to thank those redoubtable cartoonists whose work enlivens so many labor publications: John Baer, Richard Belland, the late Le Baron Coakley (Coak), John Kallas, Bernard Seaman, John Stampone (Stam) and Carl Stamwitz.

—THE EDITORS